The Journey of the Purple Heart

A First Infantry Division Soldier's Story from Stateside to North Africa, Sicily and Normandy during World War II

As Told for Him by
Robert W. Baumer

HELLGATE PRESS   ASHLAND, OREGON

I

Heroes have the whole earth for their tomb.
And in a land far from their own
Where the column with its epitaph declares it,
There is enshrined in every breast a record unwritten
With no tablet to preserve it except that of the heart.

—Pericles

AUTHOR'S NOTE

EVERY PERSON YOU WILL MEET in this book lived. Events described actually took place on the home front and on the battlefields of North Africa and Europe during World War II. In order to make the pages ahead more enjoyable for you to read, the dialogue created required some literary license, but I assure you that this is an honest representation of the individuals as I knew them, or as they were described to me.

Robert W. Baumer
January 2022

Journey of the Purple Heart

~PROLOGUE~

MY FATHER NEVER SAID HELLO when he called me. He usually didn't even say it was him. He always got right down to business.

"Robert, my Aunt Kathryn is in the hospital up in Waterbury. She's dying. We need to see her today. I'll meet you in the downstairs lobby at noontime."

I always got to where my father ordered me ahead of him. When he arrived at the hospital that gloomy March day back in 1990 all he did was nod. Then up the elevator we went, still saying nothing, until we reached the fifth floor when he just said to turn right. Seconds later we walked into his Aunt Kathryn's room.

She was conscious and sitting up. The years had certainly taken a toll on her health, but for a woman of ninety-nine years she didn't look too bad. Her white hair was combed. Her kid sister Mary Jane, not yet ninety, was standing beside her taking her pulse while watching the monitors hovering near her bed.

During her fifty-year education career Kathryn had been a beloved first-grade teacher and a school principal in nearby Naugatuck Connecticut. Mary Jane was a nurse. She served in both the European and Pacific Theaters during World War II, retiring as a 1st Lieutenant back in 1946. She and Kathryn had been living together for years; neither ever married. Another of their sisters had died back in 1973; her name was Viola and she was my father's mother, my grandmother.

We weren't in the room but for maybe fifteen seconds when Kathryn managed to tilt her head toward us. Neither my father nor I had said anything. Kathryn was the first to speak.

"Sonny, I know that's you. But Bobby, how can you be here? You were killed during the war."

Kathryn had mistaken me for my father's brother, who did die in World War II. It was the moment my life changed and gave me an important purpose.

My father had never talked to me about his brother Bob, who he and my mother named me after. The closest I ever came to his brother was the day he was buried in Naugatuck back in 1947; my mother was two-months pregnant with me at the time. My father had never taken me to see his brother's grave all through my childhood, nor to the World War II Memorial on the town green in Naugatuck where his brother is remembered, along with seventy other locals who were killed during the war.

My grandmother Viola, who had served for years as president of the local Gold Star Mothers chapter, hardly talked about him when she was alive. I had just two fuzzy recollections of the times when she did. I wasn't even a teenager; I was maybe twelve the first time. She showed me a picture of her handsome son, only adding "he fought in Africa and Europe with the toughest outfit in the Army, the First Division." The other time she opened her purse and pulled out an embroidered pouch, from which emerged what I thought to be a medal because it glittered from the sunlight coming into the window of her home.

She told me it was something called a Purple Heart. She let me hold it, but said nothing.

Now in my forties and with my father riding down the elevator after seeing Kathryn mistake me for his brother, something finally gave me the courage to speak up. We were back on the main floor when I did.

"Pop, you have never told me anything about your brother," I offered quietly. "What happened to him?"

It was pretty rare for my father to look me directly in the eye, but this time he did. "He was killed on the beachhead in Normandy," he told me before looking away. "What a waste. I don't want to talk about this. Ask Mary Jane if you have any more questions."

So I asked Mary Jane if she would take me to my uncle Bob's grave on Memorial Day that spring and she very willingly agreed to do so. I picked her up at her home near Naugatuck, and we then made our way down Route 8 towards Grove Cemetery. We turned right at the entrance and went through its stone wall-bordered gate, and then passed by the Tuttle Memorial Chapel. The narrow roadway quickly bore left, then right where we had to slow considerably to traverse the remaining rutted and non-paved surface through the cemetery's tranquil acreage. A final left turn and going down into a hollow got us to where my family's plot was located amongst several tall pine trees.

It was this first visit that awakened something else in me. It was a thirst for knowledge. I hadn't served in the military, but by now I knew I wanted to somehow figure out what had happened to my father's brother who did.

Private First Class Robert Arthur Baummer, who died when he was just twenty-three years old, lay beneath a simple flat stone marker next to his mother.

"Viola died from blood cancer," Mary Jane quietly told me as I stared at their gravestones. "Her boys couldn't have been more opposite. Your father was always serious; he was a straight-A student in high school. Bob was an easy going, happy-go -lucky kid who played hooky from school, and hung out in garages where older boys were always fixing automobiles and building race cars.

"Bob really had a big heart," Mary Jane added. "During the Depression he used to take food from the family larder and give it to less fortunate families. His father Henry was an accountant with a decent paying job at the Rubber Plant at the time. Viola was working in the factory. It was a source of friction between them, the fact that she was working rather than staying home to keep an eye on their Bob. Bob ended up at the Connecticut Junior Republic up near Litchfield. It was like a reform school is today. He went there after he got into trouble with his boyhood friend George Walker, who lived down the hill from the family's home on Oak Street."

"What did he do to end up in this reform school?" I asked Mary Jane.

"He shot out a streetlamp with his BB gun."

"Then, how did he end up in the Army? Did my father make him do this?" I wondered out loud.

"No," Mary Jane quickly answered. "Sonny assumed the role of Bob's father after Henry died, but Bob evidenced no resentment towards his brother; in fact, he worshipped Sonny. It was your uncle Bob's decision to enlist back in 1940, a year before Pearl Harbor was bombed. There is something you should know about those times. Your father was deferred during the war; he was working in the defense industry, and never had to serve. His guilt is about him not going off to war, while his brother did and was killed."

"Do you have any idea what happened to him?" I asked.

"No, Bobby, I don't. I was in an evacuation hospital in England when we invaded Normandy back in 1944, and I did ask any First Division soldier I treated if they happened to know Bob and what happened to him, but none knew him. I don't know that we'll ever know what happened."

Thus my journey began to find out what did happen to him. Staring at my uncle Bob's gravestone, I took out my notebook, and wrote down "18th Infantry Regiment 1st Infantry Division," and scribbled his date of death—June 9, 1944.

"He didn't die on D-Day after all," I then said, more as a question looking for Mary Jane to confirm that, since I remembered my father had told me he was killed on the beachhead.

"No, he did not die on D-Day," Mary Jane answered. "Bob got off the beach that day. That, in and of itself, was a miracle."

"I wonder why my father dropped one of the "m's" in our last name. Bob spelled his with two "m's. Do you know what that's all about?"

"No I don't know for sure," Mary Jane answered. "But I always suspected it was because your father wanted it to look less German."

I thought about that for a few seconds before deciding to shift the conversation in another direction. "Do you think they know we're here?" I awkwardly asked, knowing Mary Jane was deeply religious.

She just stared off into the distance, frowned in thought, and then she turned to me and whispered, "Yes, I believe they know we are here."

I said nothing; I didn't have religion like she did. We were just holding each other's hands when Mary Jane suddenly said, "I have something for you, Bobby. Your grandmother gave it to me just days before she died. Viola knew I was very fond of her son Bob. I was actually the last person to see him before he went overseas. I dropped him off at the train station in New Haven. Being an Army veteran she entrusted me with this Purple Heart. Sonny didn't want it, for reasons you'll better understand over time. But I'm giving it to you now, here in Viola's presence, knowing she'd be proud and happy that you've taken an interest in her Bob."

I was stunned. It was the same Purple Heart I had held back when I was a kid.

"Will you help me understand his life better?" I asked.

"Of course Bobby," Mary Jane answered. "As much as I can remember."

Finding out more about my uncle's time in the army proved to be fraught with one obstacle after another. First, the local Veterans Affairs Office advocated on my behalf in an attempt to get Bob's Army service records from the National Personnel Records Center in St. Louis, but all that came back was a fire in 1973 had destroyed all records "for the period 1912 through 1959." I was told complete service records could not be reconstructed, but I didn't give up and instead upped my game. I engaged my then United States Senator Christopher J. Dodd, hoping the weight of his office could pry any of my uncle's records that might have existed out of St. Louis, but that, too, resulted in nothing.

I even visited the National Archives near Washington D.C. hoping for leads. I was able to retrieve Bob's casualty file, and while it was loaded with copies of administrative paperwork about getting his body home after the war ended, the answer to what had happened to him was not there. But I did learn that he served with Company H of the First Division's 18th Infantry Regiment.

Over the next two years I went to a number of military history research centers and was able to put a timeline together which told me Bob had participated in the Invasions of North Africa and Sicily during 1942 and 1943 before he landed in Normandy in June of 1944. The record of his regiment was very impressive, but I was still unable to determine anything about his role in this, or even that of his company.

But I was still far from ready to give up.

Two things happened the following year. I was able to locate a man who lived in Goshen Connecticut, near what Mary Jane remembered as the reform school Bob was sent to when he was fifteen years old. His name was Tony Salcito, and he invited me to come to his home. He remembered Bob; quite fondly I should add. They were roommates. He regaled me with stories of the year and a half Bob spent there, and then took me over to "The Republic," as he called it, and gave me a tour of the place.

When Christmas came that year my mother surprised me with packages which very much aroused my curiosity as I stared at them under the tree in my parent's wood-stove warmed living room on Main Street in Newtown Connecticut.

I couldn't imagine what was inside them, but when I opened

each one more clues about Bob's life emerged. Pictures, letters he had sent home during the war, other correspondence related to his death, and one very moving framed tribute, "In Grateful Memory of Private First Class Robert A. Baummer," signed by President Franklin Roosevelt, fell into my hands. I never forgot the words Roosevelt wrote.

He stands in an unbroken line of patriots who have dared to die
That Freedom might live, and grow, and increase its blessings.
Freedom lives, and through it, he lives
In a way that humbles the undertakings of most men.

When my father asked to look at this he just stared at those words and said nothing. A minute or two later he glanced at my mother and said, "Laura Jean, where did you find this?"

My mother answered, "It was in the trunk at the foot of the bed in the upstairs front bedroom."

"I had completely forgotten I kept those things," was all my father said.

I had the nerve to say, "Pop, maybe your brother's life really wasn't a waste after all."

This time he said nothing.

By now Mary Jane had shared many stories about Bob with me, but I still had no idea how he died. I wanted to go to Normandy and see if I might be able to figure out that part of the mystery. Looking back, I was clearly delusional. But it was 1992 when I was given the opportunity to crew on a sixty-three-foot sailboat that was being delivered to its new owner in Oslo Norway. I worked out plans to fly to France and go to Normandy once the boat was safely in the hands of its new owner.

On Monday, June 14th of that year, I was sailing past Nomans Land Island off Martha's Vineyard in fifteen knots of wind; the boat was making 8.5 knots, and was headed on a course of 134 degrees for Nantucket Light Ship. Waypoints were laid in off Nova Scotia and Newfoundland that would get *Katya*, the boat I was helping deliver, into the Gulf Stream, across the Atlantic, and up the globe to 60 degrees-latitude. First landfall was charted to be the Fair Isle chain north of Scotland, then we would put into the Shetland Islands to re-provision before covering the last 360 nautical miles to reach Oslo.

My uncle Bob's Purple Heart made the voyage with me; *Katya* reached Oslo on July 7th after covering 2,800 nautical miles of open, and sometimes angry ocean. Four days later, I got a cab to the Oslo airport, and boarded what turned out to be an uneventful flight to Paris. A cab took me to the Saint-Lazare train station where I caught a high-speed train bound for Cherbourg. I rented a car here, and set out the next morning for Omaha Beach, the military designation for the landing zone that Bob had come into shore towards on the morning of D-Day back on June 6th of 1944.

My first stop was at a museum commemorating the landings. "I was very impressed, for this museum had much memorabilia, such as uniforms, weapons, cartons of cigarettes from the war, cards and other such things that a soldier had with him," my journal read. "Pictures depicted the landings, hour by hour. Music played; marches, hymns, and even our Star Spangled Banner. I was moved and took many pictures."

Then I drove towards the beach. At first I was confused by the absence of signs that would have helped me find my way around. The Omaha Beach area is now a quaint summer community, and I thought maybe the French people didn't want all these pesky tourists like me clogging up their roads. But I eventually found my way past several old stone Norman farmhouses, and started down a narrow road shaded by ancient hedgerows that brought me to the beach. One of the first things I saw here was a large, rusted landing craft some twenty feet from the water's edge. Children were crawling all over it, frolicking and playing, their laughter oblivious to what had happened here nearly fifty years earlier.

Next, I came to a monument; it was a large, pyramidal-shaped structure facing the English Channel. It sat on a heavy granite base in a park-like setting, alone in a triangular area surrounded by the roadway. My heart raced. Beneath a Big Red One shoulder patch emblem on one side of this monument was the First Division's motto: *No Mission Too Difficult, No Sacrifice Too Great, Duty First*. This was my uncle Bob's unit. I stepped back, and then took in the large raised-letter inscription facing the Channel; in both French and English it read: THE ALLIED FORCES LANDING ON THIS SHORE WHICH THEY CALL OMAHA BEACH LIBERATE EUROPE JUNE 6TH 1944.

Then I headed up the bluff to the United States Military Cemetery, and entered the gate. I consulted a map I had brought with me, which first led me to a colonnade overlooking the seemingly endless rows of graves. I stood in place, and took in this magnificent memorial. Centered in the open arc was a haunting, yet beautiful twenty-two-foot bronze statue which faced the simple crosses of the fallen champions who preserved our way of life. The statue represented "The Spirit of American Youth Rising from the Waves." I choked up when I saw this inscription encircling the pedestal: "Mine Eyes Have Seen the Glory of the Coming of the Lord."

My camera attempted to capture the solemn beauty of the statue, its arms reaching towards the sky, with its gazing eyes eternally fixed towards the heavens beyond. I struggled to keep control of my emotions as I thought about how young the men buried here were; they were half my age when they gave their lives for our country. I clutched my uncle Bob's Purple Heart, which I of course had brought with me, then stepped back far enough to read the inner face of the lintel. In the semicircle of this visage it read: "This Embattled Shore, Portal of Freedom, Is Forever Hallowed by The Ideals, The Valor and The Sacrifices of our Fellow Countrymen."

I then walked towards an area overlooking the beach, the same beach where I had stood before the monument with the Big Red

One shoulder patch on it. I was numb with humility by now. From this vantage point I was able to see a different Omaha Beach, the one the heavily-armed Germans saw on the morning of D-Day. A winding path lined with benches marked the advancement of the First Division up from the beach to where I now stood.

After studying this path for an hour I turned back and walked slowly through the graves, stopping frequently to read the names on the markers. This was important for me to do; they deserved to be remembered. I took the time to go down every row, along the beautifully manicured lawns, through the ten grave plots, all in rows and columns. One grave contained the remains of General Theodore Roosevelt Jr., who had been Bob's Assistant Division Commander in North Africa and Sicily. A father and a son were also buried side-by-side; there were thirty-three pairs of brothers.

Each of the graves was marked with a headstone, a Star of David for those of Jewish faith; a Latin Cross for others. The headstones were perfectly aligned. All of America was represented here; everything that made us right when we invaded Normandy. By the time I walked through the last row, the pouch that held my uncle Bob's Purple Heart was soaked through with sweat. It had never left my clutched palm the entire time I was in the cemetery.

Before I departed, I went into the chapel to say a prayer for Bob. This site of peaceful worship lay in the middle of the graves, and was surrounded by stoic columns supporting its structure. My journal said, "I approached the entry and silently watched other solemn, moist-eyed people who came here for the same reason I did. I spoke quietly to a woman from Ohio who was leaving the chapel; she told me her father died on Omaha Beach. She said she never knew him, that she was only two years old when the war took him away."

When I entered the chapel I faced the black and gold marble altar before placing my uncle Bob's Purple Heart on it. Then I stepped back, expecting to whisper the prayer I wanted to say for him. I failed to murmur any words; I just couldn't. The inscription in the center of the altar said it all for me: "I Give unto Them Eternal Life and They Shall Never Perish."

Then I left to go back to Cherbourg, still not knowing what the circumstances of my uncle Bob's death were.

The next three years flew by quickly. My research continued. I happened to be at the Military History Institute in Carlisle Pennsylvania in the fall of 1995 when I got a big break. I had spent the day digging through boxes of old records and oral histories, desperately searching for anything that mentioned my uncle Bob; nothing I found did. It was nearing the end of the day. I was tired, but I shared my dilemma with one of the research assistants, and this woman offered that I might try to write the National Personnel Records Center in St. Louis again, but to address my request to the "Morning Report Branch." She said if I was lucky and they had the pertinent morning reports for my uncle Bob's Company H, there could be names of those who served with him at the time of his death.

For some reason I sat on this, believing I'd hit another wall, and by now I was tired of hitting walls. It took until April of the following year before I decided to contact Senator Dodd's office again. The same woman who had helped me the last time was still there, and she cheerfully offered to assist me again.

A letter went out to St. Louis, and another polite response first came back using the 1973 fire excuse again, but it offered "a further response will be furnished as soon as possible." It gave me little reason to believe finding the Morning Reports would happen.

Then something incredible did happen. I received in the mail from the senator's office in early May an "Authorization for Issuance of Awards." I hadn't requested this; it turned out Senator Dodd's assistant had taken it upon herself to get all of my uncle Bob's earned medals finally awarded. I was shocked, pleased beyond my wildest expectations, and encouraged something could actually happen because typed in the REMARKS section were the words: EXPEDITE/CONGRESSIONAL INTEREST.

A box arrived just before Memorial Day, and it contained the Bronze Star my uncle Bob had earned for meritorious achievement in ground combat against an armed enemy on D-Day, his theater ribbons and medals, his Combat Infantry Badge, and Good Conduct Medal. There was also another Purple Heart.

I had them all put on a dark green background in a box-framed display case, and took it to my parent's home in Newtown early on Memorial Day to give to my father. He wasn't home when I arrived, but my mother suggested we hang the medals over the chair my father sat in on the porch, where he spent a lot of time reading, napping, or just drinking coffee in the morning and watching the birds come to the feeders outside the windows. Once we did this, I left to go back to Naugatuck so Mary Jane and I could carry on with our Memorial Day tradition of visiting grave sites.

It wasn't until later in the day when I called my mother to ask her if Pop had seen the medals.

"Yes, Bobby honey, he did."

"Did he say anything, Mom?

"No Bobby. He didn't."

Summer months go by fast in New England, but before the leaves started changing their colors that fall I heard from Senator Dodd's office again. "Enclosed is a copy of the material sent to me by the National Personnel Records Center in St. Louis," the cover letter began. I read little more, quickly turned to the Center's letter and about fainted.

"Enclosed are copies of all available Morning Report entries from June through August 1944, for Company H 18th Infantry, pertaining to Pfc. Baummer being Missing in Action (MIA) and Killed in Action (KIA). We regret the photocopies are of poor quality; however, they are the best obtainable."

Actually, in bright light with a magnifying glass I was able to create a reliable accounting of the company personnel who were not just missing or killed, but also wounded during June, July and August of 1944.

After hours of studying the Morning Reports it dawned on me that the only Company H soldier that had been wounded during the period and returned to the company roster was a Paul E. Stegall; this was recorded on July 25th. But how would I find him? Did Paul Stegall even survive the war? If he did was it possible he's already died?

I knew of only one way at the time to find out. I had the name of an Albert Jacobs who served in Company H; he was one of the few in the company who had a recorded oral history at the Carlisle Barracks. I had his address. Jacobs lived in Connellsville, Pennsylvania. I used directory assistance to get his telephone number, and called him. Albert Jacobs remembered my uncle Bob. "Knew him in North Africa," he told me. "He was a real nice fellow; he was a live wire, actually pretty comical."

I asked him if he knew how my uncle was killed in Normandy; he didn't. Did he know how I might find Paul Stegall? Jacobs remembered him too, but no, I don't know where he is, he told me.

The Internet was something I knew little to nothing about at the time. But I knew someone who did know enough about it to look up names, and retrieve what were the equivalent of the white pages in phone books anywhere in the country. She was Judy Clark, a cousin's wife. I gave her Paul Stegall's name, she did her research, and mailed me the list of results she found in January of 1997.

There were coincidently eight Paul Stegall's. But there was only one with the middle initial "E" and just looking at this gave me goose bumps. Could it be that Paul Stegall? His address was in Greenville, South Carolina.

I finally got the nerve up two days later to put together a letter introducing myself; it was brief, less than a page, and I asked Mr.

Stegall if he would kindly contact me if, by chance, he was the same Paul E. Stegall who was a casualty in Company H on June 9, 1944 in Normandy France. Before sealing the envelope, I put my uncle Bob's Purple Heart next to the letter for good luck, said a prayer, then I took the letter to the post office and mailed it.

February 5th of 1997 was an unusually mild day in New England. I happen to call my office for messages right after lunch. My secretary read them to me, and then added I had received what the last caller identified as a personal call. She told me he had told her to "tell Mr. Baumer I'm the man he was looking for," and he wanted you to know that "he remembered everything from 6/9/44. His name is Paul Stegall, here's his number, and he asked that you call him tonight."

When I called Paul Stegall that night, a soft female voice greeted me with, "Hello, we were hoping you would call. Please understand that my husband has never talked about the war, but he has been looking forward to talking with you. Hold on, I'll put him on."

I started the conversation by telling Mr. Stegall I owed him an explanation as to how I found him, and he said he was obviously curious about that. "It's a long story," I told him, "but ......"

Then he put me immediately at ease. "You'll have to forgive me," he quietly interrupted. "It has indeed been a long time, fifty-three years by my count, but I would like to tell you what I can about June 9th of 1944. First, know your uncle Bob was my best friend."

I just listened as Mr. Stegall continued to talk; I wrote down everything he said. His voice was steady, with a sweet Southern accent. I didn't know it then, but we were eventually going to become close friends.

Another two years passed, and one afternoon in March I came across a new web site that was published by the 18th Infantry Regiment Association. It had a "guest book," and I about fell off my chair when I saw that one of its more recently signed guests was a Robert E. Murphy, Colonel US Army-Retired.

An email went to the webmaster, a Vietnam-era veteran, and I asked him if this Murphy was *the* World War II Captain Robert E. Murphy, who commanded Company H. It indeed was, so I asked if I could contact him; the answer came back essentially telling me that Murphy would be notified, and if he "invited" such, I would be given his email address.

I was granted the invitation, and in one of the more carefully prepared emails I ever wrote, I told Colonel Murphy who I was, that I had a rough manuscript completed about my uncle's time under his command, and anything he might be able to recall about the circumstance of his death would be vastly appreciated.

An email came back from Colonel Murphy that very same day. Amazingly, he was able to describe the situation that brought about his order that got my uncle Bob's squad into the situation that resulted in his death.

To my surprise, Colonel Murphy asked me if I would be willing to send him a copy of the manuscript I had put together about my uncle Bob's war. Of course I would, I answered, even though it made me quite nervous wondering what he'd think of it. So off it went, and a few weeks later Murphy sent me a letter that started with, "You thought I would never get around to returning your document, didn't you?" Then he added, "I found it interesting and I might even say enlightening," closing with "I thought you did one whale of a job on your uncle's war effort. I believe he would have been very pleased."

Colonel Murphy also mentioned two other things. First, he had composed his personal history about the D-Day landings "up to the action in which your uncle was killed." Entitled "That Day," it was three typewritten pages long and rich with detail. Now I had more first hand accounts! Could it get any better than this?

Actually, it could. The other thing Colonel Murphy did was invite me to attend the Annual Dinner Reunion of the Combat Officers of the First Division, to be held that May in Washington.

Another enduring friendship was about to be formed.

Colonel Murphy eventually provided me with a treasure trove of documents he had saved from the war. He also pointed me to numerous new sources and even gave me personal war memoirs he had in his files of others who had served under him.

I was now confident I really had something more to write about, and I dared think I could march with my uncle Bob through his entire war. But where to start again, I wondered.

Mary Jane and I got together for lunch a few weeks later; it was the year before she died.

"Bobby," she said right after we had cake for dessert. "Your grandmother once told me about what she went through the night she heard about the Normandy Invasion. Would you like me to tell you about this?"

"Oh God yes, please do. Tell me what you remember."

PRELUDE
TO WAR

Journey of the Purple Heart

~ONE~

IT WAS THE LONGEST NIGHT OF HER LIFE.

Viola Baummer, a short widow in her mid-forties, first wondered who it could be when her telephone rang. It was Monday June 5th of 1944, and an unusually humid evening in the gritty factory town of Naugatuck Connecticut. Every window was open in her well-kept two-story wood-frame house, built alongside a steep hill on Oak Street.

She had just finished eating warmed up leftovers from her Sunday dinner after another long day of toiling at the rubber plant down on Elm Street; she had been working here for the past ten years. But Viola was now on the line that made the woven mesh ventilating insoles for the Jungle boots American forces were wearing in the tropical environments of New Guinea and the Philippines. It made her work a bit easier knowing she was supporting the war effort.

The telephone kept up its short rings before she finally picked up its heavy black handset. It was her oldest son. This surprised her. They had talked the night before, as had been their custom every Sunday—her only day off—for years. His given name was Edwin, but everyone in the family had been calling him Sonny since he was a boy.

Sonny was working as an industrial engineer at the U.S. Rubber Company plant in Institute, West Virginia, a sprawling complex near Charleston where synthetic rubber was being manufactured to support the war effort.

After she said hello, Viola asked, "Sonny, we just talked yesterday. Are you alright? Did you hear from Bob?"

Bob was over in England in the Army, presumably getting ready for the invasion of mainland Europe.

"No, I haven't received any letters since the one I got a few days ago, the one where he told me he was still on good terms with some blonde English girl, and was seeing her every weekend he was off."

"That doesn't surprise me at all," Viola chuckled. "He's got an advantage over there with those British lassies, his Gram Nellie being from London and a Goddard before she married a Baummer. Bob's sure got Nellie's charm, doesn't he?"

"He always had girls after him since he was a teenager Mother," Sonny gently kidded back. "I did tell you I sent a letter back to him, didn't I? Told him about having been up to see you in mid-May, finally getting the storm windows down and cutting the grass and trimming the hedges. Let him know a lot of people around town were asking about him, especially Gram. Also said I would get a box off with some cigarettes, a lighter, cards, a pair of dice, razor blades and other stuff. Will be doing that tomorrow."

"I wonder if Bob's seen Mary Jane?" Viola questioned. Mary Jane, still "Little Ma-wee" to her family since she was Viola's youngest sister, had recently left Ft. Devens—just outside of Boston—for England. A nurse by training, she had been commissioned a second lieutenant that past April and was now in charge of the orthopedic ward in an Army hospital outside of London, one sure to be populated with American soldiers when the invasion came.

"I have no idea, Mother," Sonny said. Just ten years separated Sonny from Mary Jane so he thought of her more as a big sister than an aunt. "Talked to a couple of people who knew her when I was up in Naugatuck and they said she was sorely missed, but that the Army was sure lucky to have her."

"Everyone who knows her around here adores her spontaneous and pleasing personality," Viola added.

"By the way," Sonny offered in a now more serious voice. "Bob didn't say anything at all in that letter of his about the invasion, but I sense it's coming soon."

"Why do you think that, Sonny?" Viola asked, her interest piqued.

"I just have a feeling it'll go off sooner than later," Sonny answered. "I read somewhere that the military could time the attack around a full moon period, and we have one right now."

"Something tells me you could be right," Viola said in a low, resigned voice; she dreaded thoughts of the invasion. "And the First Division is likely to be in the thick of it. They were in the invasions of North Africa and Sicily for sure. They are the best division in the Army, you know."

"Yes, Mother, I know," Sonny agreed. "It's a fine outfit and I'm proud Bob serves with them."

Viola believed this because she kept a copy of a *Time* magazine on the cluttered coffee table in her living room, right next to other magazines and several pictures of Bob and Sonny taken when they were little boys. *Time's* cover in that August 1943 edition had a picture of Bob's commanding general on it, a dashingly handsome man named Terry Allen. Inside, she had underlined the words: "There has fallen a special mark on war and history; a mark reserved for front-line fighting men, and esteemed by them. It is a mark of the greatest division in being, and the first of their kind to be publically recognized in the U.S. Army of World War II."

The Big Red One, as the division had come to be called, had stormed the beaches in Sicily and fought its way up to the steep hillside town of Troina in late July of that year. Now the entire division was back in England preparing for the invasion of mainland Europe.

Viola worried constantly about where Bob was, and what he was doing now, just like every other mother with a son fighting in the war. It had been a long year and a half since Bob first shipped out to England after training state-side, but every letter he had written to her since said not to worry about him, and that he could take care of himself when he had to.

"Mother, the real reason I called was I heard President Roosevelt was going to be on the radio tonight," Sonny said to his mother to get her attention again. "I wanted you to know in case he says something about the invasion."

"Thank you, Sonny," Viola answered while wiping perspiration off her forehead. "I'll turn the radio on now so I don't miss it. I've got to wash the dishes. I'm dead tired from work, but somehow I'll manage."

"Bye for now. We'll talk next Sunday."

~TWO~

VIOLA KEPT HER PROMISE, WENT into her living room, turned on her ten-year old but still well-working Philco Baby Grand radio to near full volume, and listened to the NBC broadcast while she finished washing her dinner dishes. It was just before eight o'clock; the sun hadn't even set. A warm breeze moved through the house, and she could hear some neighborhood kids still playing outside.

Viola was just starting to dry the dishes when she heard scratchy static coming out of her radio, then a solemn voice broke in with, "Ladies and gentlemen, the President of the United States." Suddenly Viola was glad Sonny had called; maybe there would be some news about the invasion. She darted for the living room, sat down on her well worn couch, stuffed a pillow behind her back, put her feet up on the coffee table, and stared at the radio.

Franklin D. Roosevelt, in his familiar patrician voice, one that Viola felt sounded as if the president was right there in her living room, started his address with some big news: "Yesterday, on June 4, 1944, Rome fell to American and Allied troops. The first of the Axis capitols is now in our hands." Then raising his voice ever so slightly, the president announced "One up, and two to go."

Viola knew that meant Japan and Germany still had to be defeated.

Following with a brief history of the city of Rome, emphasizing that there were still monuments there reminding everyone that Rome had controlled the whole known world in ancient times, Roosevelt made it clear to his listeners that the United Nations of today were now restoring Italy's freedom—even to the Pope. The president then credited by country the Allied forces which had been struggling across the globe to stamp out Nazism and Imperial Japan.

But the invasion of Europe was all Viola, perspiring again, could really think about. She continued listening intently, hoping Roosevelt would say something about that.

Alternately raising and lowering his voice for dramatic effect, Roosevelt instead went on to explain Italy's last twenty-five years under the dictatorial rule of the scoundrel Mussolini, then followed by saying something that finally made Viola think the president was reading her mind: "Our victory comes at an excellent time, while our Allied forces are poised for another strike at Western Europe, and while the armies of other Nazi soldiers nervously await our assault."

There it was. Something about the invasion. All Viola could now think about was just when would this strike at Western Europe begin.

She, too, was suddenly nervous.

But nothing was said about when the invasion would begin. Roosevelt instead praised Russia for its efforts on the Eastern Front before describing in simple terms how strategic islands and bases in the Mediterranean had come under Allied control before Rome fell. "But it would be unwise to inflate in our own minds the military capture of the city of Rome," Roosevelt again cautioned, then further warned, "We shall have to push through a long period of greater effort, and fiercer fighting before we get into Germany itself."

Those words made Viola shutter, and Roosevelt had still not said anything about the invasion's timing.

The president went on and explained how the Germans had been forced to retreat from countries in Africa, and through Sicily and Southern Italy, "thousands of miles" toward Germany itself. "They have suffered heavy losses, but not great enough yet to collapse." Then raising his voice ever so slightly, Roosevelt admonished, "Germany has not been driven yet to surrender. Germany has not been driven yet to the point where she will be unable to recommence world conquests a generation hence. Therefore, victory still lies some distance ahead."

Then, again without the slightest hint of any specific timetable, Roosevelt promised, "That distance will be covered in due time. Have no fear of that," adding the warning "but it will be tough and it will be costly."

But not to Bob. Viola whispered this as if she were now talking directly to the president.

A deafening silence followed after Roosevelt extended his congratulations to the Allied commanders who had led the fight for Italy's freedom, and to all their brave officers and men.

So ended the news about the fall of Rome.

Disappointed there had been absolutely no information about when the invasion of Western Europe would start, Viola decided to forego listening to the music that followed and instead go outside, walk off her anxiety, and get some fresh air before going to bed.

~THREE~

ALTHOUGH THE NIGHT HAD BECOME hazy Viola could see the almost perfect full moon hovering over the houses on Oak Street. She walked for nearly a half hour and thought about what Sonny had said, especially his hunch that the large moon could mean the invasion might happen soon. For some reason—maybe it was a premonition - she decided to stay up late. Viola knew she could never sleep when she was this worked up with nervous anticipation.

So she cut her walk short, went back to the house, and then decided to make a fresh pot of coffee. She swept the kitchen floor to keep herself busy while it percolated. Then she went from room to room, tidying up, despite how thick and sticky the nighttime air now felt. The smell of the brewing coffee kept her going; suddenly she wasn't tired at all. The time passed quickly while music played on the radio and the clock on the mantel over the fireplace in her living room ticked steadily towards midnight.

The latest *Life* magazine was lying on top of the pile on her coffee table, so she spent some time sipping her coffee and looking through it. On the cover was a big black and white picture of General "Tooey" Spaatz. Inside she saw pages of advertisements, promoting everything from Ipana toothpaste and Vaseline hair tonic to wartime support efforts by Buick, B.F. Goodrich and General Electric. Then there were pictures of Gene Kelly showing his fabulous dancing style, more ads, and suddenly she saw the cover credit in the middle of the next page.

Spaatz commanded the Army's air forces preparing for the invasion.

A piece entitled "The First Attack: Italy" came a few pages later; Viola thought this was old news, given Roosevelt's earlier address on the fall of Rome. But there were pictures that interested her. One showed tanks moving along a desolate dirt road at enough speed to leave clouds of dust behind them; another of soldiers marching through bombed out towns; then another of a destroyed Gothic-arched church, and finally one more of other soldiers in jeeps driving along a street with more collapsed buildings around them.

Pages with plenty more pictures followed, this time showing aerial photographs of destroyed Italian marshaling yards, blasted sheds and roundhouses in Florence, mangled roads and rail bridges at Giulianova, a knocked out railroad viaduct at Bucine, factory yards at Verona honeycombed by bomb craters, and a string of bombs marching across a bridge in Florence with white flecks of splashing water where debris was falling.

The next page revealed American soldiers asleep in foxholes they had dug. These upset her. It seemed to Viola that the foxholes looked too much like shallow graves, absent the dirt that would have covered their lifeless bodies if they were dead. She quickly turned the page.

She was rewarded with a glowing full-page picture of Franklin Roosevelt, taken very recently "to let the country see how well he looks." Viola nodded her approval; there had been a lot of speculation about his health. On the next page she saw hundreds of workers celebrating Boeing's Seattle Washington plant's completion of its 5,000th B-17 Flying Fortress, the Army Air Corps' dependable heavy bomber. Pictures of battleships at sea firing salvos at targets somewhere in the Pacific followed, and another one showed a group of handsome American naval fliers who had been shot down into the vast sea, but were rescued by a U.S. submarine.

Then, on both sides of the next two pages, came the first shocking pictures of Adolf Hitler's vaunted Atlantic Wall, with its fortifications somewhere along the European coastline across from England. All of Germany had been led to believe their super human forces would stop any invasion right at the water's edge, and that no Allied divisions would ever get off the beaches, wherever they made the mistake of landing. The pictures were haunting. How did *Life* get these, Viola wondered? One caption under a camouflaged fort answered that. They were released by the Nazis themselves, probably as a propaganda tool to strike fear into the hearts of anyone viewing them.

Another picture showed anti-tank obstacles somewhere along the Low Countries' shores. Then yet another revealed a huge tunnel that had been blasted through a high, rocky piece of the ocean side so the Germans could supply by rail their big fixed guns that they said could shoot all the way across the Channel into England, or into France wherever the Allied forces might dare to strike.

But one picture made Viola's heart stop; it was a terrifying shot of a huge concrete and barbed-wire-surrounded fortress, what the caption said was "a strongpoint, which can fight in all directions and will hold out even when surrounded." Its massive structure was laid into a rising slope with its big-barreled gun aimed at the beach below. For the first time Viola felt chills, despite the warmth of the now past midnight air in Naugatuck.

She next was staring at a picture of a couple strolling aimlessly through Hyde Park in London, a favorite spot for American boys to meet their English girls. Another showed a GI walking arm-in-arm with his girl amongst sheep in Kensington Garden, and yet another was of an officer with his date by a long and shallow pond in the heart of Hyde Park. Viola looked closer at the first one. She thought it might be her son Bob and his blonde English girl, but upon closer inspection she saw the young woman was a brunette.

Then Viola's world suddenly changed.

It was now a quarter to one. NBC in New York suspended its regular program - accordion, organ and guitar music being played by a New York City nightclub trio called the Three Sons—and then an excited newsman's voice said with breathless urgency, "We interrupt our program to bring you a special broadcast. German News Agency Transocean said today in a broadcast that the Allied invasion has begun. I repeat, the German News Agency Transocean said in a news broadcast today that the invasion has begun. There was no Allied confirmation."

Viola was suddenly wide awake; she gasped aloud "Oh my God," but no one of course heard her.

The resonate voice of the newsman then cautiously offered in a more level tone, "The German broadcast could be one that the Allied leaders expected would be made with the purpose of upsetting patriot plans inside the conquered countries. This bulletin has come to you from the NBC newsroom in New York. There is no Allied confirmation."

Viola was now confused. Had the invasion really begun, or not? She continued to listen, a bit impatiently now, while a sweeping fresh breeze of the now somewhat cooler nighttime air came into her living room.

"The Associated Press recorded the broadcast which said the invasion had begun from the west and that the French Port of Le Havre was being shelled," the broadcaster continued. "Le Havre lies 100 miles from the British Port of Portsmouth and is eighty miles south of the English town of New Haven. German naval forces off the coast are engaged in a battle with enemy landing craft. The German News Agency said the Allied invasion began with the landing of airborne troops at the mouth of the Seine River. I repeat, however, that there is no Allied confirmation of this claim.

"We return you now to our regularly scheduled broadcast" was all Viola heard next, and then a forlorn piano solo started capturing the gathering gravity of the day ahead.

Viola now knew she would be up for the rest of the night so she gave up any thought of even trying to go to bed. She'd pay for that at work tomorrow, but she did not care. Minutes were running together, and at 2:55 a.m., a new voice, that of Richard Harkness and ringing with clarity, broke in to tell his NBC listeners: "The German radio claims this morning that the Allied invasion has begun. There is no confirmation as yet from Washington, London or any other Allied source. If I may at this early hour recapitulate the invasion news as it has been transmitted to the NBC newsroom here in Washington. The first invasion bulletin came from London, dated Tuesday June 6. A broadcast of the German Transocean Agency said today the invasion began in the first hours of this morning. That is the original bulletin received regarding the invasion.

"May I interpolate here to say that the German Transocean Agency is the official German news agency and obviously a Nazi propaganda agent. The second bulletin which was received here in Washington at 12:43 Eastern War Time says this: London, Tuesday June 6. German radio said today that German war ships are battling enemy war ships that are landing at Le Havre."

Viola cringed when she again heard, "There is no confirmation from Allied sources," before Harkness followed by offering, "The German broadcast could be one which Allied leaders had expected would be made with the purpose of upsetting plans inside the conquered country." But listeners were also cautioned that Prime Minister Winston Churchill had previously warned that any news of a landing at places like Le Havre could be a feint, and Allied forces may land elsewhere in the main invasion.

Viola, like other Americans who were hearing this broadcast, felt nothing but total frustration. Was this real, or not?

Then the broadcast took a new turn. Harkness started delivering an analysis of the recent bulletins so he could help tamp down the angst he correctly perceived his listeners were feeling. "Now, so far, all this news is from Nazi sources. This means, without doubt, one of three things. It may mean first that the Germans are merely fishing for information. They are dithering; they want to know in the very worst way when this invasion is really going to come, and by putting out bulletins you have heard so far this evening they may be trying to find out.

"The second possibility of course is this: As was mentioned in a speech not so long ago, Prime Minister Churchill said when the invasion comes there will be feints and dress rehearsals, and false alarms. Now, if these attacks aren't in progress as the Germans report, these attacks—to quote the Prime Minister—could be feints, dress rehearsals and false alarms in advance of the main, concerted Allied invasion attempt. And the third possibility of course is that this really is the invasion and the Germans have sent out the first word over their propaganda facility. But, again, so far the War Department in Washington has said that they have no information."

Then Harkness signed off with, "That is, Ladies and Gentlemen, the invasion news up to this moment. Keep tuned to your NBC stations which are prepared to give you the fullest, authoritative news on the invasion throughout the night."

With this Viola got up and went into her kitchen, finally put away her dinner dishes, and warmed up her pot of coffee.

She had just returned to her living room when another announcement came from the NBC newsroom in New York. There was new information and it had just come in over the wires. A fresh voice gushed: "At 1:00 a.m. Eastern War Time this morning the BBC broadcast Allied high command urgent instructions to people in Holland advising them that if they were living within thirty-five kilometers—about eighteen miles from the coast—to leave their homes immediately, and also to keep off roads, railroads and bridges. These instructions from the BBC followed in less than an hour after a German broadcast announcing Allied parachute troops had landed in France. That report is not yet confirmed by the Allied sources."

Viola was then told she was again being redirected to regular scheduled programming. Holland, she wondered? Was this where we were going to start the invasion of Europe? Or was it just a feint, like Churchill said it could be?

Fifteen minutes later, with another cup of coffee in her hand, an alert Viola heard yet another bulletin come across the airwaves.

"From London, Tuesday June 6 .... three London news agencies have now reported that the Allied Invasion of Western France has begun with parachute troops spilling out of the skies at dawn over the Normandy Peninsula. One of these reports said that seaborne forces had landed in the Le Havre area. There is no Allied confirmation. Reports also said that Allied warships were furiously hitting the big German-held port of Le Havre at the mouth of the Seine River, a hundred miles west of Paris. They also said that German shock troops were hurled against Allied troops who were rushing ashore from landing barges."

Was Sonny right after all? And where, exactly, is Normandy? Viola started looking through her magazines on the coffee table for the *Hammond World Atlas* he had given her as the news broadcast continued.

"The German News agency said that Dunkirk and Calais, just across the Channel from Britain, are now under attack by strong formations of Allied bombers. The German Transocean Agency said the long expected invasion by the British and the Americans has begun." This news was then repeated with yet another cautious warning: "Allied headquarters, I repeat, has remained silent. This report had come from the German sources at 7 a.m. French time, 1 a.m. Eastern War Time." It was also reported that "no enemy landings have been made as yet at Calais or Dunkirk, and this seems to confirm that the Germans were expecting landings all along the French coast."

Then the airwaves went silent.

But not for long. After finding in the atlas where Normandy was in France, Viola suddenly was taken back to the NBC station in Washington. Richard Harkness reported, "So far ladies and gentlemen the news is this: The first word of the invasion, if it is an invasion, came from the Nazis at 1237 o'clock this morning, which is 6:37 in Great Britain." Harkness then went on to repeat, word for word, every previous announcement, again ending his segment with there were still no Allied confirmations of these reports "but that almost the entire public relations staff at the War Department had reported for duty in the big Pentagon building across the Potomac River in Virginia."

For Viola, this was now getting frighteningly worrisome.

Moments later she was told that a BBC broadcast, received in New York, had reported to the residents of France that "a new phase of the air war on the continent had begun," and they were told "to stand by for further instructions that would be dropped by leaflets from American and British planes."

Viola then heard an NBC analyst named Morgan Beatty explain that the Germans were apparently desperate for information, so if Allied forces landed in smaller garrisoned areas they would know where to send their troops and armored columns to repel the landings "when and if they were the real thing." But Beatty also pointed out that the Germans very likely had their own information about where Allied forces might be attacking, and "were careful to keep it away from us. In this situation, it is only natural that the Allied high command is not going to put out reports about our activities, if any, at this time," and this was the news that mattered, adding "so far the Allied command has indicated this is just another night."

Then this came a few minutes later.

Robert St. John reported from the NBC newsroom in New York: "Londoners were awakened in the early hours of this morning by the roaring of planes," that they saw "the largest forces of bombers and fighters ever to take the air, fighters and bombers sailing away across the Channel. The latest Berlin broadcast is one that reveals the diabolic nature of the Nazis, with their announcement in London saying this is D-Day. We shall now bring on music for the Allied invasion forces."

So the Brits are saying it really is D-Day, Viola anxiously thought. Or, had Beatty again said the Germans revealed this?

NBC did go back to its regularly scheduled musical program, but not before American listeners were warned yet again that the Germans could issue false information, thinking this would "bring patriot French forces out in the open for annihilation, but if the announcement was true this could be only a diversion, or a large scale raid."

Twenty minutes later came the first news that finally confirmed in Viola's mind that the invasion was likely happening because it originated from General Eisenhower's headquarters.

It was reported that "London radio has just issued a warning from the Allied Supreme Commander advising the French people to leave the entire coastline of France," followed by another bulletin, also from London, saying what Viola had already heard for hours now: "The German military commentator made the first comment on the reported invasion today. He said the great contest between the Reich and the Anglo-Americans has begun, which incidentally are still not confirmed by the Allies."

NBC then returned yet again to its regular scheduled broadcast, this time with music featuring accordions, violins, horns and flutes, but St. John promised NBC would continue airing full five-minute updates over its 146 affiliated stations.

Viola was now torn between being convinced the invasion had begun and the maddening reports that there was still no official confirmation that it had actually gone off. It was now well past three o'clock in the morning.

A newsworthy, yet careful announcement was made less than a

half hour later by a spokesman on behalf of General Dwight D. Eisenhower. "A new phase of the air offensive has started," Viola was now told. "It will affect the entire coastal zone areas situated not less than thirty-five kilometers inland from the French coast. People living on Europe's invasion coast will be advised by special announcements dropped by Allied planes.

"The attack will take place not less than one hour later. As soon as the warning is given, the following orders are to be followed: First, leave your towns at once. Second, choose routes out of town to avoid the main roads. Third, leave on foot, only carrying essentials. Fourth, go to areas at least two kilometers from your towns. Do not assemble in groups, in groups that might appear to be group concentrations. Keep away as far as possible from roads and railroad lines, and take nothing with you that you cannot carry personally."

The French people were again advised to leave at once, adding even more urgency to the message.

Viola's heart was now racing. General Eisenhower seemed to have confirmed the invasion news was real. She could only imagine how scared the French people must be.

~FOUR~

IT WAS EVEN MUCH FURTHER into the night when the airwaves gave way to what sounded to Viola much like Morse code, with alternating tones, some flat, others punctuated with dashes and sudden stops. Long dot, dot, dots were followed by silence before yet more rapid and closer together connected dots came through her Philco radio.

Suddenly there was this alert: "This is NBC in New York. We may be approaching a fateful hour. All night long bulletins have been coming in from Berlin saying that D-Day was here, claiming that the invasion of Western Europe has begun. Unconfirmed reports have been coming in indicating the Germans are engaged with Allied forces on the Normandy coast, and important airdromes have been knocked out."

Then, a few minutes later, an expansive voice came over the airwaves and said that a very special announcement would be forthcoming from the British capitol, "in a matter of seconds. So now we take you to London."

Viola just stared at the radio with her arms folded in her lap and waited.

First, she listened to more static that sounded this time like papers being shuffled, followed by more maddening silence that lasted for nearly fifteen seconds before Viola finally heard a British broadcaster say just the two words "expeditionary force," leaving her to believe she had missed what he said before this. But the next words carried the importance of what she was now going to be told, beginning with the announcement: "Communique Number One will be released to the press and radio of the United Nations in 10 seconds. Repeat, 10 seconds from now." British idiom was present; "now" was dragged out for effect and emphasis. Then more static followed while an agonized Viola waited yet again.

"Under the command of General Eisenhower, allied naval forces supported by strong air forces began landing allied armies this morning on the northern coast of France. The communique will be repeated." The few words were, and then the announcer simply stated, "This ends the reading of Communique Number One from Supreme Headquarters, Allied Expeditionary Force."

So, Sonny had indeed been right. This was the real thing. It's now official. Viola felt almost a sense of relief, the stresses of the past four hours giving way to a muted feeling of both reserved hope and patriotism.

Then it was back to New York, with the announcer here breaking in and very dramatically saying, "Ladies and Gentlemen, this is a momentous hour in world history. This is the invasion of Western Europe, the zero hour. The men of General Dwight D. Eisenhower are leaving their landing barges, making their way up the beaches into the fortress of Nazi Europe. They are moving in from the sea to attack the enemy under a mammoth cloud of fighter planes, under a ceiling of screaming shells from Allied warships."

Viola suddenly felt chills again. She just knew her son Bob was one of the young Americans leaving a landing craft somewhere on the coast in Normandy, and she prayed he would get off the beach alive, wherever he was.

But she nervously kept staring at the radio. Now she was wringing her hands, her fingers of one alternately squeezing the knuckles of the other.

"The first reports do not say, but this is presumed to be in the hands of American men, making the attack side-by-side with British Tommies who were bombed and blasted out of Europe at

Dunkirk; now at this hour they are bombing and blasting their way back again. This is the European front, once again being established in fire and blood, not only by the Americans and British but by the many allies in the fight against Axis aggression.

"This is the supreme test of allied spirit and of allied weapons; the world's greatest military undertaking is underway. Casualties in this mammoth operation and subsequent drive inland may reach a dreadful toll. The German war machine is still powerful and strongly entrenched, but this attack is being made with all the strength the Allies can throw into battle. General Eisenhower has promised that his forces will bring victory in Europe in 1944. The first mission of our forces will be to secure their beachheads. You have already heard the flash that came from London—the Allied announcement that the invasion of Western Europe has begun, that D-Day is here, that H-hour has struck."

Now Viola suddenly wanted to cry, but she held her tears back, fearful she would miss what was coming.

Moments later the announcer started with, "And now" but paused to catch his breath before repeating, "And now . . . for another special broadcast we take you to London, England." Static filled the airwaves yet again, then there was a quick woof sound, but a raspy voice quickly said, "Ten seconds; stand by" followed after more annoying static with "eight seconds," then "five seconds, stand by" and finally "three, two" and then a somewhat soft voice that didn't seem to fit the moment announced: "The following is the order of the day issued today by General Eisenhower to each individual of the Allied Expeditionary Force."

Viola held her breath.

Another voice, she later learned to be that of famed newsman Edward R. Morrow, started with: "Soldiers, sailors and airmen of the Allied Expeditionary Force. You are about to embark on the great crusade, for which we have striven for many months. The eyes of the world are upon you. The hopes and prayers of liberty-loving people everywhere march with you. In company with our brave allies and brothers-in-arms on other fronts you will bring about the destruction of the German war machine, the elimination of Nazi tyranny over the oppressed people of Europe, and security for ourselves in a free world.

"Your task will not be an easy one. Your enemy is well-trained, well-equipped and battle hardened. He will fight savagely. But this is the year 1944. Much has happened since the Nazi triumphs of 1940 and 1941. The United Nations has inflicted upon the Germans great defeats, in open battle, man-to-man. Our air offensive has seriously reduced their strength in the air and their capacity to wage war on the ground. Our home fronts have given us an overwhelming superiority in munitions of war, and placed at our disposal great reserves of fighting men. The tide has turned. The free men of the world are marching together to victory.

"I have full confidence in your courage, devotion to duty and skill in battle. We will accept nothing less than full victory. Good luck. And let us all beseech the blessings of Almighty God upon this great and noble undertaking."

After a brief pause, the earlier voice came back and said, "In a moment you will hear directly from Supreme Allied Commander, Dwight D. Eisenhower." Viola fixed her tired eyes on the radio again. But Eisenhower's voice was raspy, and there was a great deal of background noise, making his words barely discernable. All she could make out was that by 8:00 a.m. local time in Britain airborne troops had suffered only light losses; preliminary bombing had occurred; Navy minesweeping was ongoing; and that opposition so far seemed light. And she did hear that "All preliminary reports are satisfactory."

These reports would later prove to be untrue.

Outside, first light was awakening others in Naugatuck. Then, in a sudden rush, Viola went to the closet by her front door, took out her American flag, went outside, unfurled it, and then placed it in the bracket on the column of her porch for all of her neighbors to see.

The flag fluttered proudly in the same light breezes that had help keep her up all night.

~FIVE~

BY NOW SUNLIGHT WAS JUST beginning to appear on the east side of the houses on Oak Street. After Viola dressed for work, she rushed back into her kitchen to make a bologna sandwich, and together with an apple and some cookies placed her lunch in her big embroidered purse. Then, glancing at her small-faced Timex wristwatch, she realized she had well over an hour before her shift at the rubber plant started, so she decided to go to church and say a prayer for Bob.

As she started down the big hill on Oak Street that ran into Maple at the fast flowing Naugatuck River, she noticed the porch lights were still on at her neighbor Mrs. Walker's two-story home. Viola glanced at the gold star above the big blue "V" on the service flag in the window next to her front door, the same flag she saw every morning on her way to work, a grim reminder that it had once been a simple blue star—now covered over with that gold star - before her son George was killed in North Africa.

They usually exchanged greetings, but Viola didn't want to call out to Mrs. Walker in case she hadn't risen yet. Further down the hill was a newsstand. She stared at the headlines of the *Naugatuck Daily News* as she walked by, but there was nothing about the invasion.

Maybe it was yesterday's paper, she thought.

Once on Maple she started over the river on the Whittemore Memorial Bridge. She now knew few people were awake. She'd run into other women on the bridge coming home from the night shift at the plant most days, but not today.

Or was she just out too early to run into people, she wondered.

Striding with purpose now, it only took a few more minutes for Viola to reach the town green and walk up towards the lead-windowed, gabled St. Michael's Episcopal church where both her boys had been baptized. She had always admired the church's tall flanking square tower, with its arched windows and flared pyramidal roof that was covered with multi-colored slate pieces. Viola made her way towards the church's Baroque-style entrance, with its fluted Ionic columns and thick wooden double-door, went up the steps and opened it. Then she went through the entrance, beneath its wooden trefoil brace, and into the church where she sat down to pray in the last row of pews.

She had barely bowed her head when she felt a gentle hand on her shoulder. A bit startled, she turned to see that it belonged to her mother-in-law Nellie, her dead husband's mother. Nellie spoke quietly to her, whispering that she had heard the invasion had started, then asked if she could sit next to her so they both could say a prayer for Bob.

Viola welcomed this, so together they bowed their heads in silence. Henry Baummer Sr., Nellie's husband, had passed away six months earlier. He had been the church's sextant who maintained the magnificent church and its grounds. He had also been an officer of the church and a minor municipal figure who oversaw parishioner burials at Grove Cemetery, just south of town where Viola's husband and his and Nellie's son was laid to rest back in 1937.

After she and Nellie said their prayers for Bob, exchanged hugs and goodbyes, Viola left to go down Church Street towards the rubber plant, but a quick glance at her watch told her she still had time to go up to the north edge of the town green and stop by the neo-classical revival World War One Memorial. Her brother Edwin, whom she named Sonny after, had served in that war, survived, but came home a very sick man from the brutal German poison gassing of the long narrow trenches he was often holed up in.

He died before he turned thirty years old. Viola thought it was right to say a prayer for him, given that the First War had not turned out to be the war that would end all wars after all, and her son Bob was now settling that score for her brother somewhere in Normandy.

When she got there, Viola stood before the tall flagstaff and first stared at the pink granite slab that supported the sarcophagus-shaped limestone monument that it rose from. The early morning sun shone upon the low bas-relief figures that represented peace and war, but she couldn't comprehend at that moment the words "Victory Is Consecrated by A Righteous Peace." It just wasn't so with war raging just about everywhere now. Then she rounded the monument, first passing carvings of sacrificial rams' heads connected by fruit garlands where "Armed and Absolute Might Triumphs Through Unselfish Valor" was engraved. Then, turning to the west side of the monument she finally saw the names of the thirty men from town who had died in the Great War.

After she said her brief prayer for her brother and those who had made the supreme sacrifice during that conflict some twenty-six years earlier, she asked the Almighty to spare her son in this current war, ending with the solemn request, "Please, Dear God, never make me look at Bob's name on a memorial like this. Amen."

Although Viola didn't know it at that moment, Mayor Bernard Samuel was entering the historic foyer at the south end of Independence Hall in Philadelphia and walking towards the Liberty Bell. It had not been sounded for more than a hundred years, but Samuel was now holding a wooden mallet and preparing to tap the iconic bell. NBC was carrying the ceremony live to its listeners.

The mayor first announced: "This great bell which you are about to hear was first rung in Independence Hall in 1753. It bears the inscription from the Leviticus: 'Proclaim Liberty Throughout the Land unto All the Inhabitants Thereof.' Now, through radio, let it indeed proclaim liberty throughout the land and the return of liberty throughout the world."

It was a gigantic moment across America when Mayor Samuel tapped the bell seven times, one time for each of the letters in the word "Liberty."

Viola would have loved hearing the Liberty Bell ring, but at that moment she still had about a mile to walk to reach the rubber plant, so she started out and first saw the Salem School, set high on a brownstone foundation and constructed of brick, where her oldest sister Kathryn taught first grade. Next she passed a small park, then she crossed the walkway and headed towards the eastern perimeter of the town green, passing pink granite pollards lined with trees, and eventually made her way down Church Street, then over to Elm, arriving at the plant just in time for the start of her shift.

The night watchmen were clocking out, and were well aware of the news that the largest land, sea and air assault in military history had begun.

Viola found herself surprisingly wide awake as she greeted the women she worked with, all of whom asked her if she thought Bob was amongst the first to land in France. She gave them all the same answer: "I just pray, if he was, that he's spared from harm."

Most of Naugatuck's citizens had awakened to the news of the invasion by this time, but details about what divisions had landed where would not be learned for weeks. Some were actually skeptical when they were informed of the great event. Others, especially mothers with sons in uniform, for some reason were not. Throughout the morning hundreds gathered at the *Naugatuck Daily News* building, and the paper did its best to keep them informed. A bulletin service was even arranged so the city's curious factory workers like Viola could be kept up to date while they toiled away at their much needed tasks to support the war effort.

But there was little news from overseas. At home that fateful morning there was far more news. Across America, while Viola worked through the day, patriotism and prayers were everywhere. In New York City hundreds gathered outside of St. Patrick's Cathedral before its giant brass doors opened for the first mass at seven that morning. Five special masses were eventually said, in addition to the Cathedral's three regularly scheduled services. By nightfall 75,000 Catholic New Yorkers had worshipped in that great house of God, and Archbishop Francis Spellman had recited prayers heard by any American near a radio.

The city's powerful traders on the New York Stock Exchange were even led in a six-minute prayer with a reading that included the sixty-eighth Psalm of David, before the largest one-day volume in the past six months closed the session that afternoon.

At the Emunath Israel synagogue on West Twenty-Third Street, Jewish worshippers were greeted with a sign above its door that read: "This Synagogue Will Be Open for 24 Hours for Special Services on D-Day. All are Welcomed." Thousands came. At the Church of the Holy Cross on Manhattan's mid-town west side, candles were lit in its Victory Chapel; the walls were lined with almost 8,000 service flags, each bearing the name of a young man who had worshipped there before going off to war.

It was like this everywhere as more Americans awoke to the big news of the invasion. Bells rang in churches throughout the nation. Stores closed. The president of Lord & Taylor on Fifth Avenue in New York City, after closing its doors, ordered that a twenty-seven-by-forty-foot flag be flown from the third floor. Window displays were covered with signs that read: "The invasion has begun. Our only thought can be of the men who are fighting in it." Macy's at Herald Square also closed. That night's baseball game between the Phillies and the Dodgers at Ebbets Field in Brooklyn was cancelled. Fans instead gave blood.

In Corpus Christie, Texas, something more unusual happened.

Nearly a hundred parents of servicemen crawled for two blocks on their hands and knees in penance.

Support for the men overseas spread to the West Coast as the day wore on. Shipyard workers in Berkley California even sent a telegram to His Excellency Franklin D. Roosevelt in Washington, with a request that it be forwarded to General Eisenhower. It read: "Thousands of Negro shipyard workers pledge their unstinted support to those now engaged in the struggle to the death of democracy over fascism." It was signed by the Chairman of the Shipyard Committee Against Discrimination.

Viola knew nothing about the patriotism and heart-felt worshipping that were happening across America, but she had heard whistles going off and church bells ringing in Naugatuck as she sweated away at the plant making insoles for Jungle boots. After she ate lunch in the worker's cafeteria her supervisor came over to her as she sat down to go back to work and said, "Mrs. Baummer, you look very tired. I know it has to be hard for you to stay and work while your heart is with Bob, like all of ours are, and your mind is on the invasion. I'll clock you out at the end of the day. Why don't you go home?"

Viola merely looked up at him and answered, "Thank you, but no. I'm staying right here. The boots we're making are too important to the boys over in the Pacific. If what I'm doing now helps them kill Japs, it'll bring this damn war to an end a lot sooner. I'll be fine."

When the end-of-shift whistle finally blew later that afternoon Viola left the plant and started walking home. Her steps were slow, but her determined spirit could not be broken. She wanted to get to the newsstand on Maple to see what the papers were saying. As she got closer she noticed that the usual pile of the *Naugatuck Daily News* papers was not there. It appeared that the day's edition was sold out. But the *Waterbury Republican* headline jumped out at her; it read ALLIES LAND IN FRANCE. She opened her embroidered purse, found the four pennies the nearby daily paper cost, and handed it to the newsboy.

She also decided to take a copy of the latest edition of the *New York Daily News* with her. INVASION BEGINS was printed in large capital letters, big and bold enough to cover the entire front page above where it was folded on the table in front of the newsstand.

As she started to leave the newsboy told her that the paper had not printed its usual editorial. Instead the Lord's Prayer appeared in its place.

When she made her way up the steep hill on Oak Street, this time Mrs. Walker was sitting on her front porch. "I prayed for you and Bob today, Viola," she gently called out. Then she rose from her wicker chair, rushed down the sidewalk, took Viola by the arm, and helped her make the final difficult steps up the hill.

Mrs. Walker noticed that Viola was crying ever so gently now, so she turned and gave her a big hug when they reached 90 Oak Street. Then the two women looked directly at each other. Composing herself, an exhausted Viola just said, "You're the only person I know who can understand how I feel right now."

"Yes, I am," Mrs. Walker answered before asking, "Can I fix dinner for you tonight?"

"No, thank you, that's very kind of you, but I'll manage."

With that Mrs. Walker went back down Oak Street to her house. Viola shuffled up her short sidewalk onto her porch, glanced at Bob's service flag with its blue star that was hanging in her living room window, unlocked her front door and went inside. She came back out a few seconds later; she'd forgotten to grab the mail on the way in.

There was no letter from Bob.

~SIX~

VIOLA PUT HER PURSE AND the two newspapers down on the kitchen table, looked through the mail she did get, and was just starting to think about what she could make for dinner when there was a gentle knock at the front door.

When she opened it there was Nellie again, this time carrying a basket covered with a white napkin that smelled good. "I brought you dinner, Viola dear," she announced in her soft British accent. "I know you have had a long day, so I thought the least I could do was offer you a little company and something decent and warm to eat."

Nellie had roasted a chicken, and put together a salad. Viola was overwhelmed by her kindness so she told her to of course come in, and together they went into the kitchen.

They were eating and talking about the invasion when the telephone rang. "I better get it," Viola said. "It could be Sonny."

But it wasn't him; it was her oldest sister Kathryn, the first grade school teacher. They stayed on the phone for a few minutes, exchanged what they knew about the invasion, and then Viola went back to her dinner and told Nellie there was little news from Kathryn, but she was glad she called.

"She did say that while she was listening to her radio this afternoon she had heard someone on a command ship talking about what he could see onshore where the invasion was happening," Viola told Nellie. "Things like bombs dropping on the beaches, machineguns firing and smoke and wild fire all over the coast. It sounded awful."

They looked at each other, both knowing what the other was thinking—hadn't earlier reports said things were going well?

By the time Nellie left Viola was so tired her bones ached. She knew she had to keep herself up for maybe another hour, so she started for the front door to bring her flag in, knowing it would be dark soon, but before she could open it the telephone rang again.

"Mother," Sonny began. "I tried to reach you earlier this morning, but you didn't answer. I've been worried all day. Are you alright?"

Viola told Sonny about her day, how she had been to church before work, how Nellie had come by with dinner, and how little she really knew about the invasion. Sonny told her he was still in his office, mainly to keep his mind occupied rather than be worrying about Bob, and how relieved he was to finally hear her voice.

"The invasion news is all over the papers up here, but there's no word yet about what divisions landed where in Normandy," Viola told him.

"You should see the *Charleston Gazette*, Mother. Three quarters of the front page has "ALLIES INVADE" in huge red letters. There's just an inch or two of the story beneath it. Came out this morning. Roosevelt is going to be on the radio again at ten tonight, in case you didn't know."

"I didn't Sonny," Viola answered. "I suppose I'm going to have to keep myself up to listen." She did not want to tell him she had stayed up all the previous night because it would just make him worry more about her. Sonny asked if by any chance she had gotten a letter from Bob, and trying not to sound disappointed she told him no and soon afterwards they hung up.

After Viola put the telephone handset down, she went into the living room, turned on the radio, and sat on the couch. Her nerves felt raw, but she wasn't much of a drinker or a smoker, so she had to find another way to calm herself. Impulsively, she picked up the pictures she had on her coffee table, and started to look through them. The first was one of her favorites—Sonny and Bob as little kids. They were in cute sailor outfits and both were holding up two American flags. Viola thought back. That was the 4th of July in 1925. It made her smile. Her mind drifted back to how Bob had shown her a great deal of affection when he was a young boy, how he made strong tea and coffee for her when she wheezed and coughed during her frequent bouts with asthma back then.

Then there was another picture that must have been taken that same fall. There they both were again, standing next to the garage door. They were facing out toward the street, Sonny—a head taller—with his arms by his side looking like he was not happy poising for the picture. Bob's were clasped behind him with his fingers spread, looking like he was teasing his brother with some gesture, which explained the look on Sonny's face.

Viola thought back to how Bob had always been a happy boy. They had an extended family during those times and one of her husband's brothers owned a home on Long Island Sound in the Devon section of Milford. When Bob wasn't riding a real pony in his Uncle Rudy's big yard, his father would take him over to a nearby arcade where he could pretend he was by hopping on the Coney Island-style carousel and climbing onto the saddle of a prancing horse. Henry even bought a twenty-two-foot Chris-Craft Cadet runabout when Bob was seven-years old, and they would go out together on the Housatonic River on Saturdays when the weather was good during the summer. Most Sundays, rain or sunshine, the entire family would go over to Gram Nellie's tidy home on Trobridge Place back in Naugatuck for a cookout.

Viola gazed at other pictures as Bob got older. She remembered when he blossomed into his teen years he learned things from his best friend George Walker, including how to rebuild cars, any and all things to do with Indian motorcycles, and how to shoot BB-guns. She also remembered the time the boys played hooky from school and went to the mysterious Gunntown Cemetery down in the Millville section of town to see if it was really haunted, as the legend went. How they hitched a ride and got picked up in an old red truck by an off-duty Naugatuck cop who scared them more than the supposed ghosts did.

She even reminisced about how Bob could strum and pick at a Gibson mandolin, bang a Slingerland parade drum in rhythm to the marching music on the Philco radio she was now listening to, and blow a decent scale on a RexCraft brass bugle, all by the time he was fourteen years old. Viola laughed as she recalled how this drove her serious-minded Sonny to stay at school to do his homework, leaving Bob to continue roaming freely wherever his free spirit took him—until the night he shot out that streetlamp with his BB gun.

Wasn't it ironic, Viola thought. Her oldest boy got into Dartmouth College up in Hanover New Hampshire the same year her youngest was sent off to a reform school, that Connecticut Junior Republic place up in Litchfield. Sonny had worked his way through Dartmouth while Bob, in exchange for receiving a trade education, had to literally earn his keep by paying rent for his room, buy school books, and cover the cost for his food and other personal needs. All without her and Henry's help; the school forbade parents from offering any financial support whatsoever.

But it was OK for Henry to drive him back to the school that time Bob was so homesick he walked the twenty-five miles it was between Litchfield and Naugatuck just to see his parents and be home.

The Republic had been an exceptional experience for Bob. Viola remembered that he made both the school football and baseball teams. He even marched in the Republic's Drum Corps, and on Memorial Days dressed in his handsome gold-striped blue uniform, donned a polished chrome helmet, and marched in parades held in three towns near Litchfield.

As Viola thumbed through more pictures she thought back to that horrible fall of 1937. It was the year Henry killed himself down on the beach in Milford and made her a widow. Then Bob developed pneumonia over the following winter and was confined to the school's infirmary into the following summer. Viola thought about how she and Nellie had come to see him as often as they could, and the time the school nurse confessed to them that she was very concerned about what this confinement was doing to Bob. He had turned listless and unmotivated; she even used the word "depressed" to describe his general state of mind. He wasn't getting better. Viola was certain that Bob would do fine at home. The nurse agreed and also said she really needed his bed for other sick boys, so home he had come, bringing with him valuable lessons he had learned about life and responsibility no ordinary school could have taught him.

There were two more pictures of Bob that made Viola suddenly realize how proud of him she was now. The first one was of him in his Army uniform; he had sent that picture to her while he was in training down at a place in Florida called Camp Blanding. He was wearing his garrison cap, and holding the barrel of a rifle in his right hand with its butt on the ground next to his foot. He had leggins over his boots. . .what did he actually call those? Yes, gaiters, and they were supposed to keep mud from getting into the tops of his boots and also give him a little ankle support. His left arm was behind him in the small of his back; his uniform shirt was buttoned up to his neck. He had a gun in what looked like a holster. He had a name for that, too. That's right, he called it his personal side arm; that was strapped to his webbed belt and it hung down on his right thigh. He was also wearing an ammo pouch that was strapped to his belt.

The other picture was of Bob in the back of what looked like an open bed truck. This was also taken down at Camp Blanding, near Jacksonville in Florida, just a few weeks before he shipped out for England back in 1942. He was in a white tee-shirt this time, and his left hand held a big machine gun, aimed skyward, that was on a tri-pod base. His thick dark hair was messed up and looked like he had just run his fingers through it. Viola loved that picture. Bob had a little smirk on his face. Then she remembered that he had told her he had been trained on something he called mortars, and when he went overseas he was in what he said was a heavy weapons company.

She was hugging the next picture, an enlarged one he had sent her that was taken in some photo booth where his eyes looked sad, when President Roosevelt's voice suddenly broke the silence of the night.

"My fellow Americans," the president started in a gentle tone that made her feel he understood her own sadness. "Last night when I spoke to you about the fall of Rome, I knew at that moment that troops of the United States and our allies were crossing the Channel in another and greater operation. It has come to past, with success, thus far. And so, in this poignant hour, I ask you to join with me in prayer."

After a five second pause, the nation's president began speaking in a low, even more solemn voice. Viola held Bob's picture to her heart and bowed her head.

"Almighty God, our sons, pride of our nation, this day have set upon the mighty endeavor, a struggle to preserve our Republic, our religion, and our civilization, and to set free a suffering humanity. Lead them straight and true, give strength to their arms, stoutness to their hearts, steadfastness in their faith. They will need Thy blessings; their road will be long and hard, for the enemy is hard.

"He may hurl back our forces. Success may not come with rushing speed, but we shall return again, and again. And we know that by Thy grace, and by the righteousness of our cause, our sons will triumph. They will be so tried, by night and by day, without rest, until the victory is won. The darkness will be rent by noise and flame. Men's souls will be shaken with the violences of war."

Viola was now sobbing, but just gently.

"For these men are lately drawn from the ways of peace. They fight not for the lust of conquest. They fight to end conquest. They fight to liberate. They fight to let justice arise, and tolerance and good will among all Thy people. They yearn but for the end of battle, for their return to the haven of home."

Roosevelt's next words startled Viola; tears started streaming down her cheek as her tired mind rushed to absorb the president's startling warning.

"Some will never return. Embrace these, Father, and receive them, Thy heroic servants, into Thy kingdom. And for us at home - fathers, mothers, children, wives, sisters of brave men overseas, whose thoughts and prayers are ever with them. Help us, Almighty God, to rededicate ourselves in renewed faith in Thee in this hour of great sacrifice. "

Viola missed the next words the president offered - her sobbing drowned them out - but she collected herself in time to hear, "And let our hearts be stout, to wait out the long travail, to bear sorrows that may come, to impart our courage unto our sons, where so ever they may be. And, O' Lord, give us faith. Give us faith in Thee, faith in our sons, faith in each other, faith in our united crusade. Let not the keenness of our spirit ever be dulled. Let not the impacts of temporary events, of temporal matters of but fleeting moment— let not these deter us in our unconquerable purpose."

Then with perfect pauses, and emphasis on each word, Roosevelt closed his prayer with the nation by saying, "Thy will be done, Almighty God. Amen."

And with this Viola turned off her radio, gathered herself together, and finally went off to bed.

Others were on their way home to go to bed that night after witnessing an incredible event on Liberty Island in New York Harbor. One half hour after sunset, the 96,000 watts of floodlight that had made the Statute of Liberty so visible before war's blackout orders darkened her majestic presence shone upon her for the first time in years. Then her torch started blinking in sequences of three short flashes and one long flash, repeatedly for fifteen minutes.

Lady Liberty had proclaimed to the world "V for Victory" at the close of a very long day when Americans knew their country was never stronger, more determined and right.

Viola found it hard to sleep that night. Her eyes were constantly gazing at Bob's picture under the glow on the nightstand beside her bed.

She left the lamp on, her own simple beacon of hope that God was watching over her boy, and the last thing she remembered before falling asleep took her all the way back to that horrible time in 1939 when the world suddenly changed.

~SEVEN~

SONNY WAS JUST A WEEK away from returning to Hanover for the start of his senior year at Dartmouth when a news bulletin came through his car radio announcing Adolf Hitler's stunning invasion of Poland. It was the first of September in 1939. Sonny and Bob were enjoying their last days of summer together and were on their way back to Oak Street after visiting a nearby cousin when the big story broke.

A million and a half German ground forces, supported by more than two-thousand tanks, thundered across the border into Poland that day. Polish cavalrymen, many armed with just long medieval-like lances, were simply no match for the incredible weight of these terrifying Nazi arms.

A new art of warfare—the blitzkrieg—was about to make its debut on the worldwide stage.

After aerial attacks killed twelve-hundred Poles in the small city of Wielun, these combined German forces closed in on Warsaw. Fighter planes attacked first, and left the sides of buildings in the business district pocked after being hit with spraying bullets. Catholic crosses were knocked down by bombs in Warsaw's Novo Brodno district. In the U.S. Embassy garden, a few of its staff raised an American flag over their bomb shelter while other Americans remained at their post, even after a picture of President Roosevelt fell from the wall and landed in the tangled debris of the U.S. Counsel's office.

Forty-eight hours later most of Poland's thirty-five divisions defending Warsaw and other smaller Polish cities were either routed or surrounded. On September 13, the Polish army commander ordered what remained of his forces to withdraw towards the supposed safety of the Romanian Bridgehead in southeastern Poland, next to the Soviet border.

On September 17, the Russian army crossed into this long frontier. Hordes of horse-drawn carts filled with Red soldiers came out of the morning mist bearing white flags, and shouted warnings for the Poles not to shoot back. The Soviets led the Polish to believe they had come to help them with their fight against the Germans. It was a ruse. Within days Eastern Poland belonged to Joseph Stalin.

By this time British Prime Minister Neville Chamberlain had gone on national radio to announce that Great Britain was now at war with Germany.

Australia, New Zealand, and India followed. France also declared war on Hitler's Germany.

World War II had begun.

While Sonny was hitting the books again up in Hanover and Bob was doing chores around the house in Naugatuck when he wasn't somewhere else messing around with cars, Adolf Hitler was turning his attention towards France and England. But after talk of supposed peace with London and Paris broke down, a belligerent Hitler decided an offensive on the Western front could wait until he first invaded the weaker countries of Norway and Denmark.

On Sunday April 7 of 1940 the conquest of Norway began when two German naval groups put out to sea into gale force winds and made hard for six Norwegian cities. German merchant ships with combat troops hidden in their holds were already in three of those Norway city ports. On the rolling high seas German warships faced the threat of interception by British destroyers, but Hitler's timing of the attack was planned to catch the British fleet off guard.

In the din of darkness two nights later, with heavy seas and near-zero visibility, ten German destroyers escaped from the eyes of British watchmen and made their final approaches toward the northern Norwegian port city of Narvik, located inside the Artic Circle. By eight o'clock on the morning of April 9 Narvik was in possession of the Germans. Its local army forces never even fired a shot in anger.

Bergen, three hundred miles further south, also had fallen. Norway's largest airdrome, Sola Airfield, on its southwest coast near the port of Stavanger succumbed to German parachute troops. Kristiansand, on its southern-most coast, was also in German possession by now.

By noon on April 9 Hitler owned 1,500 miles of Norwegian coastline and control of the skies above its peace-loving people.

Oslo, Norway's capital, proved at first to be a tougher nut to crack. But that same afternoon Oslo joined the other cities on its western shores in surrendering without putting up much of a fight. It took time for the complete conquest of Norway, but an ominous shadow eventually fell upon Norwegians who had led their entire lives working for liberty and human happiness. Two hundred German civil servants and a Reich commissar, responsible only to Hitler, were placed in Oslo. Slightly under 5,000 Norwegian, French, and British forces were casualties trying to avoid this moment in history. Instead, the darkest period of her existence began for proud Norway.

Denmark, its armed forces numbering just 15,000 men, had also capitulated back on that infamous April 9, four hours after Hitler's Panzers first appeared along the rolling countryside on their way to Jutland. Copenhagen and the strategic island of Fyn fell easily. Copenhagen was bombed into submission. Danish naval vessels and shore batteries did not fire a single salvo at the German troop ships when they approached Fyn.

With Norway and Denmark conquered, Hitler again fixed his

attention on the West. France was now the principal target. He not only wanted to crush the French army, but to also gain the Channel coast, splitting France from England in advance of attacks on the British Isles. Nearly one hundred and fifty German divisions were preparing for the invasion on the Western Front.

By now Holland had also fallen. Hitler chose to subdue Holland first to divert attention away from his main attack through the hills of the Ardennes where his troops could cross the Meuse River, gain ground in Sedan, and break through the Maginot Line before moving into France.

Hitler wasted little time in this effort. On May 10, the day Holland surrendered, German shock troops crossed the Meuse and engaged French armies with a sledge hammer blow at Sedan. Three Panzer columns followed and by the morning of May 19 Hitler's blitzkrieg was within fifty miles of the English Channel. Abbeville, at the mouth of the Somme, fell the next night. With these conquests Hitler had stunningly trapped all Belgian forces, three French armies, and his own armies were closing in on the ports of Calais and Dunkirk.

King Leopold surrendered Belgium in late May. The British miraculously evacuated Dunkirk and a rescued generation of walking wounded climbed up gangplanks and back onto English soil. The hated fear of the Nazis led thousands of French and Belgian families to flee from their homes by this time, creating crawling and cursing road jams all through Flanders and Belgium. In early June German divisions unleashed their fury on what remained of the French army as the Wehrmacht continued to press towards Paris along a 400-mile front.

Within days the Germans were crushing the last weary defenders of the City of Light, and all too soon helmets littered its streets after the last French soldiers were either dragged off to prisoner of war camps, or killed. Hitler quickly received word that France wanted an armistice.

Back in Hanover New Hampshire, Sonny like everyone else in his Dartmouth graduating class by this time was asking, "What does war in Europe mean for this country and for me?"

Dean Lloyd Neidlinger even declared in the college's Aegis Yearbook, "If one single characteristic had to be chosen to distinguish the average student of the current year from the average student of other years, I would comment on his fears. Fear of war; fear of his own emotions; fear that his respect for honor and his love of liberty will sway his reasoning and make him dangerously partisan; fear of propaganda. Unlike his brothers of other war eras, the undergraduate of 1940 is neither ignorant nor indifferent to the great issues that are being dramatized, and he is sure that he wants to be a critic and not a player in the tragedy."

On June 16 Viola, Gram Nellie and her husband, Sonny's Aunts Mary Jane and Kathryn all attended his Dartmouth graduation exercises in the Bema, an amphitheater on the eastern side of campus.

Bob wasn't there. He had been working a part-time job and always on Saturdays at Mezzio's Auto in Naugatuck, where he was fixing flat tires, turning wrenches doing general vehicle repair, and making oil changes. He had also made friends with another kid he worked with, appropriately nicknamed "Savage," who owned a brand new Indian Scout with fully skirted, chrome-trimmed fenders; Bob got to ride that occasionally. But Sonny had insisted he not take time off to come to his graduation, fearing he might lose his job.

Viola started crying when Sonny stepped up onto the stage in his cap and gown to receive his diploma. They were tears of joy; she was so proud of him. He had worked very hard for this moment. There was a concert put on by the Dartmouth band after the formal ceremonies. Everyone stayed for that, and they were all walking back to the Hanover Inn when Sonny turned to his mother and said, "We have to sit down with Bob at some point and talk about his future."

Viola hastily responded, "We will, Sonny, but this is your day. We can wait on Bob."

By now Hitler had pivoted back to the task of rendering England prostrate. But with victory in Western Europe so swift, landing craft and barges necessary to cross the English Channel and storm their shores were not yet available, so the invasion was delayed. Instead, Hitler fantasized that he first could make a peace proposal offer to Great Britain and it came on July 19. It was quickly rejected by the newly appointed Prime Minister of England, Winston Churchill.

Thus, on the last day of July refined plans for Operation Sea Lion—the amphibious assault on England—started anew. Preparations followed, but an immediate attack across the Channel was ruled out. Hitler's vaunted Luftwaffe would now lead in the subjugation of England. The empire's Royal Air Force was to be destroyed first. Most of the faces of that force were young, their average age just twenty-three. They were well-trained and had mastered flying Hurricanes, Blenheim fighters and Spitfires. The heavens were their battlefields again, they were reminded by their squadron commanders, as it was with their World War One flying brethren. They would be the cavalry of the clouds like those heroic ace fliers before them. But Operation Eagle, Hitler's air war, was planned to wipe them out of the skies before Sea Lion commenced and he ordered the fire from the air to begin on August 13.

But that failed; German aircraft looses were three-times higher than those suffered by the Royal Air Force. Absent air superiority, less than a week later Hitler finally bowed to the reality that his amphibious invasion—Sea Lion—could not be launched. The strength of the British, despite the damage of the German bombings on London and other cities, arsenals, power stations and docks, had leaped up and saved England during a time Churchill said began "their finest hour."

Hitler's aggression became a major issue during the 1940 presidential election. It was a time when the vast majority of Americans did not want to become involved in Europe's war. During the third week of July, President Roosevelt became the Democratic nominee for an unprecedented third term. His Democratic Party platform perfectly reflected the mood of the country and stated, "We will not participate in any foreign wars, and we will not send our army, naval or air forces to fight in foreign lands outside of America, except in case of attack."

Roosevelt's opponent, Wendell Wilkie, still favored a peacetime draft, as did the president. Wilkie, however, predicted in early campaign speeches that the nation would be at war within five months if FDR was reelected.

"I hate war," Roosevelt reiterated in campaign stumps that fall. "I have one supreme determination—to do all that I can to keep war away from these shores for all time." In Boston, during a late October rally, the president even made clear, "We are arming ourselves not for any foreign wars. We are arming ourselves not for any purpose of conquest, or intervention in foreign disputes."

Sonny, now down in Institute West Virginia in his new job at the U.S. Rubber Company's synthetic rubber plant, was suddenly ready to base his brother Bob's future on Roosevelt's next words, which he heard on his car radio while driving home from work.

"And while I am talking to you, mothers and fathers, I give you one more assurance. I have said this before, but I shall say it again, and again and again. Your boys are not going to be sent into any foreign wars. Your boys are going into training to form a force so strong that, by its very existence, it will keep the threat of war far away from our shores. The purpose of our defense is defense."

With Roosevelt's victory a week later, Sonny's mind was now made up. It was time to go up to Naugatuck and finally have that difficult conversation Viola refused to discuss at his Dartmouth graduation ceremonies about what to do with Bob.

~EIGHT~

SONNY HAD PURPOSELY WAITED UNTIL after the draft lottery numbers drawing was held on October 29th before going up to Naugatuck. As they were lifted by a wooden dipper out of a big glass fishbowl that day, President Roosevelt announced the numbers on the radio from the stage of an auditorium in Washington. Sonny, like every other male between twenty-one and thirty-five, was nervous while he listened to his fate unfold, but his number had been high enough to put being immediately drafted aside.

The less fortunate would be notified by their local draft boards and leave their civilian lives behind for a year of military training. As he drove up to Connecticut in early December Sonny thought about what a year of serving could mean for Bob, and by the time he got past Norwalk onto the new stretch of the Merritt Parkway his mind was pretty much made up about what he was going to tell his mother. He rehearsed it in his head again before he took the Stratford exit up towards Naugatuck. As he drove along Route 8 where it paralleled the Naugatuck River he became convinced his mother would go along with Bob voluntarily enlisting in the Army. Bob was just nineteen, hadn't needed to register for the draft, but was still in need of structure in his life and a year of Army discipline and training would be good for him.

Christmas was just three weeks away so Bob could wait until the first of the year to report to the Army recruiting station up in Waterbury. This all seemed logical to Sonny. But by the time he pulled into the driveway at 90 Oak Street he had lost some of his nerve. His mother's mind worked differently, and he suddenly realized that all she would be thinking about was whether Bob could end up fighting in a war somewhere overseas before his year of service was over.

As was his custom, Sonny beeped the horn just before he turned his car engine off. Seconds later Viola poked her head out the front door, then pushed it open to welcome her son with open arms as he came up the steps. Sonny was hardly in the living room before Viola told him Bob was not home, but would be along shortly.

"Where is he, Mother?" Sonny asked.

"Oh, you know Bob," Viola started. "He's been hitchhiking back and forth to New York City for weeks, first picking up work here and there at the World's Fair in Flushing Meadows before it shut down on Halloween night. Rained like the dickens that night, and Bob was at the Perisphere where it was lit up to look like a gigantic jack-o'-lantern. The fair went broke, you know, but maybe he's still doing some work for the company that ran it. People were nervous about the war, and stopped spending money. I told Bob you'd be here today, so he promised he'd hitch a ride home tonight so he could see you."

Sonny just shook his head before saying, "He certainly gets around like he hasn't got a worry in the world. I suppose working at Mezzio's wasn't exciting enough for him. Wish I had known he was coming up from New York City. I could have met him somewhere and given him a ride home."

"Well, maybe we should use the time before he gets here to finally have that talk about his future," Viola answered. "Why don't you put your bag up in the bedroom. I'll get some coffee going."

So Sonny went upstairs and by the time he changed into some warmer clothes the coffee was made and two cups were on the coffee table when he came back into the living room. Viola never let the house get above sixty-two degrees to save money.

"I read where Americans are starting to think we should be helping the people over in Europe more Sonny," Viola offered to start the conversation. "This business of staying neutral is being heard less and less. We're already sending planes and old World War One machine guns and rifles to England."

"Yes, and a lot of people also think arming Britain is really going to do more to protect us," Sonny replied. "And the men who were drafted in October won't be going overseas because the draft legislation prohibited that unless we are attacked. We will be building up our defenses on our shores, up and down the Atlantic."

Sonny hoped his mother heard that if Bob went in the Army he couldn't easily be sent overseas into any fight.

"Do you think Hitler would dare to attack us here at home, Sonny?" she instead asked.

Sonny thought about this while he took a sip of coffee and then said, "Mother, this disease of Nazism is bound to spread unless the rest of the world starts doing what we're doing. At least we are a free economic society. Hitler's Germany relies on force. His economy is not based on supply and demand, like ours. He's devoured other economies over in Europe to make ends meet. Hitler respects nothing.

"But will he attack us, Sonny?"

"I don't know,' he truthfully answered. "There is certainly no compromise possible with Hitler. He's staked everything on one thing, and one thing only—the conquest and domination of the world by force. He's filled the German people with propaganda and fear. They are blind to the concept of truth, even justice and mercy. They do not believe in the brotherhood of mankind."

Sonny took another sip of coffee, then said with even stronger conviction, "Some say that economic cooperation with Hitler is advisable, Mother. I am not one of them. This believing that Europe's struggles are over because they have been occupied and are cooperating with the Nazis is rubbish. I do not believe for one minute that peace will become possible through any economic cooperation by the United States with Germany."

"We're so far from Germany, Sonny. Hitler couldn't even cross the English Channel to invade England. How in the world could he cross an ocean to invade us?" Viola now appeared to be thinking what Sonny had hoped for, that his educated world view and his unwillingness to not say no to Hitler attacking the states aside she, like him, very much doubted it was possible.

"What about Bob?" Viola said quietly, not so much as a question, but more about her worries for her youngest son.

"He needs structure, Mother," Sonny answered in a tone that matched hers. "We can't give it to him. You're working six days a week, and I'm over six hundred miles away in West Virginia. OK, I really don't believe we'll get into a war with Germany, unless we're attacked like Roosevelt said all fall. Down deep I think Hitler's scared of us entering the war. He's got enough on his hands already. You know I'm not a Democrat, Mother, but I think Roosevelt's right about us building up our armed forces. It will make Hitler fear us even more."

"He's got over a six and a half million-man force, Sonny. We had a bet going down at the plant about how many servicemen we have, and guess what? We've got just maybe a quarter of a million in our Army and almost that many in the National Guard."

"Mother, I know about that because I'm working in the defense industry, and we're turning out a lot of synthetic rubber to support what will be a much larger force next year. We actually have a smaller army than Switzerland right now, if you can believe that."

Sonny was in management, so he was pretty well informed about preparations going on all over the states to bolster the strength of the country's armed forces. Government officials often visited the plant in Institute and word started getting around about just how badly this was needed.

"Some training camps use broomstick handles for practice because they don't even have enough rifles," Sonny went on to explain. "Logs are mounted between old wooden wagon wheels to look like cannons. The men in training wear those old steel helmets from World War One. When they go out on maneuvers they hear klaxons sounding battle noises. Rifles are actually so scarce that rattlers are used to make it sound like something else is going on around them. Sledge hammers strike suspended metal bars so it sounds like real artillery fire. Heck, there really isn't much ammunition around either. Blanks are used when they are available. Even empty beer cans are filled with sand as substitutes for hand grenades."

"Did I ever tell you how glad I am that you don't drink at all Sonny?" Viola suddenly said.

"Liquor still doesn't set well with me, Mother. Besides, I'm too busy to go out boozing. I've got a roommate in Charleston who drinks too much, and I've seen what it's done to him. And I'm hoping Bob hasn't taken up with the bottle since I saw him last."

"No, he hasn't as far as I know," Viola answered quickly. "He's upbeat all the time again. Life hasn't been easy for him, but for some reason he's the happy-go-lucky Bob of old."

"Well, the Army could sure use men like him," Sonny said, a bit surprised this came out of his mouth so quickly. He had planned to wait until Viola became convinced that hanging around Naugatuck and maybe even getting a steady job in a factory wasn't the best thing for him, given he never graduated from high school and there wasn't any real future for Bob in that, other than to remain a factory worker all his life.

"Besides," Sonny added, "he has a lot of mechanical skills and the Army sure needs this. We're building tanks and airplanes all over the country. We're making the synthetic rubber for those down in Institute. Heck, Bob could probably tear down one of those new Army jeeps Willys is making and rebuild it with a good screw driver. Well, he might need a wrench or two, but you know what I mean."

"I do, Sonny," Viola said softly. "He's such a good boy. He's helped a lot of people around town fix things. Every time he goes over to Nellie's, he's always repairing something for her and Henry. Maybe the Army wouldn't be that bad for him after all."

"He's not a boy any more, Mother."

Viola was about to say something when they both heard the back door off the kitchen open.

"Mom," Bob yelled out. "I'm home." Then, when he came into the living room, Bob reached for Sonny's hand and shook it vigorously. Young men didn't hug in those days. Viola got a big one of those instead.

Sonny looked over at his brother and watched Viola give him a kiss back on his cheek. He couldn't help but notice that Bob was at least two inches taller than he was, and a lean, roughly 160 pounds. No, he sure wasn't a boy anymore, Sonny said to himself.

"What's for dinner, Mom?" Bob asked. "If you're too tired I'll go ahead and make it. Seems like you and Sonny are deep in conversation, judging by the coffee cups."

"Well, we were," Viola said. "Where have you been?"

"Ah, just in the city. No big deal," Bob sheepishly answered.

"You got a girl there?" Sonny shot out, smiling for both Bob and his mother to see.

"Heck no," Bob laughingly said back. "I've got enough trouble with too many of them right here in Naugatuck and up in Waterbury. How about you, Sonny? Dating much? Are those southern gals after you?"

"I don't have time for them," his older brother answered back. Bob didn't say what he was thinking. His brother really wasn't the dating type; he was so damn serious all the time.

"Bob, Mother and I have been talking about your future," Sonny suddenly said. "We'd like to talk to you about this."

"Well, I've been thinking about my future too, Sonny. Matter of fact me and some guys down in New York City got to talking about that draft drawing back in October, and we all agreed it wasn't fair us nineteen year olds weren't being asked to step up to the plate and serve our country."

Viola just gasped. Sonny was taken back, but he listened carefully as Bob kept talking.

"So we went to the National Guard armory on Park Avenue of all places. That's where really rich people live. But it's also the home of the Seventh Regiment. They had these make-believe barriers on the floor. They use those to toughen guys up, give them agility training. Best is they have .22 rifles, and they teach you how to shoot them. Pay's not all that good. If we joined up it's just a dollar per drill night, but people come to watch the fun. Pay goes up to a buck-and-a-half for field training. Heck, if there was a natural disaster or something else and the Guard's called up there's even extra pay."

"We have something like a National Guard right here in Connecticut, Bob," Viola said. She was thinking more of herself, and having him close by.

"Naw, New York City would be far more exciting than this rusty old state," Bob laughed.

But Sonny sensed his brother was giving him an opening he never expected so he decided to take advantage of it.

"Bob, I'd like for you to consider joining up with the regular Army. It pays better, $21 dollars a month actually, it's more like a full-time job, and you'll likely get a chance to travel the country during your training."

"You mean I could?" Bob shot back. "I thought you had to be twenty-one to get in the Army."

"Not if you volunteer Bob," Sonny quickly pointed out. And then he said nothing else, allowing Bob to give that some thought.

After a short pause, Bob looked at both Sonny and his mother, shifting his eyes from one to the other before he simply said, "One thing I learned at the Connecticut Junior Republic was life is not so much about one's self as it is about doing good for bigger purposes. What bigger purpose is there than serving my country? That's where the work is for me. We're German immigrants but Americans now, right? I remember you telling me, Mom, when you Kamerzel's came to this country the whole family walked from Ellis Island all the way to Baltimore because that's where the work was. Sonny, you didn't have to go to college to be so smart, but you did. You worked hard and you make me proud, even if you can't get a date because you're still working so hard. I'll work hard in the Army, but I'll date all the girls I can."

Sonny was not one to tear up. Nor did he laugh much. He hardly ever showed any emotions at all. Viola was different. She ran into her little boy's arms. Sonny noticed Bob was the one tearing up now.

"OK," his younger brother said while looking over at him. "That settles it. I'm gonna' also talk to George Walker. Me and him kicked around serving already. He got a good draft lottery number, being old enough. He doesn't have to go into the Army, but I'm guessing if I go, he will too."

Then, looking right into his mother's eyes, Bob told her they'd probably go up to the recruiting station in Waterbury the following week.

"This could mean I'll be in the Army before Christmas," Bob said. "But there will be other Christmases I won't miss."

Viola simply told Bob she loved him, and was proud of him.

Sonny just shook his hand, thinking this was a lot easier than he thought it was going to be, and said, "OK, how about I take us out to dinner to celebrate Bob's going in the Army."

~NINE~

BOB DID ENLIST IN THE ARMY in December but he wasn't ordered to report to Ft. Devens up in Massachusetts until January. It was an eye opening experience, from the moment the bus that had taken him on this new journey in life began. The fort's grounds were massive, and had been carved out of four quiet towns northwest of Boston back in 1917. Many of its 5,000 acres and nearly seven square mile layout were now built up with 1,200 wooden buildings that were surrounded by snow-covered farmland. Ft. Devens was the new home of the famous First Division, the oldest division in the regular U.S. Army, which had just arrived here after maneuvers in upstate New York.

By this time red brick Georgian Revival structures had replaced some of the older wooden buildings, but the first one Bob saw was the brick and slate-roofed Verbeck Gate, the main entrance to the fort—just steps from where he got off the bus. Once he was cleared through this checkpoint Bob soon became a number, and no longer just a name; he was now Army Serial Number (ASN) 11-012-180, aka Private Robert A. Baummer. Within an hour his head was shaved and he was also stripped of his civilian clothing and other personal belongings, which were tagged and shipped home to Viola.

Bob then stood in line for further processing with other new enlisted men and draftees, all of whom were butt-naked and shivering while they waited to be issued Army regulation shirts, pants, shoes, socks and underwear. They were also given a steel bucket filled with everything from toilet articles to sewing kits. Everyone was charged $25 for what was issued to them, $4 more than they would be paid when they received their first Army paycheck.

Bob was grateful Sonny had sent him the $25 he needed for that purpose before he reported to Ft. Devens.

Next up was a physical examination, plus intelligence and proficiency tests. One of the many problems the new enlisted men like Bob faced was a clash with career Army soldiers who had stayed in the service after World War One. The old timers regarded anyone now entering Ft. Devens as a possible societal reject, or some other form of misfit who was simply using the Army as a place to get away from their problems in civilian life. There was solid basis for these Regular soldiers to feel this way. Half of the men examined at Ft. Devens after the draft act was passed in 1940 were deemed unsuitable for service, many because of prior criminal records; a full twenty percent of others because they were illiterate by Army standards.

Those deemed satisfactory like Bob were now called GIs. "GI" didn't mean general infantry; it meant government issue. New recruits were sometimes even called dogfaces—because they were now being tagged like dogs needing to be trained, and they would soon all indeed be wearing metal dog tags for identification purposes.

But Bob was happy with just being derisively known as lowly Private Baummer; he knew he would prove himself to be the best the Army could train in due time.

That training began two days after he arrived at Ft. Devens and continued for weeks. Bob's first exposure to the Army's way of explaining things came when he read the lead paragraph of the foreword in his *Soldier's Handbook*:

You are now a member of the Army of the United States. That Army is made up of free citizens chosen from amongst a free people. The American people of their own will, and through the men they have elected to represent them in Congress, have determined that the free institutions of the country will continue to exist. They have declared that, if necessary, we will defend our right to live in our own American way and continue to enjoy the benefits and privileges which are granted to the citizens of no other nation. It is upon you, and the many thousands of your comrades now in military service, that our country has placed its confident faith that this defense will succeed should it ever be challenged.

This was followed with words that said the transition to military life would be challenging, but "you are repaying your obligation to the United States for all the benefits of the past and are declaring your faith in our future." Continuing to read, Bob was told "making a good soldier is no different from making good in civilian life. The rule is the same and that is—know you own job and be ready to step into the job of the man ahead of you." More followed about obedience and being loyal, especially obeying "promptly and cheerfully all orders of your commissioned and noncommissioned officers" and sticking by your organization "through thick and thin."

The training goal for each new trainee was the attainment of proficiency, not academic but practical, so Bob would be qualified to satisfactorily perform his duties in the field—wherever that field may be.

There was a one-hour history lecture during Bob's first week of training that was academic but it presented the reasons the Army was preparing the new men for a possible war that would involve the United States. It started with the signing of the Versailles Treaty back in 1919 and covered events through the Invasions of Poland, Norway and Denmark, up to the fall of Western Europe and the evacuation of Dunkirk.

The Army lecturer explained how Adolf Hitler helped form the National Socialist Party, and how he wrote *Mein Kampf* while he languished in a prison cell before he was appointed Chancellor of Germany in 1933. The lecture covered other interesting topics to give the men a sense of how Hitler's aggression was birthed, from his increasing the size of his army to his ordering the re-occupation of the Rhineland in order to make Germany invincible in that borderland between France and Germany. The lecture even covered how Italy had manufactured a war to conquer Ethiopia, the effects of the Spanish Civil War on Europe, and how Hitler and Mussolini divided Europe and Africa into the zones they now reigned over.

When the lecture ended Bob had a good understanding of why he was being trained to build up the Army of the United States.

Bob's first organization at Ft. Devens was the 26th Infantry Regiment. Deployed with the First Division during World War One, the regiment was the first to enter combat, first to sustain a casualty, first to take the offensive, and amongst the first to enter Germany after the Armistice.

It was a hastily rushed into combat unit that one veteran recalled "was less impressive than any other army outfit I have ever seen. In intelligence it was probably a little below the American average, in education certainly. It spoke a dozen tongues and, I have no doubt, maltreated them as sadly as it did their own. Its manners were atrocious, its mode of speech appalling, its appetites enormous, its notions of why we were at war rudimentary, to say the least."

But with virtually no pre-deployment training and arms they received from the French only after their arrival in St. Nazaire France, the 26th Infantry Regiment indeed became the advance element of the American Expeditionary Force.

Bob would eventually become thoroughly indoctrinated in his regiment's history while he grew accustomed to his training. It started at 5:30 a.m. sharp every day. The goal was to turn the wide variety of individuals who Bob entered the service with into teams of fighters who could work seamlessly with one another. Bob's basic training taught him to think of himself less as an individual and more as an integral part of his unit, something less difficult for him to adapt to than it was for others because of the structure and discipline he had learned at the Connecticut Junior Republic.

He and his fellow recruits slept, ate, learned together, and did hours upon hours of physical fitness training. They were taught how to salute, when to salute, and when not to salute. They practiced things over and over, like marching, and especially loading, unloading, and cleaning their World War One surplus 1903 Springfield rifles. Drill instructors, in Bob's case an older sergeant with two rockers on his shoulder patch who never left the First Division after World War One, used tough in-his-face methods—always staring more at his forehead than into his eyes—to force him to become attentive to every detail.

Bob was careful not to ever show his trademark smirk when this crusty old sergeant got so close to his face that he could smell the cheap whiskey on his breath the veteran soldier drank the night before.

But the Army wanted bulldog stick-to-it attitudes like this sergeant had to prevail at all times. Bob's tough drill instructor constantly hammered home that never giving up meant winning battles in real war, the "greatest game of all" as he would often bark out to everyone. Teamwork was everything; all the new recruits were taught teamwork was like a football game where everyone had to pull together to win. Basic training, Bob and his fellow soldiers were reminded again and again, was the single-most holy rite of American maleness, and the Army was going to make real men out of them.

Bob took this to heart and soon perfected close-order drill. He spent endless hours staring at the back of another soldier's head, and kept perfect cadence during every strenuous exercise. He learned to take steps precisely thirty inches straight to his front at the rate of 120 a minute when marching. He even learned to swing his arms in natural arcs and to keep them inside an imaginary barrier six inches in front of his body and three inches behind his back. He quickly felt the stimulation that came with being part of a well-oiled and perfectly working mass of men.

Because he was agile and fit before reporting to Ft. Devens, on most days Bob excelled at everything he was ordered to do and he became particularly adept in negotiating obstacle courses. Most every day he was exhausted but happy before his supper was served at 6:30 p.m., and when it was lights out after taps sounded at 10:00 p.m. he slept well.

He was just what the Army wanted; he had a strong body, a good disposition and a natural respect for authority—something else he learned at the Republic. Bob actually liked being in the Army and was fully expectant of giving it his all during his one year of service.

Bob completed his basic training at the end of March and was given leave for three days so he went back to Naugatuck for a visit with his mother. Viola was overjoyed by this and had even called Sonny, hoping he could get Friday off and come up from West Virginia for the weekend Bob was there. His older brother happily complied and the family reunion revealed the Army hadn't taken away the same old Bob they always knew and loved. Sonny was greeted warmly by his brother when he arrived at the house on Oak Street, and Bob wasted little time before he began talking about his basic training at Ft. Devens.

"So Sonny," Bob started when they settled into the living room. "Let me tell you how far that steady $21 a month pay you were telling me about before I enlisted gets spent."

Sonny braced himself. Bob had that familiar smirk on his face, so he knew he was in for a ribbing.

"First, I have to pay for my own laundry and dry cleaning. The Army requires that I wear clean clothes every day, by God. That's about a buck a week, mind you. And on top of this I have to fork over the money for toiletries, things like soap, razor blades, toothpaste and then there's of course cigarettes. Those together are about $4 a week. That adds up to almost $20 a month."

"Doesn't leave much," Sonny levelly pointed out.

"Nope, but the Army did pay me an extra .44 cents a day ration money for this three-day furlough," Bob laughingly shot back. "And I'm getting a raise now that I'm out of basic. Pretty soon I'll be earning $35 a month. That ought to help cover the bus fare next time I come home."

Sonny, always very conscientious about money, asked, "What are you going to do with all that extra dough, Bob?"

"Well, I'm going to have to buy a field jacket for starters, and that's going to cost me $6.50. But I'm not complaining. Remember, I had to pay for my own room and board at the Junior Republic by working in the mechanical shop. At least the Army provides that for free. Maybe I'll be able to spend a little on entertainment, but come to think of it Ft. Devens is in the middle of nowhere and its too expensive to go into Boston."

Viola had just been listening to this but was startled when Bob added, "So, what I'm going to do is send Mom $5 a month to help her with expenses around the house."

Tears started streaming down his mother's cheeks moments later. Sonny was shocked.

"Bob, that's awfully generous of you," he quietly said. "I really respect you for offering this, but it's not necessary."

"Yes it is Sonny. Mom's been alone for almost four years now. There used to be two paychecks that came into this house. I know you've helped out here and there, and there's no way I'm not going to do what I can, too."

Suddenly Sonny was speechless. He couldn't help but admire his younger brother's new sense of responsibility, and he now wasn't about to take away the joy it gave Bob to do something to help their mother.

"OK, that's settled," Bob said. "Now let me tell you about the new orders I received."

"What do you mean, Bob?" Viola asked. "You're not being transferred to some base far away, are you?"

"Nope, but I've received orders to report to Captain Bays, commander of Company H in the 18th Infantry at Ft. Devens. Apparently my proficiency tests said I'd be good with machine guns and heavy mortars, so I'm to report to him as soon as I get back from leave."

"What are mortars, Bob?" Viola questioned.

"You know how they shoot clowns out of barrels at the circus, Mom? Well mortars are kind of like that. There's a smooth barrel, a baseplate it rests on, and a bi-pod stand that gets angled in a way that determines the distance the mortar shell will go. It's sort of like pitching a softball underhand to a catcher. You have to lob it just right to have it land in his mitt. The heavy mortars, the bigger ones I'll be training on, work kind of the same way, except the shells can travel over 3,000 yards and fly a few hundred feet in the air before they hit their targets."

"Sounds like this would put you behind the rifle companies if we ever had to fight a war, supporting them with these mortars, Bob," Sonny commented.

"Maybe," Bob said. "I really don't know yet. I asked around before I left Devens, and that may be the case with mortars, but I was also told that machine gunners in the company actually get what they called imbedded with the rifle companies, which means they are right up there in the front lines with the riflemen."

"Scares me either way," Viola said nervously. "By the way, have you seen George Walker?"

"George was assigned to artillery so I haven't seen him much. But Mom, don't worry about me. If we ever get into a shooting war, I'll be able to take care of myself."

"Well, I suppose you will," Sonny answered. "But let's hope we never have to find out."

"OK, enough about me and training. Let's go out somewhere and celebrate my raise. Word at the base was it's likely the only one I'll ever get no matter how long I serve in the Army, so let's celebrate. I'm buying."

"What do you mean you're buying?" Sonny asked. "How you going to do that on your .44 cents a day furlough pay? I'll buy."

"Nope, I'm buying," Bob shot back. "Didn't tell you about how I made a little extra pocket money during basic, did I. Well, a bunch of other guys can, the ones I looted shooting craps and playing poker. I can smell the hot dogs over at Blackie's in Cheshire, and can just taste their homemade relish. Make you a deal Sonny. You drive and I'll buy, OK?"

"Deal," was all Sonny said.

So off to Blackie's they went, Bob instead driving Sonny's recently new to him, but bought used black '37 Buick Century convertible with Viola sitting between them beaming with pride.

The rest of the weekend was spent tidying things up around the house, picking up the yard, visiting all of the relatives and eating great lunches and dinners together. Bob was always the center of attention and as such bombarded with questions about Army life. He, in turn, regaled everyone with the adventure of it all every time.

The weekend ended too quickly, and when Sonny dropped Bob off at the bus station in Waterbury Sunday afternoon he turned to him and said, "You are making your Mother and me very proud. Now just keep your nose clean, and keep watching out for yourself. Before you know it your one year of service will be over, and I'm already angling with some people at the rubber plant about starting you in the maintenance department. With your mechanical skills, you should be a shoe-in, and in time you'll be a foreman."

"Thanks Sonny. And hey—good luck finding a date down there in Charleston. The new car should help…" was all a smirking Bob said as he hopped out of Sonny's Buick and walked into the bus station in his neat, clean Army uniform that his mother had washed and pressed for him.

When Bob got back to Ft. Devens and reported in to Captain Harold Bays he thought he was being kidded with when his new company commander told him he'd have to first report to Paul Revere and get some of his paperwork finished before he could be processed in to his new company.

"Sir?" Bob questioned. There were other officers and a couple of sergeants with Bays at the time. All were staring at Bob. And they looked dead serious.

"Baummer, yes, I said Paul Revere," Bays reiterated. "That would be Captain Paul Revere over at regiment."

Bob was still standing rigidly at attention when Bays broke into a broad smile and everyone else started cracking up.

"At ease, son," Bays ordered.

Bob assumed the position.

"Welcome to Company H."

It turned out that Captain Paul Revere was a very real person and rumored to be a direct descendent of the famous silversmith who made the midnight ride through nearby Lexington and Concord to warn the colonial army that the British were coming at the start of America's Revolutionary War.

The present day Revere was the personnel adjutant for the 18th Infantry Regiment. Somehow Bob's life insurance paperwork had gotten lost, and he had to fill the forms out again before he returned to his new company.

Bob couldn't help but notice the good natured, lightly kidding way the entire regimental staff related to each other as he filled in Viola's name as his beneficiary, should he get killed in the line of duty.

"I'd take you back over to your company on my horse, if I had one Baummer," Captain Revere joked when they were done with the paperwork. "But truth be told, the animals scare the hell out of me."

Apparently the officers of the 18th had a lot of fun with the fact they had a Paul Revere serving in the regiment, and he, too, also got a good laugh out of that.

Bob left feeling pretty sure he was going to like his new home.

~TEN~

ON MAY 3, 1941, THE 18TH Infantry held its 80th Annual Organization Day at Ft. Devens. It was a clear crisp morning, and the barracks were humming with activity. Bob, like many others, had attended an enlisted man's dance at the First Division hostess house the night before and stayed too late, but when the review started at 10:00 a.m. he looked like a real soldier as he stood in his crisp Class A dress uniform wearing his garrison cap before the large assembly of guests in the reviewing stand.

The regiment's colors, garlanded with battle streamers awarded for participation in numerous battles and engagements during its long history, snapped sharply in the brisk winds of the day. The bleachers were filled with wives, families and friends of the soldiers, but Viola had to work and wasn't there. Seated in one row on the hard benches were several important senior Army officers, including the commander of the First Division. Next to him was the oldest living veteran of the 18th Infantry and Honor Guest, 101-year old retired Brigadier General William H. Bisbee.

After Chaplain John McEvoy gave the invocation, the band struck up the regiment's traditional marching music—oddly called "Happy Heinie"—a compilation of two old German songs set to a jazz-march tempo which ensured that Bob and every man in the 18th would march with a lively step as they passed before the assembled dignitaries in the reviewing stand. A short welcoming introduction by the regiment's current commander, Colonel Eley

Denson, followed the march, and then Master Sergeant William Lepski provided a brief sketch of its history.

The regiment's roots went all the way back to the War of 1812, but its authorized formation was officially ordered by President Abraham Lincoln on the 3rd of May in 1861. During the saddest war in the nation's history that followed streamers were added to the regiment's colors for participation in Civil War battles across Mississippi, Kentucky, Tennessee and Georgia.

General Bisbee's participation in the Battle of Stones River at Murfreesboro Tennessee during June of 1862 received honorable mention, as the then-lieutenant had distinguished himself by personally rescuing his battalion's colors to keep them from falling into Confederate hands. He was also credited with participation in the fighting at Chickamauga, Mission Ridge and Atlanta, all battles whose names were embroidered on the battle streamers that festooned the fluttering regiment's colors on the parade grounds during this Organization Day.

After the Civil War ended, the regiment was deployed to Georgia and South Carolina for duty during the Second Reconstruction where its mission was to suppress the Ku Klux Klan and enforce new federal laws against slavery. But before this the regiment had briefly served in the Northwestern United States where its men fought against numerically superior forces of Sioux, Arapahoe and Cheyenne warriors around the Dakota Territory.

During the 1880s and 1890s the regiment was again on the western frontier, and its companies were scattered far and wide at isolated Army posts stretching from Montana to Texas. When the war with Spain broke out, the regiment was transferred to the Presidio of San Francisco and then transported to the Philippine Islands where the officers and their men participated in the Battle of Manila. The regiment remained in the Philippines for several years but in 1914 when the situation along the U.S.-Mexico border grew critical, the 18th was deployed to Douglas, Arizona. Here they came to the attention of then-Brigadier General John J. Pershing and when he put together the American Expeditionary Forces for service in France in 1917, Pershing selected the 18th Infantry, one of the better field-hardened regiments under his command, to comprise the newly-organized First Division.

Like the 26th Infantry Bob had first served with at Ft. Devens, his new regiment had fought at Cantigny, Soissons, then Mont Sec during the St. Mihiel offensive and later amongst the tangled stands of trees in the Argonne Forest. As part of the Army of Occupation, the regiment was selected to pass through the streets of Luxemburg where it was reviewed by General Pershing. Then, the 18th was the first regiment to cross the Rhine, and amongst the first American troops to ever enter Germany.

Together with nearly 3,500 other men of the regiment standing before the bleachers and red brick buildings by the parade grounds for this memorable Organization Day, Bob had every reason to beam and now wear on his uniform's shoulder the regiment's distinctive insignia, emblazoned with its motto, *In Omnia Paratus*— In All Things Prepared.

Following a short message by First Division commanding officer General Cubbison, Colonel Denson's remarks were also brief, but poignant. To the surprise of many, including Bob, he said that wartime duty would undoubtedly be thrust upon the regiment once again, and that its record in both peace and previous wars was something everyone could be proud of. Then, turning to General Bisbee, Denson added, "Those of us to whom the future is entrusted will see that the regiment is always ready, and that we will not fail those who have gone before us."

The benediction followed, and when the band played the National Anthem to close the Organization Day ceremonies Bob got goose-bumps.

Viola, on the other hand, thought she might get hives because of her constant worrying about Bob. She read newspapers and still listened to her radio almost every day after work. Opposition to intervening in the war over in Europe had taken on new twists. Results from a Gallup poll that spring revealed eight-five percent of Americans believed the United States would have to get more involved in the war, although that same poll reflected her and most other mother's sentiments—almost the same number were opposed to getting into the actual fighting, even if it meant Great Britain fell to the Germans.

When a woman she knew at work who was originally from Somerville Massachusetts showed her a piece in the *Boston Herald* that had been published the week after Bob's Organization Day celebration, even Viola instinctively knew the Army was convinced it was only a matter of time before the country would be drawn into the conflict over in Europe.

The article covered an exercise up at Ft. Devens she knew Bob had to be involved in; the paper called it "the largest maneuver ever staged in New England and the first extensive action of its kind since the World War."

Viola became very confused and got a pit in her stomach when she read that "casualties were light, considering the scale of the attack."

It was certainly a massive affair. It began the week after Organization Day, first with a seventy-five-mile motor march through central Massachusetts and southern New Hampshire to stage for maneuvers involving the entire First Division in war games that pitted two mythical forces against each other. Lengthy columns of what the Army called "serials" spanned ten straight miles on those highways before the big matchup between the "black" and "blue" forces took place back closer to Ft. Devens.

In preparation for that fight Bob wore the same black brassard every other soldier in the 18th Infantry had tied on his upper left arm. The regiment first conducted a night maneuver that went through Ayer, Groton and Townsend before bivouacking near West Groton. Bob's opponents, elements of his old 26th Infantry and the 16th—the other regiment that comprised the First Division—had by this time occupied assembly areas east of Ft. Devens near Hell Pond in the small town of Harvard, before shifting closer to the scene of the upcoming battle in a wooded area opposite Bob's 18th.

The 18th Regiment's objective was a piece of high ground near Whittmore Hill in Sherman. Bob's battalion fought off a surprise attack by several of the 16th's companies as they marched closer to this objective and the 18th was harassed yet again, this time by Bob's old unit, the 26th, as they got nearer to Lancaster. But Colonel Denson took more aggressive actions than his opponents and called for a mock barrage of artillery fire which the umpires ruled wiped out their opposite numbers. Bob's battalion then rapidly advanced into Sherman and after a clever, unexpected flanking maneuver they seized the crest of Whittmore Hill and became the victors in the first maneuvers of their kind in over twenty years.

Viola read with interest an after-action observer's disclosure that the 26th Infantry's commander, Colonel Theodore Roosevelt, Jr., the oldest son of the former president, had "feinted with a few companies and sent his main force under the cover of trees and bushes into which the men vanished like shadows, up the north and east sides of Whittmore Hill," and how Colonel Roosevelt's "face was streaked with sweat and dust" with him "in the front at all times."

What interested Viola were two things. First, Bob's unit had apparently outwitted Roosevelt's. Two, and disturbing, was the fact that Roosevelt had been in the fight. A month earlier she had read where he and his wife had helped organize an anti-war event at Carnegie Hall in New York City.

Now here Roosevelt was in uniform, like he had been in World War One, and he was back with his old unit—the First Division. And now Bob was at Ft. Devens. For Viola this was a bad omen.

Later that month the First Division had its first formal review since the end of the Great War. The 15,000 men of the division and its 2,500 motor vehicles staged a smooth pass in review on the parade grounds at Ft. Devens in front of more than a hundred veterans and their families. It started at 2:30 in the afternoon to commemorate the exact time the division began its historic attack on Cantigny back in 1918.

That same night a surprised Viola heard President Franklin Roosevelt on her radio in Naugatuck when he told the American people "what had started as a European war has developed, as the Nazis always intended, into world war for world domination." She listened intently as the president warned her that the war in Europe had now become an American war and "unless the advance of Hitlerism is forcibly checked the Western Hemisphere will be within range of Nazi weapons of destruction."

Roosevelt concluded his speech by issuing a "Proclamation of Unlimited National Emergency," leaving Viola fearing that war clouds were now indeed forming over the United States.

Maybe the Army really knew what it was doing up at Ft. Devens, she thought.

Viola read in the papers a few weeks later that leaders on Capitol Hill in Washington were heatedly debating an extension to the Draft Act, which was set to expire in October. Her fear of war was growing. She fretted more than ever, likely because she hadn't heard from Bob since he went back to Ft. Devens earlier that spring. Little did she know that the entire First Division had been preparing for large-scale maneuvers down at Fort Bragg in North Carolina.

On August 12 she was listening to her radio and just getting ready to make dinner when news broke that Congress had renewed the Draft Act by a single vote—203-202. Panicked about what this could mean for Bob, she called Sonny.

He answered with "Baummer" because he was still at work.

"Sonny, did you hear Congress renewed the Draft Act?" Viola asked with alarm in her voice.

"Yes, Mother, I did," Sonny answered. "I'm sure you're worried about what this might mean for Bob."

"Of course I am."

"Mother, it's really not entirely clear," Sonny offered back. "But it does appear that Congress extended the period of service for eighteen more months. There are exemptions, I believe, but on the whole it looks like Bob will stay in the Army after this December."

"Oh my God, Sonny," Viola exclaimed.

"Mother, think about it. Think about all the training he's been through, all to ready us if we end up in a war that seems more and more likely now. If the Army lost everyone they've been training this year, where would that leave us?"

"Defenseless, I suppose," Viola conceded.

"Mother, I'm sorry. I don't know what to say."

There was nothing Sonny could say to help Viola that night.

Another month went by and Viola had still not heard from Bob. It was the evening of September 12th, she was trying to settle down after work and had just sat on her couch to listen to the famed airman, but firm anti-war pacifist Charles Lindberg, deliver what was billed as a speech which would lay direct blame on President Roosevelt for escalating America's chances of getting into the European war. She was surprised when the announcer told her that the first speaker would instead be the President of the United States himself.

In one of the liveliest speeches of his presidency, Roosevelt, after greeting his fellow Americans, suddenly announced that a Nazi submarine had attacked a U.S. destroyer "which was doing nothing more than carrying American mail and flying an American flag."

Viola, like everyone listening, was stunned.

"In spite of what any American obstructionist may prefer to

believe," Roosevelt rang out in an obvious shot across the bow of Lindberg and his ilk, "I can tell you the blunt fact that the German submarine fired first upon this American destroyer without warning, and with the deliberate design to sink her. This attack was no localized military operation in the North Atlantic.

"This Nazi attempt to seize control of the oceans is but a counterpart of the Nazi plots now being carried on throughout the Western Hemisphere," Roosevelt said in a raised voice. "They are all designed toward the same end, for Hitler's advance guards—not only his avowed agents but also his dupes among us—have sought to make ready for him footholds and bridgeheads in the New World, to be used as soon as he has gained control of the oceans.

"The danger is here now," Roosevelt made clear, "not only from a military enemy but from an enemy of all law, all liberty, all morality, all religion."

Then, in words that fell just short of declaring actual war on Germany, Roosevelt said sharply, "When you see a rattlesnake poised to strike, you do not wait until he has struck before you crush it." After proclaiming that Nazis were the rattlesnakes of the Atlantic, the president told his startled listeners he had ordered the U.S. Navy "to shoot on sight" any Nazi warships that threatened an American vessel.

Roosevelt then closed his speech that was later learned to have been heard by nearly a billion people in the United States and throughout the world with, "The time for active defense has come and if German or Italian vessels of war attack ours they do so at their own peril."

The former Assistant Secretary of the Navy and lifelong sailor stole the wind out of Lindberg's sails that night. Polls just days later revealed Americans overwhelmingly supported their president's "shoot on sight" order to U.S. naval commanders.

It was also the moment when Viola put aside any reservations she had about getting into the war if the country had to.

And something told her Bob felt the same way.

The 18th Infantry took part in the Carolina Maneuvers a month later. There were two phases, both involving the Army Air Forces and newly formed tank and airborne divisions, as well as infantry units like the First Division. Army's basic purpose was to test its new formations in corps to corps mock battles, and determine their readiness for war.

The outcomes from the Army's perspective were generally disappointing, although published press reports at the time were positive. Viola read some of these articles, and while they did not hesitate to point out observed faults and deficiencies they left her with a feeling of both pride and admiration at how far the Army had come, considering the fact that there were two decades of virtual disarmament after World War One and this was being made up for in what amounted to less than two years.

Some writers even went so far as to compare the 1941 U.S. Army with Hitler's supposedly invincible war machine and the comparisons were not altogether unfavorable, leaving Viola a bit less worried about Bob's chances to survive a real shooting war if one were to come.

But Army leaders were less optimistic. "Are the troops ready for war?" was the question repeatedly asked in Washington after the maneuvers ended. Some said yes, provided they could be given the equipment they needed. Others said losses would be unduly heavy against the Germans.

More critical was the readiness of what the Army called "small units" like Bob's Company H. While this criticism was not directly aimed at his company, in general it was concluded that small units behaved as if they did not know how to protect themselves and showed little regard for defensive tactics in the face of staged hostile fire. One critic even said, "Secure in the knowledge that only blanks were being discharged, soldiers would maneuver openly in the face of small arms fire, rather than utilize cover.

They often ignored artillery fire and sometimes stood in the open to watch air attacks that would have killed them in real war."

Said bluntly, the new infantry doctrine developed by higher headquarters in Washington was generally not being adhered to at company levels.

But Bob's 18th Infantry made a decent showing during the maneuvers. In one exercise the officers and men of one battalion conducted a successful reconnaissance mission and spoiled a surprise attack by the opposing 1st Armored Division, and in doing so was able to avoid a massive tank ambush, thereby earning a victory. The First Division also captured the town of Lancaster, South Carolina on November 27th and held it the next day, despite strong pushes by their opposing force at the defensive perimeter on the edge of town where the division's men had set up artillery and anti-tank guns to stop them.

After the Carolina Maneuvers Bob rode in the back of a very cold Army two and a half-ton truck, which the soldiers called "deuce and a halves," all the way up to Ft. Devens. He arrived during mid-afternoon on Saturday December 6, and caught a bus back home that night; Bob, like everyone else in the 18th, had a three week leave coming and he was very happy knowing he'd be home for Christmas.

~ELEVEN~

BOB'S AUNT MARY JANE PICKED him up at the bus station in Waterbury that night and it was close to midnight when she dropped him off at the house on Oak Street. Bob went right to bed and it was after ten the next morning when he started to smell bacon and eggs. Viola had decided a good breakfast was just what her son needed to start his first day away from Army life.

After he ate Bob spread the Sunday funnies out on the living room floor as he listened to Sammy Kay's *Sunday Serenade* on the radio. He got caught up with Dick Tracy and Tess Trueheart as they trekked through the snowy weather of upstate New York. Joe Palooka was getting ready for another championship bout. Skeezix was doing his best to start his car repair business in "Gasoline Alley." Mutt and Jeff were up to their usual shenanigans.

Bob was in no hurry to do anything, but he did want to listen to the New York Giants football game that afternoon. They were playing against the Brooklyn Dodgers. Brooklyn—a football team then—was favored to win, but Bob was a Giants fan so he was hoping for an upset. It was a lazy Sunday in Naugatuck, cold and dreary outside, but it was the first time in weeks where Bob didn't have anything he had to do. So he tuned the family's Philco radio to WOR and got into the game when it started airing at two o'clock.

It was scoreless after the first quarter, and Bob was just coming back into the living room with a bottle of Coca-Cola when Pug Manders scored a touchdown for the Dodgers. Then the game was suddenly interrupted. It was announced that a news bulletin would follow and when Viola heard this she asked Bob to switch back to NBC just in case it was something important they should know about.

Seconds later they were again listening to *Sunday Serenade* and then a newscaster suddenly broke in with: "From the NBC newsroom in New York. President Roosevelt said in a statement today that the Japanese had attacked Pearl Harbor Hawaii from the air. I'll repeat that. President Roosevelt says the Japanese have attacked Pearl Harbor Hawaii from the air."

Neither Bob nor Viola knew what to make of that.

"We will interrupt our program to give you the latest news bulletins. Stay tuned to this station."

This big news was being heard all across America, but the initial reports that followed were fragmentary at best and often misleading. Several bulletins came in, including one Bob and Viola heard at 3:24 P.M. announcing that the Japanese had even torpedoed an army transport carrying lumber 1,300 miles west of San Francisco. Then in a precursor of things to come for Bob, fifteen minutes later Secretary of War Henry Stimson ordered the entire U.S. Armed Forces in uniform—estimated now to be about 1,600,000 men—if not already at their bases to report to their posts on Monday.

"Ladies and Gentlemen we also bring you this announcement," Bob and Viola heard as they continued to listen with real alarm. The NBC announcer this time told them that the police and sheriff departments in New York City had been placed on twelve-hour shifts and that all auxiliary personnel had been directed to stand by for emergency service instructions.

"The regular county defense program is functioning in an orderly manner and citizens are urged to remain calm and avoid all necessary confusion because of hysteria," the announcer continued. "Citizen volunteers are asked to go quietly to their nearest police or fire stations and offer their services if they wish to help.

There is no immediate cause for alarm and coolness will accomplish more than anything else.

"We return you now to Hollywood." Dance band music followed and after loud applause a Jello ad was broadcast.

Both Bob and Viola still had their eyes trained on the radio; neither had said anything to the other yet.

Then suddenly came "Go ahead Honolulu..." and a voice there said: "Several planes have been shot down. Anti-aircraft gunnery is very heavy. All lines of communication seem to be down between the various Army posts. Everyone here on the islands were surprised by the enemy attack, and even yet it is difficult for some people to believe an air raid on these beautiful islands has actually happened and that lives have been lost. After the attack on Pearl Harbor, several squadrons of Japanese planes came in from the south dropping incendiary bombs over the city. One bomb dropped in front of the governor's mansion. Traffic is almost at a standstill. At Pearl Harbor three ships were attacked. The *Oklahoma* was set afire. There is great activity there now clearing the debris.

"The governor has proclaimed a state of emergency. The Army has issued orders for all people in the civilian population to remain off the streets. After machine gunning Fort Island, the first Japanese planes moved to Hickam Field. There were 350 men killed in a direct bomb hit on the barracks at Hickam Field."

Viola finally turned to Bob and said, "Oh my God, this probably means we are really going to war."

"It sure sounds like it," Bob answered back. "Looks like I'll be heading back to Ft. Devens real soon. I'm going to try to get a call through to see how soon they want me there."

Irving Yarock, a lieutenant in Company A, was the only officer in Bob's regiment at the base he could get through to. Yarock was visiting relatives in nearby Worcester when the news flashed over their kitchen radio. He had immediately returned to Ft. Devens.

"Lieutenant Yarock," Bob started. "I'm in Company H. Do you know if they need me up there right away?"

"I'm the only officer in my company that's here," Yarock told him. "There's been a flood of telegrams and telephone messages from my men who are on leave, asking if they should return immediately. I have no specific orders. I told them to stay where they were and if we wanted to cut their leaves short I would notify them."

"Sir, I heard that Secretary of War Stimson said we had to report on Monday," Bob informed the lieutenant.

"I heard that, but nothing official has come down from regiment yet," Yarock answered.

"Thank you, Sir," Bob replied before ending the call.

Unknown to Lieutenant Yarock was that the Pentagon had already contacted the First Division commander, General Cubbison. Developing contingency plans in preparation for important expeditions to foreign lands was standard operation procedure for a division commander, but the call Cubbison received just hours after the attacks on Pearl Harbor was a first—even for the oldest division in the Army.

The Washington caller started the terse conversation with General Cubbison by asking, "When can your division start for the West Coast?"

"Tomorrow," the First Division commander answered.

"What additional equipment do you need?"

"None," Cubbison confidently responded. "We have been completely equipped for six months."

"How long after you detrain can you begin to operate?" was the next question from the Pentagon.

"We will get off the train fighting," Cubbison answered this time.

Early that evening NBC correspondents Drew Pearson and Robert

S. Allen summarized the events up to the moment and started giving predictions of what was likely to come. They were certain declarations of war against both Japan and Germany were imminent. Shortly following this came an announcement that an estimated 104 Army personnel were killed in the attacks on Pearl Harbor.

Then more interruptions to the regular NBC broadcast followed. The first was a local California announcement about civilians reporting for volunteer duty and another warning about hysteria. Then at 8:00 p.m. it was reported that Fiorello LaGuardia, the Mayor of New York City, had ordered all Japanese men and women be confined to their homes.

Bob and Viola went nowhere. They stayed in the living room and continued listening to the news as it broke. The *Dinah Shore Show* was being broadcast when it was announced that Canada had declared war on Japan. A startling report followed shortly afterwards informing Americans that a total light blackout would occur that night along the entire U.S. West Coast, from Mexico to the Canadian border.

Then, at 10:00 p.m. the *New Adventures of Sherlock Holmes's* "Mystery of Mrs. Warren's Lodger" was interrupted to announce that President Roosevelt would address a joint session of Congress the next morning.

"That settles it, Mom," Bob announced. "I'm going back to Ft. Devens tomorrow for sure. There will be nothing less than a formal declaration of war and I need to be where I can do the most good."

"I understand," a very sad Viola answered. "But promise me you'll write whenever you can, OK?"

"I will Mom. I love you."

"I love you, too, Bob. We better try to get some sleep. It's going to be another long day tomorrow."

Sonny called after Bob went upstairs. Viola was tidying up when the phone rang.

"Mother," he said sadly, "I never expected it would come to this so soon. I feel horrible and guilty about talking Bob into joining the Army."

"Sonny, stop talking like that. Bob is proud to be in the Army, and if he hadn't gone in when he did he'd be getting drafted real soon anyway."

"But Mother . . ."

"Sonny, I said stop. I never want to hear you talking about feeling guilty again."

Bob got an early bus back to Ft. Devens the next morning and was on his way there when Viola heard during her lunch break at work President Roosevelt address the Congress and the nation at 12:30. It was just a six-minute address and it began with the clearly angered president proclaiming that December 7, 1941 would be "a date which will live in infamy." But it really was a speech, interrupted several times by loud applause, that made every American aware that the United States was no longer looking at looming war clouds; rather the country was going to be shifting to a state of firm and determined war footing.

For Viola the most memorable words the president spoke came near the end of his speech—after Roosevelt announced that 2,403 American lives had been lost at Pearl Harbor—when he said in a raised voice, "With confidence in our armed forces—with the unbounding determination of our people—we will gain the inevitable triumph—so help us God."

President Roosevelt then declared that a state of war already existed between the United States and the Japanese empire because of their attack on Pearl Harbor, and asked Congress to formally declare war on Japan.

The Senate unanimously approved the resolution an hour later, right after the House had weighed in with 388 yeas and just one dissenting vote.

Japan reciprocated by declaring war on the United States. Germany and Italy declared war on the country four days later, and the

American people were thrust into a gathering conflict that would become the largest in world history in both scope and ferocity.

By this time Bob was back at Ft. Devens. The First Division wasn't going to the West Coast. Instead guards had been placed on twenty-four-hour watch around the officer's quarters that Sunday night, and after war was declared on Monday Colonel Denson put a series of emergency plans in place. Bob's Company H got prepared to deploy machine gun squads to various points around the base, in case there was an attack. Rife companies were put on high alert and were ready to take up concealed positions in wooded areas around the post. Some platoons were ordered to immediately start patrolling the area around Ft. Devens's perimeter to look for saboteurs.

Like every one of his fellow soldiers, Bob was full of vigor and seriousness of purpose. Every man in his 18th Infantry now believed the declaration of war would result in their eventual assignment somewhere overseas in a full combat role.

~TWELVE~

WHEN CHRISTMAS CAME SONNY GAVE his mother tickets for the New Years Day premier of the comedy film *The Man Who Came to Dinner*, starring Monty Woolley, Bette Davis, Ann Sheridan and Jimmy Durante. It was playing at the Strand Theater in Times Square in New York City. Sonny wanted to take Viola's mind off her worries about Bob, so together they set out in his Buick for the train station in New Haven, and by the time they got to Grand Central Station they still had a good hour to spare before the show started.

It was about ten blocks to the Strand, which was on the northwest corner of 47th Street and Broadway, and Viola wanted to walk there. It was a very cold day, the skies were overcast, but Sonny went along with what his mother wanted. They were soon strolling along 42nd Street by Bryant Park and both were quickly reminded the war had already come to New York City. Through the iron fencing and beyond the stone balustrades of the park they could see an Army anti-aircraft detachment on the lawn, not too far from the Lowell Memorial Fountain.

Sonny happened to notice a Skyline taxicab was nearby and first in a line waiting to pick up passengers, so he got an initially reluctant Viola to agree to take this yellow, red-fendered DeSoto the rest of the way. It really was cold out and their heavy overcoats and gloves helped keep them warm, but the wind was biting. Five people could sit in the back of the long cab, but it was all theirs and the first thing Sonny asked the driver was whether there was enough time to go by the Empire State Building and still get to the Strand before the show started. He wanted to give his mother a tour of sorts, see some of the Christmas decorations that were still up along the city's streets, and the ride would do just that.

"It'll be tight but we's can do 'dat," the fiftyish taxi driver said in his clipped New York accent.

"Thanks. That will make my mother happy," Sonny offered back.

"Wish we had time to go up to the observation deck when we get to the Empire State Building," Viola chimed in.

The taxi cab driver just looked at Sonny through his rearview mirror and wondered what he'd have to say about this.

"Mother, I don't even know if the floor the observation deck is on is open any more," the driver overheard. "You saw that anti-aircraft detachment back in the park. Well, where do you think they have their eyes and ears that spot airplanes for them?"

Viola said nothing. The cab driver was looking more at Sonny through his rearview mirror than he was the traffic on 5th Avenue now. How could this kid in the back of his cab know anything about that he wondered?

"I know the top of the Empire State Building is being used for anti-aircraft surveillance," Sonny explained. "The stairwells in the middle of the skyscraper are air raid shelters now, they even do drills during the work week, and the windows are blacked out at night. Isn't that right, driver?"

"Yea, 'dem windows are dark at night, but how'd ya' know 'bout the 'utter stuff, kid?" the fast talking New Yorker asked.

"Well, I work for a company that has its headquarters in Rock-efeller Center and people there know the Empire State Building is now central to the defense of the city," Sonny answered. "Word gets around."

"Damned if I knew bout 'dat kid," the driver fired back.

"Damned if I knew that myself," Viola said with a little laugh. She was getting into that New York frame of mind and now really enjoying herself.

"Mother," Sonny said. "You shouldn't use that kind of language."

"Hey, kid, if I were yous I'd let ya' mutta say anyting she's wants ta'," the driver kiddingly threw in.

Sonny smiled, but said nothing.

After they went by the Empire State Building, the driver shot across 33rd Street, then got on 7th Avenue and headed back up towards Times Square. With minutes to spare they arrived at the Strand. Sonny reached into his pocket, got out the forty-cent fare and gave the driver, now smoking a cigarette, a quarter tip.

"Hey big spenda'," the driver said. "Thanks, kid."

"Let's hurry so we're not late...big spender," Viola, now having the best time she'd had in a while, said to Sonny. "Thanks, Mr. Driver. And thanks for keeping my kid in line."

Seconds later Viola was staring up at the glazed terra cotta exterior of the Strand Theater and heading towards the ticket window. After Sonny handed their tickets over to an attractive red-haired woman in the box office—who threw a wink at him—they entered the very impressive theater, which sat almost 3,000 people. Viola took in the tiers of box seats set above the main level on both sides of the lower seating area; they were beautifully decorated with mural paintings. The interior stonework was fine marble and all of the decorations—including the ceiling art—were done in French greys, rose and gold.

Sonny had managed to get seats near the center of a row about fifteen back from the big screen, even though there were no columns or other obstructions where the cheaper seats were that could have possibly interfered with their line of vision. The aisles were wide and there was plenty of space between the rows, so after being escorted to their row by an extremely polite uniformed usher Viola sat down in her very comfortable seat and stretched her legs out. Within minutes the first reel of *The Man Who Came to Dinner* started after the glow of starlight was thrown off by the house lights being dimmed.

"Thanks big spender for this grand gift," she said to her son.

And then she and a beaming Sonny just stared at the screen and laughed through the entire movie.

Dinner later was at the Oyster Bar back in Grand Central Station where they both had its famous pan roast before they warmed their stomachs up for the train ride home with steaming bowls of oyster stew dashed with Worcestershire sauce, paprika, celery salt and a pat of butter.

The day had been the perfect escape for Viola. The film had none of the patriotic themes others had at the time, but it sure had its funny moments. She loved Monty Woolley as Sheridan Whiteside, even though at times he was crude and a bit obnoxious. She hoped the masterful Bette Davis would do more comedies. The beautiful Ann Sheridan in that mummy's tomb was spooky. Jimmy Durante's cameo appearance was goofy, but she thought great overall.

It was late when Viola and her son got back to Naugatuck, but the day had turned out better than Sonny ever expected. He drove back to West Virginia the next morning a very content kid.

Neither Viola nor Sonny knew that Bob was also in New York just over a week later. He had come down from Ft. Devens by truck and embarked onto a transport ship in Brooklyn with the rest of the First Division for what the Army called "amphibious landing exercises" that were scheduled to take place at New River in eastern North Carolina.

Fortunately for Bob the stormy January weather forced a change of location for the exercises to closer Cape Henry, near Virginia Beach, Virginia. Like the maneuvers back at Ft. Devens seven months earlier where black or blue brassards were worn, the forces at Cape Henry were either blue or red and the results during land-ings were mixed, but generally disappointing. Getting boats ashore in the rough seas proved troublesome during the first day; many came in on the wrong beach areas. One battalion—not Bob's— was judged to have suffered fifty-percent casualties amongst its men that day.

A second dawn landing was more successful and this time Bob's regiment captured a large number of their opposing forces before they "strategically withdrew." On the third day the wind was blowing a steady forty knots and the seas were very choppy. Whitecaps helped the Higgins boats the men were on towards shore, but the breaking waves swamped most of them as they tried to land on their designated beaches. Luckily no one drowned. The Navy finally called the exercises off and Bob's was amongst the fortunate companies that had never left the ship they were on.

Instead, his transport made its way northward that night and after rolling around in heavy seas Bob arrived back in New York Harbor on January 18th. The same deuce and a halves that brought him and the rest of his regiment down from Ft. Devens took them along the snowy and icy roads on the Merritt Parkway through Connecticut and back up to the fort.

Bob suffered a mishap during those exercises. Another soldier had stepped hard on his right hand when they were going down the nets off their transport to jump into a Higgins boat during the second day of the exercises. He required stitches, and the wound left a memorable scar that would even be recorded on his Army ID card the next time one was issued.

But it could have been far worse for Bob. The war had come to the Atlantic frontier off the U.S. coast. German U-boats sank thirty-five American ships in the sea lanes between Cape Hatteras and New York City during that January, sending 200,000 tons of steel and hundreds of American Merchant Marines to watery graves often within eyesight of safe harbors.

The First Division convoy was indeed fortunate not to add to the tally Nazi U-boat commanders were radioing back to Berlin on a daily basis.

January had also been a tough month for Viola to get through. She received no letters from Bob, and while she tried to understand that he had to be a very busy with training, it still left her wondering why he couldn't find a few minutes just to write and let her know he was alright.

February passed and Viola finally found in her mailbox a letter from Bob in March when she got home from work. She rushed inside, sat at her kitchen table and when she opened the letter up she saw that he had written it on Ft. Devens stationery and it was dated Thursday, March 19th.

Dear Mom,

Just a few lines to let you know that I am at Camp Blanding down in Florida now. There are rumors going around that we are leaving for Africa pretty soon, but I don't know what is going to happen as yet, but will let you know as soon as I can.

It is starting to get hot as heck down here, in fact the temperature was up to 92 this afternoon, and I already got a good suntan, and it may be called the land of sunshine, but we sure do get a lot of rain.

Finished firing the rifle this week and got a 176 out of a possible 200, so I am a sharpshooter, which isn't bad but I should have made expert.

Give my love to all the relatives for me, and I will probably see you again when the war is over, so don't worry about me mom, cause I can take care of myself.

Will close for now, and I hope to hear from you soon.

Love,

Bob

PS: Give my love to Son too

Viola laid the letter down, then after putting a lit wooden match to the pilot light in her gas oven so she could bake some rolls to go along with the salad she was going to make for her dinner, she read it again. Then she called Sonny.

"You must have heard from Bob," Sonny said as soon as he heard his mother's voice. "Otherwise, we'd be waiting until Sunday to talk."

"Yes I did. At last. Guess where he is?"

"Still at Ft. Devens?" Sonny ventured.

"Nope; he's down in Florida getting a suntan."

"Well, lucky him," Sonny responded, knowing there had to be more to be said about what he was really doing in Florida. "Where in Florida is he? Did he say?"

"Some place called Camp Blanding, but I'm not sure where that is," Viola answered.

"Did he say what he was doing?"

"How about I read you the letter, Sonny. It's not that long."

"OK, I'm all ears, Mother."

After Viola slowly read the letter to him, Sonny asked her to read the first part of it to him again.

When she got to "There are rumors going around that we're leaving for Africa pretty soon," Sonny stopped her.

"Mother have you said anything to anyone else about that?" he asked in a very concerned voice.

"No, you were the first person I called and I didn't talk to anyone before now."

"I have no idea how the business about going to Africa soon got through Army censors," Sonny carefully said. "They should have caught that."

"What do you mean, Sonny?" Viola asked. "Bob didn't do anything wrong did he?"

"No, certainly not intentionally. But I don't want you to show his letter to anyone. In fact, I'm asking you to hide it somewhere and when you tell people you heard from Bob to not say anything about the rumors he may be going to Africa soon."

"I don't understand, Sonny. But if you say so, I'll do what you're asking."

"Mother, I don't mean to sound far-fetched. I'm just being very cautious and here's why. Just suppose our forces were really going to Africa soon. Who would benefit most from knowing that?"

"I'm still not sure what you mean, Sonny."

"Hitler, Mother. Or Mussolini. If they knew we were going to land in Africa they would be sure to put their armies there to meet Bob and the rest of the First Division."

"OK, I understand now," Viola finally said.

"Look, I'm just being very cautious. We have extra security down here at the plant, and one day about three weeks ago I was in a briefing where two men in dark suits—they were Edgar Hoover's FBI agents, Mother—were warning us about Nazis who could be in our midst. They said they could really be anywhere and that they might actually be spying, trying to learn anything they could about our war plans."

"It sounds pretty far fetched actually, to think a rumor from Bob about going to Africa soon would be taken seriously by the Germans, or even those damn Wops, Sonny."

"Mother, let me be as direct as I can. Again, I may be overreacting, but I'm asking you to play it safe. There was an article in the *Washington Post* in mid-February, and this is what got all this tightened security business started. Walter Lippman wrote it, and he was saying national security should preempt civil rights. He was in strong support of interning Japanese people on the West Coast, but now that we are at war with Hitler and Mussolini this same sentiment is being directed at German and Italian immigrants. And don't call them Wops, Mother. Please."

"That really upsets me, Sonny. I meant the bastards fighting for Italy—if you'll pardon my French—about the Wop reference. But I get your point," Viola said in a still animated tone. "It seems hysteria is getting out of control. Are you saying that because I'm a second generation German immigrant with a son in an American Army uniform that someone in a dark suit could come and take me away if word got around our forces were going to Africa! And if it got back to it being me who was saying that, that I'd be accused of helping our enemies and taken away, called in the Naugatuck paper a spy, and locked up somewhere where you'd never hear from me again?"

"That, Mother, is what I meant about sounding far fetched, but it's also why I said to play it safe and just say nothing about Bob's letter—the part about the rumor the First Division was going to Africa soon."

"You've always been very pragmatic Sonny," Viola said back. "OK, I'll hide the letter and say absolutely nothing to anyone about Africa."

"Just imagine if that's where the First Division is actually going, Mother. We just don't know who could be lurking in our midst anywhere in a public place. Or frankly at the plant here in Institute, or the rubber plant in Naugatuck where you work."

After a long pause where Viola said nothing, Sonny said, "Mother, are you still there?"

"Yes I am. Need to get back into the kitchen and finish making dinner. And I'll be watching out the windows for Hoover's FBI men in their dark suits."

"Mother. . ."

"And I'll show the bastards the pictures I have of Bob in his Army uniform, and give them a piece of my mind if they dare show up here."

"Mother. . ."

And then the line went dead.

~THIRTEEN~

BOB HAD ARRIVED AT CAMP BLANDING back on February 21st.

The complex awed him; it appeared to have no beginning or end. Word quickly got around that work began to construct the largely scrubbed oak 28,200-acre site back in 1939, and after Roosevelt federalized the post in 1940 the camp mushroomed into 170,000 acres of grounds that became a huge tent city.

Kingsley Lake was in the center of the camp and its ankle-deep sandy beaches forced the construction of wooden duck walks so soldiers like Bob could get back and forth to their quarters. His new home was actually underneath a hole laden canvas-covered roof that hung over a pyramidal-topped wooden building which billeted him and eleven other men; a wood burning stove sat in its center, but wasn't needed when the warmer Florida weather settled in. Bob was here as a breeze flowed through his screened quarters while he sat on his cot and wrote the letter home to his mother the day he made sharpshooter at the rifle range.

Bob's training had been very focused and time consuming from the time he arrived. What he endured were mostly lectures at first. Some of the subjects were interesting; some not so, but were required because the Army knew best what a soldier had to know, and no one dared challenge that.

All the lectures were in classrooms, and quite thorough. Everyone appreciated the eight hours the Army lecturers put into learning how to identify anti-personnel mines and booby traps where they could loose a leg if they happened to step on one. Gas warfare was common in World War One, and the Army made sure enough time was devoted to chemical warfare training; the men grew to appreciate the importance of carrying their gas masks and stopped seeing that newer regulation as a burden. The full day spent on the fundamentals of map reading and interpreting aerial photographs was interesting; the half day on tent pitching, equipment and clothing, less so. But the Army stressed the importance of getting through inspections so everyone listened carefully.

Their attention was certainly piqued the day the lecture was delivered on identification of armored vehicles and the Army's aircraft, less they not know the difference between friendly support and an enemy tank or plane; this took up another half a day.

A lengthier time—over two days—was spent on what was billed as military sanitation, first aid and personal hygiene. Without healthy soldiers an Army could not function. Absent how to administer first aid in combat could make the difference between dying, or surviving a treatable wound in the field and getting further care by medics in an evacuation tent. Even the lecture on personal hygiene made sense; many of the men wondered why their hair had to be cut so short. They learned it was to prevent them from getting lice. Watch out where you sleep was also stressed; avoid laying down on hay or straw, for critters could get into your underwear, and crawl up your back; worse—into your crotch. Before you knew it you'd be scratching and swearing like a proper soldier shouldn't, and this would be followed by being stripped naked, shaved everywhere, and fumigated with the insect killer DDT.

The sex hygiene and morality lecture boiled down this: your battalion chaplain will tell you not to have sex, unless you were married, and then only with your spouse. If you made the mistake of having sex with someone you didn't know and got syphilis or gonorrhea, the battalion surgeon would tell you how to take care of yourself. Everything possible would be done to keep you from being discharged from Army service. But the worse part was the hell you would catch from your company commander, and the punishment that would follow because you didn't do what the chaplain told you to do in the first place.

The takeaway from that lecture was first to resist temptation, but if you succumbed to it use a prophylactic and don't get caught.

Other lectures used blackboards, charts and sand table models to depict what Bob's Company H mission would be like in actual combat; this followed a boring two hour talk on the organization of the Army. But the lectures eventually trickled down to how Bob's mortar platoon he was assigned to fit in, what the role of the company's individual squads would be, and what his actual personal responsibilities were as an ammunition bearer.

During the first lecture Bob learned that the mission of his heavy weapons company was basically to give fire support to the rifle companies when it got to the real fighting. He was told decisions on the tactical use of his company were made by his battalion commander and he would determine the best mix of the company's machinegun and mortar fires in order to give maximum support to the assaulting rifle companies. Army doctrine deemed his heavy weapons company not capable of independent action, in other words what Bob got from that session was his Company H could not take or hold ground without assistance from the rifle units.

This left him feeling grateful he wasn't in a rifle company because they would be in more direct contact with the enemy. But it also gave him a feeling of vulnerability because without their support his mortar platoon could be easily overrun if an enemy force were to attack their position.

A welcome smoke break followed this lecture, but it seemed to Bob that he was next going to learn in more detail just how he personally fit into all this.

He wasn't disappointed. The next lecture did cover the organization of the mortar section he would serve in. It consisted of a sergeant who would be his section leader, a gunner, an assistant gunner, a driver for the squad's specially-fitted jeep weapons carrier, and five ammunition bearers—of which Bob was one— who would bring the 81mm shells from the weapons carrier to their mortar's location.

Bob's personal responsibility as an ammunition bearer was to assure that an adequate shell supply was at the mortar itself at all times. By now Bob was already familiar with the big 81mm mortar; earlier classes he had taken back at Ft. Devens covered this, but it had to be gone over again for the new guys in his platoon. The weapon consisted of three basic components, or as the Army called them "loads." The three-inch, smooth-bored barrel was one load; it weighed just over forty-four pounds, was slightly under fifty-inches in length and was 3.2" in diameter. The barrel was a seamlessly drawn-steel tube fitted at the breech end with a base cap, within which was a firing pin that would propel the mortar shell out of the tube.

The other two loads consisted of a rectangular pressed steel base plate and a tubular steel bipod which formed the legs for the mortar barrel to rest on.

The mortar was also equipped with a sight which included a collimator, elevating and lateral deflection mechanisms, plus longitudinal and cross-levels. This assembly, which was supported by its own bracket and fit on the mortar yoke, provided accurate laying for elevation and deflection adjustments; this is what controlled the direction and angle of fire in order to hit the designated target.

Each 81mm heavy explosive shell Bob would most often carry— which included over a pound of TNT bursting charge—weighed just under seven pounds, which meant his normal load of six shells in the tan canvas carrying vest he would wear would be just over forty pounds.

These shells, which were dubbed HE-light, had a point-blank

detonating fuse and a fin assembly to give them stability in flight. The other mortar shell Bob might have to carry was filled with stinging, blinding white phosphorous. Both shell's ranges were anywhere from 100 to 3,290 yards. When either shell hit an enemy location their center blasts could spread for roughly a hundred circular feet. A third shell—HE-heavy—weighed fifteen pounds and would be transported by the squad's weapon carrier because it was too heavy to man-pack.

Bob knew by now that if he were ever hit, with the six shells— be it either heavy explosive or white phosphorous—he had to carry in his apron vest, he would be killed instantly. Telling his mother about his rifle shooting was one thing; he wasn't about to explain the dangers of being an ammunition bearer to her.

Bob's specific role after he delivered the requisite number of shells to his mortar's location would be to assist with the barrages, which meant handing the shells to the assistant gunner, who would in turn place them in the barrel of the big mortar. He also had to be prepared to take over alternate and supplementary po- sitions, in other words assume the duties and responsibilities of anyone who was wounded or killed. This meant he had to know how to fire the mortar itself should the occasion arise.

There was no question that being in a mortar squad meant hard, risky and demanding work; just why the Army was training him to be in peak physical condition that he sometimes bitched about was now becoming very clear to Bob.

Next up for Bob was the tactical training phase and the Army made every attempt to make it represent actual battlefield condi- tions in the wooded areas and winding streams on the Camp Blanding grounds. Live ammunition was used. Artillery shells were even fired to illuminate simulated battlefields during night exercises.

To Bob it was starting to feel like the real thing; the Eastern Di- amondback rattlesnakes he saw in the scrubbed oak made it even scarier. His mortar section engaged targets when ordered; their mortar delivered live covering fire for mock offenses and strategic withdrawals. He had to carry 81mm shells for hours to his mortar's emplacements in the hot spring weather he told his mother about in the letter he sent to her.

Preparation for hostile air attacks was also rehearsed; foxholes were dug and his mortar was lowered into one of the them during this exercise. Critiques were leveled if too many 81mm shells were stacked too close to one another, less any of their positions were hit by enemy fire; Bob's section avoided this criticism by spacing twenty yards apart the shells they unloaded from their weapons carrier.

By now Bob's mortar section was taking on an identity birthed in some new but soon-to-be tight friendships. Ralph Sproull, another ammunition bearer in Bob's section and brand new to the unit, was from Rockmart in the corner of northwest Georgia; Willy Driscoll came from Poughkeepsie New York; Louie "The Rub" Rubado lived way up the state in Watertown near the Canadian border before he enlisted; Carmen "The Charmer" Giello recently left a Philadelphia Pennsylvania suburb and his big family behind to join the Army. Corporal Walter "Slugger" Szelugoski , who like Bob came from Connecticut, was their lead gunner. "Gentle" John Murga, out of Trenton New Jersey, was Slugger's assistant; Bob and John got along well because both loved talking about cars, no matter how exhausted they were from their rigorous training schedule at Camp Blanding.

Together the five men who would carry the 81mm shells into the fight when all hell broke loose dubbed themselves the "Bearer Boys."

~FOURTEEN~

IN LATE MAY THE BEARER BOYS left Camp Blanding to head up to Fort Benning in Columbus, Georgia; it was a hot, sunny day. General Cubbison had left the First Division by this time; he was deemed too old at age sixty to command troops in combat. Brigadier General Teddy Roosevelt, who had become the division's assistant commander, was placed temporarily in charge when Bob packed up his field equipment, slung two bags of clothing over his shoulder, and fought to keep his balance as he loaded all of his belongings onto a deuce-and-a-half for the trip north.

The trucks traveled 150 miles to Moultrie that day. Rain had started coming down during the afternoon and the fairgrounds on the edge of town where the Bearer Boys were to encamp were full of mud by the time they arrived; Bob ate his cold supper off a regulation tin plate in his pup tent during a downpour. After a fitful night of sleep, he left this drab setting the next morning for the last 100 miles of the trip. By nightfall his company finally arrived in a heavily wooded area near Cusseta, which was off the crowded Fort Benning's main post. It was also what at first seemed to be a much better place for Bob to pitch his tent and finally get a decent night's sleep.

Training started anew. Bob's days consisted of close order drill, digging foxholes and filling them up, road marches, swatting constantly pesky mosquitos, and worrying about how he was going to wash his uniform after negotiating obstacle courses where he had to leap into a large muddy hole, do a roll, get up and keep going. Word started spreading saying that the real purpose of this latest phase of training was to make Bob and all of the Bearer Boys so mad that they would actually look forward to getting into a real fight anywhere overseas just to get away from Cusseta, Georgia.

Many new officers—derisively dubbed Ninety-Day Wonders—joined the 18th Infantry in Cusseta after being trained at the Fort Benning Infantry School. Speculation about going overseas abounded and when the men were told they had a new commanding general most figured the day they would ship out was growing closer; his name was Terry Allen. Word started getting around that General Allen was a charismatic but somewhat devilish officer who had flunked out of West Point, fought Pancho Villa's army on horseback in the cavalry along the U.S.—Mexico border before the Great War, commanded an infantry battalion during that fight, and somehow managed during the inter-war years to get his first star on the same day his friend George Patton did.

Bob also got a new company commander; he was a dark-haired Irishman from a railroad family in a town so far up in Maine it was on the U.S.—Canadian line. He made a good first impression. Captain Robert Murphy quickly demonstrated he could be demanding when necessary, but criticism was delivered in a way, usually with a congenial splattering of humor, where Bob and his fellow Bearer Boys somehow got the message their clear-thinking captain wanted them to without making them feel like they were being talked down to, or ridiculed.

Bob finally got to see the main post at Fort Benning after Allen and Murphy assumed their commands. There was a review which he was told would have his company passing in front of both American and British military dignitaries. Everyone figured something big had to be up, and after the Bearer Boys marched in route step, fully combat loaded in front of their distinguished guests so they all could see what they looked like, new orders came down in mid-June to prepare for a move up to Indiantown Gap in Pennsylvania, the Army's major staging area for units awaiting shipment overseas.

The move was uneventful, except for the confusion that arose on the rainy morning Bob left Cusseta; it was still pitched black out when he packed up. Everyone seemed to find a way to stumble over everything they would have to take with them as they tried to assemble in an orderly fashion. After waiting for trucks to pick up his platoon, Bob's move out was delayed until Captain Murphy checked off everyone on the Company H roster. He had a clerk who could do this for him, but it was Murphy's style to look each of his roughly 190 men in the eye as his name was checked; to him it was simply about showing respect for even the lowly privates he commanded.

After the trucks finally got rolling, it wasn't too long before Bob's platoon reached the nearby railroad yard and headed for the train that would take them up to Indiantown Gap. Most everyone slept or were playing cards right after they boarded. After spending the night weaving through the Carolinas and hilly Virginia, then Maryland, it wasn't long before the Bearer Boys reached the railway yards near Indiantown Gap; it was again before first light. They were picked up by trucks and driven to the reservation.

The stay at Indiantown Gap found Bob seeing two more important command changes. The first was the promotion of Frank U. Greer, who had been the number two in the regiment, that put him in direct command of the 18th Infantry; he replaced Colonel Sherburne, a soft spoken, cordial officer who had taken over the regiment back in late 1941; Sherburne wasn't a fighter. Colonel Greer was just the opposite. He was tall, tough, bald, and had a very dominating personality. He was so overbearing that after meeting with him for the first time one officer came back and said to others, "Colonel Greer seemed to give you a fifteen-minute reprimand every time he looked at you."

The other promotion had a direct impact on Bob. Another tall and rugged looking officer with a high hairline and a buzz-cut took command of his mortar platoon. He was from a tiny town in Coryell County Texas and had a real Texan's twang; his name was an odd one that was difficult for Bob to at first pronounce. But Lieutenant Waldemar Hobratschk won Bob's immediate respect; he was the only officer in the entire regiment who had recently been shot at. Hobratschk had been a machine gunner stationed in the Schofield Barracks during the attacks on Pearl Harbor; he also spoke German. He was an ideal compliment to Captain Murphy. Murphy's Irish wit and Hobratschk's dry sense of humor were often on full display in front of their men, especially one time after they came back from a meeting with Colonel Greer in late July and Hobratschk cheerfully announced to his new platoon, "You boys are dang lucky. We're a fixin' to go overseas rehel' soon."

The next day the company's continuing training program was suspended. Identification cards with photos were issued. Everyone received a new dog tag. Bob turned in his light weight khaki uniform and had another issued to him that was made of heavy wool and was Army olive-drab in color. He received a new M1 Garand rifle to replace his old World War One-era Springfield; he was also issued a new bucket helmet after he happily surrendered his dented, round steel helmet somebody else had worn during the Great War. Before too long barbed wire was placed around the battalion area and military police were constantly patrolling the perimeter to keep anyone from leaving. One somehow did in Company H, a private named Wright who had done wrong and Captain Murphy later noted as AWOL.

Everyone else was examined for communicable diseases and given inoculations to prevent them for getting smallpox, or typhoid. Bob also received a tetanus shot and a short haircut to last for the duration of the trip that lay ahead. Everyone now believed it would be to the British Isles, and not to the Pacific. The rumors were still going around that they would eventually end up in Africa.

Then on the last day of July the company gathered in the dark on the gravel road outside of Murphy's orderly room while he and Lieutenant Hobratschk used their flashlights to check off everyone's name in Bob's mortar platoon. After these formalities, which were blended with some good natured kidding from Captain Murphy, Bob joined the rest of the Bearer Boys, sat down on his pack and smoked a cigarette. A few minutes later trucks arrived and Hobratschk's flashlight and a few more wisecracks guided them into their back cargo area.

It was finally light out when they boarded a train and a few hours later Bob found himself at a railroad station in what he knew to be Brooklyn. After Captain Murphy checked his name off on the full Company H roster again—what Murphy called his Gangplank Roster—Bob received a paper bag lunch and staggered onto a dock to board a ferry boat. Some curious civilians, New York City cops and Service and Supply soldiers, were gazing at him and his fellow Bearer Boys. As one nearby officer wondered, "Where was the traditional panoply of war that greeted the brave defenders of the Republic departing for the front? There were no blaring bands, no cheering thongs, and no pretty girls throwing roses!"

Bob was standing straight up after he boarded the ferry; the boat was jammed with too many soldiers and their heavy bags, so there were simply no places to move around to or sit down. But everyone stretched their necks and turned their heads when they passed the charred hull of the French ocean liner *Normandie*. It was lying on its port side in ugly ruin; Bob had no idea how that came about. Maybe it was sabotaged, he thought. But the once well-appointed luxury liner that had brought American tourists to France during better times had actually fallen victim to a careless welder's torch that ignited a pile of debris and set off a massive fire which destroyed the thousand-foot long vessel a few weeks earlier.

The ferry finally arrived at another dock a few minutes later where Bob and the other Bearer Boys disembarked and lined up with the rest of the men in their mortar platoon; Lieutenant Hobratschk then led them into a gigantic shed where all they could hear were loud stevedores shouting out orders to other workers manning swinging booms as big crates and boxes were loaded into what first appeared to Bob to be an opening carved into a gigantic gray wall. But when he got a closer look, the gray wall turned out to be the side of another ship. When he saw soldiers in clean lightweight khaki uniforms checking off unit names he swore and wondered who the hell they were; by this time his heavy wool uniform was soaked with his sweat from the muggy Brooklyn heat. Beyond this checkpoint he made out a long gangplank, and he could finally see the soldiers in the company ahead of him shuffling up into the ship.

When Bob got aboard he heard British accents that reminded him of his Gram Nellie; it turned out they were blue-uniformed stewards now trying to provide further directions. One consulted with Lieutenant Hobratschk. All eyes were now on him; he led the Bearer Boys as they clambered down stairwells where there were plenty of other soldiers cursing while they kept weaving down into the ship's maze of smelly passageways, trying to find their assigned bunks and a place to dump their heavy bags.

Finally, after more twists through other gangs of soldiers, Bob found his bunk outside of a companionway next to a NO SMOKING sign. He was deep in the ship's hold, well beneath the officers' cabins—which were normally populated with just two paying passengers—but were now each fitted with double-bunks that would accommodate ten of those far above Bob's rank during the sea passage ahead.

It wasn't long before Bob learned that the ship he was on had been a noble tribute to man's imagination when she embarked back in 1936 on her maiden voyage out of Southampton in England. When the war started four years later she was painted a camouflaged gray, her luxurious furniture was removed, and this "Inevitable Ship," the pride of the British Cunard Line, was now re-designated simply as "HMS *250*."

But there was no mistaking the fact that the ship Bob was on was the same luxury liner Hollywood stars like Clark Gable and Bob Hope, as well as British nobility and Winston Churchill had made ocean passages on. She was rumored to be the fastest ship on the seven seas.

The Bearer Boys were going to cross the Atlantic Ocean on the *Queen Mary*.

By this time the sinking of merchant ships along the Atlantic Coast beneath New York were far fewer due to an interlocking convoy system that had finally been inaugurated by the U.S. Navy. But the Germans quickly adapted and shifted their deadly U-boats to the vast North Atlantic to cut off the flow of supply and troop ships being sent to England. There were about 15,000 First Division soldiers and crew aboard the *Queen Mary*; it was her largest manifest ever and twice her normal passenger carrying capacity. But she was indeed fast, on her way to deliver soldiers destined to fight Germans, and would be a tough target for the far slower U-boats.

Nevertheless, the first day the Bearer Boys spent aboard the *Queen* was filled with instructions about abandoning ship, and actual drill was conducted in lifeboats during shifts on deck; they all had to don big Mae West life vests. Even what to do if there was an air raid was rehearsed. There was an abundance of caution being taken. Orders even came down that required every man to sleep fully clothed; otherwise they'd freeze in the North Atlantic air if they were fortunate enough to get into a lifeboat should the *Queen* get hit and abandon ship orders came down. There was absolutely no smoking allowed below decks. Armed sentries were even placed at the companionway down in the hold the Bearer Boys were in to be sure every rule was strictly adhered to.

On their second day aboard there was a tremor that told Bob

the ship was coming to life; it was mid-morning. The *Queen Mary* slipped away from Pier 90 at 10:45 and tugboats help point her bow down the East River. It was August 2nd of 1942, and after a year and a half of Army training Bob was finally heading off to his war. He was below deck so he never got to see the Statue of Liberty before the *Queen* left New York Harbor, headed out to sea and was met by two Navy blimps off Long Island that were performing maritime reconnaissance; they would spot U-Boats if they were on the surface in U.S. territorial waters. Two destroyer escorts also patrolled to the *Queen's* port and starboard, but by the time she reached her cruising speed of some thirty-five knots the Navy destroyers were slamming into waves, falling behind and loosing sight of the much faster gray troop ship; they veered off, reversed course and headed back into New York Harbor.

But no U-boats appeared and the five-day voyage was limited as far as training programs were concerned. Lieutenant Hobratschk was still required to be on duty in the hold at all times, except when he slept; he even had to conduct a personal reconnaissance so he could lead his men to mess and find their way back. He also held daily weapons inspections which Bob never had a problem with; his name was always checked off after Hobratschk shined a flashlight into his M1 rifle's breech and down its bore to be sure it was properly cleaned. And Hobratschk's attention to detail didn't end here. Bob especially enjoyed the instructions his lieu-tenant gave him in calculating how many shillings equaled a pound in English currency and what the exchange rate was for a pound in U.S. dollars; it was $4.03. He knew this would come in handy when he shot craps or played poker after he got to wherever it was he was going.

When it came time for meals the Bearer Boys were marched up into the mess hall and their platoon was lined up alongside the tables. A whistle signaled when they could sit down; twenty min-utes later another signal blew ending mess and everyone had to stand back up and march out, even if they hadn't finished their meals. The good news for Bob was his battalion drew KP duty and as such Lieutenant Hobratschk had to furnish kitchen help; Bob was one of the fortunate ones selected so he managed to get plenty to eat while the *Queen* was at sea. So far going to war wasn't all that bad; he even had time to get a couple of smokes in during the day. Because the ship was overcrowded, everyone had to remain below decks, but there were one-hour airing periods in the mornings and afternoons when the Bearer Boys were rotated out of their hold and allowed to go up on the main deck.

Bob and a couple of the Bearer Boys happened to be topside when planes were suddenly seen approaching the *Queen Mary*; it was their fifth day at sea. At first they thought they could be German bombers, but it turned out they were British planes; it was actually a squad of escort aircraft providing cover for the *Queen's* approach into the Western British Isles. Again no U-boats appeared in these dangerous waters as the graceful vessel steamed towards the rugged coast of Scotland, made landfall, then passed through the deep coastal waters of the Firth of Clyde and eventually got closer to the old Cloch Lighthouse where the *Queen Mary* was met by tugboats that helped guide her through the early morning mist into a dock in the little seaside town of Gourock.

Gourock was dotted with brick and stone buildings and surrounded by lush green hills; silver barrage balloons, tethered by heavy steel cables, hung in the sky to help defend the area from German dive bomber attacks. Launches were darting back and forth from the dock area out to freighters and other small vessels. Bob saw none of this until he gathered up all of his heavy gear, filed out of the *Queen's* hold with his buddies, crossed a gangplank and shuffled down into the bowels of a waiting ferryboat. There were numerous delays, but after the ferry boat eventually tied up to another dock Captain Murphy got the entire company in lines of two abreast. The first things Bob saw when he reached the street were railroad employees, some curious civilians and a bunch of not particularly attractive women who were working as freight handlers; there was no warm welcome. There were no donuts or bitter British coffee, nor was there any band playing patriotic songs to cheer the arrival of the Americans in his platoon.

It really didn't matter because by now the Company H men were lined up in columns of twos again and marching down the street to a railroad station. Soon they piled into narrow aisled coach cars, and after a few warning toots the train pulled away from Gourock for somewhere unknown; the Bearer Boys passed through stations on their way to wherever it was they were going, but there was no telling where they were along the way because all of the station signs had been removed so a German spy couldn't report the Yanks were there and reveal the direction of their movements.

At least the food was somewhat decent; Bob was issued a K Ration and it contained a can of American cheese, soy bean meal crackers, gum, candy and even three British Chelsea cigarettes. The Bearer Boys settled in and played poker, and enjoyed looking out at the gentle, rolling countryside but when night came all the window blinds in their coach were closed so German pilots wouldn't see the long line of train cars and interrupt the journey by strafing them.

They rolled into another train station at seven the next morning. The usual confusion was present before Bob and the rest of the Bearer Boys finally disembarked from their coach, lined up in columns of twos yet again and marched for a good half hour through a small village, then down a tree-lined winding road and finally into a concrete courtyard surrounded by two-story brick buildings. Bob had arrived at Tidworth Barracks on the Salisbury Plain, close to prehistoric Stonehenge and about sixty-five miles southwest of London.

Bob settled into a squad room with the other Bearer Boys that had two coal-burning stoves at either end, the first solid and warm surroundings he had been in since his time at Ft. Devens over a year earlier. The food got better; regular British rations were served in the mess hall and usually featured things like mutton, cabbage, Brussels sprouts, boiled potatoes, heavy dark bread, and even tea. Bob got to go into London the first weekend he was at Tidworth Barracks, and he had to carry his gas mask with him. It was standing room only on the train he took that Friday. Along one platform on the way into Waterloo Station were the first signs Bob saw that told him he had allies for the fighting sure to come; they were tall and erect, immaculately battle-dressed soldiers of a British Guards Regiment.

He also saw signs of war as the train got closer to London. There were gutted buildings surrounded by piles of brick, charred black pieces of roofing material and scattered glass; all the structures were victims of the ongoing bombing campaign by the Germans.

When Bob got off the train it was close to nine that night and London's blackout orders left the streets dark; he didn't bother to sleep and even though the next day was rainy he got to see Piccadilly Circus, which reminded him of Times Square back in New York City. He found a pub he liked that night where there were women in blue Royal Air Force uniforms and others he learned were called "Wrens" who wore black stockings and commanded his full attention. But the competition for their affection was fierce; too many officers were in his and the other Bearer Boys' midst. Even Carmen the Charmer Giello's lines didn't work. Louie the Rub Rubalo's advances fell flat. Slugger Szelugoski struck out; the women gravitated to their higher ups. Bob didn't even try. He was the kind that let women come to him first before he turned on the charm; none did.

Sunday was also a big letdown; it rained again and by the time Bob dried out and got warm next to the coal stove in his squad room back at Tidworth Barracks he was ready for a good night's sleep.

Company H's mortars were packed in cosmoline back at Indiantown Gap and had not arrived yet; Bob actually hadn't seen a mortar since he left Camp Blanding, back in Florida. But training started anew. Colonel Greer wanted every man in the regiment to get his conditioning edge back and hikes would do just that. One was a full twenty-five miles with just ten minutes of rest per hour where Bob and the other Bearer Boys had to carry their full forty-pound packs. Trucks brought the noon meal. It was an all day affair, not ending until late in the afternoon when the soldiers in the tired column were finally told that the drill period was over. Calisthenics, equipment inspections, close-order drill and even air raid rehearsals—made real when the whine of air raid sirens signaled actual German bombing runs—were the typical routine most days the Bearer Boys stayed at Tidworth Barracks.

One day was particularly memorable; it was a Wednesday. A regimental formation was held in the gymnasium. Bob was called to attention after everyone was assembled, and he then witnessed General Roosevelt enter the room and make for the boxing ring in the center of the gym. His walking stick pushed aside the ropes and the well-liked general then stood fully erect and greeted everyone in his booming voice with, "Men of the 18th, I'm damned glad to see you!"

The applause that followed shook the building. Morale was indeed high, a lot of training was behind them, and the Bearer Boys were now really itching for a fight with the Germans.

~FIFTEEN~

PRESIDENT ROOSEVELT AND PRIME MINISTER Churchill began discussing the invasion of North Africa six months before the Bearer Boys crossed the Atlantic on the *Queen Mary*. U.S. military leaders had their doubts about the value of sending U.S. Forces into North Africa, and some even argued that their chances of succeeding were low. But the formidable Roosevelt preferred the first American offensive be in North Africa because it afforded an opportunity to take the fight to the Germans; the equally formidable Winston Churchill had also argued that a "Germany First" doctrine be adopted; Great Britain, after all, had been fighting Germany alone for two years without direct U.S. troop help.

Thus revised, highly secret plans for the invasion of North Africa were tentatively approved back on the 19th of February; amazingly the "rumor we are going to Africa soon" letter Bob sent to his mother was penned just a month later—to the day—back at Camp Blanding. Rumors sure had frog's legs in the United States Army.

As with most higher-level planning, nothing was cast in stone until the commander-in-chief gave his final approval. For months Roosevelt had to contend with his military advisers' arguments for a more direct, bold assault on Hitler's conquered European shores; they really saw North Africa as a side-show to the main goal of driving into Germany and quickly ending the war in Europe.

But British planners were dead-set against a cross-Channel invasion at the time for two primary reasons: One, the U.S. nor Britain were ready for such a large-scale attack; maybe they would be in 1943. And two: the infamous "Desert Fox," Erwin Rommel, was driving toward Alexandria and the Suez Canal. Rommel had to be stopped; British forces were fighting with their backs to the wall in Egypt and were in danger of being pushed into Tunisia and thrown into the Mediterranean Sea.

And there was also the matter of Russia. The imperturbable Soviet Commissar Molotov had been constantly complaining about impotence on the U.S. and Britain's part to committing to the opening a Second Front. Pressure needed to be taken off Hitler's quest to conquer Russia, and diverting German forces elsewhere was the only thing that would satisfy Joseph Stalin.

It was mid-September when President Roosevelt and Prime Minister Churchill gave their final approvals to the invasion of French North Africa; it was really a compromise between the political realities of fighting a global war and military expediency.

North Africa was now to be invaded before the winter rains set in during December. General Eisenhower would be in overall command. But questions remained: Would the African French resist the American landings? Eisenhower was led to believe they would not. Would the Vichy government—exiled officials from France—welcome the U.S. Army? American diplomats thought they would.

But the pragmatic First Division commander, General Allen, wasn't buying into either of those sentiments. He expected the Vichy French forces in North Africa would fight; failure to do so could result in brutal retaliation by the Germans on their families back in France. To plan otherwise would be military folly. In Allen's opinion, Vichy French officials would simply stick with whoever won the fight.

Bob and the other Bearer Boys knew nothing about the Army's decision to make the landings in North Africa, or when it would go off. Despite all of the training Bob received over the last year and a half, one very important maneuver had not been practiced since his time on the rough seas off Cape Henry, near Virginia

Beach way back in January: amphibious landings from troop ships onto a hostile enemy shore.

So this training was going to be next.

The Bearer Boys were really looking forward to spending the first weekend of October in London when an unexpected alert order came down from regiment; they would be leaving Tidworth Barracks that coming Sunday. Saturday was spent packing, then they were hurriedly loaded into trucks the next morning and driven to the nearby train station. Rain now seemed to always accompany every one of their moves. This one delivered downpours that drowned out conversations inside the cars of the seven-train rail convoy as the Bearer Boys traveled through the rolling English countryside all the way up to their destination—Rosneath in Scotland.

Rosneath Base had been taken over by the U.S. Navy back in August; it was now the main training facility for future amphibious landings. The base was located on the Firth of Clyde opposite Gourock, where the Bearer Boys had disembarked from the *Queen Mary* a few weeks earlier. The ten kilometer Clyde shore-lochs just to the north of Rosneath was where the actual amphibious landing practices would be conducted.

When the Bearer Boys reached the Rosneath train station late in the afternoon that Sunday Lt. Hobratschk first lined them up; their raincoats kept them from getting soaked while they waited for what was next.

Hobratschk tried to cheer everyone up; he joked that the downpour reminded him of home since it was "coming down like a Texas heffer pissin' on a flat rock." That got a lot of grins. Everyone finally boarded trucks a half hour later, and they were soon weaving through country roads at a brisk clip. A harrowing twenty minutes of this passed and the men were finally dropped off in a heavily wooded area called Green Isle.

The Bearer Boys were then directed to one of the hundreds of Nissen huts on these grounds, all of which looked like a giant sliced in half Campbell's soup cans. These would serve as their new quarters. Bob shuffled through the mud and went into the thin wooden doorway of his hut first: he pulled open the heavy burlap drapes that covered the two small windows next to the door, then he turned on three naked light bulbs so the rest of the Bearer Boys could see their accommodations better.

They weren't all that bad. There was a British coke and coal stove in the middle of the hut with a stack that ran up through the roof; at least this would take the damp chill off. Their beds were wooden-framed and had decent four-inch cloth strapping they could spread out their bedrolls on. It only took about a half hour for the Bearer Boys to settle in, get the stove lit, unpack, light up their cigarettes and start playing poker.

Lieutenant Hobratschk disappeared the next morning. The Bearer Boys had the day off until he showed up that night after they finished having mess on the main post. They had eaten well. The Navy sure served better food than the Army did. The Bearer Boys hogged down juicy slices of roast beef, scooped up the extra gravy that came on their mashed potatoes with fresh white bread, and then they settled back and drank real American coffee. But the best treat was the ice cream dish they had for desert; it reminded them of home and was certainly delicious.

"OK, men," Hobratschk suddenly began after he came into the hall. Everyone jumped out of their chairs and came to attention, but his next words told them this was going to be an informal briefing.

"'Y'all gather round and sit here," Hobratschk said while pointing his finger. It was to an open area away from the long plain wood tables they just ate off of. All sixty men in the platoon complied and sat in a semi-circle in front of their commander. Six rows of soldiers, ten to a row, were eager to find out what was up.

"Boys, tomorrow we're a fixin' to go down to the beach," Hobratschk said with a smile. "Y'all won't need suntan lotion. Matter of fact, you landlubbers aren't even going to have a chance to go for a swim. Any questions?"

Bob looked at the other Bearer Boys and smirked. Their lieutenant was putting them on, and they knew it. The weather that day was clear for a change, but damn chilly. They had been issued knitted wool caps with a small visor that afternoon and everyone was wearing theirs to stay warm. No one had the least desire to get their feet wet.

"Ok, then. Listen up," Lieutenant Hobratschk bellowed out. "First, don't let me catch you again with those new caps on y'all are wearing without your helmets over them. That's the rule now. Break it and y'all will get a fine. Break it twice and every one of you will be peelin' potatoes for a week. Now. Any questions?"

Hobratschk had his wool cap on and wasn't wearing his helmet, but rank did have its privileges after all. Nevertheless, sixty of America's finest soldiers first remained silent, then Private Billy Fencil in the front row stood up and timidly barked, "Sir, yes Sir." Fifty-nine others jumped up a second later, saluted and repeated the same.

Their commander smiled then said, "At ease, men. Sit all your sorry asses back down and relax." The men in the front row started taking their new caps off; others began to do the same, but Hobratschk chuckled and said, "That rule is effective tomorrow. Otherwise I'd have my helmet on. Keep them caps on for now and y'all stay warm."

Everyone was eager to learn more and Lieutenant Hobratschk didn't disappoint them. "OK, men," he said in a now far more serious tone. "Captain Murphy and all the rest of us officers in the company, plus some non-coms, got a briefing today over in the auditorium. We all were shown the important points of how to make amphibious assault landings. Our instructors were fine Brit commandos who survived the Dieppe Raid over on the French coast a few weeks ago. That went badly. There were 900 men killed, almost 600 wounded and just under 2,000 captured. Over a hundred Royal Air Force and Canadian planes were shot down. Three U.S. Army Rangers were killed, and one was a Louisiana fella'. He was the first American killed by German forces in this war."

All eyes were fixed on Lieutenant Hobratschk as he continued on.

"But lessons came out of that, and y'all are going to be the lucky ones to learn more about those in the coming days. All us officers got to see a mocked-up beach today. It was a model on a big table with miniature assault craft, signal devices and more. Problems we could confront when we all land wherever the hell it is we're going were worked out."

"Any questions yet?"

Everyone remained silent.

"OK then, tomorrow we start practicing. We're going to the beach and you boys will learn how to pack into LCVPs. Y'all know what those are, right?"

A few shook their heads indicating they had no idea what they were.

"These are the boats that y'all will go to shore on when we land wherever, like I was saying, the U.S. Army in its infinite wisdom sends us," Hobratschk told them. "We're going to start by just getting you all off the boats onto the beach. Eventually y'all will learn how to climb down a net off the side of a bigger transport, and jump into them. That's later. Tomorrow y'all see how we pack roughly three dozen or so of you brave men into each boat. They're flat-bottomed and some are made of wood, the better ones good Eastern Texas oak. There's a ramp in the front of 'em. It's taller than me; seven feet or so. It goes down and that's where y'all will get off. We'll practice that, too."

Bob thought back to the amphibious landing practices at Cape Henry and how badly those went, but didn't say anything.

"Still no questions?" Lieutenant Hobratschk shot out, fully expecting there would be.

"Just one, Sir," "Gentle" John Murga said. "How early tomorrow can we get started?"

That made Lieutenant Hobratschk's smile almost as wide as he was tall. "We depart from the cozy huts y'all are in at 0800. Get a good night's sleep. Lights out at 2200. And don't forget I never want to see any of you all wearing those wool caps again unless they're underneath your helmets. 'Course I'm not going to be watching you sleep tonight. Full gear tomorrow, though. It's going to be a long day."

The LCVPs—Landing Craft Vehicle Personnel—at Rosneath were better than the ones Bob went to shore on back at Cape Henry. The machinegun positions on those were located at the bow of the craft. The ramps were narrow, which made disembarking difficult. It was near the noon meal when LCVP orientation on the new ones ended. Lieutenant Hobratschk got the entire platoon lined up, but before they marched off to mess he put his hands on his hips, spread his legs as if at ease, and broke into a wide grin.

"Y'all got any questions now?" But again there were none.

The next few days were spent perfecting amphibious landings from stationary LCVPs. Captain Murphy split the entire company into thirty-five man groups, and the Bearer Boys were paired with a Company H machinegun squad and a few squads from a rifle company. Lieutenant Hobratschk sometimes oversaw their progress; other times Murphy did. Neither seemed to be in a joking mood.

For some reason not known to the Bearer Boys there was only one amphibious landing rehearsal scheduled in the Clyde shore lochs. It came on October 19th. They were loaded onto a bigger LCT—Landing Craft Tank—this time, a 117-foot steel boat with a thirty-two-foot beam that normally carried five tanks, or 150 tons of mixed-cargo. But for this exercise the Bearer Boys were five soldiers amongst 345 other men.

They were all packed into the long hold where the tanks would normally be. They had no cover. The skies were cloudy when the LCT departed Rosneath and hours were spent on the open water circling in station orbits waiting for the cover of darkness to finally sneak over to the shore lochs. Fortunately, the waters were calm, but a cold, damp wind soon sprang up and made conditions miserable after night fell. Men shivered, many swore and most prayed this would end soon. It didn't. The Bearer Boys waited all night; smoking was prohibited, as was having any conversations the whole time.

The only voices that could be heard were British. One started calling out soundings—the water depth—as the LCT finally approached shore just before first light. Next was the banging of iron bars, accompanied by the loud swearing of others as the LCT's ramp fought being lowered. Then there was a sharp jar when it collided with the pebbly beach edge. Now it was the Americans' turn to curse as they stumbled forward and shuffled down the ramp.

The Bearer Boys disembarked behind a rifle squad from Company F and followed these men up a narrow path across the stony beach that connected to a brush-lined road about 200 feet away. They assembled like good soldiers should, awaiting further commands. The Company F commander, Captain Jack Williamson, finally showed up; he led the column groupings off the road, and up the side of a hill to what everyone presumed was their ordered destination.

But the only order that came down was to halt. All of a sudden the maneuver was over. That quick. The Bearer Boys had to wait until full daylight for anything to happen, and after it came they marched through a small village, were watched by some curious early risers with coffee mugs in their hands, and then they shuffled back to the beach where their LCT was drawn up alongside others.

As Company F Lieutenant John Downing, whose rifle and light machinegun squads the Bearer Boys were marching up the ramp with, remembered at that moment, "I hoped an actual landing would work out better than this maneuver. Our confused stumbling around blindly in the dark of early morning did nothing to increase my confidence in my ability as a combat leader."

When the Bearer Boys got back to Rosneath Lieutenant Hobratschk was there to greet them. "I've some good news and bad news for all y'all," he started. "The bad news is we won't be doing amphibious landing practices tomorrow. The good news is we're all moving out of these nice Nissen huts y'all are staying in so we don't get too comfortable before we head for wherever the Army in its infinite wisdom decides to send us for more training."

~SIXTEEN~

GLASGOW, THE BIG PORT CITY on the River Clyde in Scotland's western lowlands, was the next stop for the Bearer Boys. Or so they thought. The train they found themselves on actually went through the city and finally stopped at a small depot. As usual, rain was pouring down as they disembarked. The Bearer Boys assembled in columns of twos, standard formation they didn't even wait for an order to do, and before too long they were marching by some buildings along what signs said was Corkerhill Road. They arrived at their new home when the concrete paving gave way to a sea of mud.

The Bearer Boys had arrived at Pollock Estates, which featured a big two-winged three-story stone mansion and once had a golf course on its grounds. Nearby was Old Pollock, where people moved out of Glasgow to before the war in order to escape the city's depressing slums. The golf course was now a military tent city; they were British conical type canvas tents everywhere. The Bearer Boy's new home was placed on a gentle sloping knoll that they had to first wade through ankle-deep mud to get to. The nauseous odor of decades of sheep droppings—once sweet fertilizer for greens and fairways—filled their nostrils.

Their tent slept eight, and there was a duckboard the cots rested upon so their legs didn't sink into the mud. The five Bearer Boys, Slugger Szelugoski and Gentle John Murga took one look into the tent, and Charmer Giello spoke for them all when he said, "You've gotta' be shitting me. We sleep head-to-head in a circle in the middle of this muck, with our feet sticking out to the sides to catch rain? With the way Louie snores? You gotta' be shittin' me. Gimme' a break."

It only got worse. The closest latrine was in a sheet-iron shed partitioned off with stalls but it had no doors; iron honey buckets were placed in holes beneath the raw, flat board seats. Washrooms were in open sheds; at least cold running water was available for showers. Mess was in a hospital tent, surrounded by even more mud; long wood tables and benches were here for the Bearer Boys, but there were no lights.

Word soon came down saying Lieutenant Hobratschk and Captain Murphy were going to hold an orientation in the mess hall an hour before supper was served. The Bearer Boys put their raincoats back on and left their new accommodations early enough to compensate for the slow going in the churned up, soupy mud.

"Men, welcome to Cokerhill Camp," Captain Murphy began when everyone assembled. "Starting tomorrow, we'll pick up here where we left off back in Rosneath, which means you will have the good fortune to receive more tactical and amphibious training."

Then trying not to smirk, Murphy added, "To make your stay here more pleasant, the Army will issue rubber overshoes to you in the morning. That's about it. Wally, do you have anything you'd care to add to this?"

Lieutenant Hobratschk certainly did. "Men, we're sure to be here for some time, given how miserable this camp is. But the Army has sent us here for a reason. Any questions?"

Bob had the nerve to ask, "Lieutenant, Sir, how far away is Glasgow?" This drew uncomfortable laughter.

"It's twenty minutes by tram once y'all waddle through the mud to get back to the depot," Hobratschk shot back before he started grinning. "But even that may be a problem for y'all. First, we'll be settling in to our training routine, as Captain Murphy just told you. And if you do eventually get leave, y'all will have to wear your dress uniforms when you depart for those nice pubs in Glasgow. You are representing the United States Army after all."

Colonel Greer and his staff officers disappeared a few days later to represent the 18th Infantry during some meeting in London. Rumors abounded; most were just guesses as to what the secret mission could be about. But training continued, and when Army-issued pyramidal tents showed up for the regiment's officers speculation about going anywhere else soon started dying off.

After Captain Murphy and Lieutenant Hobratschk left during their second week at the camp, no one was particularly surprised; well-sourced rumor on that was they had just gone over to Rosneath for more lectures on amphibious landings. But when the Bearer Boys received an alert order the next day, everything changed. They were also going back to Rosneath, this time to board a 550-foot Dutch liner that rivaled the *Queen Mary* in appointments and luxury before she was also painted a dull gray and converted into a troop ship.

The Bearer Boys were aboard the *Reina del Pacifico* two days later; they were actually in quarters deep in the ship's hold staring at blue lights to keep their eyes accustomed to darkness. Turned out that Murphy and Hobratschk had spent their time away in a conference room where they were briefed on a simulated landing maneuver that would have their 2nd Battalion operating against the British Number 9 Commandos. The Commandos' formation was birthed in 1940 to answer Churchill's desire to have specialized forces that could "develop a reign of terror on the enemy coast." Their latest raid back in late March had provided assistance to another commando unit in demolishing port facilities on the heavily-defended Normandie dry dock at St. Nazaire in German-occupied France. The Commandos would now be providing assistance with the training of green American troops who had yet to land on a hostile enemy shore. The Number 9 Commandos would defend a small peninsula located near the Scottish towns of Dunoon and Inellan.

All the Bearer Boys knew was their mortar section would be supporting Company F during what was now being called "the landings," rather than another maneuver. Landings sounded more like the real thing. Lieutenant Hobratschk told them that their order to move out would come over the ship's loudspeaker, and that they'd load up after serial 135 was called. They would then be mustering at sally port S-1, descending down an iron ladder and boarding a waiting assault craft.

"Couple of other things y'all need to know," Lieutenant Hobratschk added. "We'll all be going to shore on LCAs and not the LCVPs you're familiar with. Your new landing craft is not a standing room only vessel. Being the refined Brits came up with these LCAs, you all will have places to sit. There's actually three bench rows. One's in the center; the other two are to either side and y'all who get to sit in these will be under the cover of the top deck. A bowman-gunner will let the ramp down when we hit the beach. Any questions?"

There were none.

"OK, then. There's more. Even though we won't have our mortars with us, our squads will be positioning to support F Company when they attack. Major Ben Sternberg will be overseeing the operation. For those of you who don't know him, he's our S-3, the battalion's operations officer. He's from Florida. Actually Starke, where Camp Blanding is, for those of you who were there back in the spring. Know, too, that Major Sternberg is a West Pointer. And he's a tough man. He played football and lacrosse at the academy. But his favorite sport was boxing. He was on the team that won the Eastern Intercollegiate title."

The Bear Boys just looked in awe at Lieutenant Hobratschk, but said nothing. Bob remembered that Major Sternberg was in command of Company E when they were at Ft. Devens nearly two years ago.

"Assuming again there are no questions, just stay put until I come back for y'all. I've got to be certain the exit route out of here gets us to the right sally port when our serial is announced over the loudspeaker."

There were no questions. The Bearer Boys just saluted Lieutenant Hobratschk, but he left them less in the dark about what was going to happen as they stared up into the blue lights, nodded off and waited for their serial to be heard.

"All officers assemble in the troop compartments" was their first warning the show was on when it came over the ship's loudspeakers early the following morning. The next thing the Bearer Boys heard were shouts and heavy footsteps. Then there were thumps against the sides of the *Reina del Pacifico* as the LCAs were lowered into the water. Serials started belching out. Serial 135 was soon called. Company F's riflemen departed. They were next.

When Lieutenant Hobratschk got the Bearer Boys on deck it was still well before dawn. The skies were a lead gray, but at least it wasn't raining. Before they knew it they were climbing down the iron ladder on the side of the ship and into their LCA. They settled in with two Company H machinegun squads, and moments later the Bearer Boys were churning over the choppy waters off Dunoon towards shore. In the distance Bob could see the reflections of colored lights. His LCA was bouncing in the waves, but within minutes there was a thud and his landing craft hit the beach. Then the bowman-gunner lowered the ramp.

The Company F men were already moving off the beach along a narrow dirt trail. The Bearer Boys followed them up to a rutted road, and then through another trail before the riflemen ahead of them fell out in a field. They were apparently waiting for more boat groups to arrive. And as if on cue, the few visible stars disappeared and heavy rain started coming down.

The column got moving again after the rest of the Company F rifle and light machine gun squads showed up. Bob could see that the men were stumbling and slipping; he was about twenty yards behind the back of their column. It looked like some were holding onto the belts of the man ahead of him; others farther up the line were bumping into those in front of them. The long olive-drab line of soaked soldiers that the Bearer Boys were supposed to support looked like a sorry bunch as they marched up a wide trail carved into the side of gently-rising hill. Then, to Bob's amazement, what must have been the platoon at the head of the column circled back and was now marching directly towards him.

An officer finally got the column re-organized and this time it took off in another direction and went down a country road. First light had lit up the horror show by this time, and after the somewhat better disciplined column started climbing another hill that was overgrown with tall weeds and brush, they ran into a larger group of officers. When the Bearer Boys caught up what they saw startled them. Bob just smirked; he couldn't believe what he was witnessing. Soldiers were resting. Some were sleeping. Others were smoking. Most were eating K rations.

But somehow these soldiers got organized again and before too long the head of the column reached the crest of the hill. Down the other side the long line went, past some British tents and then onto a dirt road that led up yet another hill. Finally, enemy fire rang out, but it turned out that supposedly captured commandoes were just shooting blank cartridges to pass the time.

A carrier jeep suddenly roared up and met the Bearer Boys. Somehow, their mortar had arrived. Bob just scratched his head. Hadn't Lieutenant Hobratschk said they wouldn't have their mortar for this maneuver? Nevertheless, the timing was excellent. The Company F column had worked its way up another grassy hill to an area that appeared to be surrounded by swamps. The Bearer Boys and their jeep followed them and together they were going down the other side of the hill when the driver yelled out, "Just got our orders on the radio. See those guys deploying along that stone wall down there? Lieutenant Hobratschk wants us to go onto the backside of that damn slippery hill, get in defilade, set up and be ready to render support."

The Bearer Boys and a determined looking Slugger Szelugoski twisted around first. Murga followed them; Gentle John, the assistant gunner, didn't appear to be all that fired up. Maybe it was because he was omniscient for it wasn't long before the jeep's radio crackled again and new orders came down calling the entire maneuver over.

LCTs eventually took everyone back to the *Reina del Pacifico*. There was a lot of officers dressed in their dress pinks in the ship's bar that night. Plenty of whiskey, British gins, and scotch and sodas flowed. Dice rolled and rollicking ballads were sung. "A great feeling of well-being and comradeship, along with cigarette smoke and liquor fumes, filled the air," Lieutenant Downing in Company F remembered before he fell out just after midnight.

Downing was awakened from his slumber several hours later by an irate British officer. Downing was told that some American troops had invaded the British sailors' quarters, and wouldn't leave. It turned out the Bearer Boys had gotten into some mischief with a few British naval ratings and this had apparently set off an international incident. Ralph Sproull, the Bearer Boy from northwest Georgia, was actually passed out when Lieutenant Downing arrived. Bob and the rest were still throwing dice, so they gathered up their winnings and went back to where they belonged. Ralph wasn't so lucky. His crime was giving Downing a sullen look and moving too slowly after the lieutenant kicked him awake. He was guided off to the brig and put in a cell, only later to be retrieved and taken by a guard back to the Company H compartment. It was Captain Murphy's decision as to whether or not to prefer charges.

"Private Sproull, I have just one question," Murphy began when Ralph stood rigidly at attention in front of him. "Were you up, or had you lost some money before you fell out?"

"Sir, I was up plenty," Ralph answered.

"Good," Murphy replied. And with a gleam in his eyes he followed up with, "At ease. That's good for company morale. We here in Company H are winners. Now listen up. We just got a message from battalion headquarters. Says we must remain on this ship until LCTs come out again and get us. Seems they think we could walk on water to get to shore, so I want you to deliver this message to the rest of your gang."

"Sir, yes Sir. I will make that perfectly clear."

"Very well, Private. And let 'em know that the next time we storm a beach, we aren't going to skip on water to get there. We in Company H won't even get our boots wet. We'll part the sea if we have to."

That story made the rounds as did a couple of other rumors about the Dunoon landings folly. The juiciest one had started in the officer's lounge when they discussed the lessons they should have learned from the confusion that marked the maneuvers inland. The source was Major Sternberg, who remembered the dark and rain when other companies in the battalion were loading into their LCAs. "It was a scary moment," he told the near-numb rollicking officers standing around him. "I had an observer with me. We went down the ladder together into our bobbing landing craft. We sat down, and he turns to me and says, 'You know, I just peed in my pants.' Guess who that was?"

"Major Powers?" a particularly buzzed lieutenant guessed. John L. Powers, their ruddy-faced battalion commander, was standing right there amongst them.

"Wasn't me," Powers assured them while he laughed real loud. "Who was it, Ben?"

"Major General Terry Allen, our division commander."

The other rumor wasn't quite as funny. Another general had come up from London where he observed the troops of the First Division—as the story was told later—"lying in combat loaders in the lochs who were to disembark from their landing craft at numerous points, under the cover of darkness, with the objective of taking the 'enemy' airdromes, coastal batteries, and in general practicing the kind of operation that lie ahead."

From his vantage point this general observed what he labeled the faults of the lieutenants, captains and major grades, who did not seem to know what to do after the troops got to the beach. Even General Roosevelt's cheery assessment didn't sway the visiting general's thinking. Roosevelt had told him, "The troops captured the airdrome, bypassed an enemy position and had all but choked Hitler."

But the visitor's naval aide later noted, "Having seen most of the operation, Ike was inclined to discount that report. As a matter of fact, the whole demonstration was disappointing, and Ike felt pretty low on the return trip."

When General Dwight D. Eisenhower got back to London he had a cold, and the unsatisfactory showing up in Scotland led to what he described as a "state of jitters." He said he couldn't even concentrate, but there were a lot of other reasons for that.

The invasion of North Africa was scheduled to go off in two weeks.

The Bearer Boys went back to Corkerhill Camp the day after the failed invasion of Dunoon; it was raining, of course, when they arrived. Still, activity picked up. More Army regulation canvas pyramidal tents showed up, as did Sibley stoves and cots. The entire camp suddenly resembled a construction site. Unfolded British tents were scattered around everywhere, making for an ongoing logistics nightmare as more Army tents were pitched to make the stay—which now seemed like it would be for a long time—more pleasant.

Sightseeing started anew. It wasn't to Glasgow, however. With each passing day hikes got longer, but they were along narrow Scottish highways that were so scenic that vacation planners could have sold Corkerhill Camp's surroundings as a tourist destination.

Colorful visitors did arrive at the camp one day in late October. They usually wore coveralls and overseas caps, but these soldiers also donned British helmets and battle dress jackets when they did their high spirited "jog-trots." Their canvas leggings were cut so their trousers puffed out above their boots, which no Bearer Boy would have ever dared to do without being fined. To avoid getting their boots muddy, this new bunch pulled wool socks over them, then left these piled on the wet, muddy edges of Corkerhill Camp so they could take leave in Glasgow's dancehalls and strut their stuff in shiny boots.

"Who the hell is that bunch?" Bob wondered out loud to his fellow Bearer Boys while they were eating their K-ration breakfast on their cots the day after these visitors arrived.

Charmer Giello said, "You don't know? I'll give you a hint. They're on our side, even though they stole the Brit commando's way of showing their battalion designation with those flashes they wear on the shoulders of their blouses."

"Yeah," Willy Driscoll added. "There was a rumor going round they even wanted to put up their sergeant's tents in their officers' row, but that got nixed by the higher-ups."

"That and they address each other by their first names," Louie the Rub said in a bewildered tone. "There's none of this 'sir, yes sir' business we have to abide by. Can you imagine calling Lieutenant Hobratschk 'Wally,' and getting away with that?"

"OK, I give up," Bob said. "Who are they?"

"The 1st U.S. Ranger Battalion," Ralph Sproull answered. "Veterans of the Dieppe Raid. Or just a fraction of 'em, so the rumor goes. Cocky bunch, huh? And to think I could have spent a lot of time in the brig just 'cause I looked at that Lieutenant Downing funny when we looted those Brits of their pounds shooting dice back on the *Reina*."

"They call themselves Darby's Rangers," Slugger added. "Maybe they'll come in handy wherever it is the Army in their infinite wisdom sends us."

"You sound like Wally now," Bob laughed. As did all of the Bearer Boys.

"Hey, we better get our asses moving," Slugger Szelugoski yelled over their giggling. "We got gun drill at 0900."

There was no gun drill that morning. A different buzz filled the air. Word got out that Colonel Greer was back from his secret meeting in London, so something big could be up. Instead of boring gun drill, the Bearer Boys were marched over to an open field where they joined every other company in regimental formation. Greer mounted a platform and started by confidently saying the regiment was going to be given the opportunity to uphold the fine record of the First Division in the last war. Then he said the words that Bob had spent twenty-two months in the Army getting ready for.

"Men of the 18th," Greer bellowed, "we're goin' a fightin'!"

Journey of the Purple Heart

COMBAT:
NORTH AFRICA

Journey of the Purple Heart

~SEVENTEEN~

THE ALERT ORDER TO LEAVE Corkerhill Camp had already come down on October 24th. The Bearer Boys could not have been happier. The camp had been home on and off for almost a month and a half, and by this time the grounds looked like the aftermath of the Mississippi River flooding the surrounding lowlands after a torrential spring rain.

New equipment had been issued. Each of the Bearer Boys received anti-gas ointment, shoe impregnate and oilcloth gas capes to protect them from mustard gas. They were also given water purification tablets, and sulfa tablets to take if they were wounded during the upcoming fight. Insufficient ammunition for older Springfield rifles resulted in others finally being issued new M-1 Garands.

Little known to the Bearer Boys, Colonel Greer had asked General Allen for an early decision as to what other equipment had to be taken with them "in order that a prompt disposal of excess could be made." Apparently their division commander had harkened back to the waste-not habits of the Depression-era Army and was reluctant to leave anything behind, less they might need it for reasons yet to be determined.

As a result, when the Bearer Boys waded out of Corkerhill Camp for the last time they were afraid they'd collapse because of the two hefty duffle bags of gear each had slung over their shoulders. But they were going off to war, and this was not the time to get weak knees. When they reached the hard road surface on the edge of the camp, the Bearer Boys bent over and took off their rubber overshoes, buckled them together and left them in a big pile before putting on their boots and heading off to wherever it was the Army in its infinite wisdom was sending them.

They were quartered down below in the prow of the *Tegelberg*, a Dutch transport ship manned by an East Indian crew, when it weighted anchor and departed from Glasgow two nights later. There was no particular excitement in the air at that moment. They were simply going off to war. None of the Bearer Boys could look at each other and even begin to imagine any of them would be dead soon. But they became a high-spirited bunch when they heard the *Tegelberg's* horns blast as she headed for a rendezvous with the rest of the ships participating in the upcoming invasion.

Their squad's jeep was manifested with others on a 5,000 gross ton cargo ship whose name reflected the mood they suddenly were in; it was the *Empire Confidence*. Thankfully no one knew it had already been captured once back in 1939. The First Division convoy became huge as it formed up. It consisted of sixty-one escorts—mainly British corvettes and destroyers—plus eight other assault transports and thirty-four merchant ships. They were scattered all over the Bay of Biscay and heading into the open waters of the Atlantic.

The Bearer Boys by now were pretty certain Norway was their destination. Had to be there, or at least somewhere where it was cold. Maybe even Poland. They were still wearing the wool uniforms they were issued when they left stateside and both of those destinations were plenty cold this time of year. The rumor about going to Africa had not been heard in a while, therefore least likely ports of call were there, or somewhere in Egypt because the Army would have certainly provided light-weight khaki uniforms to them so they could fight like soldiers should in the warmer weather on those shores.

Just the opposite hit the invasion armada when the ships made for the expansive waters off Scotland's coast. Surface temperatures dropped. A low pressure system, amplified by the open North Atlantic, suddenly blew in. Dark clouds sat so low the rest of the sky disappeared. Strong, raking winds worked the sea, and their long fetch soon made for big, rolling forty-foot waves.

The next three days were the most miserable the Bearer Boys faced since they put on their Army uniforms. The *Tegelberg's* bow rose and fell the entire time, and it felt like the seas were lifting them up into a suspended cloud, only to be dropped like rocks onto concrete a few breathless moments later. All they could do was hang on to the overhead pipes in their hold and try to maintain their balance and not be thrown around.

Some gave up. Rolled up hammocks that were neatly stacked before the storm hit were sliding back and forth now, and being prone on them looked inviting. But the rocking motion didn't cease. There was nothing to steady their eyes on. Bob knew that staring at the horizon was the best way to avoid seasickness; his father had taught him that when they went out on his Chris-Craft runabout during the summers back in Connecticut. But nothing was fixed to stare at down below in the prow of the *Tegelberg*; the closest thing to that were the blue lights that hung from the ceiling above the pipes. Bob tried to use his imagination, and pretend they were not moving, but soon sweat and dizziness took over.

Out on the churning sea the skippers of the convoy's ships somehow maintained their courses, changed at intervals according to blinking lights, or signal flags brave East Indian mariners ran up their ship's swaying halyards. The convoy was zig-zagging to avoid German submarines. Down below on the *Tegelberg* conditions remained the same, the only improvement coming the fourth day into their sea odyssey when one the Bearer Boys was well enough to empty the puke in their helmets into a larger galvanized trash can that others were still vomiting in. Becoming healthy enough to storm a hostile shore seemed as distant as going home.

But the seas finally calmed down, and when the shaky Bearer

Boys got a chance to go on deck the next morning to get some fresh air they were greeted with warmer weather. They noticed ships everywhere, as far as their eyes could see, all now seemingly heading in the same direction. Bob took a bearing off the sun; the armada was heading south. So much for landing up in Norway or Poland.

The following day was spent trying to get their sea legs back by doing calisthenics on the deck of the *Tegelberg*. Later in the afternoon air raid, fire, and the all important landing drill were rehearsed. Days started running together, the air was getting warmer, and nights brought the glow of a waxing moon as the Bearer Boys eagerly awaited seeing land.

Then on the night of November 6th the convoy passed over a resting sea through the Strait of Gibraltar. An officer on a nearby transport remembered, "Not a light showed aboard our ship. The dusky shapes of the other troop ships, appearing and disappearing in the varying light, seemed terribly vulnerable to submarine attack." Aboard the *Tegelberg* those on deck could hear the soft slapping of waves against her hull as the transport ghosted along in waters so calm the ship didn't even rock; some saw the dim outline of the real Rock, the northern-most of the famed twin Pillars of Hercules that guarded the Atlantic Ocean and the Mediterranean Sea in ancient times. A peak in Morocco, the southern pillar, wasn't visible, but others on the starboard side of the dull gray troop transporter could make out the Morocco city of Ceuta—an early casualty during the Spanish Civil War six years earlier. Barely visible above pinpoints of light, Ceuta now appeared to be a dull beacon of neutrality far more concerned about more Italians, rather than Americans invading its shores.

Aboard the nearby *Reina del Pacifico* the next day, General Allen was absorbed in studying his overall battle plans one more time before his staff officers came into the ship's lounge. When they did, Allen was standing before a large map marked TOP SECRET and moments later, with a pointer in his hand, it became clear the convoy was headed for North Africa.

> We are the Center Task Force. Oran is our primary objective. Another landing will be in Casablanca; another in Algiers. The 16th and 18th Combat Teams will land to the east of Oran near Arzew. The 26th will land west of Oran at Les Andalouses. By D+1, the main body of the division will gain and hold a beachhead line extending from the heights of Djebel Khar, a prominent feature located between Pointe Canastel and St. Cloud, through Fleurus, along the northern end of a salt lake and road junction south of En Nekala, before carrying back to the Golfe d'Arzew just east of La Macta. The 26th will capture Djebel Santon and Djbel Murdajadjo, which dominate the western approaches to Oran. The landings near Arzew will be supported by the 1st Ranger Battalion, which will send parties up Cap Carbon to take one coastal battery and into Arzew Harbor to capture another. All three of the First Division's infantry regiments will converge on Oran from several directions to force the surrender of the French garrison.

With the formal briefing concluded, Terry Allen then smiled and simply closed with. "Now you know it."

An hour later, the *Tegelberg's* loudspeakers crackled to life.

> Attention all personnel. We are about to embark upon the first phase of America's partnership with our English allies as we engage the enemy on the shores of North Africa. You men are the fuel that will ignite the torch of liberty. It will be the honor of the First Division to be the first to halt the tide of Nazism and stamp out the evil it

represents. The morning of November 8th 1942 will go down in history as the turning point of the war against Germany. You all have been through a vigorous and extended training period to prepare you for this moment. Those of you who are here today have proven your ability and I am sure you will defeat the enemy at every turn. Remember the great history and traditions of the Big Red One are also at stake. The world will have its eyes on you. Your company commanders will fill you in on the details. As you go forward into battle, remember the division motto: "No mission too difficult; No sacrifice too great; Duty first. Good luck and may God be with you."

Captain Murphy and Lieutenant Hobratschk arrived in the hold of the *Tegelberg* a short time later; they were carrying maps and intelligence summaries. Murphy led in briefing the Bearer Boys and the rest of the men in their mortar platoon about the 2nd Battalion's mission. It pretty much came down to hurry up and wait. The battalion would be in reserve and wouldn't land until the situation became better defined. At that point they would either assist the 3rd Battalion in their mission to seize Arzew, or the 1st Battalion in taking St. Cloud, a mysterious town between where they would hit the beach and Oran. Intelligence reports indicated both St. Cloud and Arzew were "lightly defended."

"Know your password, men," Captain Murphy cautioned them. "If challenged with 'Hi-yo Silver' it doesn't mean the Lone Ranger wants to have a beer with you. It means someone isn't sure if you are friend or foe. You better respond with 'Away-y-y' or face getting shot. Maneuvers are over. This is the real thing. Lieutenant Hobratschk and your new section leader Sergeant Horn will provide you with further details."

Bob just looked at Slugger Szelugoski after Murphy departed, smirked, and then said, "Hi yo' Slugger. Away we go with our 81mm mortar shells. Rumor has it our motor train may not be able to keep up with us, so it looks like we Bearer Boys will be man-packing those shells for you to shoot. No mission too difficult...no sacrifice too great..."

That's when Bob got cut off as the rest of the Bearer Boys together cheered, "Duty first!"

At one the next morning men on the nearby transport ship *Ettrick* began loading into their landing craft. One company aboard the *Tegelberg,* led by Captain Cliff Raymer and participating in the initial assault, also departed. Aboard the *Reina del Pacifico* General Allen was observing more First Division soldiers going down nets into their assault boats. He remained on deck with a war correspondent who wanted to get the story of the landings through the eyes of the man commanding them. As the combatants neared their designated landing areas in Arzew, Allen was able to discern a light on the outer end of the town's main dock, seemingly indicating that the landings would be a surprise and the defenders—if any—would be easily overrun.

Moments later President Roosevelt's steady patrician voice was heard over the airwaves on shore; he was delivering a planned message to the Vichy French his advisors had recommended. "We come among you to repulse the cruel invaders who would remove forever your right of self-government," the president began. "We come among you solely to defeat and rout your enemies. Have faith in our words. We do not want to cause you any harm."

The same message was heard through the loudspeakers on the ships offshore. The Bearer Boys looked at each other and just cringed. So much for the element of surprise.

Moments later the loudspeakers on the *Tegelberg* bellowed, "The first assault craft have reached the beach with no opposition."

By 4:30 over 1,200 U.S. soldiers were ashore. Forty-five minutes later General Allen was able to see a prearranged Very-light flare signal—green and amber—that confirmed the Rangers had seized the main dock facilities in Arzew. Another white flare shot up indicating the 3rd Battalion was now safely on the beach. As was the 1st Battalion; these men were regrouping into formation for their march up to St. Cloud. All appeared satisfactory, and an anxious Colonel Greer was already making plans to head to shore, rather than be holed up on the *Reina del Pacifico.*

It was a different story ashore. With the aid of the first rays of light, U.S. forces of the 18th's 3rd battalion, under the command of well-respected New Jersey native Lieutenant Colonel Courtney Brown, headed for the French army barracks in Arzew, where his men were greeted by cracking enemy rifle fire and ricocheting bullets. Alerted by these sounds of war, other French forces on the south jetty the Rangers hadn't yet subdued used their machineguns to spray bursts of tracer bullets at their supposed liberators. Snipers added to the mayhem, and before too long three Americans were dead and seven had been wounded.

These gun flashes—and the muffled roar of explosions in the main Oran harbor—quickly came to the attention of the commander of the Oran garrison, and he immediately dispatched a platoon of charcoal engine-powered armored cars to investigate the situation. The first of these ran right into the American battalion heading up to St. Cloud. Four other armored cars followed, and were eventually knocked out by U.S. soldiers firing anti-tank grenades. Two French combatants were killed; fourteen more were captured—some just wounded—but an American staff sergeant's war was cut short and he was now dead along the side of the road the French armored cars had come down.

But one armored car had escaped the ambush; thus the fate of the others was reported to Major General Robert Marie Jules Camille Boissau at his post in Oran. The 16th Tunisian Battalion and a battalion of the French Foreign Legion were already on their way to save the day for the people of St. Cloud, but the apparent American aggression in-force prompted Boissau to also dispatch a battery of his African Field Artillery to help out. In this they succeeded. Their 75mm guns greeted the Americans when they got closer to St. Cloud. The A Company captain was hit, and was lying near death in the middle of a cemetery on the edge of town. His replacement was wounded by shell fragments, and a third officer was hurriedly rushing forward to take command of the company.

A lieutenant in Company B was nevertheless trying to lead his men into St. Cloud. One of his privates had already been wounded by a gunner in the sole surviving French armored car, and when these American forces reached a crossroad just outside of the village it only got worse. They were stopped cold by a well-aimed barrage of French shells. Colonel Greer's headquarters company was inbound towards St. Cloud when the shells exploded, and Major Sternberg—who was with Greer at the time—heard him shout, "Get away from the crossroad! They are zeroing in on us!"

Although the French troops might not have been tinged with the collaborationist spirit of the Vichy, they were clearly fighting back.

~EIGHTEEN~

THE *TEGELBERG* WAS CLOSER TO shore by this time. Arzew had fortunately quieted down. The small naval base had been overrun and a dozen seaplanes were grounded. Over 120 French fighters had put their hands up over their heads and surrendered. One held out, an Arab in a long flowing robe; he came tumbling down a hillside plenty dead after an American rifleman shot him. A captain in the French Foreign Legion who had been roused from his sleep was taken prisoner and carted off to the battalion command post. People were now coming out of their white, pink and tan plastered homes and staring over their tiled roofs to survey the damage. The local church tower and the smokestack of the sulfur refinery had survived the American attack. They could only hear an occasional rifle shot.

But the earlier fighting had given Colonel Greer cause to to have the Bearer Boys' 2nd Battalion disembark from the *Tegelberg,* and as the situation around St. Cloud worsened it became their mission to come up and assist their fellow Americans in subduing the stubborn French fighters still clinging to the village streets.

The alert order came down just after sunrise. Lieutenant Hobratschk had just finished watching Sergeant Horn give the Bearer Boys their daily yellow atabrine pill. They were now undergoing a last minute inspection. All were wearing their field jackets; they had the requisite American flags sewn on between their left elbows and shoulders. A white brassard was tied around their same arm just above their elbows.

Their blanket rolls and barrack bags were stowed; they would be brought up later. Sergeant Horn made each of the Bearer Boys open their combat packs they would carry with them to be sure they contained no papers bearing the regiment's identification so the opposing forces ashore would not know the unit they were with if anyone got captured. Personal items were checked; Horn made sure they had their D rations, water purification tablets and sulfa tablets, plus spare clothing. A couple of old garrison passes and driver's licenses were surrendered. They were allowed to keep pictures they had of their families; Bob would take his mother's picture he had in his wallet with him into combat, along with his .45-caliber personal side arm and his knife and canteen that were strapped to his web belt. He had no rifle now. Each Bearer Boy also had to show Horn his gas mask and cape.

Then Captain Murphy showed up to personally inspect their combat load.

Slugger Szelugoski was holding the sight for their 81mm mortar; he would carry that with him into battle. Murphy nodded his approval. Gentle John Murga would be weighed down with the mortar tube itself; that was resting like a rifle at his side. Captain Murphy smiled. The bi-pod and base were in the hands of others. Then Murphy turned to Bob and inspected his ammo apron. He was bearing six 81mm high explosive shells per regulation, three on his chest and the other three on his back. Murphy adjusted his tan apron where it fell over his shoulders—the load on it alone was about forty-five pounds—so it would not gall or chafe Bob's neck or shoulders as he marched off to war.

Bob stared straight ahead the whole time; he was starting to sweat, not because he was scared but more so because of the hot stuffy air in the hold. His captain continued on and inspected the other Bearer Boys. Satisfied, Captain Murphy stepped back and stared from man to man as they began saluting. He did not salute back. He said nothing at first. Instead he reached out and shook their hands, looked each of them in the eye, and then finally stepped back and said, "You boys make me damn proud. I am honored to be your commander. Good luck, and may God be with you."

Moments later their serial was called out on the loudspeaker. Lieutenant Hobratschk started leading them to their sally port. It was the one closest to the bow on the starboard side of the *Tegelberg*. In the distance the Bearer Boys could now hear a few rifle shots. Then there was a dull explosion, followed by a geyser of water spurting up about thirty yards in front of the ship. They climbed down into their LCA just as another shell whistled overhead and then exploded in the water just aft of the stern. A sole German plane—clearly so because of its Iron Cross markings—was overhead, but it didn't drop any bombs; it was likely on a reconnaissance mission. Not good. But the Bearer Boys knew the shore was close; it was actually about 800 yards away. The waves sparkled; the early Sunday morning sun made their reflections look more like gorgeous silver points of light than dangerous waters that more enemy fire could be skimming over.

As soon as their LCA was loaded, the Bearer Boys were waved away from the Tegelberg by the loading officer. Lieutenant Hobratschk was all the way forward, with his back up against the ramp that would be lowered when they got to shore; he was wearing a white brassard on both of his arms. The Bearer Boys braced themselves for more fusillades of enemy fire, but none came. Instead, the LCA's diesel engine roared as they headed towards shore. As they got closer to the beach everyone kept their thoughts to themselves. Getting off onto dry land certainly had to be one of them.

Then a few minutes later the LCA's coxswain yelled, "I can't go any farther. I'll run aground and won't be able to back off to pick up other serials on the ship. You'll have to wade ashore from here."

The ramp came down. Lieutenant Hobratschk stepped off first

and was in water up to his waist moments later. The Bearer Boys followed; the water was cold. Their boots immediately filled with water. Their pants first puffed out; the filling salt water soon deflated them, and their strong legs carried them to shore. Gentle John had their 81mm mortar tube on his shoulder to keep it dry. The base plate and bi-pod were above two other's heads. They kept wading in, then they hit the beach and moved up to the railroad tracks that ran into Arzew. No opposition. They had just crossed over the tracks when a runner suddenly appeared and told them the battalion assembly area was in the large field just ahead of them.

The Bearer Boys were on solid ground, and finally off to war. It was 7:30 in the morning on November 8, 1942.

There were three lone trees in the center of the assembly area; riflemen from F Company were already deployed in ditches to protect its perimeter when the Bearer Boys got there. But time was lost getting organized and into columns of companies for the march up to St. Cloud, and it was close to nine by the time the battalion finally got its act together. Company E, led by Captain Murphy's good friend Carl Randall, went first; a heavy machinegun platoon of Company H was attached to Randall's riflemen. Square-jawed and rugged Virginian Captain Charles Penick's F Company was right behind this group. Lieutenant Downing's platoon was on their tail, and about ten yards behind where his men were lined up was the battalion command group; Captain Murphy marched with these officers.

Another twenty yards away were the Bearer Boys and the rest of Company H. Bob was far enough forward in this column to see Murphy, and this gave him both comfort and confidence; Lieutenant Hobratschk was just off to Bob's and the rest of the Bearer Boys' left. Their lieutenant kept staring into the low bushes with his rifle at the ready to blow away any snipers. G Company, under the command of Anne Arundel County in Maryland-native Captain Warren Bonnett, formed the rear of the battalion formation as the line got closer to moving out. Bonnett was sturdy, dark-haired and often teased about being too good looking to get shot at. The African sun was getting plenty hot, and it didn't take long before sweat started pouring off everyone's head and trickling down inside their heavy wool uniforms. The gas impregnate coating on their field jackets killed any hope of ventilation.

With an average load of over sixty pounds per Bearer Boy, it was certain to be a difficult march. Their pants were already causing their legs to be itchy because of the salt water they had waded through to get to shore. Wet socks were sure to cause blisters. Thankfully, orders came down to lighten their loads and pile their combat packs in a stack so they could be brought up later.

When the battalion finally started moving out it was along a narrow dusty trail that led onto the main road that ran up to St. Cloud. Locals knew it as National Highway One. The pace quickened as the men mounted this two-lane hard surface roadway, but before too long many were totally out of steam. Some of the men in F Company ahead of the Bearer Boys started falling out; a few sat down. Most of their faces were red and soaked with sweat. Shirt collars were opened in an effort to cool off. But the Bearer Boys struggled on; Bob's sweating produced black stains under his arm pits. Other's collars were the same color. More men in front of them started dropping out in increasing numbers. Disorganization grew. Companies started getting intermingled.

St. Cloud was at least another five miles ahead. And it only got worse. The men in F Company started to discard their field jackets, leaving them piled up near boxes of ammo. But officers took control of the situation and the journey soon became more of a forced march than an organized movement of well-trained men eager to get into a fight. Bob wiped the sweat off his face with his white brassard, and poured some water from his canteen on his forehead to cool off; he passed the time counting telephone poles as the column continued to struggle on. Before too long they reached Renan—scene of the earlier ambush of the French armored cars.

Arabs wearing red fezzes and long robes stared at the Bearer Boys as they marched past the faded pastel-tinted concrete block houses in the small village. A few of their French owners gave them looks that evinced little emotion. One was carrying a bible, a woman apparently on her way to church. The Americans were not greeted as liberators. One soldier remembered their demeanors showed neither happiness nor hatred. "What a sorry spectacle we must have afforded them, struggling down the street, hot, tired, dirty and disorganized," Lieutenant Downing, roughly fifty yards or so ahead of the Bearer Boys, honestly remembered. "We were a motley string of shuffling soldiers passing by a phlegmatic populace followed by screaming native children noisily begging for candy."

The louder sounds of war could soon be heard from the direction of St. Cloud—occasional crumps of exploding mortars and echoing rounds of artillery fire. But as the Bearer Boys passed a house with a hole in its roof and every window smashed out, the war suddenly became much closer. A soldier was lying to the side of the road. His arms were aimed upward and they were stiff; the rank patch on his shoulder revealed he was a sergeant. His face was dirty and waxen, except for the hole in his head. He was very dead; he was the one killed when the French armored cars were ambushed just a few hours earlier.

It was a sickening experience for every one of the Bearer Boys; now they were starting to get angry, and Bob was suddenly mad as hell at the Germans who got him into this mess. Up ahead was Captain Murphy, but he was still marching forward, obviously focused on the mission. Lieutenant Hobratschk made a brief stop to salute the fallen soldier, but then he moved on. The Bearer Boys kept step, and watched as an old French ambulance flying a Red Cross flag come down the road; a young girl and a man retrieved the body of the fallen American soldier and drove off.

Then Bob saw a jeep careening towards the battalion command group. Two lower ranking soldiers were sitting in the back and one had his rifle at port arm with his finger on its trigger, ready to shoot. Maybe they were body guards, Bob thought. But there was no mistaking that the one in the passenger's seat was a general; the star on his helmet confirmed that. It was Cliff Andrus, the commander of Division Artillery, and the next thing Bob could make out was, "Get your men forward as quickly as possible. The French are preparing to launch a counterattack down this road."

A few minutes later a seemingly unconcerned American on a bicycle came down this same road. Someone up ahead yelled out to him, "Look out for snipers!" When he drew closer, he started waving to some of the officers in the F Company line. One who finally recognized him waved back as he peddled by, still being warned by others to watch out for enemy bullets. "But he continued peddling slowly along, as if he hadn't heard or didn't care," Lieutenant Downing told others later.

The man was on a mission. It was Major Sternberg, who was anxious to get to the battalion command group and start coordinating their support for the 1st Battalion, which was still trying to plant their boots on St. Cloud's streets.

The F Company commander, Captain Penick, was sitting in a ditch studying his map when Sternberg peddled by on his way back to Colonel Greer's makeshift CP on the outskirts of St. Cloud. Captain Randall's E Company was still at the head of the column; he ordered his riflemen to fix their bayonets and move out towards a field off to the left of the road they'd come this far on. From here they would pick up a trail, bear right on it, and head into a vineyard next to St. Cloud to meet the enemy.

Penick had spotted this vineyard on his map, and after Major Sternberg passed he stood up and yelled out to his men, "Let's go!" The F Company rifle platoons lined up in squad columns, spread far enough apart to not be hit at the same time by enemy artillery or their mortar shells. Lieutenant Hobratschk did not appear to be all that excited; he turned to the sixty men in his mortar platoon and just said, "Y'all stay steady." Then he pivoted around toward the waiting field of battle and gave them a perfect Ft. Benning "Follow Me" high-handed wave. The Bearer Boys and the rest of the platoon followed. Captain Bonnett, who at that moment could not begin to imagine he was soon going to receive one of the battalion's first Purple Heart of the war, got his Company G moving so his men could keep up with the hardened and muscled heavy weapons soldiers of Company H.

None of the combatants who fought at St. Cloud ever forgot the vineyard they assembled in for their first fight with an armed enemy. It looked nothing like a field of trellises with lush grapevines ready to yield the fruit for a great wine year. Instead they saw straight rows of low bushes no more than a foot and a half high as they faded down a gentle slope; it would yield no protective cover. The ground wasn't fertile; it was sun baked and as dry from thirst as the Bearer Boys were.

As Captain Murphy explained later, "The ridge we'd arrived on was between 500 and 700 yards south of St. Cloud. The village cemetery occupied the eastern two-thirds of the ridge, closer in. A four to five-foot wall surrounded the cemetery. What we could see of the village looked typical North African, in that the whitewashed houses were built side-by-side around the edge of town. The back of each house formed the wall that protected St. Cloud. We couldn't see it at the time, but in the center of town were the market and all the buildings of the public offices."

~NINETEEN~

THE MEN IN F COMPANY were closer to the cemetery wall and they were already taking fire. The zip-zip of bullets forced many to hit the dirt. One remembered he could see other riflemen making short rushes toward the low white wall. These were men in a platoon of B Company.

"We were spread out behind that wall," Lieutenant Ed McGregor, this platoon's commander, explained later. "By prearrangement we attacked using neither mortars nor an artillery preparation, so as to spare the civilians if we could." But when McGregor blew his whistle and jumped over the wall, none of his men followed him. After threatening to shoot them if they pulled this again, his thirty-five men followed and they finally went over the wall.

"There was no fire on us at first," McGregor remembered. "We advanced quickly. Then spasmodic firing erupted. Snipers. One man behind me was killed instantly. My company commander, First Lieutenant 'Toot' Plante, and I climbed up on a rooftop to see where the firing was coming from. We didn't see much. The men were working their way along the streets—moving very slowly, cautiously. The company commander and I got through the southern part of town, up to the main north-south road, which made a crossroad with the east-west road to Oran.

"We were crossing that at a run. The French had a machinegun in the square that opened up. It hit Toot Plante right in the head. The bullets ripped part of his face away, and when I dropped beside him his last words were, 'Keep going Mac.'"

A Company's new commander—their third—was now Lieutenant Irv Yarock, the officer Bob talked to about returning to Ft. Devens when Pearl Harbor was attacked nearly a year earlier. "I could see McGregor behind that stone wall before his men jumped off," Yarock told others later. "We were in the cemetery. It had crypts— little houses—in it, with iron grating as gates. With all the shooting going on—you couldn't tell where from—some thought French soldiers were sniping from behind those grates.

"As our men went by them, a soldier threw a grenade into one of those dark openings, but it hit a bar and rebounded. Our 2nd Platoon commander, Lieutenant Bob Goddu, saw it, yelled, and was able to get all the men down, but was a little slow himself. A fragment from the blast went through Goddu, and he was shipped out—ended up in England."

Three A Company officers were now out of action, as were Toot Plante and Goddu. And there were others. "We heard our Lieutenant Gerry Williams was wounded," Captain Morris Shapiro, who commanded the medical team, relayed to others later that night. "Williams was a forward observer; he had been wounded and was still under fire in a roadside ditch heading into St. Cloud. The ditch was in full view of a steeple in town, from which I believe they were firing on us. French shells were coming in. I couldn't see the guns doing the firing. Sergeant Larkin and I crawled into the ditch, and over the crest until we reached Lieutenant Williams. He was dead white; a bad wound in his upper arm. I put on a tourniquet, and we worked him back upgrade, prone and in the ditch until we were out of enemy sight."

Disorganization was spreading. "I commanded Cannon Company," Captain Frank Colacicco, a 1940 graduate of West Point, remembered about that day. "We were a small company with two full-track self-propelled 105mm guns, and six half-tracks with 75mm guns. We never got the 105 guns until we boarded ship at Glasgow. We could only fire them by bore sight—looking down the tubes—because the sights were not with the guns. We came off the ship fighting. But, we lost one half-track when it fell off a hill.

"We gave the 1st Battalion the full-tracks at St. Cloud to use as assault guns. When one came back, turned out our own infantry shot it up and ruined the recoil mechanism on the 105. Remember, our guys had never seen a full-track 105 gun before. Another 105 we lost when the clutch burned out. So, that was a fiasco. Our guys had never seen, much less operated, these self-propelled guns before that day."

Captain Malcolm Marshall was Harvard-educated, and the forward observer for the field artillery battalion supporting the 1st Battalion on that school of hard-knocks day. Marshall was with his battalion's command group on the way up to St. Cloud; their first contact with the enemy was a wine truck out making its morning deliveries. As it clanged closer, everyone thought it was a French tank and opened fire. Wine sprouted out of the truck's tank; its alcohol fuel added a sweet smell to the air. The driver was caved over and his bloody head started falling towards the ground; he was full of bullets, and plenty dead.

But when he was a quarter of the way down the hill into St. Cloud Marshall captured that moment knowing "my first lesson in combat firing was coming up. Open fields on either side revealed no French, but sporadic shots came our way from town. Some of our artillery, 105mm guns, had finally landed behind us, and our fire direction center told me to register on the center of town so all three batteries could converge their fire accurately."

After Marshall got farther forward he called in adjustments as the firing of 105 salvos roared overhead; he thought the first might have been long, and the second too far left, but he later reflected, "I had the sense to tell the fire direction center I was in a poor position to judge overs and shorts. I was making some big mistakes."

A 6x6 GMC supply truck pulled up a few minutes later. Luckily the driver had bailed out, for a French anti-tank gun found it, hit the truck's radiator, and sent it up into a ball of flames.

"We were lifted off the sand by the concussions," Captain Marshall told everyone, remembering very clearly it was "typical sad action by inexperienced troops."

By the time the Bearer Boy's 2nd Battalion reached the draw behind what Captain Murphy called Cemetery Ridge, all three of the 1st Battalion's rifle companies had withdrawn from the streets of St. Cloud. Captain Randall's E Company moved up closer to the cemetery's wall to extend the line of Lieutenant Yarock's A Company. Penick's F Company was sent nearer to the railroad tracks just south of the cemetery. Soon afterwards his lead platoon was close to a couple of soldiers who looked the worse for wear; they were hunkered down in a culvert cut through an embankment a few yards away. Lieutenant Downing had just leapt over this embankment and was catching his breath when one of the soldiers yelled to him, "You better stay down.

"That town is full of troops," the soldier also warned. "Our company is all shot up. We lost our company commander. You better watch out. Those snipers will get you."

Downing asked them what company they were with.

"1st Battalion, Company A," came the answer.

Major Sternberg was making most of the calls for the 2nd Battalion because he was closer to the action; Major Powers, the battalion commander, had set up his command post somewhere behind E and F Companies. Sternberg ordered Captain Bonnett's men to pass through the Bearer Boy's company and with this Captain Murphy sensed more combat was coming. The first thing he did was call out on his 300 radio to Lieutenant Hobratschk and the commander of his machine gun platoon, Lieutenant Ed Butkiewicz, and told them to join him.

"Listen, I don't know much about what's happening, but we know where the rifle companies are," Murphy told them when they reported to him. "Ed, I want you to put your sections in partial defilade on the ridge between the cemetery and the highway. Wally, position your mortar platoon right here in the draw, look at your map to get the data you need, and get ready to place harassing fire just inside the house line beyond the cemetery."

And with this Murphy wished them well, picked up his radio and called Leo Hennessy, his recon sergeant. Hennessy was from Brooklyn, New York and accustomed to moving fast so he quickly found Murphy and together the pair left the ridge and headed for the cemetery to better appraise the situation.

The first officer they found was Major Bob York, the 1st Battalion's S-3. He was an Alabaman who had graduated from West Point with Ben Sternberg and the two were the best of friends. York greeted the Company H commander with, "Murph, I'm going to make another try at the town. Can you give me any support?"

"My machine gun and mortar platoons will be ready for action in fifteen to twenty minutes," Murphy answered. "But I'll have to check with Major Powers first."

"Go ahead," the lean, mustached and handsome York said. "I'll be around here when you get back."

So off Murphy and Hennessy went, first down a trail through the cemetery, past its eerie crypts, and just as they were leaving this bad omen behind there lay A Company Captain Joseph Hill's body, the first officer in the regiment to die in the war. Murphy and Hennessy looked at each other, but said nothing; there was nothing to say. They continued on, with fire still coming out of St. Cloud in their direction, and found both Powers and Major Chase, his executive officer, in the far section of the vineyard a good hundred yards behind the battalion's rifle companies.

"We're back over on the ridge on the other side of the cemetery," Murphy started. "Major York has asked us for support. He's planning to attack again. We're ready, but this could be a strain on us, especially our mortars, since the motor train is not up here yet. All the machinegun ammo was hand-carried up from the beach. And the 81mm ammo bearers—all they have is the mortars they brought up in their apron vests. Nothing else. But we'll be ready to go."

"OK, proceed, Murph," Powers said. "We'll be attacking too, but Bob York's targeting will be the most effective since he knows where the French bastards are. Just call me on your 300 before you open fire."

With this Murphy and Hennessey left and as they were passing through the cemetery again they found Lieutenant Butkiewicz waiting for them; he showed them the data he had used to position his machine gunners, and pointed to an area about thirty yards beyond the right wall of the cemetery, close to where the 1st Battalion rifle companies were assembling. Murphy could see Butkiewicz's machineguns were in partial defilade behind the top of the ridge.

"Our guns are going to register on the intersection of the Arzew road and the one on the edge of town," Butkiewicz informed him. Satisfied with this, Murphy told Butkiewicz to stay where he was while he contacted Major York. He and Hennessy quickly found York plenty forward at his outpost right up against the cemetery wall closest to the village, and Murphy told him the situation.

"Our machinegun ammo supply is good enough. Best if we give it to you on demand, and I recommend we traverse the houses facing the street so our fire masks your advance," Captain Murphy told Major York. "I'll pass the word to the mortar platoon to register one section inside the wall on the road coming in from Arzew, and have the other sections lay rounds to the southeast in front of our 2nd Battalion."

"Murph, we'll also need covering mortar fires on the road ahead of our attack," York told him. "If you have your men start laying smoke rounds in front of our riflemen, and keep it ahead of them as they move in, that would really help. And when my men get halfway there, lift the smoke and then have your boys lay their heavy explosive mortars right inside the house line."

"Consider it done," Murphy answered. "Leo, go tell Lieutenant Hobratschk what we're doing, and have him send a forward observer up here for Major York to work with."

"Thanks, Murph. And do it as soon as possible," York urged. "It's getting late and no one wants a night fight in the village. We're going to attack at 1600. That's fifteen minutes from now."

Hobratschk sent his Staff Sergeant Ray Roof up to York's forward outpost; from here Roof could see the road leading from Arzew into St. Cloud. He made radio contact with Sergeant Horn; he was with the Bearer Boys—actually Horn was behind their mortar position in the draw so he could hear his 300 radio over the mortar's firing blast, but close enough to be heard by Slugger Szelugoski when firing directions needed adjusting. It was their squad's mission to place the covering fire along the road when the 1st Battalion rifle companies jumped off.

It was definitely going to be challenging. Rolling cover fire had to stay well enough in front of the riflemen to prevent them from being seen by the French machine gunners who likely had the roadway sighted in. The mortar's impact would create a smoke screen, and block the American riflemen from view as they advanced. Shorts could be deadly, and kill the men they were trying to support.

Gentle John Murga would feed the mortars into the barrel; he was standing just to the right of the tube, ready to put the shells into it. Slugger controlled the firing angle and direction; he was standing to the left of the mortar where he could see the sight, control the elevating hand wheel, and traverse it if the firing had to be adjusted to the left, or right. Firing data was already placed on the sight; elevation was adjusted to lay the first round forty yards in front of the riflemen when they advanced.

Willy Driscoll, Carmen the Charmer, Ralph Sproull and Louie the Rub unloaded their mortars first. They were spread out in rows of six; not stacked. Bob was last to unload, so he was first in line to pass the mortars to Gentle John.

Their squad was ready. Only an occasional rifle shot could be heard from the direction of the village. Then, in the distance were sounds none of the Bearer Boys would ever forget hearing—the clock in the church steeple chimed four solemn times, announcing it was four o'clock.

Unknown to them, French machine gunners in the village's main square indeed had their weapons perfectly sighted on the roadway the Bearer Boys' squad was about to deliver covering fire on.

Seconds later Horn's 300 radio came to life.

"Commence firing," Sergeant Roof barked.

"Fire mission, base point," Horn yelled out to Slugger.

Gentle John loaded the first mortar into the tube. It hit the firing pin.

"On the way," Horn yelled into his 300 radio.

"Perfect," Roof radioed back as he saw the mortar hit the road in front of the attacking riflemen. "Adjust elevation, and give us another round."

"Slugger, adjust elevation downward and fire again," Sergeant Horn called out.

Slugger dialed the elevation drum down a few mils; Bob passed Gentle John another mortar. He placed it in the barrel, and seconds later it blasted out of the tube.

"On the way," Horn yelled into his radio.

"Another good one," Sergeant Roof radioed back as he watched smoke hit the roadway again. "Adjust twenty yards left and drop the elevation some more with the next round."

Slugger traversed the hand wheel, turning it just enough for the adjustment, lowered the tube a few more mils, and peered into the sight. The bubble was level. Bob put another mortar in Gentle John's spread hands, then he dropped the mortar in, and off it went.

"On the way," Horn screamed out for a third time.

Bob's hands were wet with sweat now; he rubbed them on his pants and picked up another mortar. Then he tore off his white brassard and tossed it to Gentle John so he could wipe his hands and prevent the next round from slipping from his grip.

"One more time," Roof called out through his 300 radio.

"One the way," answered Sergeant Horn. Bob, now sweating like a pig, was bent over reaching for another round; Gentle John had his arms stretched out, ready to receive it. Slugger waited for more adjustments, thinking the riflemen had to be moving closer to the village by this time. He figured the next fire mission order would likely have him adjusting the mortar to blind the French inside the wall, rather than on the roadway.

"Cease fire," came instead.

Bob stared at Gentle John; Slugger turned towards Sergeant Horn, then asked him, "What's going on?"

"Damned if I know," their squad leader shot back.

The answer came later from Captain Murphy, who had been with Bob York the whole time. "The French were well-armed, and they sure knew how to use their weapons," he later told his platoon leaders. "Their fields of fire were excellent; they had their damn machine guns aimed—pre-plotted—for hundreds of yards on the incoming roads from every side of town. It was getting too dark, and from what I could see we weren't making much progress. Major York called the attack off."

"You guys got off some good fire missions," Lieutenant Hobratschk nevertheless told the Bearer Boys and the rest of the squad that night. "The other sections waited to fire at the wall while you all covered the road. Combined, we all in the platoon fired just thirty-two rounds. We had eighty-four available. But don't let that fool ya'. We'll need 'em eventually.

"Just so y'all know, Captain Murphy was keeping a closer eye on the machine gunners. The dang French fire still kept coming when we thought they would all stop fighting. Three or four bursts he told me; took one of their guns out. Remember the guys that came through here being evacuated? Your captain saved one of their sorry Yankee asses. Their squad leader thought he had done gotten everyone out, but one guy was lying flat next to the machinegun, trying to duck the fire. Captain Murphy got him out of there just in time; said he'd never forget the look on the man's face. He told me the next round would have got him.

"Y'all also are gonna' hear this soon enough, the way word spreads," Hobratschk added in a more solemn tone. "The G Company commander, Captain Bonnett, was killed today. He's gone. Direct hit someone told me. And y'all know Corporal Kroener in our 3rd Section. Well Stan was wounded, but thankfully he's going to make it.

"Now try to get some rest," Lieutenant Hobratschk offered, then warned: "Stay alert. We don't have orders for tomorrow yet, but they're as sure as a Texas thunderstorm with plenty of lightening and damaging winds to come.

"And you boys, remember this," Hobratschk added while staring from man to man. "A piece of steel will do just as much damage to y'all, whether it's fired as token of resistance or in mortal hatred."

~TWENTY~

THE BEARER BOYS HAD NO way of knowing that seventeen of their fellow soldiers who had been engaged at St. Cloud that day were killed, or that fifty-two others had been wounded, one of whom later died. Nor could they have known that the French fighters in the village had proven to be the most difficult of the enemy forces encountered by the entire First Division after they landed on the beaches earlier that morning.

In the tiny native schoolhouse two kilometers west of Arzew in Tourville that was serving as the division's command post that night, General Allen and his staff were busy using pocket flashlights dimmed with red tissue paper to look at their maps and study the day's overall progress. Two Army photographers—anxious to get a couple of pictures—were lying on the floor, dead tired from their day's work snapping pictures and making Technicolor film recordings of the landings and the capture of the seaplane base at Arzew. Guards surrounded the schoolhouse, and Allen's personal bodyguards hovered around him while he and his most trusted officers decided what to do about the heavy resistance up at St. Cloud.

Glancing at his map, Allen could see the division's left flank was well-protected and its advance along the lines he had pointed out on his map during the briefing aboard the *Reina del Pacifico* two days earlier was progressing satisfactorily. The high ground near Fleurus had been taken. St. Cloud was clearly the main problem the division was facing before Oran could be subdued.

To address this, Field Order Number 2 was issued just after nine o'clock. The attack would go off at seven the next morning. The 18th Infantry was to hit St. Cloud again. To assist Colonel Greer with this mission, General Allen added the support of a company of the Ranger Battalion, and a rifle company native to the 16th Infantry. A battery of the division's 5th Field Artillery would also weigh in. Mindful of the fact that friendly fire had caused some of the casualties during the fighting earlier that day, Allen added to his order, "careful instruction to prevent shooting into own forces be adhered to by all officers."

After a runner was sent off to deliver the order to Colonel Greer, the division staff settled down, had a few drinks, then spread out on the floor of the schoolhouse to try to get some sleep. That was difficult. "Bullets pinged on the walls and thumped in the schoolyard," famed war correspondent Ernie Pyle wrote. "The soldiers in the schoolroom were nervous all night. In the darkness they could hear the click of cartridge clips in pistols."

By the time Colonel Greer received General Allen's order the occasional flashes of gunfire from the direction of St. Cloud had pretty much ceased. But Greer wasted little time before he called his battalion commanders together and issued corollary orders an hour before midnight. They were straightforward. First, an artillery preparation would begin at 6:45 the next morning "on that part of town known to be unoccupied by our troops." Then the 1st Battalion would attack from its present positions east of St. Cloud while the Bearer Boys' 2nd Battalion attacked from their current location south of the village. Greer also added Courtney Brown's 3rd Battalion forces to his scheme of maneuvers; their work in Arzew finished, his men would now hit St. Cloud from the north.

The gunfire in St. Cloud may have quieted down, but for the Bearer Boys that first night trying to sleep on what they clearly remembered as a battlefield was miserable. Their itchy beards were near two days old, and they were still moist with sweat when darkness finally came. Their bedrolls hadn't come up from the beach; they had no soap or toothpaste. All they had to eat was their D-rations, but there was little left of them. Bob hadn't even opened his, so when he took out his knife, cut open the box it came in, and pulled away the cellophane-wrapped bar he first asked who else was hungry.

"I am," Louie the Rub said.

"You always are," Bob smirked, knowing a little laughter would help ease the tension none would ever admit to having.

"Yea, and you eat it too fast, and always belly ache about your stomach hurting," Ralph Sproull joked.

"I wouldn't feed a chunk of that crap to a date," Carmen the Charmer threw out.

"No problem there," Wally Driscoll threw back. "Back in England you couldn't even get one."

"Well, if you came from Connecticut like me and Bob, you'd be wishing right now that you could have a Peter Paul Mounds candy bar," Slugger offered.

"Or a date," Bob deadpanned.

"Army says these D-rations are a lot better for us; more calories," Gentle John weighed in with.

"Slugger's right," Bob chimed out. "Remember, I'm from Naugatuck where they make the Mounds bar. I'll betcha' before too long my mother or my grandmother will ship a box to us, but we're stuck with this D-ration at the moment. So who's hungry?"

Turned out they all were, so Bob broke off the six pieces that came in the package and shared his D-ration with everyone.

By now the night had turned chilly. There was no waning or waxing moon; it was pitch black out. The occasional chatter of rifle fire from the direction of St. Cloud broke up the monotony of hearing the clock in the church steeple chime every fifteen minutes. Every now and then a dog would bark. The Bearer Boys stayed up for another hour and kept bullshitting, but they were dead tired, so one-by-one they finally started buttoning up their field jackets, laid down on the ground, put their helmets over their heads and tried to get some sleep.

Then it started raining.

It wasn't like the torrential rains they experienced back at Corkerhill Camp, but it drizzled all night. The clock in the church steeple kept chiming, sounding out on the hour what time it was. Then a rooster crowed and woke Bob up. Some dog yelped. Bob yawned. Then the chime rang five times.

"Time to get your sorry asses up," Bob said as he started shaking his fellow Bearer Boys. "We got a war to fight."

The whitewashed buildings in St. Cloud looked peaceful that morning. But the fifteen-minute artillery preparation designed to wake up the French fighters changed that. The American 105mm tubes first laid in rounds of smoke, and then the artillery men followed this with three volleys of high explosive shells. Two French 75mm guns were later learned to have been neutralized, but it turned out there were more dead horses that had towed these guns into place than there were French fighters killed.

Frank Colaccio's Cannon Company then made a quick foray into the village where three of his halftracks ended up in the midst of the enemy's 75mm guns that had not been knocked out. Colacicco later told a couple of this fellow infantry officers that "we threw grenades at the French before we realized we couldn't get out. We had to break out behind them to come back. As we pulled out, the French directed fire at us. They hit our first halftrack, but we got the other two out."

An infantry platoon commanded by a tall Michigan native was the first to launch a ground attack. Lieutenant Clem Van Wagoner had determined that the French were using the village's post office as an observation point to direct their machinegun fire from. He came close to losing his life when a round barely cleared his head before busting up the door of the building right behind him. His men got even for that when they saw a Frenchman peering out of a window in the post office; a rifle grenade shattered its glass and several of the American's opposite numbers came out with their hands over their heads.

Van Wagoner lined them up shoulder-to-shoulder and tried to use these French fighters as human shields while his men advanced behind them towards the machinegun causing all the trouble. But their own gunned the French fighters down, leaving Lieutenant Van Wagoner and his men exposed; they dived into buildings to avoid more of the determined French machinegun firing.

By this time more 1st Battalion riflemen had joined in the fight against the stubborn French defenders. Captain Sam Carter, another Alabaman like Bob York, was commanding the battalion's heavy weapons company and his mortar sections had been working over the French artillery positions. His men were just getting ready to fire more rounds when York raised hell with him on his 300 radio, yelling "Captain Carter, cease fire! McGregor is in there where you're shooting."

Turned out Ed McGregor and eight of his men had set out the night before to try to find some of their B Company men who were missing. Instead they got lost. When first light came the rescuing party found themselves twenty-five yards in front of the French main line of resistance west of the village. Cries by McGregor offering in broken French "We've come to save France" were answered by a bitter French officer in equally broken English with, "Why do you attack us? We're neutral!"

But it turned out McGregor and his men weren't in St. Cloud; they were in an open field on the other side of the road into Oran and now being watched over as prisoners of war by French officers in dress uniforms. They commanded Berbers, which the American soldier called "Ay-rabs."

"Then, our own mortar and artillery fire started landing on us, sporadically," McGregor later told Major York. "A couple of our men were wounded."

York had made the right call when he told Sam Carter to stop firing his company's mortars. As did Colonel Greer. The no-nonsense commander had seen enough. He witnessed several failed attempts by other platoons to gain solid footing in St. Cloud from his forward outpost, and when runners came back with reports of more dead and wounded, Greer weighed their modest gains versus his losses in men. Later in the morning he issued orders for all troops to be withdrawn from the village.

The Bearer Boys never got a mortar round off until this order was issued. But when they did their smoke was directed into the courtyard just over the wall past the cemetery where a factory building sat; French fighters were in there. Colonel Greer knew he had help on the way from the Ranger company, the 16th Infantry rifle company, and his own 3rd Battalion. And that battery of field artillery promised by General Allen was getting into place. Greer would hit St. Cloud again, this time with a thirty-minute deluge of artillery fire. Then later that afternoon the American infantry would strike St. Cloud again.

But they would have less mortar support. It was going on two that afternoon when Lieutenant Hobratschk radioed Sergeant Horn and told him to move his mortar section out.

"OK, we're outta here," Horn told the Bearer Boys. "We're moving over towards that belt of small trees. See all those vineyards past them? The paved road leading away from them goes into Oran. The main attack is behind schedule. We're going to make up that time. So pack up your mortar, and let's get going. Jeeps are on the way, but for now you'll have to carry everything again."

The Bearer Boys were marching away from St. Cloud an hour later. The sun was still beating down. Gentle rolling hills were ahead of them; looking at picturesque farmhouses broke up the monotony of their move.

"What the heck's going to happen back there in St. Cloud?" Bob asked Sergeant Horn as they hit the top of one of those small hills.

"Damned if I know," Horn answered. "But word came over the radio from Lieutenant Hobratschk saying General Allen didn't cotton to that artillery strike Colonel Greer was planning. Said it would kill too many civilians, and leave a bad impression on the French we came here to liberate."

Moments later the piercing scream of a French shell broke the relative quiet of the afternoon. It hit, throwing dirt all over the Bearer Boys. They dove into the ditch on the side of the road. Then more shells whistled in.

Bob yelled out to Sergeant Horn, "Tell the lieutenant those shells are hitting us like a Texas heffer pissin' on a flat rock! So much for being greeted as liberators."

French shells were of much smaller caliber than an American 105 and they tended to burst upward, rather than sideways in every direction. So the Bearer Boys were lucky; no one was hit. Instead they marched up another hill, in line behind F Company like they were on their way up to St. Cloud. They had many miles to go to reach Oran. Sergeant Horn told them his map said it was a good ten or more miles between the two towns. There was no clock chiming anymore to give the Bearer Boys some idea of what time it was, yet there was no denying the sun would soon set.

But there would be no rest for the weary soldiers. Lieutenant Downing, who was up ahead of the Bearer Boys, appeared to be staggering like someone who was drunk. They weren't doing much better. They took turns carrying their mortar's barrel, and would rotate the thirty-pound baseplate and the bipod mound—which weighed almost the same—amongst the five of them to give Slugger and Gentle John breaks. Sergeant Horn stayed near, and he helped out, too.

Night moves were safer because they obviously couldn't be seen as well. The last thing Bob remembered as dusk started settling in was another hill range emerging out of the low valley they were struggling through. The hill was already shadowed but it looked like it was covered with trees and he imagined this might be where they'd settle down and get some sleep. He sure hoped so. Bob could even see that some of the Company F riflemen out ahead of him were now starting to drop like dead flies. He couldn't imagine how anyone could go much farther.

Bob could also see Sergeant Horn on his radio, and this made him wonder if he was getting orders from Captain Murphy or Lieutenant Hobratschk about definitely stopping for the night. Something had to be up by the look on the sergeant's face.

"OK, men, gather up here real quick," Horn said seconds later. The Bearer Boys did, and then he told them, "See that line of trees up ahead? That's where we're going to halt, dig in, maybe get some rest and be ready to attack in the morning."

"Any word on who we'll be attacking?" Slugger asked the sergeant.

"Actually it may be the other way around," Sergeant Horn answered. "Major Sternberg got word that the French Foreign Legion could be expected around daylight."

"Holy shit," Slugger moaned. "They are the stuff made of legends."

"Well, we don't know anything for sure, except they are supposed to hit us," Sergeant Horn offered. "I do know that when Captain Murphy and our lieutenant came back with all their maps and briefing books before we landed that there was mention of the French Foreign Legion. But given we were told by the way-higher-ups that our landings would be something like a walk in a park and we'd be planting our colors against—don't laugh—token resistance, I know the Old Man and Lieutenant Hobratschk were pretty skeptical about the French Foreign Legion not fighting."

The Bearer Boys knew the "Old Man" was Captain Murphy. Company captains getting called the "Old Man" was pretty common lingo in the rank and file by now.

"What we do know is this, and we trust the information because Major Sternberg gave it to us," Horn continued. "The Foreign Legion is about a thousand strong and are supported by a field artillery battalion of maybe another three hundred men. Major Sternberg is pretty good at getting the dirt on what their morale is. He's convinced their leadership is pro-Hitler, so it doesn't matter what the rank and file soldier thinks like. They have to fight.

"As we saw back at St. Cloud the French units are not our friends. Major Sternberg thinks some are actually for us, but most are afraid to come out either way because they don't know how this is going to end yet. Now let's get moving."

It turned out the trees on the hill up ahead were low pines planted in sandy, chalky ground. But it looked inviting to the Bearer Boys, even without their bedrolls to keep them warm. They dug slit trenches and settled in; there was no smoking allowed because of the danger of a flickering match being seen, and giving their position away. So Bob, like everyone else, buttoned up his field jacket and got ready to lie down and try to nod off.

"I want you guys to have one of you stay awake at all times to guard this area," Sergeant Horn told them. "I'll go first, and since Baummer is first in the alphabet of this fine mortar squad you'll be up next.

"You better have bullets in that Colt-45 of yours, Bob," Horn told him. "Now listen up, all of you. We lost a guy in the Old Man's headquarters company last night. Apparently he was roaming around and the men were jumpy. Rumor goes he was challenged with the password by the 1st sergeant, and he didn't answer quick enough.

"He shot him. He's dead."

Rain started coming down a few minutes later.

The Bearer Boys were cold, wet and miserable the next morning; none had slept well. Occasional firing broke out during the night. They were distant echoes followed by unsettling silence, and it happened often enough to keep everyone on edge. They were a sorry bunch, but they lined up in columns of twos with the rest of the mortar platoon before first light, moved off the hill that had been home and onto a dirt road surrounded by plowed fields. By the time the sun came up they were back on the paved highway that led to Oran, fully expecting they'd soon be fighting with the storied French Foreign Legion.

Word spread saying General Allen was pretty worked up about hitting Oran. "Nothing in hell must stop or delay the First Division" was in the actual orders he had dictated to his orderly the night before.

The motor train had finally caught up to them, so their mortar was something the Bearer Boys didn't have to hand carry. More 81mm shells came along on one of the company's weapons carriers, finally assuring the Bearer Boys they'd have enough mortar shells for whatever lay ahead. The battalion supply officer even showed up; he had C-rations for them, but they would have to be shared—one for every three of them in the section, which meant just two rations had to go a long way. They were eaten rather quickly.

Before too long there was a sense of urgency evidenced by the F Company officers out in front of them. Then Lieutenant Hobratschk came down the line and told the Bearer Boys there was a town just ahead that was going to be attacked.

"It's a small village down the slope off the road and it's surrounded by vineyards and truck gardens," their lieutenant told them before he added, "We're going to set up after we pass over the crest of the next hill. Sergeant Hennessy is going to recon the area, but I suspect we all will fire only on demand, depending on the situation. Cannon Company is going to fire a few rounds first."

About that time a mule loaded down with machinegun ammunition passed by. Then the column moved on. But the French soldiers in the little village of Arcole didn't want to fight. No shots were fired at them when the American riflemen climbed over the stone fence surrounding the village. "A few French civilians just stared at us stoically," Lieutenant Downing explained when he got back from this foray.

Turned out the gunners of the 105mm tubes of the regiment's artillery battalion were ordered to fire a couple of high explosive rounds into the village after Cannon Company's welcoming fire—just for good measure—and this had persuaded the two hundred stunned French soldiers in the village to simply surrender. Additional persuasion from the firepower of the Bearer Boys' mortar wasn't needed.

The column instead reformed and again started out on the highway towards Oran. By now the sun was beating down, and after passing through endless vineyards the spires that marked the big Algerian city could finally be seen in the distance. But at that moment the Bearer Boys were just wondering where the French Foreign Legion was.

Lieutenant Hobratschk came back from what must have been a hurried meeting farther up the line a few minutes later, and let them know that the capture of Oran was still on.

"There could be a lot of trouble ahead, men," he warned the Bearer Boys. "Snipers, street fighting, you name it. We all are going to support the rifle companies as usual. Your squad will give F Company any help they need. They all have one of the city's squares as their objective. Captain Randall's E Company is going to cross that road over there, and hit Oran from another direction. G's behind them.

"Now listen up . . ."

But before Lieutenant Hobratschk could finish whatever it was he was going to say some civilians approached. Dazed at first, the Bearer Boys looked at them as they told anyone who would listen in halting English, "There be no opposition. People eager to welcome you."

Hobratschk just looked at the Bearer Boys and said, "Y'all know they could just be saying this to fool us. We have specific orders to shoot any civilians who shoot at us. They could be setting us up for a trap. Stay alert, and if you have to use your .45s."

The lead platoon of F Company was deployed into attack formation when it entered Oran just after ten that morning. Their squads took up positions with every man's rifle at the ready. But civilians were indeed crowding sidewalks and squares, some wildly waving and cheering. The Bearer Boys came in behind F Company to this unexpected greeting. Women, many friendly olive-skinned black-eyed younger girls, passed baskets of oranges and cheap wine to them. Some gave them hugs. The happy throng continued to cheer and clap as the Bearer Boys kept marching towards a square where the local population purchased their needed goods; more bottles of wine, fresh oranges and even French cigarettes were handed to their liberators. Then a jeep forced its way through the streets and an officer started shouting the official word: "An armistice has been signed. No more fighting!"

But the jubilant Bearer Boys continued to march while their own jeeps followed and the freed citizens of Vichy French Oran kept showing their appreciation. People cheered wildly on both sides of the street into the afternoon. The Bearer Boys eventually closed in on a square, and it was here where Lieutenant Hobratschk ordered them to assemble in a thatch-covered marketplace surrounded with iron gates; it was lined with stalls and barred windows near one gate. Women with babies were hovering outside of it looking for milk to give their infants. Barefooted Arabs in disheveled baggy pants wearing red skullcaps were also squatting outside of the gate, begging for food.

Rumors started quickly spreading. Apparently the big French 16-inch guns on the cliff edge overlooking Oran Harbor had been overrun. With this, the last hope for defending Oran had faded. Thankfully, for whatever reason the French Foreign Legion was a no show. But when small boys raced through the streets to welcome the Americans some were shouting, Hi-yo, Silver," seemingly indicating word spread fast amongst the French too.

It soon got to be late afternoon, the excitement had started to die down, and a sleep-deprived and scraggly bearded Bob had just finished eating a can of hash and a can of biscuits he washed down with wine; he was taking a drag on a French cigarette when he sat on an 81mm wooden ammo crate to write a letter to his mother so she would know he was alright.

November 10, 1942
Dear Mom,
I guess it's time I finally wrote to you, but it's the first time I have had a chance to. I am down in French North Africa now, but I can't tell you anything we are doing. I am still getting along slow but sure, and I am hoping for this war to end so I can get back home to see you and the rest of the folks. Seeing the world is all right, but as the old saying goes there is no place like home.

I am having two war bonds sent to you every month and I hope that you are getting them. I haven't written to Sonny for some time now, but tell him you have heard from me and I am all right.

I guess this will be another Christmas that I won't be home, but I'll sure be thinking of the good times I could be having if I was there. But there will be other Christmases I won't miss. Don't worry about me, cause I can take care of myself when the occasion arises. Try to write to me and let me know what's happening around town, and if possible send a paper or two.

The food we are getting is pretty good, but it couldn't compare to a nice juicy steak or a roasted chicken like you make at home.

Well, Mom, I shall have to close now. I shall be thinking of you all the time that I am away. Don't forget to take real good care of yourself.
All my love,
Bob

~TWENTY-ONE~

VIOLA WAS PRETTY SURE BOB was somewhere in North Africa. She just knew he had to be after reading the newspapers, especially the *New York Daily News* final edition dated November 10th where the front page above the fold read: ALGERIA AND MOROCCO SURRENDER; END OF CAMPAIGN FREES YANKS FOR DRIVE ON AXIS IN TUNISIA.

Viola simply had no way of knowing that her son Bob's regiment experienced three officers killed and that four had been wounded during its three days of fighting in the hottest spots around Oran. Nor could she have possibly known that thirty-four enlisted men like Bob had been killed, and that one hundred and thirteen of his fighting brethren had been wounded. The Army simply did not release such information.

But the worst part for Viola was not knowing Bob's fate, and waiting to hear from him was filled with emotion only a mother understood. Her worst fear was getting a telegram from the Army saying he was missing or killed.

Bob didn't even know what his fate would be when he woke up on the floor of the thatch-covered market the day after the French forces in Oran surrendered. It was well before first light, but by the time the sun rose up around eight o'clock Bob could see the same scraggly Arabs still begging for food outside of the market's gate.

Hope abounded that he would be able to stay in Oran and maybe get some deserved time off. Bob knew it was a big city, and there had to be a lot to explore. Rumors even got around that Oran had trendy cafes where one could sit outside under palm trees, sip wine and feast on a good hot meal. He had been able to make out office and apartment buildings and lots of stores past the wild throngs of people that had greeted him the day before. He imagined shopping and maybe even getting his mother something he could send home to her. He thought about meeting a girl; maybe he could get the attention of one of those French black-eyed olive-skinned beauties he saw when he was being greeted as their liberator, but then he reminded himself that they were nothing like the pretty girls back in the good old U.S. of A.

"You got to be kidding, Bob," Louie the Rub teased when they kicked around sipping wine and meeting some women that morning. "But, I get your point about saving yourself for some girl back home. Word's already started spreading saying that we could be heading back stateside soon to help train green troops that can't even imagine what real combat is like. They say we're going to show them how amphibious landings are done right."

Bob and Louie were just starting to light up French cigarettes and thinking about cleaning up when Lieutenant Hobratschk appeared and yelled for a reveille report. It took a bit for everyone to gather up; Bob was thinking about shaving his three-day beard off when the order came down. Others were returning from the luxury of using the public latrine outside of the gate.

When they finally assembled their commander announced, "Listen up y'all. We're a' goin' to march out of town in a bit to go on outpost duty."

The men exchanged disappointed looks. Some swore, but not loud enough for Lieutenant Hobsratschk to hear them.

An hour later the Bearer Boys' mortar platoon was lining up with the rest of H Company. Captain Murphy even looked glum, which was rare for him. He walked the line, counting off his men. There was no Irish sparkle in his eyes.

A few minutes later Murphy started shouting commands and

the Bearer Boys joined their fellow soldiers in loathsome columns of twos and marched out of the market gate for wherever it was the Army in its infinite wisdom was now sending them.

Company captains like Murphy were carrying staffed American flags when the column marched out of Oran. Regiment had ordered this practice during marches when the landings began, but the directive had been largely ignored because many thought it was something not done since the American Civil War, and only then at a battalion level. Many of the officers actually thought it was silly; probably some idea that came out of Washington. It made themselves and the men they commanded good targets. They weren't going to risk that, and no one enforced the order.

But now that they were liberators and being embraced, the American flag was an asset. When it fluttered in the light morning winds off Captain Murphy's shoulder, every French and Arab cheered wildly as their saviors passed by them on the hard road surface near their modest homes. Then the cheering stopped. An hour into the march, the column headed off this road and over toward some farmhouses, here to await further orders from regiment about the big move.

It was a drab setting. The morning sun had warmed up the day, and before too long the Bearer Boys learned their first lesson about Arab customs. Sheep feces had been traditionally used for fertilizer over the years, and the field they were in was starting to smell far worse than Corkerhill Camp back in Scotland. Their platoon was bivouacked near one of the farm's outbuildings, and the constant presence of flies also added to the smell of dung, so much so that many feared getting infected with some disease.

Sleep was impossible. None of the Bearer Boys even tried to fall out. They were mad as hell at the Army for putting them here instead of letting them cut loose in Oran. Some riflemen had even rebelled and Bob could see them riding bareback on a horse they apparently borrowed to pass the time. Arab children even showed up, begging for food again. Out of the corner of his eye Bob could see Arab farmhands relieving themselves in the alley next to the outbuilding. A jeep brought up C-rations for the noon meal, but Bob and most everyone else by now had lost their appetites.

The afternoon was loosing light when new orders finally came down; it was near dusk when the column got moving again, and by the time it got dark the Bearer Boys were marching into yet another field where sleep was all they could think about. And as if on cue, a company jeep came up and deposited their bedrolls and packs they had left behind on their way up to St. Cloud. Joy turned to anger, though, when the Bearer Boys found their packs had been looted; cigarettes and some personal items were missing. Bob was particularly angered when he saw the Zippo lighter Sonny had given him was stolen.

And before too long Lieutenant Hobratschk also disappeared. Sergeant Horn explained to the Bearer Boys that their commander had left on a reconnaissance mission, apparently to reconnoiter the route to their next stop which—as rumor put it—was to be their "objective," which in Army parlance meant the likely next dreary place they would be staying for awhile.

Sleeping that night, however, was made comfortable with the arrival of their bedrolls so the Bearer Boys got their first decent rest since coming ashore. But when they got up the next morning, they were greeted by a very worried Sergeant Horn. Lieutenant Hobratschk was not back from his reconnaissance foray, and Horn even said he was worried that their lieutenant may have been captured, or killed.

But the mission came first. Just after the sun came up the Bearer Boys moved out again, this time in a single marching column that made the line of olive-drab soldiers longer. As it got hotter, the road got dustier because of the wind and dry air. Sweat was dripping down everyone's foreheads and stinging their eyes. Cussing was common. Sergeant Horn nevertheless urged them on as best he could, and when Bob saw him looking to the rear and suddenly start smiling he thought his section leader was losing it.

There was Lieutenant Hobratschk, but he was not smiling. Instead he'd been running to catch up with the platoon after what he was about to explain was a pretty bad night.

"We all made it to where we're headed men," Hobratschk began as he started catching his breath. "It's up ahead, about eight miles from here. It was damned cold out last night, and I'm ashamed to admit we got lost coming back. That was the easy part. The bad part was my jeep ran out of gas, and if it weren't for that resourceful Lieutenant Downing in F Company managing to find us a gallon of fuel, we wouldn't be here. His jeep even ran out of gas, but he put the gas he got from a French railway worker in his tank and towed me back.

"Enough of that. Y'all are going to see some French tanks up ahead, but don't worry. They all are shot up. A supply truck is a burnt skeleton of a mess near them tanks. There's even an American half-track we came across that was hit by what appeared to be an artillery shell. Y'all will also see a French tank with the muzzle of its gun pointed at you, but again—don't worry. It's deserted. Breech block was open, spiked."

The Bearer Boys were obviously happy to see their commanding officer, but were less happy when a runner came up on a horse with word that battalion wanted them to pick it up and move more quickly. But that was a hard order to follow. Everyone was groggy, and the sun was still beating down. There was no shade, just dry fields and endless rows of vineyards to either side of the dusty road they were on. Instead of hurrying up, the men in the long column began to fall out into ditches. Then a new order arrived: words to the effect take it easy, help was on the way.

It arrived in the form of two and a half-ton trucks. Regiment had come through. The Bearer Boys were going to be shuttled to their destination. Mules carrying loads were suddenly and happily relieved of their duties. When the trucks had everyone packed in, off the convoy went, passing all of the sites Lieutenant Hobratschk had told them about. Before too long they reached a little town called Les Trembles. Its citizens greeted them as liberators, passed them wine, and waved madly as they drove through.

Then they came to a farmhouse on the edge of town. The Bearer Boys de-trucked. More deuce and a halves showed up; these had pup tents for the men. And more C-rations, too. Lieutenant Hobratschk pointed to a field next to a farm house. Off they marched and before too long their pup tents went up and Willy Driscoll started a fire to heat up their stew. When night came the Bearer Boys were a happy bunch. Wine was flowing. Guards were on the perimeters of their new camp, keeping them safe. A light wind was blowing the smell of the farm's manure pile away from them.

One by one the Bearer Boys fell out, closed up their pup tents, kicked off their boots and then went to sleep in their uniforms, grateful of the generosities shown to them by the U.S. Army that day.

The Army issued soap, razor blades and toothpaste to the Bearer Boys the next morning so helmet baths, shaves, brushing their teeth for the first time in three days, clothes washing and on and off sleep consumed the bulk of the day. Housekeeping was pretty much the task for all the companies, and the battalion's officers were finally reunited with their bed rolls and hand baggage. A none too pleased Captain Murphy discovered his bag had been looted, but Lieutenant Hobratschk's musette bag apparently wasn't because he was in a particularly good mood when he called the mortar platoon together during mid-afternoon.

"Y'all need to know a few things, so let's start at the top," Hobratschk started. "First, your commanding general thought you all did a good job over the past few days. He extends . . .

"Well, let me just read it to y'all. General Allen extends his deep appreciation and personal thanks to every officer and enlisted man. I also want to thank you. You didn't cower. You did the job given to you.

"Now, I know rumors have been going around about us being

all done with combat and going on a training mission back in the states," Lieutenant Hobratschk said in a serious tone. "So let me again quote General Allen. What we did since we landed is just the initial phase in a long series of operations. So men, happy to say y'all be seeing—again in General Allen's words—rapid offensive operations in the near future.

"The sooner we get this war over with the better. Meantime our job is to get re-supplied, and the trucks coming up with our equipment already shows we've made a good start. General Allen has further directed us to resume combat training and perform maintenance on our equipment, which means we'll be inspecting our mortars soon.

"Also, our good commanding general—he's from El Paso Texas, just so you know—expects you to exhibit the highest standards of soldierly behavior, and let me add to that with he underlined 'highest' and 'soldierly behavior.' He wants us to carefully observe sanitary regulations, and with your all nice clean, shaved looks you've gotten a good start on that. Y'all will be getting pills to purify the water around here, and you will start taking those atabrine pills again so you don't get malaria. We're going to need your fighting strength. Last but not least General Allen wants us to establish cordial relations with our allied forces and the civilians we meet, which means y'all have to really behave yourselves.

"OK, men, I've got this stack of little booklets here that will acquaint you all with African culture and customs. It's just sixteen pages, and I expect you to read it."

"Any questions?" Hobratschk added.

There were just glum faces and there were no questions. Instead everyone fell out, and the Bearer Boys were heading towards their pup tents with their booklets when they heard the loud sounds of horses' hooves on the street at the edge of the farm.

"Wonder what that's all about?" Bob asked.

"Maybe we should just go take a look and find out," Ralph Sproull said in his thick Georgia drawl. "Sounds like there's a lot of horses going someplace. I can hear wheels turning, too. Maybe we can see if they are one of our allied forces."

"Sounds good to me," Slugger said. "Let's go and be cordial to whoever it is. We'll just be obeying orders."

That drew laughs as the Bearer Boys started running towards the street.

"Oh my God," Louie the Rub yelled out when they saw the spectacle. "Can you believe this?"

The Bearer Boys were watching a battery of French artillery troops on a march towards Oran. Clearly proud officers wearing tall, flat-topped and beaked kepis and non-coms in blood-red chechias were mounted on well-groomed Arabian chestnut horses. Others were pulling World War One 75mm guns, carts with hay for the horses and rations for their soldiers.

Louie suddenly yelled out, "*La France vive encore!*"

One of the French officers called back, "*Viva a la France!*"

"*Bonjour!*" Louie called out, spreading his arms in greeting.

The Bearer Boys just stared at Louie with awe before Bob smirked then asked, "Where'd you learn French, Rubado? I know you 'a speaka' the Italian, but French?

"Long story, but I'll give you a hint. Needed to know a little French when I visited Montreal before enlisting. Wasn't far from where I grew up in upstate New York. Beautiful French-Canadian girls up there in Montreal. Some even called me Frenchie. Get my drift?"

Everyone was breaking out in laughter, and some of the French soldiers joined in before one yelled out, "Hi-yo-Silver!" and another screamed, "Away!"

"I sure as hell hope they are on our side now," Gentle John said as the colorful battery kept going towards Oran.

~TWENTY-TWO~

OFFICERS DISAPPEARED THE NEXT DAY. Rumor had it that they were checking out the cafes in Les Trembles, and when Lieutenant Hobratschk came back that afternoon word quickly got around that a near quart-sized canteen of wine was going for just seven cents.

The Bearer Boys weren't so lucky. They hadn't received permission to leave the camp so they spent the day studying their Arab customs booklets. Coincidently a bunch of Arab boys had decided to check out their bivouac area and before the day was over they had found friends in some soldiers who gave them their C-ration chocolates, and enemies amongst the American soldiers who had their clothes hanging out to dry, only to see their personal items stolen by a few of the small kids.

"Wonder who wrote this booklet," Carmen the Charmer said to start discussions amongst the Bearer Boys. All of them had pretty much kept to themselves during the morning, but they became a chatty bunch after their noon ration.

"Whoever it was probably didn't spend too much time here," Bob offered along with his trademark smirk. "See where it said there's little rainfall along the coast? Seem to remember it came down a lot at night after we landed."

"I liked the part where it said mirages are frequent occurrences," Gentle John kidded. "Says they occur early in the morning."

"Yea, it'll be just a matter of time before Carmen starts thinking he's seeing French broads in his pup tent," Slugger joked.

"You Yankees are pretty funny," Ralph laughed.

"See the part about there being no places to spend our pay?" Willy Driscoll asked.

"Sure did," Bob answered. "Said we should ship seventy-five percent of it home. I already send my mother five dollars when we get paid, and a couple of war bonds every month. I think I'll just save up. You guys better too. I'm gonna' loot you when we play cards and I don't give out I.O.U's."

"Funny, Bob," Carmen the Charmer deadpanned. "I've got a big family back near Philly, so I just might send 'em some money and win the difference off you."

"I thought the more interesting part of the booklet was all those do's and dont's if we ever visit a mosque," Slugger volunteered. "Don't enter one was the first rule. What else do we need to know?"

"Well it said we can't even hang out around them," Willy threw in. "But if we did, no smoking is another rule."

"That and no spitting," Bob reminded the Bearer Boys.

"Apparently bread is holy to the Arabs," Slugger added. "Says we can't even use our knives to cut it, and we have to break it with our hands."

"And not let any crumbs drop on the ground," Bob threw in.

"Did you see where it said we can only eat bread out of our right hands Slugger?" Gentle John pointed out. "You need to re-member that since you're a southpaw."

"My favorite part of the booklet was the thing about not killing snakes, or even birds in the presence of an Arab," Ralph said. "In Georgia we shoot snakes all the time."

"Yep, says Arabs believe snakes and birds are the souls of their departed chieftains," Bob noticed.

"And remind me not to take a dog into any of their homes," Slugger added. "That's forbidden, too. Oh, and did you see the words and phrases we're suppose to learn so we can try to speak Arabic when we're in their presence?"

"Let me give that a try," Louie the Rub said with gleam in his eyes. "Ready?"

"Laaaailltack, cee 'da ada' 'em sic be hair," Louie gave them. "It means good night."

"You don't have to worry about memorizing that Louie," Bob laughed before finishing with, "Doubt any respectable Arab woman would ever want to get close enough to you for you to say good night to her."

But that night was one dreams were made of. There was no rain. Stars danced in the clear sky. It was chilly, but there was little wind and the Bearer Boys were plenty comfortable in their pup tents. Bob was dozing off with Willy Driscoll when a dog started howling. Bob couldn't resist a wisecrack.

"Funny how we can't bring a dog into an Arab's home, but theirs can bark all night around ours."

Rumors in plain English spread fast the next morning. Word had started going around about the Bearer Boys' battalion commanders and how Colonel Greer was going to sack Major Powers and his number two, Major Chase, and give Ben Sternberg command. None of the Bearer Boys really knew much about Powers or Chase, but the rumor had it that Greer wasn't pleased with their command and control during the fighting back at St. Cloud. Sternberg, on the other hand, had gained the reputation of being fearless, commanding from the front, always knowing what was happening and being aggressive.

Another rumor making the rounds was there was more combat ahead.

The discussion amongst the Bearer Boys outside their pup tents that morning—where they actually drank coffee—centered on all this rumormongering and they tried to sort that out.

"So, maybe we won't be going home to train new guys on the finer points of making amphibious landings after all," Louie started.

"But I heard the division will get broken up, and we might be reporting to the Brits," Carmen the Charmer said, dead serious this had to be what was really going down. "Why would they be replacing our commanders, supposing that's true, if we didn't have more fighting ahead of us?"

"We're going somewhere for sure," Willy added. "Some are still saying we'll likely train troops stateside for combat. Not sure I believe that one, or the one about getting handed off to the Brits."

"I've got you all beat," Bob laughed. "A pretty believable rumor I heard was the cream of the crop amongst our officers and we men are going to be shipped home so they can set up a recruiting station in Central Park in New York City. I've already put in for that assignment."

But Captain Murphy had others assignments in mind. They included close order drill, digging by the book foxholes around the Bearer Boys mortar, camouflaging their weapons carrier's tracks, and even performing some agility exercises to prove to their good captain that they hadn't lost any of their nimbleness; they also had to show Murphy that they still had their routines down pat about moving shells, plus stacking them up correctly so they could be efficiently handed to Gentle John when he fed them into the mortar's barrel. After a full first day of this in the hot African sun, Lieutenant Hobratschk called them to a platoon briefing that was held in the field an hour before sundown.

"OK, men, listen up as you all always do," he said in a tired but still expansive voice. "Two things y'all need to know. First you're going to get your mortar ready for a show-down inspection, which means you'll have the good fortune and honor this time tomorrow to evidence to me and Captain Murphy that y'all still have everything the Army issued to you, and it's all in good working order.

"Any questions?" Hobratschk added, almost daring someone to speak up.

"Yes, sir," I have one," Sergeant Horn said. "Since we haven't done this in the field yet, I just want to be certain about the level of maintenance you'll be looking for."

"Good question sergeant," Hobratschk answered. "We're limited by the tools we have on hand. So, we expect you to use what we've got, disassemble what you have to, then inspect, lubricate and replace anything necessary—assuming we have the parts. Our carriers do have the usual spare parts. Obviously, if we don't have all the parts we find we'll need I'll have to requisition them. That's the point of the exercise. If your mortar needs work beyond what we can do here in the field, it'll have to go off to the ordnance shop.

"Men, consider how fortunate you all are. The mortar is your weapon of war. Y'all need to develop the confidence you can keep it functioning at peak because we all could get called into battle at any time, we have to be fully prepared, and here in Company H we always will be.

"Any further questions?"

There were none, but there were a lot of men with confused looks on their faces, and this led Lieutenant Hobratschk to say, "Cheer up men. All y'all have all day to work, and you won't have to deal with me or Captain Murphy 'till this time tomorrow. That's when we'll be inspecting each mortar.

"Now, the second thing I promised you. Sergeant Roof, bring me that oblong wooden box up here, please," Hobratschk ordered with a mischievous look on his face. Roof did while everyone looked on, wondering if the box had a new style of 81mm mortar in it.

"Thank you. Men, Sergeant Roof went all the way over to Captain Murphy's CP, then back here with this so I can show you your new ration. What we have here is a complete daily ration for fourteen of y'all fine soldiers. It's a British Compo Ration."

Carmen the Charmer poked Bob when he heard this, and said, "See I told you we were going to be fighting with the Brits!"

"Private Giello!" Lieutenant Hobratschk shouted. "You got a question?"

"Sir, no Sir."

"OK then. This box contains little delicacies like canned beef and chicken stew, steak and kidney pudding, vegetables, sardines, cereal stuffed sausage and bacon. There's also oxtail stew, complete with jointed bones, plus powdered tea. Sorry, no American coffee. But the British have been kind enough to include Players cigarettes and even matches. Means you can have seven smokes a day. Each of you.

"And for snacks there's boiled sweets, which looks like hard candy to me, and chocolate bars. And don't let me forget desert. We have for y'all treacle pudding and rice pudding. Add salt when you please, and know, too, that the Brits were even kind enough to remember toilet paper.

"Any questions?"

"Sir, I do have one after all, sir," Carmen the Charmer confessed. "Does this mean we are going to be fighting with the British?"

"Damned if I know where the United States Army in its infinite wisdom is going to send us," Hobratschk answered. Truth was rumors were going around in the officer's quarters that they would be, but he wasn't going to spread that around just yet.

"OK, assuming there are no other questions, Captain Murphy and I will be back to see you at 1600 tomorrow."

There were no further questions.

The Bearer Boys woke up early the next morning, tried eating a cereal-stuffed sausage and bacon out of their new Brit ration, decided they weren't all that great, and then quickly split up into teams and go to work on their mortar.

"I'm only observing," Sergeant Horn told them. "But seems to me you passed the first thing I'm supposed to see. Something about showing initiative, absent leadership direction."

"Huh?" Slugger dared to suddenly question, then lightened up with, "Sarge, I'll speak for the whole squad here. We're kinda' growing to like you, but please don't hold that against us. We even think you're a good leader."

"As long as I'm not dead," Horn shot back. "Point being if you lose me, you boys still have to perform. Understand?"

The Bearer Boys just looked at each other; no one could imagine Sergeant Horn dead. Instead they got right down to the task at hand. Bob and Gentle John teamed up first to inspect the mortar barrel.

"OK," Bob started. "You and me have worked with our hands on cars before John, so I'm thinking what the Old Man and Lieutenant Hobratschk are looking for really boils down to this. There's no way we can break everything down. We ain't going to have time to rebuild anything. I'm guessing we have to be sure the barrel's clean, free of rust, burs and scores. No rough spots. No bare metal, 'cause it will shine and make us a good target. We're going to have to check the firing pin, too."

"Well, let's have at it," Gentle John agreed.

Everyone else stood back and watched.

Bob unscrewed the firing pin from the end of the mortar tube's base cap. He left the base cap in place to maintain the proper seal. He inspected the firing pin vent, and it looked clean, so he screwed the pin back into the end of the base plate plug and tightened it.

"There, that's gastight," Bob said. "Hand me a dud 81, John."

Gentle John gave Bob the dud, the opposite of how they would interact when they actually fired a mortar in combat, and he watched Bob hold the barrel level in his hands and then tilt it back and forth so the dud slid freely through the tube.

"It's as smooth as The Rub thinks he is with women," Bob smirked. "No burs on the quadrant seat, unlike the women's butts he never got. And look here. The aiming lines are visible. Louie's lines never work, but our mortar tube's lines do. Wonder why. Who's up next?"

"I am," Willy Driscoll boasted. "Let me have a look at the baseplate. Stand back everyone. I have to show Bob up."

Willy checked to be sure the baseplate's latches were operating smoothly, and that it had not warped or developed deformations when it was fired back in St. Cloud. Then he got real confident and said, "OK, Ralphie, you snake shooting hillbilly you, get your sorry Southern ass down here and let's check out the legs on this 'sumbitch."

"Charmer never got that far with his women," Ralph shot back. "But watch me work this bitch's legs and show you Yankees how it's done right."

The laughing died down as the Bearer Boys looked at Ralph while he used the shadows from the sun like a smart Georgia farmer would and angled each leg just right to be sure they were straight, holding each one at the end of his arm with both adjusted so his eye aim could declare it so. And with that decided, Ralph made sure the chains and straps that might be needed to hold the base in place were secure and the clevis pins that held the feet to the legs were locked tight.

"Now let's check out the shock absorbers while we're at this," Ralph said.

While everyone watched—somewhat in awe because they had never done this before—Ralph called out: "Guides smooth. Check. Smooth as a sweet Georgia peach's...never mind. Check. No worn components; no need to replace them. Check. Clevis and mount attachment ring has no damage. Check. We losing you on this Carmen, you charmer you?"

"You're so full of it, Ralphie. And I'm not a leg man, so it don't matter to me, hearing you pretend like you are."

"OK boys, calm down," Sergeant Horn laughed. "I can't take too much more of this, OK?"

"OK," Slugger said. "Since I have to aim this thing, now that I know the barrel's smooth and the legs on this bitch work I suppose it's time for me to see just how well she dances. Men still lead, right?"

"Don't ask the Charmer," Bob wisecracked, and then they all finally settled down and watched Slugger as he started traversing the hand wheel back an eighth of a turn to check on the backlash.

"OK, here we go," Slugger said before getting on his knees and working the elevating mechanism. "No binding here. Bevel gears mesh. No wear on the spindle. Oil caps are clear and still circled in red paint. Traversing screws look normal. Well, maybe there's a little bit of wear on this one. I'll tighten the bearing ring nut to compensate for that. No cracks in the screw on the hand wheel. No damage or markings on the sight level vial.

"You guys seeing all this?" Slugger asked.

"No we trust you, Slugger," Bob deadpanned.

"One more time. You guys trust me?"

"Yea, yea," all the Bearer Boys said in unison.

"OK, I'm gonna' position the traversing spindle to make sure the lubricating hole lines up with the oil cup in the yoke," Slugger said. "OK, it leads right. And finally I'm seeing if the shock absorber tube slides easily through the yoke. Yep, sure does.

"We're ready to lob a few round of mortars on Adolf Hitler himself boys."

At four that afternoon Captain Murphy and Lieutenant Hobratschk showed up just like they said they would. They first visually inspected the mortar from a few feet away, and then moved in for a closer look; they now seemed to be looking for excess grease, oil or dirt because Murphy had a clean rag in his hand.

"How are you on spare parts?" he instead asked Slugger.

"If we had to I s'pose we could rebuild this mortar Captain," he answered with pride.

"Do you have adequate stocks of cleaning and preserving materials?" Murphy followed that with.

"Yes, Sir," Slugger answered.

"Works for me," Captain Murphy finally said to everyone's relief. "Sergeant Horn, if you'd read me the serial number off the mortar, I will sign off on this inspection. Doing so means this mortar assigned to the second squad, third section is properly functioning and ready for immediate use.

"Now gentlemen," Murphy began with what seemed to be the last he was going to say. "I have. . ."

By this time the entire squad had sprung to attention.

"I have just one last question."

"Sir?" Slugger responded.

"At ease, all of you. Who has the carrying handle for the baseplate in their pocket?"

"I do, Sir," Gentle John sheepishly answered.

"Thank you men. This completes your inspection. Keep this up and we may find a way to get you a little R&R one of these days."

Murphy and Hobratschk both grinned, and then left.

"Nothing gets by the Old Man," Bob was the first to say. "John, you saved us! How'd you remember you had the handle for the baseplate in your pocket?"

"Cause Louie dropped it, and I picked it up," Gentle John answered back. "We're a team, guys. I fessed up to the captain right away so Louie wouldn't fumble around looking for it in his pockets and maybe get one of them steely looks Lieutenant Hobratschk gives us on occasion."

"I owe ya John," Louie said with a straight face before everyone cracked up. But that didn't mask the lesson they just learned. They really were a team, and they had each other's backs.

Thanksgiving was coming. To keep the cordial relations with the French going, hand bills inviting them to join company tables were distributed to civilians in nearby towns. The invitations to join the soldiers for the holiday explained the origins of America's Thanksgiving, and were even written in French. The Bearer Boys all volunteered to go into Les Trembles to work the French population there and continue to build up cordial relations, but poor Sergeant Horn had to explain to them that there were too few French in town, and officers had already staked their claim on them, especially the women.

Thanksgiving came, but for the Bearer Boys there was no turkey dinner. Turned out more French citizens from l'Oggaz and Perregaux showed up than were expected, and there weren't enough servings to go around to offer any to some of the soldiers outside of Les Trembles who helped free them.

December arrived a few days later, as did the start of the rainy season in North Africa. Training went on; the usual hiking in the countryside surrounding Les Trembles kept everyone in shape. Captain Murphy and Lieutenant Hobratschk came back from battalion headquarters the first Thursday night of the month in what appeared to be very subdued moods. Turned out one of the rumors still going around was true. Majors Powers and Chase were actually leaving the battalion for some unspecified duties in Oran. Then the next day all the company-level officers disappeared for what turned out to be a little R&R in Sidi-bel-Abbes, home of the French Foreign Legion.

A few new rumors made their way through the ranks when they got back. One was the story on why the Foreign Legion didn't attack the Bearer Boys when they were marching on Oran. Turned out they had been strafed by some planes on the road they were taking to get into the fight, and had simply received orders to return to Sidi-bel-Abbes.

But the best rumor was attributed to Lieutenant Hobratschk, and it was pretty funny. He and Lieutenant Downing in F Company had befriended a few of the Legionaires over drinks and they both at the same time needed to use a bathroom to relieve themselves of the copious amount of wine they drank.

"The latrine, like a lot of French toilets, had the letters 'W.C' painted on the outside wall," so the story went according to Downing—as Lieutenant Hobratschk retold it. "This was their abbreviation for 'water closet,' the name the French gave to bathrooms. An officer told us that when the Germans were there they permitted the abbreviation to remain and put out propaganda to the effect that the letters stood for Winston Churchill and that the initials were located very appropriately."

More rumors started up a few days later. Downing had also been on another reconnaissance mission, which usually meant another move was coming.

This rumor proved too good to believe when it came true. The Bearer Boys were finally going to move out for a little R&R. Passes were handed to them for twenty-four-hour leave, and they were headed to a fair-sized town called Mascara, where a red wine was manufactured. The town was a hotbed of intrigue just two weeks earlier when it was found by American patrols to have been the location of a German transmitting station. Further investigation revealed there had been a strong pro-Nazi feeling in Mascara, and it had even been called by some of the Jewish locals "little Berlin."

But now Mascara was going to be invaded by nearly a thousand U.S. soldiers because their population was reported to be taking the occupation of their country by American troops with considerable calm and friendliness. Louie the Rub even anticipated friendly greetings. He couldn't help telling the Bearer Boys that mascara was also something women wore when they made themselves up, so even Carmen the Charmer might have a shot at finding a girl.

The Hotel de Ville was supposed to be one of the more proper places in town, but there were plenty of seedier bars too. For some reason there was a big contingent of military police when the Bearer Boys arrived, and this got everyone's curiosity up. Then another rumor started spreading. There were brothels in Mascara, and the MPs were there to enforce higher headquarters' orders to keep American soldiers from patronizing ones run by Arabs, although it appeared the Army was OK with those staffed by Europeans.

Guards were posted outside the two Arab brothels, but when the U.S. soldiers arrived a soon to be record business started up in the sole European house. Guards even had to maintain order and supervise a growing queue as afternoon turned to dusk. The Bearer Boys had pretty much behaved themselves, and they were all pleasantly buzzed and full of food by this time. Still, their curiosities got the better of them, and they had to check things out.

The brothel was in an enclosed patio courtyard, replete with nice shrubbery and a fountain. The light-flooded patio was surrounded by balconies, and heavily made up blondes and brunettes in skimpy kimonos were leaning over the rails. A prophylactic station was even set up, manned by the MPs to be sure every soldier used one, and word was medics would show up later.

The brisk business was still going, and a line was formed up all the way out to the street when the Bearer Boys got there that night. A session cost thirty-five cents in American money. Some soldiers were falling out—from too much drinking—but the queue was moving. As soon as one soldier came down the balcony another went up. Fights started breaking out because some unruly soldiers didn't close the queue up fast enough.

Slugger took this all in, and was the first to say he had no interest. The Bearer Boys looked up to him not just because he was a corporal but also because he had standards that they respected. Everyone was in their early twenties and none of them were prudes, but Bob was the first to peg the line, "Guys, we can do a lot better than this. Let's get the hell out of here."

It was about ten by this time, they were all plenty happy and had even been smart enough to fill their canteens with wine at the last bar they hit. The trucks that had brought them to Mascara were lined up on the edge of town, ready to take them back at midnight. Some soldiers were passed out and lying on the ground next to the deuce and a halves. Others were already in the back of the trucks in much the same condition.

"I say we just walk back," Bob told everyone. They all agreed and went merrily on their way, sipped their wine, sang songs and weaved along the side of the road on their way back to Les Trembles.

They were good and hung over the next morning. Bob was talking about their R&R outing, and everyone was laughing when

Sergeant Horn suddenly appeared and told them to pack up. They were moving out. So they packed up and re-boarded the same trucks that had delivered the battalion's drunks the night before.

The countryside along the road to wherever it was the Army was now sending their hung over throng was full of the usual vineyards and fields, but after passing through a few small villages the Bearer Boys started seeing something different—cactus plants.

"Maybe we're heading for the desert, boys," Slugger joked. "Maybe the Sahara. Maybe we'll get to see the Nile River."

"Nope," Bob yelled over the sound of the truck's deuce and a half engine. "I got it from good sources that we're headed for the Atlas Mountains."

They were all wrong. They were headed for a town that in Arabic literally meant "camp." The Ottomans built the first military garrison here two hundred and forty years earlier, and it was now home to the 9th Regiment of the Chasseurs d' Africa, a French African cavalry unit. Bob was close to being right; the town was near the southern slope on a range of the Atlas Mountains. It was Denis-du-Sig.

They barely had time to settle in before word got around saying that the Red Cross had arranged a little entertainment for their battalion the following night. It was to feature all French talent and it was going to be held in the local theater. It turned out there were just two actors when the vaudeville show went off, and they were a husband and wife team. The husband played a magician and performed some clever illusions, but the Bearer Boys got to see something that was far from the illusions their Africa guide books had warned them of. In plain sight, his wife wore just a brassiere and shorts. She got all of the attention and drew their hearty applause.

But there was no further entertainment. A few nights later another alert order came down; they were moving out again in three hours. They were to take only their bedrolls and light packs. Their company kitchen broke up. Trucks showed up again. Rain started coming down. The trucks were uncovered, so everyone swore about that. Finally, just after midnight, the wet, tired and miserable Bearer Boys moved out.

It rained more all the following day, and through the night. They had already traveled nearly 300 miles. The next day they finally reached l'Arba—twenty miles south of Algiers— where they bivouacked near a grove of large cork trees.

~TWENTY-THREE~

BY NOW GENERAL EISENHOWER HAD made up his mind about the next operation, and it was to seize the important ports of Bizerte and Tunis in Tunisia. Time was of the essence. The African winter would soon envelope the area and bring with it heavy rainfall, miserable cold and ankle-deep mud. Eisenhower knew that absent control of these two ports, the German buildup in North Africa would continue and give Hitler the time he needed to control the skies in the region. As worrisome, with vastly larger numbers of tanks it would also allow him to gain the upper hand in future mobile operations.

Hitler's thinking obviously centered on hindering any renewed Allied advance. Estimates had 19,500 German and 11,250 Italian fighting troops with about 2,500 German Air Forces personnel and 5,000 service support troops already in Tunisia. Thousands more German forces were scheduled to arrive by air transportation and troop ships.

The British had brought ashore just a single infantry division, short a brigade, and one tank regiment when they landed in Algeria back in November. Their forces had already tried to seize Bizerte and Tunis, but after hundreds of casualties had been suffered the British ceased offensive operations in early December. Now their communication lines were fragile, and bringing supplies forward was dangerously close to collapsing.

Additional British forces were on the way, but they would not arrive in sufficient force or time to mount a creditable attack towards the important Tunisian ports that General Eisenhower badly wanted. Thus the Allied Commander had no choice but to re-examine the cards he held, and when Eisenhower showed them to his planners it was far from a good poker hand. He simply needed more troops. Terry Allen felt it was a literal flush of his First Division, for Eisenhower mandated that the Bearer Boys' proud commander had to make a choice about which of his regiments could be handed over to the Allied cause for what amounted to a supporting role in what would feature the British as the main characters on the Tunisian stage during this second hurried attempt to take Bizerte and Tunis.

General Allen had only one card in his hand at the time, and that was the Bearer Boys'18th Infantry.

Somewhat tongue-in-cheek, the soldier's newspaper *The Stars and Stripes* noted in its December 15th edition that there were just ten shopping days left until Christmas. That same day started unusually for the Bearer Boys. They were introduced to a British custom when they lined up for breakfast at seven that morning, and it came in the form of a rum ration. It was still plenty cold and rum sure warmed the soul, so each of them put their allotted teaspoon in their cups to jumpstart their day.

Rumor had it that a definitive order had come down from Eisenhower's headquarters in Algiers and this was confirmed when officers started shouting out for everyone to board the regiment's trucks again. When the sun came up the Bearer Boys found themselves heading east, past brown hills covered with scrubby trees, for wherever it was the Army was now sending them. They did have some company. Alongside the road, Arabs in flowing robes riding sideways on donkeys were being followed by their veiled wives and children, all carrying bags of grain.

After the noon meal rain started coming down. It was light at first, but it was pouring by mid-afternoon. The roads were not very good to begin with so the convoy had to slow down, but the frustrating part for the Bearer Boys was just sitting in the back of their truck and being stopped in the open when it needed gas. Five-gallon cans were all that were available, the refueling was slow and frequent, but the convoy still managed to cover over 200 miles before pulling off for the night into a field near the old trading city of Setif.

But the Bearer Boys had their pup tents back, and it took little time to pitch them and fall out. The wind picked up during the night and at 3,500 feet above sea level there was plenty of cold air to mix with the downpour.

It was still raining in the morning when the convoy took off again, but it cleared up by noontime. That night the Bearer boys slept in a field near some Arab mud and straw huts about twenty miles east of Constantine, the ancient city created by the Phoenicians before they lost it to the Romans during the Third Punic War. The sounds of warfare were present again, and it kept them awake. Planes were heard overhead towards midnight; they had to be German. The muffled roaring of their bombs hitting somewhere nearby kept the Bearer Boys on edge, but the planes didn't come back, and everyone settled down and got what sleep they could.

The convoy wound down a long hill onto a broad plain late the following afternoon. This usually lush green oasis with its fields of crimson poppies was barren because winter was coming. The Bearer Boys had finally reached Ghardimaou, in northwest Tunisia, and they were now about 120 miles from Tunis. They set up their pup tents in a large grove not too far from the rail line that ran along the nearby Medjerda valley.

Strict blackout orders went into effect. Branches from olive trees were gathered up to camouflage their bivouac area. No one even dared to smoke; occasional rifle shots could be heard while the Bearer Boys tried to sleep. They were the angry firing of sentries enforcing the blackout order.

More rumors started up again the next morning. Word had it

that some of the regimental staff had taken off to report to the British in Beja, roughly another forty miles closer to Tunis. Something big was going down. Later that day—it was now just four days before Christmas—official word arrived.

The 18th Infantry was now attached to the British First Army and would operate under their 78th Division. More orders were coming and direct combat with the Germans was imminent.

Captain Murphy and the rifle company commanders were called to Colonel Greer's headquarters the following morning. Here they received their orders, then they returned to their respective company areas. Murphy, as was his custom, decided to first go over the order with Lieutenants Hobratschk and Butkiewicz.

"I don't like what we're being handed," Murphy started. "We're moving up to Medjez-el-Bab. That's about thirty-five miles southwest of Tunis. The attack we are going to be part of is going to jump off on the night of the 22nd. We'll be bypassing the 1st Battalion, which will be relieving the Coldstream Guards on what they call Longstop Hill. After they supposedly take it. The Guards just arrived from England, and they are just one battalion in strength so I'm worried they'll have enough troops to do the job. Longstop's actually six miles northeast of Medjez-el-Bab. All we were told about Longstop is it's a five-peaked rocky hill mass, about 900 feet high, and supposedly lightly defended. The Brits say maybe 300 Germans. Longstop is definitely key terrain. It dominates the main road towards Tebourba, and we heard on a clear day you could see the whole Medjerda Valley and most of the plain towards Tunis from the top of it.

"Our job is to seize a 750-foot hill the British call the Bou," Murphy continued. "The Bou is almost directly across a river opposite Longstop, about six miles from where we'll jump off. We'll establish an antitank position on the Bou, and together with Longstop Hill and having the Bou this will dominate the valley and control the road to Tebourba from both sides. That is supposing a Brit battalion of the Northamptonshire Regiment is successful in taking Djebel el Aroussia farther up on the other side of the river. Courtney Brown's 3rd Battalion will pass through us and seize Djebel el Guessa, another piece of high ground opposite el Aroussia on our side of the river. We will occupy these hills mainly to screen the advance of the Brit's tanks. Their tanks will need Longstop, the Bou, el Guessa and el Arouissa taken before they roll out and secure Tebourba.

"At Tebourba the Brit's 1st Guard Brigade and their 1st Parachute Brigade will join the tanks we set free and drive into Tunis and get all of the glory. Easy as that."

Captain Murphy then paused, which was his way of inviting questions.

"What's the timing of our attack?" Lieutenant Butkiewicz asked. "Do we attack simultaneously with the 1st Battalion, or wait until Longstop Hill is secured?"

"That's the part I don't like Ed," Murphy answered. "The Brits are calling the shots, and we have no idea yet as to exactly when they'll order us to jump off. I've been told it will be after Longstop is secured, which suggests it will be the morning of the 23rd."

"Probably means we won't know what our continuing mission will be," Lieutenant Hobratschk guessed. "Seems like we'll be held in reserve once the Brit tanks pass through, then depending on what they run into we'll hear what's next for us."

"That's another thing that bothers me Wally," Murphy grimaced. "The command and control is very unclear. We know we can always rely on Major Sternberg to get the best information he can, but there's a new player at 1st Battalion. Some Lieutenant Colonel Fricke took command. I remember he was a loading officer when we left Scotland. Rumor is he's a friend of General Allen's. Fine, but Bob York's a closer friend of ours, and someone we already know can work with Ben and coordinate our move. Wished Colonel Greer had made York battalion commander; suspect Fricke got shoved on him, though."

"I have another question," Hobratschk said. "With all these Arabic names for towns and djbels—what we call hills—where did the plain name Longstop come from?"

"It's actually Djebel el Ahmera to the locals but the Brits named it Longstop Hill," Captain Murphy answered. "Apparently they've been fighting to get it for weeks, thus it's been a long stop for them. Either that, or what one British officer offered. It's also supposedly some cricket term.

"Any other questions?"

There were none, even though Hobratschk and Butkiewicz were clearly baffled by the cricket reference, so Murphy closed the briefing with, "Ed. . .Wally, what I really don't like about this is the timing. Not because it's Christmas, but because the 1st Battalion is supposed to relieve the British up on Longstop at night. Around midnight to be exact. We don't do this, but the Brits apparently do. Our doctrine calls for a relief never to be performed at night because counterattacks could hit at first light before we could get reorganized, familiar with the surroundings, and ready for them. It's going to be a very difficult way for the 1st Battalion to meet the British for the first time. And, another thing. We have no intelligence on whether there's Germans on the Bou. Plus, it's wide open to air attack.

"OK, that's it for now. We move out tomorrow. And I don't want anything said to the men yet. Let's wait till we get to Medjez. Maybe the order will make more sense by then."

The move did go off the next day, but not until dusk and the regimental column was under strict black out orders when it rolled out of Ghardimaou. To the Bearer Boys riding in the back of their deuce and a half again, the move was far more frightening than any they had been on since landing in North Africa. An eerie near-full moon faintly lit up the hilly countryside. There was none of the usual rain that accompanied their every move, so the convoy was traveling at a speed far faster than usual. It was also cold. When the sun came up there was fear German planes would see them, and the throbbing of aircraft motors they soon heard was real; distant echoing of their winged-machineguns rattling at some targets was not imagined. Unfamiliar deep pumping sounds were also within ear shot. They were muffled pup-pup-pups of quick-firing British Bofors antiaircraft guns out there somewhere responding to the German threats in the sky.

The road became bumpier as the Bearer Boys got closer to Medjez; it was getting close to dark again. The convoy slowed down some and there was no mistaking more sightings of recent warfare. Bomb craters were on both sides of the road; when the dim low-hanging moonlight rose it cast a queer glow on British troop carriers and armored vehicles that were burnt up. Dead mules lay near them, their legs pointing stiffly upward.

The Bearer Boys could now hear the sounds of detonating shells as they echoed off the rock-combed hill ranges on both sides of the Medjerda Valley. They could also see rich green farmland light up when the shells exploded. Then the pale moonlight started to disappear, and the flashes of fire started revealing a thick, gloomy cloud cover. A storm was on the way, ahead of a front that was going to produce downpours for days, the likes of which the Bearer Boys hadn't experienced since their time back in Scotland.

The convoy kept going and the Bearer Boys soon felt the rumbling of their deuce and half as it crossed a bridge; the strange thing about that was seeing the truck's tires leave a splashy wake behind. They had crossed a partially submerged bridge, purposely built by British sappers to camouflage the crossing. British MP's wearing white gloves and steel helmets were guarding the bridge, and pointing where to go. The market town of Medjez-el-Bab lay just ahead. It wasn't long before the Bearer Boys smelled faint hints of rosemary and juniper while they looked at busted up tobacco stands as they passed through Medjez-el-Bab's rubble-strewn streets. Then they felt their truck mounting onto the narrow paved road on the outskirts of the village before they finally saw treed farmland near a big barn that was to be their bivouac area.

~TWENTY-FOUR~

ARTILLERY OBSERVERS ATOP LONGSTOP HILL had already spotted the 18th Infantry's movement through Medjez, so the Germans knew they were encamped on the farmland just to the east. The element of surprise, essential to the plan to take the hill, was gone. The Germans were already well prepared and were still putting the final touches on their defenses. Using pneumatic jackhammers, picks and spades, they were carving out more trenches on the backside of Longstop Hill, finishing what had been started by labor camp-enslaved Jews moved to the area weeks earlier. German forces could hide in these trenches when any preparatory artillery strikes were fired at them.

Once this fire lifted, the Germans planned to move to connecting trenches so they could flank their attackers and annihilate them. It was a tactic they used extensively during World War One, and it was not lost to their successors on Longstop Hill twenty-five years later. The British estimate of 300 Germans lying in wait was way off the mark. A couple of infantry companies and a platoon of engineers did occupy the hill, but other combat groups had recently arrived to reinforce them. One had three more infantry companies; another was an armored reconnaissance detachment from the storied 10th Panzer Division; a heavy tank battalion with 75mm self-propelled guns could also weigh in. Four hastily thrown together replacement units also lie in wait; they had recently arrived in Tunis and were now deployed near Longstop Hill. Three were infantry companies and one was a heavy weapons company with machineguns and mortars like the Bearer Boys' Company H.

Thus, the overall attack was doomed to failure before it began. And when it went off it became a disaster. When the final casualty counts for the 1st Battalion were confirmed by regiment it revealed 219 Americans were either killed, captured or missing—over a third of the battalion's strength. Irv Yarock's Company A was hit the hardest; he and his men were tasked with the relief of the Coldstream Guards and the company recorded 144 loses. They started the fight for Longstop Hill with 168 men.

Numerous errors were made by the British. When anyone on a reconnaissance mission before the attack looked at Longstop Hill what was seen was a long, low hog-backed hill mass. They failed to see a 260-meter high spur named Djebel el Rhar that was just behind Longstop Hill; it was separated from Longstop by a deep valley. This hill was not quite as high as Longstop, but it was certainly within a German machine gunner's eyesight range. The British missed both of these important features. It cost them; they suffered 178 casualties. German causalities were unknown, but their commander noted that Arabs took from the bodies of the dead anything they could get their hands on, even stripping them of their uniforms and underwear.

By noon on Christmas morning what was left of the battalion was gathered in a farm settlement southwest of Longstop where the dejected men shared rations together. Regiment was still standing by, waiting for orders that never came. It was later learned that, due to the heavy rains, General Eisenhower had called off the ambitious Allied plan he had forged to reach Tunis and Bizerte. Bob's 2nd Battalion had not been ordered to take the Bou but thankfulness for that turned to sorry when he heard about the 1st Battalion's casualties.

"We had Christmas music on our radio," a medic who treated some of the 1st Battalion's wounded told Major York a few days later. "I was able to tune into the German propaganda broadcast in Tunis.

They featured a girl who played our American songs. We called her 'Gertie from Bizertie' and she talked about the battle of Longstop Hill and even mentioned the names of some of the men who were captured. She said we were loosing the war and should give up."

Giving up was the last thing on Captain Murphy's mind after he and Sam Carter talked following a company captain's meeting at Colonel Greer's headquarters a few days later.

"What really happened up there on Longstop, Sam?" Murphy started when he took Carter, the D Company commander, aside after the briefing. The two had known each other since they served together in D Company back at Ft. Devens in 1940. Sam Carter was not one to hold back when it came to expressing himself.

"It was pitiful, Murph," he said with still simmering anger. "None of us were ever briefed on the overall plan. The maps we got were awful. We had no idea as to what part of the hill we were to take, or just where it was the British would screen us."

"Did Major York at least get a briefing before the attack?" Murphy questioned.

"No way. He was given no plans to work with, but he did his best to give us company commanders some direction.

"We never got a chance to study the terrain in advance, even with binoculars from any outpost," Carter went on." The attack really needed a full day of planning. I know Colonel Greer would have never approved the attack had he really known how our battalion was going to be used. We should never have been moved up to relieve the Guards until they had accomplished their basic mission. They hadn't.

"Dammit, Murph," Carter said in a now raised voice. "The British commander Stewart-Brown came, he saw, but he did not conquer Longstop Hill."

"How did Archie make out?" Murphy asked. He was the "just give me the facts" type. Archie Cameron was the B Company commander.

"Archie lost about fifty men. Herb Scott-Smith, our C Company commander, was supposed to keep his men in reserve, but some of them got antsy and tried to help us. I know he lost at least an officer, a non-com and about a half dozen enlisted men. I suffered some losses too, Murph."

"What happened, Sam?"

"I lost a squad that was trying to set up their mortar," Carter answered. "Then I almost lost my own command group. The Germans walked in on us. They had one of my captured men in front of them, and the apparent commander of the Krauts had his pistol in the middle of my man's back. Ordered us to surrender, but I gave my corporal—the one with the pistol in his back—an order in English to duck and we killed that damn German commander and instead made his entire patrol prisoners.

"But back to C Company's story," Carter shifted. "Some Guards showed up where Lieutenant van Wagoner was, said they wanted to help but they first had to have their tea! Clem told me he was coming off the hill later and found our battalion commander, Colonel Fricke, behind a boulder shaving. Said he wanted to look presentable when he saw Colonel Greer. Claimed that the Germans had wasted a lot of ammo shooting at him."

"Where was Fricke when Irv Yarock's company got wiped out?" Murphy asked, again looking for the facts.

"Don't know for sure, but rumor has it Fricke actually was pinned down by machinegun fire."

"I can only imagine Irv trying to reach Fricke on his radio to get some help, only to receive silence instead," Murphy offered while he stared off into nowhere. "And Irv's a Jew, at best not dead or maybe even worse off. A prisoner of the Germans."

"Colonel Greer said he didn't even know about A Company's fate until much later that afternoon when a German prisoner told him what had happened," Carter said to Murphy before he, too, looked away.

When Captain Murphy got back to the H Company bivouac he found Lt. Hobratschk in a pensive mood.

"What's the matter Wally?" he asked. "You don't look yourself."

"I'm fine Captain. Well, maybe I'm feeling a little guilty about being able to feed our men fresh meat and vegetable stew for Christmas while the 1st Battalion was getting all shot up. How'd the meeting go at regiment?"

"It was pretty grim, but I am certain we're going to learn something out of this, like how the Germans should be fought with," Murphy answered, then gritted and added, "Or maybe how the British should be fought with."

Then Murphy said, "OK, it isn't official yet, but it looks like we're going on outpost duty again. We're going to relieve an armored infantry battalion outside of Medjez and take up their defensive sector just in time to celebrate the new year. And we're going to be reporting to the British 6th Armoured Division."

Hobratschk just grunted.

"Here, I need you to see something," Murphy added. "At the meeting we had with Colonel Greer we company captains had to go down our rosters and check off names so they could be transferred over to the 1st Battalion. I couldn't cherry pick the list. It was a random thing. Here's the results."

Lieutenant Hobratschk went down the list then said, "I'm glad we're keeping Baummer. He's the most popular man in the mortar platoon now. His grandmother sent him two big boxes of Peter Paul Mounds candy bars for Christmas, and he passed them around to everybody. Told me to give one to you, too. Here you go. Merry Christmas."

"Well, next time I see him I'll have to thank him," Murphy chuckled as he pulled the wrapper off the bar and bit into it.

Captain Murphy had already thanked Bob. As luck would have it, none of the Bearer Boys, nor Slugger, Gentle John or Sergeant Horn were transferred out.

~TWENTY-FIVE~

VIOLA HAD NO WAY OF knowing about the total disaster up on Longstop Hill that December. Christmas for her was very low-keyed. Sonny wasn't able to get home because he had to work and could only get Christmas Day off. But Viola did share the morning on Oak Street with her sisters before spending time that afternoon over on Trobridge Place with Nellie and Henry, along with their daughter's and son-in-law's twins.

Viola and Sonny talked every Sunday after the new year and they did the best they could to cheer each other up. Bob hadn't written to his mother, although Sonny did mention he'd sent a couple of letters to him.

Viola wasn't much of a letter writer. She knew how important it was for Bob to hear from her, but she had grown so worried about him that she was afraid her letters would do little to cheer him up. She wrote irregularly, usually once a month. Oddly, it was Bob who was doing his best to cheer her up whenever he got time to write, and it was of course big news anytime anyone got a letter from him.

When Nellie received a V-Mail letter from Bob thanking her for the Peter Paul Mounds for Christmas, she called Viola the minute she got home from work and then came over to see her.

Viola cried after she read her son's letter.

January 26, 1943
Dear Gram,
Received your big package OK and I want to thank you very

224

much for it. I am sorry for not writing sooner but I am in quite a "hot spot" but I don't mind it much cause you get used to it after a while.

I am getting along alright and I hope that you are too, and I shall be looking forward to seeing you when and if I return. Received some letters from Sonny, and I can see that he is doing all right as usual, but he still seems to be having the same old women trouble no matter where he goes!

I am getting to see most of the world, which includes London, Glasgow Scotland, and now North Africa. Where I go from here God only knows, but maybe the next stop will be the good old U.S.A. I hope.

Give my love to Reina, Gramp, the twins Harold and Jackie, and of course Mom when you see her.

All my love,

Bob

"*If* I return. . ."

This was the hardest thing any mother had to endure; it was far worse than simply wondering when he would come home.

One thing Bob was not getting used to that January were the new British rations. While the Brit's jam tasted really good on their hard biscuits, the ration's canned meat, kidney pudding and oxtail stew were all bland. Too much salt had also been added, leaving him constantly thirsty.

And Bob was certainly trying to keep Nellie and his mother from worrying by saying that while he was in a "hot spot" he got used to it. The mission he was part of was to hold the area around Medjez-el-Bab so another try for Tunis and Bizerte could go off when spring came. But he had been living that January in a covered hole trying to stay dry during the rainy Tunisian winter. Some days there were high winds and thunderstorms; some nights brought violent hailstorms. He always slept in his wool uniform to stay warm; he seldom even took his boots off.

Staying clean was a real challenge. His washcloth was always full of mildew. His one towel was smelly; it never dried. He used his helmet as a cold water wash basin when he could, and it was a real treat when he was able to get a little gasoline in a ration can and start a fire to heat water up for himself and the other Bearer Boys so they could at least shave.

The Bearer Boys were actually lucky in one way; they had what was regarded during outpost duty that month as a sign of wealth—toilet paper. As a medic who treated some of their fellow soldiers noted, "You either got used to this life, or one of two things would happen. You could go into a nervous state and be sent back to a hospital, or you could take an extreme measure and shoot yourself."

At the start of the new year Bob's 2nd Battalion relieved a British unit eight miles southeast of Medjez-el-Bab, just like Captain Murphy told Lieutenant Hobratschk they would. The companies took over the trenches and foxholes the Brits had previously dug into a horseshoe-shaped stand of trees that overlooked a curved intersection with three legs that either went up to Massicoultt, down to Goubellat and over to Medjez; it was dubbed Peter's Corner. The crescent ridge out in front of the Bearer Boys' bivouac area—it came to be called Banana Ridge—afforded direct observation on Peter's Corner, and therefore the intersection and low foothills around it became focal points to be watched over.

Then, just as Bob had said in his last letter, things really started to heat up. During the second week of January, the Luftwaffe began what was to become a daily mid-afternoon routine of bombing the area from Banana Ridge, all the way up to Medjez-el-Bab.

It was the first time the Bearer Boys endured sustain attacks from the air. The strikes were first warned by the terrifying distant drones of multiple Stuka engines, then after they closed in at 250 mph the formation would break up and each plane would nose downward at a target somewhere. When they dove their sirens grew louder and would be howling by the time the German pilots pulled up and banked away, leaving smoke, dust and destruction wherever they dropped their 500 pound bombs. The Bearer Boys were lucky; none of these bombs hit in their immediate area.

But at noon on the 11th columns of smoke rose all over Banana Ridge when twelve heavier German bombers—twin engine JU-88s—hit the 2nd Battalion area. The black planes were just 500 feet off the deck when they dropped their bombs, and while there were casualties in the rifle companies the Bearer Boys lucked out again.

It rained the next couple of days and the German bombing thankfully let up. Nights were pitch black; there were no moon or stars to look at. On the 15th there wasn't even enemy activity in the Bearer Boys' area. The Germans began evidencing more interest in Medjez-el-Bab. Heavy artillery shelling hit here, and Bob sometimes even heard distant dull thuds when the German shells exploded.

Major Sternberg used the following week to send out patrols most every night, but they were not full platoons; they were usually just seven to twelve men. There was an olive grove about a mile and a half to the northeast of Peter's Corner, and one night Sternberg wanted to be sure no Germans were assembled in it. The Bearer Boys had been ordered to register their mortar on this olive grove, and they were prepared to lay heavy white phosphorous rounds on it if they got the request, but it never came. No suspicious sounds were heard, and as the patrol made ever-widening sweeps of the area the men inspected rock outcroppings and even cactus patches; there were no signs of Germans. But one lone farmhouse, surrounded by a stone wall that also enclosed storage sheds and a barn, was left unsearched; it was a mere couple of hundred yards outside of the barbed-wire fence that protected the battalion area from insurgents, but whoever lived there seemed to be quite at peace with the war going on around them.

The Bearer Boys got to take their first shower since mid-December a few days later. It wasn't a hot shower; it was a cold, portable shower they used. The Brits had provided it so everyone could be checked for lice while their clothes went through a steam delousing unit. All came up clean except Slugger; he struck out again and had to be shaven from his head downward to his feet. A medic daubed him with ointment, and as if this wasn't bad enough, when it came time to get dressed he had to put on British underwear and one of their uniforms, giving him the instant new nickname of "Sir Slugger."

But it wasn't all grins when Bob and the rest of the Bearer Boys put their own uniforms back on. A lot of the grease had disappeared from their field jacket's collars, armpits and cuffs, but being made of wool their jackets and pants had shrunk to the point where they barely fit.

Bob still managed to slip his new I.D. card into his wallet; he was pleased that he still weighed in at 150 pounds, considering how little he was eating. It showed his rank—now PFC—and noted the scar on the third finger of his right hand that he got when it was stepped on while he was going down the net off the ship way back when he participated in amphibious training off stormy Cape Henry two years earlier.

It was fairly quiet on Banana Ridge during the last week in January. Patrols went out every day and returned safely. Gas was in short supply, and the British had ordered the regiment to minimize the use of any fuel; pirating a can of gas to boil water and heat rations had to stop. A feeling of "hurry up and wait" settled in. What the British called the "Bubble and Squeak" raid happened a few days later; its purpose was to determine if the wet Goubellat Plain could bear the weight of their tanks. Eighteen ventured out. It went poorly; more than half bellied down in the soupy mud, and their crews had to abandon them. German artillery found these hapless tanks, and the ones their big shells didn't get were blown up by Royal Engineers that night.

It was relatively quiet when February arrived, but that didn't last. Captain Murphy's telephone rang just before dawn on the 3rd; he immediately recognized that it was his reconnaissance sergeant, Leo Hennessey, on the line.

"I'm up here at the outpost, Captain, "Hennessey started. "That farm out there past the barbed wire, you know the one. I just saw at least a half dozen armed men going into it."

"Did you have enough light to tell if they were Germans?" Murphy quickly questioned.

"I had some dim light, Captain, but I couldn't tell for sure."

"Alright, here's what I want you to do Leo," Murphy announced. "First, keep the farm under observation. Two, notify the machine-gun platoon that's up there with you. I'll get back to you."

And with this Captain Murphy crawled out of his bedroll and called battalion operations. Major Sternberg was on the line a few moments later.

"Do we have any patrols down by that farm?" Murphy asked before he gave Sternberg a brief rundown of what Sergeant Hennessey had told him.

"No, but it sure sounds like we need a patrol out there now," the battalion commander answered. "I'll get E Company to bring in whosoever out there. Can you have a mortar section ready to lay some heavy explosive on that barn if we need it Murph?"

"I'm almost certain Wally's ready for that but I'll check," Murphy answered.

With this plan in place Captain Murphy called Lieutenant Hobratschk and he assured him that he indeed had a section ready to go.

"They are up in the trench on the backside of Hennessey's OP right now, Captain."

"Good. Wally, have them get ready to lay heavy explosive with delayed fuse down on the barn in that farmstead over the ridge.

Captain Randall's going to send a patrol down there. Have your other sections ready to render normal support. Hennessey said he saw about a half dozen what must be Germans going into the barn, but if there's more out there we'll want to shake up their morning."

The Bearer Boys, Slugger and Gentle John were all in their trench behind Hennessey's OP, just as Lieutenant Hobratschk had said. They had been there since midnight. When Hobratschk radioed Sergeant Horn with the alert, it only took a few minutes for Slugger to get their mortar registered on the barn and the heavy explosive shells were already stacked up and ready to go.

Twenty minutes passed. Then E Company's Captain Randall called Murphy and told him, "I've got a patrol ready to cross the wire in ten minutes. What do you think, Murph? Can you hit the barn? I'm sure Germans are holed up there."

"We sure can."

"Can we get some covering smoke? It's broad daylight out there now," Randall pointed out.

"The only smoke we have is white phosphorous, but I think it's a little too dangerous for this situation, Carl."

"Alright. We're going to open the wire and pass through in two minutes."

A minute later Gentle John laid a mortar in the tube and Slugger fired the first round. Seconds later Captain Murphy was watching the barn through his field glasses and he saw tiles on its ridge pole fly off. The round was perfect. It even set off something inside the barn that caused tiles to burst skyward on the far side of the roof.

"Two more for good measure," Murphy ordered, and Lieutenant Hobratschk relayed this to Sergeant Horn.

The next two rounds finished off what was left of the roof. By this time Captain Randall's patrol had reached the gate that went into the farmstead; his men were greeted by a warrant officer commanding the German patrol who came out of the barn with his hands up and surrendered.

The German told his captors that half of his men were killed; others were wounded. And in perfect English added, "You took the fight out of the rest of us."

It seemed the Americans had taken the fight out of far more Germans, for it became quiet all across Banana Ridge through the rest of the week. Patrols went out, but came back with no reports of finding any more of their opposite numbers.

On the night of February 13th the regiment was finally relieved after spending forty-eight straight days in the line. A convoy loaded with the 1st and 3rd Battalions started heading for an olive grove in Teboursouk. The Bearer Boys had to wait another day before their 2nd Battalion departed for Beja.

The Bearer Boys' respite was well deserved, and they were of course looking forward to it. Despite the burnt out wrecks they saw on their way to Beja, they had heard it still had great places to discover, and if they were real lucky they might even get to swim in warm bath waters and write some letters to the folks back home.

But two days later, before they even had a chance to wash the mud off their grimy bodies, a sudden order came down to move out again. Word had it that Field Marshall Erwin Rommel's Afrika Korps was pounding the hell out of the thinly-held Allied line in central Tunisia at the Kasserine Pass. The Bearer Boys were now going to move by truck yet again and help stop Rommel's ferocious tanks from breaking through another pass located to the south of an Arab town called Sbiba.

~TWENTY-SIX~

BY NOW THERE WERE TWO things Bob really didn't like about Army life. He was growing to hate the cold, and after experiencing the haunting dive bombing on Banana Ridge he dreaded being attacked again by German bombers. He got a lot of the first on his way to Sbiba. Bob and the other Bearer Boys didn't even talk much as they loaded up for the trip; they were packed into the back bed of their open deuce and a half, and by the time they pounded through Siliana they were shivering and their feet ached. It was an unusually bright, clear night. The African moon was casting dim shadows over the surrounding landscape. In the half darkness Bob could see Djebel Serj and even make out the gap between its two peaks. When he went over the heights of the ancient Roman city of Maktar he saw mysterious rolling fields in the valleys all around him.

Then, as the convoy got closer to Sbiba the road became flatter and the surroundings more barren. Gone were the green grasslands of northern Tunisia. Instead, there were rolling sand dunes, ghostly shadows of hundreds of shoulder-high "elephant ear" cactus patches and other spiky plants growing amongst olive trees and crumbling stone walls. All were visible on both sides of the road.

Once Bob got through Sbiba's uneven streets and past its ramshackle dwellings with painted wooden doors, off to the west he could see a mountain range that looked like it rose up over a thousand feet. The white-peaked Eastern Dorsal Mountains were even visible further in the distance to the east. There was more light now but the wind had picked up, bringing with it new rushes of cold air.

Then clouds of dust sprouted up ahead of the regiment's convoy. Suddenly there was competition for the roadway and the truck Bob was riding in had to pull off to the right and stop. But the sounds of other motors grew louder, and soon it became clearer about just what was happening. Battered American tanks, trucks, even Harley-Davidson motorcycles, were all going in the opposite direction. The soldiers Bob could make out looked exhausted and demoralized. After his truck got moving again, on the east side of the valley Bob spotted a sloping hill that rose up gently to about a hundred feet. To the west he could now make out another mountain crest; the sunlight was hitting it. It looked like the valley ended here, for the slopes of the mountain faded to lower and flatter foothills on the valley floor.

But his 2nd Battalion was not going to occupy either of the higher ground locations. Instead, the 18th's trucks dropped all of the companies off about five miles south of Sbiba; the open ground to the south seemed to stretch on for another mile or so, but this was the end of the journey for Bob. He and the other Bearer Boys were suddenly in the open, in the mouth of the valley, dead in the center of the avenue of attack where Rommel's tanks were expected to probe for openings and attempt their breakthrough.

Major Sternberg placed Captain Russ Spinney's F Company rightmost on the line the battalion would be defending; Spinney's flank was anchored on a small knoll just to the west of the road. Carl Randall's E Company was on the other side of the roadway. G Company provided some depth; these men were dug in as a reserve force about a hundred yards behind Randall's men.

Captain Murphy faced a real challenge; he had to place his two heavy machine gun platoons in positions to cover the battalion's entire line, and he lucked out. "The defense at Sbiba was as near to textbook as I can remember seeing during the entire war," he later noted. "Each machinegun platoon supported the rifle companies with interlocking final protective lines which extended clear across the battalion front. Each gun, when laid on the line, was able to fire at the maximum range at which the trajectory of a bullet would not rise higher than a standing man's head."

Said another way, any German who might venture within range of one of H Company's .50-caliber machine guns was a dead man. Murphy set up his command post with Major Sternberg behind Spinney's F Company, and it was then decided that the Bearer Boys' mortar platoon would emplace their tubes about a hundred yards behind Spinney's men. After each section laid their mortar in Lieutenant Hobratschk ordered the men to register their tubes to cover both of the line companies. Their main mission was to lay fire on any Germans within range who accompanied Rommel's tanks, or others that might venture past the barbed-wire concertina into the mine field that was being put in place out in front of the rifle companies.

The Bearer Boys' mortar was set up in a trench they dug close to the road; their shells were stacked under the thick branches of the elephant ears in a close-by cactus patch. Foxholes were dug out nearby, under other cacti. Their position faced directly south, and beyond clusters of esparto grass they could now make out the Meftah Ridge about a mile away; two peaks to either side channeled the roadway. It was here they expected Erwin Rommel's attack to start from.

The only immediate anti-tank protection the Bearer Boys had was a battery of British 17-pounders. But to complete the regiment's defensive position, Colonel Greer put one of his battalions close to the flat rise on the left side of the mile-wide line; another would defend the right side. A battalion of the Grenadier Guards and another of the Coldstream Guards were on the high ground along the base of the tall mountainside to the Bearer Boys' right. Other infantry battalions from an American division were up on the low hill to their left. Four battalions of artillery had their trails on the ground on both hillsides, lying in wait for Rommel's infamous Panzers.

When Greer was questioned by one of his staff officers about holding the line in the valley the British were giving to them his answer was direct. "There will be no additional support, and the regiment will hold," Greer bellowed. "By God we will. We must!"

When word of this trickled down to the Bearer Boys they heard for the first time since landing in North Africa words to the effect that the Sbiba Pass had to held "at all costs."

Unknown to anyone on the Allied side, Rommel was probing the Sbiba Pass to determine if he could break through here and drive to Le Kef, seventy-miles northward. Le Kef was at the junction of one of the British First Army's main supply routes. If Le Kef fell into Rommel's hands, the First Army's position in all of North Africa would be threatened.

The Desert Fox did not keep anyone waiting. A thick mist early the next morning provided cover when a column of his tanks, led by a previously captured American Sherman, stopped at the minefield the British had laid down in front of Meftah Ridge. German engineers quickly started clearing a lane so the Panzers could pass through; they were successful at this before the mist lifted. But when it did the Bearer Boys witnessed their own artillery greeting the Germans with thundering salvos that temporarily stopped Rommel's tanks.

The Desert Fox was at an outpost where he was observing the attack; he wasted little time deciding what to do next. Rommel, it would be learned later, was personally overseeing the attack being made by Generalmajor Hans-Georg Hildebrandt's 21st Panzer Division. But it was Rommel, knowing the misty weather and poor visibility would deprive him of air support, who ordered an all-out concentrated thrust be immediately renewed; it came at mid-morning and Hildebrandt's Panzers again attacked though the gap made in the minefield off Meftah Ridge. Allied artillery was not as effective in stopping them this time. As Colonel Greer suddenly saw it, "the German tanks appeared like they intended to probe here and there, looking to penetrate into our line."

Greer was right. At 11:30 a company of German engineers was spotted leaving their armored carriers right in front of the Bearer Boys' 2nd Battalion barbed-wire protective barrier; it was clear the Germans' intentions were to enter the minefield that had been laid in and sweep out a path for their Panzers to bust through. Hildebrandt's Panzers were indeed behind their engineers when everything Greer had at his disposal let go. Artillery shells rained down. The Bearer Boys fired their mortars at the Germans who had ventured into their regiment's minefield, or away from their carriers; the company's heavy machineguns also took direct aim at the German engineers, and their opposite numbers were again slowed down.

But Hildebrandt quickly spread his tanks out so they could probe for a weaker spot along the regiment's wide line in the valley. It now became evident to Colonel Greer that the German commander's plan was not to force an opening in places where his tanks and ground forces drew fire; rather it looked pretty certain that Hildebrandt was going to use them as decoys while he kept probing for supposed weaker spots in the Allied line.

Colonel Greer was right again; by noontime semi-circles of German tank groups started popping up everywhere. Ten were seen a half hour later coming towards the Guards brigade's position in the hill to Greer's right. "Shells whined, hissed and exploded around us," one of the British soldiers remembered. "Bullets whispered over our heads from both directions. From behind us, American 'Long Toms' opened up with seven-inch shells. They adjusted their range and along with our guns soon several Panzers were on fire."

With no breakthrough here Hildebrandt tried the American line again. From his outpost Greer saw six tanks out in front of Captain Cliff Raymer's K Company at two-thirty that afternoon, advancing and firing at point blank range; fifteen minutes later another dozen tanks approached closer to the Bearer Boys' 2nd Battalion line. This time more of the Brit's 17-pounders and Frank Colaccio's

Cannon Company engaged the Panzers, and they were stopped again. Then at three, seven more of Hildebrandt's Panzers were spotted emerging out of a hidden labyrinth of wadis and starting to advance directly towards Company F, right in front of the Bearer Boys. Their mortars joined the loud chorus of ringing artillery fire; one of the British seventeen-pound guns got two of the Panzers this time. The Bearer Boys' mortars killed some of the German Panzer grenadiers who were fighting alongside their tanks. Hildebrandt was stopped again.

But the German commander still wasn't ready to give up. At four-thirty Colonel Greer saw another thirty of his Panzers coming down the valley and eventually stopping six-hundred yards in front of the 1st Battalion. The minefield halted the first two tanks, then as others tried to bypass these wrecks, Greer's supporting artillery started to shower them once more.

The Bearer Boys' mortar tube had turned red hot by now. Mortar after mortar was being shoved into the tube by Gentle John as Bob and the other Bearer Boys kept Slugger constantly supplied with shells. They weren't a bit worn down. Adrenalin and knowing they were stopping the German onslaught provided all the motivation they needed to keep doing their part.

And they succeeded at this; later that afternoon Hildebrandt called it a day.

Colonel Greer ordered patrols out just after dark to finish off the remaining German tanks before their crews could recover them; a few had been able to start withdrawing back towards Meftah Ridge, but before the rest could get away the Americans knocked out at least two more with their bazooka guns. Captain Spinney's F Company men managed to set three other Panzers on fire that night. A total of seven were destroyed before midnight, and then Greer used the rest of the night profitably by ordering more mines and barbed wire be laid in, fully expecting the 21st Panzer Division would again try in the morning to break through the regiment's line.

Fog and rain hung over the valley floor again at first light, but no one doubted Hildebrandt's tanks would soon appear. When they came just after eight-thirty he first struck the British battalions with thirty-three Mark III's and six Mark IV's, supported by 1,200 Panzer grenadiers and a battery of artillery. Colonel Greer deduced that the Germans now intended to avoid the strong resistance evidenced the day before by his 18th Infantry, and instead make wide sweeps around the regiment's flanks, permitting their Panzers to take the ridges to either side of the valley, then cut the road behind the 18th's positions, effectively encircling them.

But it was another bad day for the 21st Panzers. When Hildebrandt's tanks and Panzer grenadiers got within small arms and mortar range of the Brit's position the Guards brigade let them have it. Allied artillery fire also weighed in and quickly stopped the attack on this side of the valley.

Another group of Panzers tried to break through on the other side of the pass, but four were quickly disabled by the anti-tank weapons of the American division defending this side of the Allied line. Hildebrandt then appeared to hesitate, but late in the afternoon another group of his Panzers made a third try for a breakthrough by veering off into the 1st Battalion's lines, only to suffer the same fate again. The Bearer Boys even had some fun with the Germans; their mortar section joined the others in H Company and mauled Hildebrandt's Panzer grenadiers; a later count cited Hildebrandt suffered close to one hundred casualties here. Some were killed by a reinforced combat patrol Bob York sent out. Eight more German tanks fell victim to Allied artillery fire, and no fewer than thirty other armored vehicles—personnel carriers and weapons carriers—were also destroyed.

By dusk the open plain to the south of the Bearer Boys was quiet again. That night they shared high-fives as they watched thick, black smoke rising from the charred wreckage of even more German Panzers out past the minefield.

Little movement could be seen up on Meftah Ridge the next morning. A few small groups of Panzer grenadiers probed the Allied lines again, but none of Hildebrandt's tanks followed them. Suspecting the Germans may have withdrawn, General Charles Keightly, the British commander, decided to send a reconnaissance in force up onto the ridge to better determine what Hildebrandt was up to.

Seven brand new Churchill tanks with infantry mounted on their decks started out later in the day from the Coldstream Guards position on the west side of the valley. A smoke screen was laid down to cover the move. The Bearer Boys watched in awe; the tanks were less than a mile from them. It was a wonderful sight at first, but after the smoke screen lifted things quickly went bad. White streaks of light burst from German anti-tank guns. Then machinegun fire forced the British Tommies to abandon their tanks. But the Churchills kept rattling towards the top of the ridge and the Bearer Boys soon saw they were silhouetted against the sky line. One of the Churchills quickly fell victim to what must have been more anti-tank guns, then flame up; two others were knocked out by German 88s. The rest left to avoid being ambushed.

Another troop of Churchills came up to the ridge from the British left flank a few minutes later. The Bearer Boys could see that this group was also in trouble. One of their Churchills was hit by German anti-tank guns, sending a thick column of swirling black smoke into the sky. Two more were set on fire in quick succession. No one could come to the aid of the wounded because the blazing on the ridge became so fierce. But the remainder of the Churchills in this group were able to get back behind the Allied lines where their crews were served whisky, as one Tommie put it, "because no one actually expected us to come back from our suicide mission."

Rommel also may have thought further tries to break through

the Sbiba Pass would be suicide for German forces. By the time the Churchills got back to their lines he had already weighed in; he knew he had been denied the pass. Rommel actually halted Hildebrandt's operations and ordered him to send his reconnaissance battalion to Kasserine. Rommel felt his better opportunity was to exploit the gains his forces had already made back in the Kasserine Pass, push ahead from here, then eventually encircle the stubborn forces that had just rebuffed his 21st Panzer Division.

Rommel planned to do this by attacking from Thala northeastward to Rouhia, and then drive back southward towards Sbiba. General Keightly, however, was determined to outwit the Desert Fox. He planned to trap Rommel's advancing armor at Thala and not even allow him to reach Rouhia—never mind Sbiba.

For the Bearer Boys this meant another move. Orders came down on the 22nd of February—George Washington's Birthday—to pack up. Right after dark, Colonel Greer ordered a massive artillery barrage on Meftah Ridge—what he later admitted was three week's worth of shells—to cover the regiment's withdrawal. The Bearer Boys then moved by truck the twelve miles it was to stop Rommel at Rouhia—if he even got this far.

They couldn't imagine that the new line the regiment was establishing would be any more inhospitable than the one they had just left, but it was. Gone was the softer sand; small rocks and gravel were instead what they had to first move with their shovels so they could dig their foxholes and a trench for their mortar. The Bearer Boys were again in the open, while their British friends took up safer positions in the mountain heights on both sides of the valley. But minefields were again laid in to their front; barbed wire was strung up. The Bearer Boys were ready.

Amazingly, no Germans appeared where they were because Rommel got pinned down at Thala. Allied artillery had stopped him from moving. Overextended, and with supplies dwindling, the Desert Fox finally accepted that he was beat. He had done plenty of damage to the American forces in the Kasserine Pass, but to the shock of many Rommel simply retreated from Thala, and left Rouhia unchallenged.

Thus the Bearer Boys went back to the valley south of Sbiba on the 25th of February, and this time they got to set up their tents next to a beautiful rocky stream in the hills to the east; going for a swim was the first thing they did. Unknown to any of them, the *New York Times* headline that same Thursday proclaimed: ROMMEL REELS BACK, POUNDED BY PLANES, ARMOR SHATTERED, FOE MAKES FOR COAST.

Praise for their part in making this headline reached into the ranks of the 18th Infantry. It came from British Commander Keightly. His message read in part, "The enemy tried to find the weak place in our defences to push his main force through. The fact that he didn't do it at Sbiba is a high tribute to the efficiency and fighting ability of you all."

"The successful stand against a major enemy offensive at Sbiba witnessed the growth of our boys into men," Colonel Greer justifiably claimed. It had come at a fairly low cost. While ten of the regiment's men were killed, just three had suffered serious wounds; twenty-one others had only been slightly wounded.

~TWENTY-SEVEN~

BOB RECEIVED HEARTENING NEWS IN early March when orders came down from General Terry Allen directing his regiment to rejoin the First Division in Bou Chebka, a forested area about eighty miles southwest of Sbiba. Bob certainly grew into a man while he was under British command, but next to going back to the States being reunited the rest of the men he had come overseas with was as good as it could now get. He felt great pride in his 18th Infantry, and he just knew that if the Germans tried to hit them again this time they would have to face the full fury of what he understandably felt was the best division in the U.S. Army.

Bob had now been in North Africa for going on five months, and he found it somewhat interesting that actual combat had consumed what seemed to be a fraction of his time. Nevertheless, Bob had grown to hate the Germans, and had no qualms about killing them. It fascinated him to realize that he now saw war as an absolute necessity, that what it was really all about was preserving the American way of life. He didn't feel at all like he was just fighting England's war, or that what he was doing was only about freeing North Africa, or maybe even mainland Europe some day from Nazism.

Even though the good old USA was far from Germany, Bob had seen enough of Hitler's war machine to believe that it could only be stopped by destroying it. He vowed to keep doing his part, and he even knew that what he had experienced and was still expecting to do was something he would be proud of for the rest of his life.

The friendships being forged with his fellow Bearer Boys meant a lot to Bob. Sure, they kidded each other unmercifully, but it was all in good fun and an important way to make the hardships of war easier for them to bear.

And they vowed to keep those friendships going when—not if—they got back to the States.

Slugger was from a town like Bob's in Connecticut and they had both talked a lot about their upbringings. Slugger grew up in New Britain, which was only about an hour's drive from Naugatuck. One plant in Slugger's hometown had made the fuse head for mortars during World War One, and he'd bragged that was why their current mortars were so good. Another factory was now making mess kits and canteens; Slugger swore the ones they were using in the field came from New Britain.

They had grown close enough to talk about their families back home, even what it was like growing up in Connecticut. Bob confessed how he'd ended up at the Connecticut Junior Republic after shooting out a streetlamp with his BB gun when he was just fifteen years old; he even told Slugger about how his father had committed suicide while he was there, and that his mother was living alone and working six days a week at the rubber factory back in Naugatuck. He bragged about his older brother, and how he was working in a different synthetic rubber plant in West Virginia that was doing its part to keep the Army moving, but that Sonny was expecting he'd eventually be drafted.

It amazed Slugger that Bob could be so outgoing and free-spirited, more happy-go-lucky than anyone he'd ever met before, considering how rough life had been for him growing up.

But now there was a mutual dependence on one another that only those who have fought in a war together could understand. To Slugger Bob was the glue that kept the ammo bearers working together. He was strong, agile, intelligent and unstoppable; his wisecracks spurred everyone on. Bob had grown to admire Slugger's skill in firing their mortar, how he handled it with ease and precision. He had watched him while they were defending the Sbiba Pass. There was an all-in, steady way about Slugger; nothing fazed him. He was very cool under pressure.

The move to Bou Chebka covered two days. Engineers had gone out ahead of their convoy to sweep the roads that took the Bearer Boys there from mines Rommel left behind. The weather again was what it always seemed to be when the 18th Infantry moved; it was an all night affair and it rained pretty hard.

Some roads were rough; they were particularly muddy as they traveled through wooded areas. In other places they were steep, and the going was bumpy and slow. But when daylight came, there was sunshine. The roads dried out, and when they arrived in the beautiful forest of fir trees in Morsott on the plateau of Bou Chebka all Bob and Slugger could think about was getting more rest and something better to eat than their British rations.

Their stay at Bou Chebka consumed ten quick-passing days. Bob spent the time mostly resting, but there were inspections and some tough training, mainly to allow the replacements that had shown up to integrate into their units. General Allen handed out awards and medals one day when there was a parade; it was he who announced the arrival of their new II Corps commander, General George Patton, to them.

But by the time Patton formally visited the 18th Infantry he was already disliked. A well-sourced rumor had gotten around about the new commander's first visit to Terry Allen's command post in his tent-filled oasis. The story went something like this: Patton was staring at the slit trenches Allen and General Roosevelt would have used if the Germans hit their CP from the air. It was a valid concern. Stuka bombers had been coming into the area late in the afternoon every day since the First Division's arrival; at night they dropped flares, lighting up the area. But this did not concern General Patton. Others present had him mumbling something about the trenches being cowardly retreats before he asked

General Allen which one was his. When given the answer, Patton supposedly urinated into the First Division commander's trench, and then yelled to him, "Now try to use it."

The rumor proved to be true. It was Patton's odd way of sharing his friendship with Terry Allen.

The new corps commander had also decided that other troops he had seen lacked discipline, and Patton had taken steps to change that by instituting fines to any soldier or officer who failed to wear a necktie, his leggings and especially his helmet. The fines were a steep $25—half a month's enlisted man's pay—and they were usually administered by Patton's military police. The Bearer Boys, now hardened combat veterans who had stood up to Rommel, thought this policy was nothing more than nit-picking chicken-shit.

It didn't take long before everyone was calling Patton "Gorgeous Georgie" to his back and joking that the fine system was a silly "$25 Derby." The wool hats the Bearer Boys still wore would even be confiscated if anyone was caught with them on, but they managed to dodge Patton and his MP's on this one. The only one who suffered was Slugger; he lost his "Sir" title. He had to surrender his British uniform that he was given back when he got the lice treatment a couple of months earlier; Patton's supply people had thoughtfully ordered new clothes for him, but they were a tight fit.

Bob teased him about this; he told Slugger he looked like he was going out on a date, but she'd have to pay because he couldn't even get his hands into his pockets to get his money out, although his new pants had a nice crease in them.

Others found the new commander a bit harder to take than Slugger did with Bob's wisecracking. Word spread like wildfire after Patton himself, escorted by motorcycles, wearing full battle dress and standing up like Julius Caesar, rode in his scout car into Cannon Company's bivouac area one day, went past it, then turned around so he could personally administer fines to several men who were digging foxholes but weren't wearing their neckties.

Nor did officers escape Patton's attention. Captain Murphy and Lieutenant Hobratschk managed to always wear their requisite ties and leggings, but Patton had ordered that they also paint their insignia of rank on their helmets. This would make them desirable targets for sure, as the Germans knew that killing American commanders would drastically affect overall control of their units, but this also mattered little to George Patton. He maintained that it was part of the job of being an officer, and he expected those under his command to lead from the front. They were expendable in Patton's thinking. Murphy and Hobratschk complied with this order by painting their rank insignias on their helmets in black; it was far less conspicuous against their dark, muted olive drab helmets. It was also another example of their black humor and when the Bearer Boys caught wind of it they really thought it was funny because less crafty officers had painted their helmet insignias a far more noticeable white.

Therefore, it was no small wonder that Patton, after lunching with General Allen and visiting the 18th Infantry on March 12th, actually left that inspection impressed with the officers and men he had seen.

Perfectly reflecting how they had stood firm at Sbiba and the way they now regarded themselves, Patton wrote in his dairy that night, "The 18th has done well and is quite cocky."

During the third week of March the First Division's mission was to retake Gafsa; it was a large Axis supply dump that had been occupied by the Italians during Rommel's Kasserine offensives in February. In the big picture the new attack was designed to draw German forces away from the British armies fighting to seize the Mareth Line, fifty miles to the east. Capturing Gafsa would also give the Americans a forward logistic base from which to conduct future operations to mainly support the British; however, Patton's initial order did not provide for sending troops—except for reconnaissance forces—beyond Gafsa, which was thought by Patton's intelligence section to be defended by no more than 7,000 Italian troops of the Centauro Division.

The large oasis settlement was located forty-five miles to the south of Bou Chebka on the northern edge of the Sahara Desert. Patton's intelligence people compared the Gafsa garrison to a citadel; a machinegun and artillery fortified series of bare hills roughly 400 feet high covered the terrain. Gafsa itself was in an exposed position, but unfortunately the maps given to First Division commanders were inexact; important topographical features were not accurately represented. Moreover, the Italians could summon reinforcements from nearby El Guettar; these reserves were estimated to be about the size of Bob's battalion. But within a day German troops from as far away as Gabes, a seashore town on the western side of the great gulf that forms the Libyan coast, could be brought to Gafsa—provided they were not needed for the impending fight for the Mareth Line, which the British were not expecting to begin until the next full moon period which was still days away.

Bob moved in a big hurry by truck on the night of March 16th to the First Division's assembly area for the Gafsa attack; this was in the olive-grove surrounded hamlet of Feriana. His battalion's role was to come off the saw-toothed ridge near the Feriana-Gafsa road, then along a railroad line and into Gafsa from the east. An air strike plus an artillery preparation would soften up Gafsa's defenders. Dubbed OPERATION WOP by Patton's headquarters, it was set to go off at eight o'clock the following morning.

But fog delayed the attack from the air, and Bob didn't jump off until ten, and only after his artillery support had also thoroughly pounded the garrison. It was quite a show to watch, but the overall attendance was much lower than expected and Bob saw no combat.

The Italians, which was later learned to be a much smaller force of 1,200 men, had already abandoned the oasis supply dump. They had cut and run eastward. General Allen wasted little time and sent out reconnaissance patrols towards El Guettar to find them. Two days later an officer from Patton's headquarters arrived at Allen's command post with an alert message that would find Bob in one of the hottest spots of his war, far hotter than Sbiba. It read: "Dear General Allen; Please make all necessary plans, including areas for emplacement of your artillery, for an attack along the axis Gafsa-Gabes. If this attack comes off, you may be called upon to put it into effect tomorrow."

~TWENTY-EIGHT~

BOB'S REGIMENT HAD ALREADY DISPLACED to a bivouac area behind Lortess that was four miles closer to El Guettar. It was here Colonel Greer, fresh from a meeting with General Allen, met just before dark with his battalion commanders to go over the plan of attack. Ben Sternberg wasted little time after the briefing, and got his company commanders together to go over their orders.

"OK, listen up," Sternberg started. "First, the big picture. The basic mission is to open up the road that runs to Gabes so the British can be resupplied from Gafsa when they break through the Mareth Line. Now look at your maps. See El Guettar? Just past it the plain is divided by a mountain mass in the center, and it's walled in by another to the south; thus two defiles are formed. Along each stretches a road; the northeastern fork has an unimproved road called the Gumtree Road, while the southern fork is the continuation of the hard-surfaced highway from El Guettar to Gabes. Our area of operation is in this southern fork."

Sternberg then went on to explain, "In order to control the area east of El Guettar the First Division needs to seize the heights on both sides of the road. There are three immediate objectives; first, Djbel Ank, a knife-like ridge about seven miles northeast of El Guettar. It will be taken by Colonel Darby's Ranger Battalion. The center objective is a horse-shoe shaped hill mass called Djebel Mcheltat; it's eight miles more directly to the east but still north of the Gabes Road. Courtney Brown's 3rd Battalion owns the responsibility for taking this position."

Sternberg then laid out the 2nd Battalion's mission. "We are eventually going to occupy the area around Djebel Berda, a massive hill mass eight miles to the southeast," he announced. "That is our primary objective. It's the enemy's southern anchor, the key to controlling the division's move further down the Gabes Road. We'll be doing this with the 1st Battalion. But before we cross the valley we are first going to secure the northern part of Qued El Keddab; it's marked as Hill 336 on your maps. 336 is easier to pronounce. York's men will take the southern part of this hill, it's really the foothill area, then we'll head over to Djebel Berda. Central to the overall mission is absolute control of the road; like I said our regiment owns this and together we will not fail.

"Alright, we saw the terrain with Bob York and his company captains from Darby's outpost on Friday. We know our route of advance on the road from here is going to be in the open, and there's little to no cover—rocks nor bushes—on the way to 336 once we get by El Guettar. Surprise is key. We know our enemy is the same Italian bunch who ran away when we got to Gafsa; probably about a regiment in size by now. They are dug in around the hills out there in the valley and have as many as two battalions of artillery supporting them, as well as some anti-tank and anti-aircraft weapons. We know the Italians are good with their artillery, so that's why the element of surprise is key. If we're lucky we'll catch 'em sleeping and capture the bastards, their equipment and their forward artillery observers before we cross the valley and head for Djebel Berda.

"There you have it," Sternberg suddenly said. "We go off at 2200 tonight. Any questions?"

"Yes. What's the situation in El Guettar, in the village itself, since we have to go through it first?" Captain Randall asked.

"Bill Darby's Rangers already took it, Carl; it shouldn't be a problem to get through," Sternberg answered. "And patrols found weak activity further to the east. They observed lots of Italian trucks moving around, the large van-type variety apparently bringing in supplies. The enemy used their anti-aircraft guns whenever one of our planes flew over the last couple of days; that Darby's guys saw. The good news is there was no reported tank activity."

"I have another question, Sir," Captain Jeffrey said. "It's about four miles to El Guettar from here, and another four or more miles to our first objective. That'll be a lot of marching."

"Good point, Gordon," Sternberg interrupted. "Should have mentioned this. Thank you. Colonel Greer decided that our trucks are going to take us as far as El Guettar. Bob York and I were wary of that, fearing the noise might get the attention of the Italians, but it started to make more sense and worth the risk because the men will arrive fresh before we head for Hill 336."

"What about our jeeps?" Captain Murphy asked. "Do those stay with us?"

"Yes, Murph," Sternberg answered. "One jeep and trailer per section when we head for 336, but we may have to carry the mortars and their ammo shells when we cross the valley. Tell Ed that his machine gunners will be attached to the rifle companies so they are going to have to carry their guns when we get off our trucks at El Guettar."

"Russ, you have any questions?" Sternberg asked.

"No, Sir. F Company is raring to go," Captain Spinney shot back.

"Alright then. Head back to your companies, brief your men and then try to get some sleep before we board up at 2200."

It had rained for the past three days. Bob had spent the time holed up in a wadi, a shallow ravine out of enemy sight near the 1st Battalion's bivouac area. It was a defensive posture he was in, with boulders and rocks all around him. A sheer wall protected the battalion's left flank, but their other flank was exposed. Thus Bob's time was spent on alert and his section's mortar was ready to fire if any Italians appeared from that direction. Their wadi had become very muddy, and with the rain being as steady as it was, others had actually flooded. But the Bearer Boys, Slugger and Gentle John had been lucky; even though the conditions were miserable they had stayed comparatively dry. The sun came out the day before, so moving out at 2200 would find them on dry roads.

When Captain Murphy got back from his briefing and told Lieutenant Hobratschk what the attack plan was it wasn't long before the Bearer Boys got their equipment together and loaded it up into their jeep carrier; they had plenty of mortar shells. Rations were issued, and Sergeant Horn told them they had just five hours to rest up before they jumped off. But uneasy rest was about it; sleep was near impossible, given combat was just a few hours away.

And it came all too quickly. The moon rose at about the same time the Bearer Boys finished loading up and the trucks started departing for El Guettar; the traffic ahead was already noisy and heavy. The moonlight illuminated the landscape; ridges along massive Djebel Berda could be seen through the light haze, but there was no way for Bob to make out Hill 336 until he at least got by El Guettar. And while everyone was worried about Italian artillery fire finding them, the loudest thing Bob heard on his way to the village was an American half-track out ahead of him exploding after it ran over a mine. When his battalion finally got past El Guettar, the rifle companies unloaded near a large dirt wall where the only sounds that now filled the air were dogs barking and the occasional chatter of bewildered Arabs. So far so good. It was well past midnight, and while there were still several marching miles to go in the open valley there was enough time to reach Hill 336 before daylight.

Bob couldn't help but notice the moon glow sparkling off Chott El Guettar, a huge salt lake just off the road he was about to march over. He was the first in line behind his section's jeep, and while he was plenty alert the beauty of the plains—even without any scrub brush or trees nearby—was more like watching an illusion, or having a dream; entering a fight seemed queer at that moment.

Bob York's 1st Battalion was a quarter of a mile ahead. Sam Carter later told Captain Murphy they had definitely and most assuredly drawn the route most dreaded, the open plain, with nothing but a prayer between us and bullets if we were spotted. There actually was fire that Bob heard coming from the direction of Hill 336, but it turned out the distant muffled exchange of machinegun clatter was planned because the Italians expected American patrols at that hour. To make them think nothing unusual was up, the patrol appeared right on time; things quieted down after this as Bob and his fellow Bearer Boys marched into the dust and wind at an increasing clip, still spread out with ten yards between them so they wouldn't all be taken down at once if Italian artillery shells suddenly found them.

It was about an hour before first light when Bob's battalion finally reached the wire that marked the minefield the Italians had laid in front of Hill 336; it was cut and a path to mount the hill had already been cleared by the regiment's dependable engineers. Sternberg sent two of the rifle companies around the eastern side of the hill, but they didn't find any Italians. Close by was Sergeant Horn; he was on his radio and it wasn't too long before he came over to Bob's mortar section and said, "We're going to stay where we are, right here on the northern slope of this hill."

"What's up, Sarge?" Slugger asked.

"Shhhhh. . .whisper guys," Horn warned. "OK, here's what we know. We sent patrols further up onto the part of 336 we're suppose to take, and guess what? Right, no Italians there. So the artillery strike has been called off. Leave your mortar in the jeep; we are not going to need it right now."

After a pause while Horn listened to his radio, he suddenly said, "One of the 1st Battalion companies apparently got antsy. Well, seems as though they may have actually gotten lost because they hit the part of the hill our E Company was going to seize. They went right up the backside of it. Caught most of the Italians there sleeping, by God. Some were eating breakfast. Others raised up white flags; I heard someone say it looked like it had snowed, there were so many. Now I'm hearing that Bob York is sending another company up to be along side the one already up there. Amazing. This fight's over."

Actually it wasn't. All of a sudden the unmistakable whine of artillery shells was heard coming in, followed by a salvo hitting less than two hundred yards from where they were.

"Damn it!" Sergeant Horn screamed. "That's our guns firing. OK, I'm hearing their forward observer yelling to cease fire."

Seconds later another thunderous salvo landed on the hill.

"Oh my God. This has to end," Horn started mumbling. "Wait, hold on. Now I'm hearing Bob York yelling to stop the damn firing. He's telling the battery it's his men up there."

But then another round of artillery fire crashed down. "OK, now I'm picking this up," Horn shared. "The battery is saying they are sure it's Italians on the hill, that it has to be because the attack wasn't even scheduled to go off until 0600, and that's still five minutes away."

The groans of the Bearer Boy's and the bewildered stares of Slugger and Gentle John were all Sergeant Horn took in as he kept listening to the radio traffic.

"Well, that's that," he suddenly said. "Bob York just gave that battery a piece of his mind. He was plenty pissed. Told them again it was his men on the hill."

An awkward silence followed. But Hill 336 now belonged to Bob's 18th Infantry.

The sun hadn't even risen over towering Djebel Berda yet, but there was enough light to see around now. Colonel Greer had wasted little time, and knowing the Italians were caught off guard on top of 336, he ordered Courtney Brown's 3rd Battalion to rush up and complete the encirclement of the hill. Bob's battalion continued around the eastern edge to assist in this, and before noon Greer's hoped for double-envelopment was complete.

It was very fortunate the element of surprise had achieved the hoped-for results. From his new position Bob could see more minefields and barbed wire entanglements the Italians had put in place to protect themselves from further attack. As he mounted the lower ridges he even saw machinegun positions, and elaborate foxholes with connecting trenches; dugouts honeycombed the entire side of the hill. But they were void of Italians, and their guns could now be used by the Bearer Boys if they had to protect themselves.

And they certainly had to. As the morning wore on, Italian artillery found their position. But the Bearer Boy's were safe because they had jumped into their foxholes and were even trying out captured Italian rations. Unknown to them, Colonel Greer had come up from his command post back closer to El Guettar to personally observe the progress, and upon seeing what he did he wanted to take the nearby horseshoe-shaped spit of hill marked as Djebel Mcheltat; Bob's battalion was again ordered to assist Courtney Brown's men with this mission.

It didn't take long; within an hour the second djebel was theirs without a fight. Greer was with Bob York and Ben Sternberg by this time, and all were anxious to continue the attack; Greer ordered a patrol to head out towards Djebel Berda, the prize in the regiment's scheme of maneuvers that day. The patrol encountered heavy artillery fire but before they returned these men saw that enemy forces were strongly entrenched not just on rocky Djebel Berda, but also on the eastern tip of the hill mass on the lower ridges of Berda's neighbor, Djebel Kreroua.

Colonel Greer was not one to shy away from a fight. He quickly ordered Bob York to attack across the south side of the valley and over to the ominous hill so his men could get there before dark. But minutes later artillery fire found Greer's location at the base of Hill 336. The shells began falling rapidly, so much so that Ben Sternberg later told everyone that York had said it sounded more like continuous machine gun fire than high explosive shelling.

Sternberg vividly described how it had struck too damn close, and after Greer's jeep was hit and his radio operator was wounded their regimental commander decided the attack over to Djebel Berda had to wait.

Another story about how commanders were good targets that day started spreading like artillery fragments as the morning wore on. George Patton had come to General Allen's command post near El Guettar to see first-hand how the battle was progressing. He wanted to get closer to the action, so he and Allen found their way out onto Hill 336, and arrived alone in Allen's jeep. The division commander had been driving while Patton stood straight up with his hands holding the top of the jeep's windshield so he could balance himself and be seen. Somehow they found Sam Carter; he was fully aware of the artillery that was hitting nearby at the time, and he warned both senior officers that the Italians had his location zeroed in. "As soon as I said this," Sam later told Captain Murphy, "*wheeee, boom, boom, boom, boom*; a battery salvo hit the road behind us real close to their jeep."

Then with a glint in his eye, Sam told a devilishly entertained Murphy, "I was the first to dive into my foxhole; I dug it just before they got there. It was behind a two-foot bank of dirt. Next thing I knew General Patton was on top of me; Terry Allen was trying to get to the bottom of the hole.

"Never had so many stars around me," Sam smirked. "Then Patton said, 'Terry it's too damn hot. Let's get the hell out of here.'"

It got even hotter that day. Italian tanks were reported during the late afternoon to be just to the east of Djebel Mcheltat, and friendly artillery fire needed to address that problem before Bob's battalion could move again. His squad's mortar was hurriedly set up to support the fire mission. Sergeant Horn knew mortars could not do much to stop a tank—if they were really out there—but his orders were to be prepared to fire stinging white phosphorous shells and ruin the day for any Italian foot soldiers who might accompany their tanks through the valley.

American 155mm artillery batteries were about a mile behind them, and they were also being alerted to render fire on the Italian tanks when Bob started to see distant specks in the eastern sky heading for him. The shape of gull wings appeared seconds later, and all too quickly he could see a dozen or more terrifying twin-engine German Stukas screaming into the valley; they were being escorted by ten Bf-109s.

Sirens wailed as the Stukas roared down no more than 500 feet over Bob's head, broke away from their lined-up formation and hunted for the American artillery locations further west, closer to El Guettar. But a couple of the German planes circled back and headed for a 105mm battery that had already displaced into a position right behind Hill 336. A Stuka destroyed one of the battery's guns when its bomb hit the top of its quadrant; the fragments from the gun shield tore off a gunnery sergeant's leg, killing him after he bled out. Fires started and threatened the battery's ammunition dump; the gun's tires flamed up. Powder bags started to explode. Further to the rear, jeeps and other guns were being hit, but the biggest tally there was the dozen men wounded.

The Stukas found their next victims along the northern ridge of Hill 336. This is where Bob had been just a few hours earlier. A lieutenant now in that position told everyone later, "I saw these planes, about thirteen of them, making a U-turn over the valley to go back towards the east. And in the course of that they were passing almost overhead."

The German planes were now targeting the lieutenant's tank destroyer platoon that had displaced near Hill 336 to support the First Division's continuing attack. His halftracks were World War One era equipment but they had machineguns. The lieutenant selected this weapon to try to defend his ancient tank destroyer from one of the modern Stukas, and he opened fire as the sleek bomber dove down towards him. The result was more terrifying than watching the black 500-pound bomb leaving the plane's fuselage.

"So I fired several rounds, then the machinegun jammed," the lieutenant later explained. "I cleared the jam, fired it again. It jammed again." Just before the bomb hit to his right, the lieutenant jumped out of his destroyer but it was too late. "Fragments went under the halftrack and hit me in three places. I landed on my face and looked at my two hands and my fists were closed. . .oh, but my arm was still attached."

Others were not as lucky; two nearby soldiers were killed. Bob had been luckier. While he witnessed the entire air strike from his foxhole where he could see an immense column of black smoke rise up over Hill 336, his location was not hit. But the smell of the German bombs, and the dust it kicked up blew in his direction.

Something just wasn't right. Bob wondered where the hell his own air support was.

~TWENTY-NINE~

A FULL PATROL BOB YORK sent out after things quieted down reported seeing fifteen tanks about two and a half miles to the east. These may have been the tanks that Bob's mortar section had been alerted to watch out for. But General Allen's staff saw otherwise and three hours later called the sighting a false alarm. Still, a reconnaissance patrol went eight miles eastward to set up a screen and provide an early warning if any tanks actually did appear.

Terry Allen visited Colonel Greer's command post behind Hill 336 just before dark and reviewed the overall situation with him; during this meeting Greer requested that a minefield and barbed-wire be laid in along the front of the hill. Allen concurred, and the division's engineers tied in four thousand mines and three trucks of wire with the minefield the Italians already had in place. This would definitely slow up any of their tanks that might venture up the Gabes Road into the regiment's lines.

The night was fairly quiet so Bob, Slugger, Gentle John and the rest of the Bearer Boys got a decent night's sleep. But the next morning brought a buzz of activity that started when Patton raised hell about getting over to Djebel Berda, and this was quickly followed by a flurry of orders. They were confusing. Greer now wanted York's battalion to move out and occupy positions on Djebel Berda in force, and for Ben Sternberg's companies to come in on their right flank. The attack would go off at one that afternoon and commence with a covering artillery fire mission. Presumably both battalions would attack abreast, in the open during broad daylight, exposed to the Italians answering back with their own artillery.

But this changed; Greer decided to send Bob York's battalion first, and alone. Bob waited the entire afternoon before his 2nd Battalion finally got their own orders to cross the valley. The time of their departure still wasn't certain; it would now depend on what was reported back from the other side of the valley. The answer to that came just before five when thundering artillery fire bounced off Djebel Berda and echoed into the valley; it became evident York's men had been discovered by someone, and a few minutes later York indeed let Greer's command post know that artillery was shelling his column as they approached the hill mass. There was some confusion about just where it was on the hill that York's forces were heading to, but that was sorted out when the position was later described by York to Greer as a "flat crescent that was overlooked by the top of Djebel Berda—a sheer climb a thousand feet over our heads."

Sensing trouble, Colonel Greer now wanted Bob's 2nd Battalion to cross the valley. It was nearing six o'clock by this time. When the order reached Captain Murphy, all he could do was grumble. The actual time they would jump off still wasn't specified; Ben Sternberg had simply been told by Greer to "attack the enemy position tonight" and both he and Bob York had been further warned to be careful not to shoot each other up.

It was after ten when the alert order to move out finally came down from regiment. All Captain Murphy knew now was the 2nd Battalion was going to extend the flank of Bob York's position on a low ridge. This rise wasn't even marked on Murphy's map but 2nd Bat's job after crossing the valley was to cover the road junction to the northeast and disrupt access to the valley from this direction. Sternberg assured Murphy and the rifle company commanders that their own artillery batteries were displacing another mile closer to support their crossing; if any Italian tanks did break through, this defensive setup would stop them.

"What about air support?" Captain Randall asked. Sternberg's confidence aside, all the company commanders had learned by this time that no question was too sensitive to ask him; Ben Sternberg was a no bullshit kind commander. He didn't talk down to anyone, was never intimidating, and always gave answers only if he knew what he was talking about.

"All I know is this," Sternberg offered. "Supposedly three air missions have been ordered up by Patton's staff. But just when they'll fly in to support us is unclear. It certainly won't be tonight when we cross the valley. And there's no preset time when we'll see them tomorrow."

"Have we got any news on when we'll get started?" Russ Spinney asked.

"Bob York's sending guides back to lead us over," Sternberg answered. "That's now scheduled to happen after three. It will still be plenty dark, and we should have enough time to get into position before first light. Murph, your machinegun sections will march with the rifle companies. And Murph, sorry, but the jeeps and trailers stay on this side of the valley; your men are going to have to carry their tubes, and the ammo bearers will need to fill up their aprons with their heavy explosive 81s. We'll get more mortars over by jeep later.

"OK, if there's no further questions, let's get going. Head back to your companies and get them lined up. I want an extended formation, with one platoon at a time marching out. Carl, your company will go first and follow the guides Bob York's sending to us. Russ, you go second. Murph, you'll stay with me and the rest of my command group; we'll follow F Company. Gordon, your G Company is last in line.

"And let's pray we all make it."

"That shooting star is a bad omen," Bob wisecracked as his section lined up for the movement to the other side of the valley. The sky was indeed clear, the moon was still up, but it was the fear of artillery shells streaking through the sky at them that had the Bearer Boys most worried; a shooting star was nothing.

A few minutes later they started marching through a six-inch carpet of yellow daisies and poppies towards Djebel Berda.

Two things surprised them about the move; they were in a gulley depression that made the column invisible to the enemy, and no one shot at them. The route of advance—it was a little over eight miles to the other side of the valley—actually had enough defile to make the Bearer Boys feel like they were walking through a tiny valley within a valley. The only things they saw along the way were some occasional tracers and flares shooting into the sky to the east. Sporadic sounds of artillery fire also rang out in the distance, but it did not drown what appeared to Bob to be the steady droning of engine motors as they got closer to the other side of the valley.

He sensed someone was warming up for something.

He and Gentle John looked at each other. "You hearing what I'm hearing, Bob? The pitch. Whatever it is that's moving, there has to be a lot of them."

"I don't think they're trucks, John," Bob answered back. "The rumble's too deep. Sounds more like twelve-cylinder engines to me."

"Whatever it is, forget about it," John yelled. "We got more important things to worry about right now. We're almost there. I can see E Company up ahead in the moonlight already deploying."

It was going on five-thirty now. Ben Sternberg was being guided off the dust-whipped plain to Bob York's command post; minutes later they shared the plan for the continuing attack. There would be no rest for the weary. A five-minute artillery preparation would go off in ten minutes. Communication wires were already in and strung across the valley back to Colonel Greer's command post beneath Hill 336. Both Sternberg and York could report their progress to regiment, which in turn would be communicated to

General Allen's CP so he would have up to the moment information when—not if—the demanding George Patton called.

"We're supporting F Company again," Sergeant Horn told Slugger, Gentle John and the Bearer Boys. "F's in reserve during this first show, so we are too." Bob was soon struggling around a rock cropping, with Slugger, Gentle John and Sergeant Horn following him carrying the pieces of the squad's mortar. They hoped to find some cover. They didn't. Then artillery fire rang out. Theirs. The last round was white phosphorous. The attack was on.

It was a short show. The first heavy explosive artillery rounds had landed on top of the enemy positions. After stinging white phosphorous shells were laid in two of Bob York's companies went forward with their gas masks on and captured just shy of 200 dazed Italians whose eyes and skin were burning.

Captain Murphy had been with Ben Sternberg during this time; just where the companies would be positioned was decided. Captain Jeffrey's G Company would hold the ground next to a wadi that was on the long spur of Djebel Kreroua and extended towards the northeast; this was the position Murphy didn't have on his map. A war correspondent described it as "three-hundred yards of almost bare rock with scant cover of clay shot through with gravel and a few weary weeds. It was naked if ever a position was." Jeffrey's men nevertheless would tie in here with York's companies and form the rightmost anchor on their line of defense. Carl Randall's men were sent over towards the eastern side of Djebel Berda; his E Company was the anchor tenant here.

Company F was in the center; Captain Spinney's men, a platoon of Murphy's heavy machine gunners, the Bearer Boys, Slugger, Gentle John and Sergeant Horn would directly overlook the Gabes Road.

Everyone started digging shallow foxholes in the mostly shale slopes, expecting orders to renew the attack at first light. But those sounds of engines were still out there somewhere amongst the ridges and washes in the valley. The Gabes Road was no longer visible, even with the moon arched lower; the road was a little over 2,000 yards to the north, and it was shrouded in mist.

Stars still washed the skies above the low eerie mist cover. York's men had finished mopping up the Italian position that had surrendered and were returning to Djebel Berda.

Bob was dead tired, but he suddenly turned to Gentle John and said, "Do you hear that?"

"Hear what?" John asked back. "Stop spooking me. All I can hear are those same sounds we've heard for the past hour. Engines out there somewhere."

"I think I'm hearing something different," Bob offered. "It's higher pitched and sounds more like flat-twin engines."

"Whatever it is, we're best off where we are, right here in our foxhole."

"Yea," Bob smirked. "And don't forget to put your tie on. You never know when Gorgeous Georgie Patton might show up."

~THIRTY~

TRACERS STARTED SHOOTING INTO THE sky minutes later. Bob could see they were red, white and blue as they exploded out of the mist in the valley. It was like a fireworks show back in the states on the 4th of July. The engines he heard earlier were revved up now. Then green, yellow, purple and orange tracers flew up. Higher-pitched whining, grinding, and muffled voices shouting commands suddenly filled the air.

Faint light a half hour later revealed the dim shapes of tanks—German Mark IIIs and Mark IVs—all lined up for everyone on the south side of the valley to see. Ahead of them were armored half-tracks loaded with Panzer grenadiers; Volkswagens with flat beds carrying ammunition were mixed in with motorcycle-mounted infantry in rows of twos. The disciplined column—a bit more visible now—moved westward, following the sheaf of fire ahead of them. The Panzer grenadiers soon dismounted their halftracks and steadily advanced through the folds in the terrain. The tanks broke into three columns behind them; one headed for Hill 336. Another kept moving next to the Gabes Road; the third column broke off towards Courtney Brown's 3rd Battalion on Djebel Mcheltat.

Right where Bob had been a few hours earlier before crossing the valley.

Radios started lighting up; the first call came into Greer's command post at six from the division's tank destroyer battalion. "Ten tanks and two enemy companies coming down Gabes Road on our front; left front being attacked by tanks." Another report a minute later from the artillery battalion commander to Greer revealed, "32FA position attacked from the northeast." Fifteen minutes later a breathless runner came into Greer's command post and announced, "Twenty-three tanks have broken through and are approaching."

At half-past six Ben Sternberg got through to Greer and said, "The 2nd Battalion needs help; request some tank destroyers be brought over to our position." Five minutes later, Bob York weighed in: "Thirty enemy tanks and infantry de-trucking on road northeast of us. Request air and Long Toms."

"K Company is yielding some ground," Greer was told next before learning minutes later that the entire 3rd Battalion was being withdrawn slightly. Then, encouraging news was received at ten minutes ahead of seven from Bob York: "Tank attack here is repulsed by our artillery; seven tanks are knocked out," followed minutes later by an already-wounded Courtney Brown with: "3rd Battalion will not withdraw."

But at seven that morning more came into focus. Apparently all hell was breaking loose. The reconnaissance patrol sent out the night before to look for tanks reported to Greer: "At least one hundred tanks and scout cars now in front of our position. Twenty still in front of 1st Battalion and the remainder all over the rest of our front."

Bob's battalion, as well as York's men, were now in danger of being cut off from the rest of the regiment; this is why Sternberg had already requested help. But as the minutes went by the situation became better defined. The German commanders were intent on only blocking the Americans on the south side of the valley, and after receiving a small amount of enemy artillery and self-propelled gun fire here it died away and Bob got to watch in awe the 10th Panzer Division's continuing attack.

"The precision and timing of the huge iron fort moving down the valley was a thing of magnificent beauty," Sam Carter later said for Bob and everyone else on their side of the valley that morning. "Few persons will see this once in a lifetime, and the majority will never have an opportunity to see something like this." Bob York added to that by saying, "Tanks, armored vehicles, artillery, everything just as far as the eye could see, and we had a ringside seat on the edge of this tremendous arena. The hugeness, clockwork and precision of the 10th Panzer attacking made me temporarily forget our precarious position."

Those across the valley would never forget the precarious position they were in. Brown's battalion was actually being overrun. Tanks rolled over his men's foxholes, and when their treads cleared, Panzer grenadiers pointed their rifles at some Americans and killed them; Brown's machineguns rattled back. German mortars mauled the battalion's positions before more halftracks unloaded even more Panzer grenadiers; Brown's heavy mortars responded with 500 rounds within minutes. One of his companies did pull back, but only to get into a better position behind a ridge where the men couldn't be seen; from here they hurled grenades at the Germans. At one point the attacking force massed just fifty yards away from the battalion's final protective line. "You could look in the air and see between thirty and forty grenades at the same time," one participant remembered.

But a German later told his captors, "Behind us on the plain our tanks were spread out; not all could get up on the steep slopes we were on. Very soon we were completely stopped. We made no progress; just lay there."

The Mark III's and IV's instead veered to the left and tried to find the American 105mm artillery guns. Greer heard about this at 7:20: "Fourteen enemy tanks reported to be moving around right flank vicinity of artillery positions." Greer responded by saying: "601 TD sent by division to meet them."

It became a duel where the odds were not even. The 601st's tank destroyers were no match for the German tanks, but they hovered in defilade positions along the ridges in the valley until the Mark III's and IV's appeared. Then the American destroyers popped up, took shots with their 75mm guns at the German armor, and then they backed down until another group came along. But when the German tanks approached in larger numbers it forced the tank destroyers to stay in place on the top of the ridges in order to continue their work, leaving them in perfect positions to be molested by both the German tank commanders and their supporting artillery. Several fell victim to the onslaught; others were able to hit the German tanks with flank shots that tore into their less-armored sides.

Some American field artillery batteries were displaced in wadis, presumably out of sight, in front of Brown's battalion on Djebel Mcheltat so they could also help out. They were suddenly rendering support to his men, firing their tubes like rifles, at times so determined that buckets of water had to be poured on their guns' flattened tubes to cool them down. Some of the 105's batteries were eventually ordered to stop firing because their muzzle blasts were giving away their locations. German artillery now had them bracketed, the men couldn't manhandle their guns into safer positions, and one section was ordered to spike their gun; the crew put thermite grenades down the tube hoping the molten metal would fuse the breechblock to the breech.

Two other section chiefs even poured gasoline on their guns and started setting them on fire while they screamed for their men to run for cover. Brown's heavy mortars, the same Bob, Slugger, Gentle John and the other Bearer Boys used, even expended what remained of their available 81mm mortars trying to stop the attack. But the First Division had depth. Even though some of the big 155mm Long Tom crews closer to El Guettar also had to spike their guns, others continued firing.

It was actually a miracle the Americans were surviving the attack, but they were doing so by exhausting the Germans with their super human efforts. Right after Greer's command post was hit with enemy mortar fire answering in anger to the red-hot barrels of Brown's men, encouraging word started trickling in; a little after nine an outpost reported: "Enemy seems to be retiring." Twenty minutes later, Brown confirmed this report: "Tanks appear to be withdrawing. 3rd Battalion still holding."

If this wasn't enough to steel Colonel Greer's resolve, watching a German prisoner crying while he was being interrogated hardened his determination even more. Asked why he was weeping, the Panzer grenadier said, "This is the first time we've ever been stopped by infantry and artillery."

But there was no doubt the Germans would come back, and Colonel Greer wasn't about to let up. At one minute before ten he sent a message out to his commanders: "Bombing mission at 1000 hours consisting of A-20s and B-25s. Do not fire on them."

A dozen showed up a half hour later. They flew in from the west and Bob watched as they swooped down over Hill 336 before they dropped their loads on the Germans; plenty of black smoke rose up in the valley, but he couldn't make out whether they made direct hits on any of their tanks farther to the east. What he could make out were some still smoldering tanks near Hill 336; a couple were flaming but others Bob couldn't see were being hooked up to trucks and towed back to wherever the Germans were now getting reorganized.

What Bob never heard, nor did Ben Sternberg or Bob York, was Colonel Greer's attempts to get messages through to their 1st and 2nd Battalions' switchboards or via radio ordering them to withdraw from the south side of the valley. Greer actually told division over the phone just before eleven that he was convinced the Germans were preparing for an attack on the south side of the valley, but "I can't get messages through to York or Sternberg. They are still south of the road, running short of ammo."

Greer was acting on messages he did receive nearly an hour earlier when Bob York reported "seven tanks and ninety enemy now on our right flank. Tanks seem to be moving into gullies." It was York who first requested more air support. Fifteen minutes before Greer got on the phone with division Ben Sternberg also relayed: "Company F reports thirteen tanks in front of their positions."

Colonel Greer emphasized to division that "the tanks between us and them" were complicating resupplying York and Sternberg, and trucks would be unable to reach their isolated battalions and deliver badly needed rations, ammo and mortars. "I don't know the actual size of the force in front of them," he told General Allen's representative, a colonel who was his chief of staff. "The whole plain is apparently covered with tanks and vehicles in large groups. I got that from the Cannon Company outpost."

This same colonel wasn't happy with what he was getting from General Patton. Right after he got off the phone with Colonel Greer, he pressed a II Corps' staffer for more air missions, diplomatically asking, "If you can in any way influence keeping fighter support over us we would appreciate it."

"We'll take it up," Patton's man said.

"I think things are getting reorganized on both sides. We'll need the air support, and badly," Allen's chief of staff answered as firmly as he dared to. "I want to get it lined up in advance. Fighter support is the main thing we are asking for."

"They are short," the voice at Patton's headquarters explained. What he meant was scarce U.S. Army Air Force assets were on other high priority missions.

"But we'll take it up again," Patton's man said before he hung up.

Bob, Slugger, Gentle John and the other Bearer Boys were hunkered down in their eighteen-inch deep foxholes when Sergeant Horn came over to them and said, "Listen up."

Their mortar was set up behind a rock cropping on what there was to the backside of their front row seats overlooking the battlefield. Just under fifty mortars were piled up near their tube;

they were woefully unprepared to repel any sizeable attack if it came into the south side of the valley.

"We just got word that the Germans are going to hit again at 1600. That's an hour from now," Horn said. "Word came through regiment once we got the wires fixed. Apparently division intercepted the German orders, if you can believe that. Word is they will concentrate their artillery fire on both sides of the Gabes Road. Division has requested air support. We don't know what the hell is really going to happen, but Lieutenant Hobratschk wants you at your mortar and prepared to fight back just in case the Germans decide to make us targets. If it's artillery they use on us, we're just going to have to grin and bear it and hope our planes knock their batteries out. If it's their infantry coming at us, we're going to have to fire away.

"Any questions?"

There were none. But when 1600 came and there was no attack Bob asked, "Where the hell are they, Sarge?"

"Damned if I know," Horn answered. "Hold on. Wait."

"We're waiting," Slugger assured him.

"OK, here's the latest dope. Seems the Germans are going to bomb the area before they attack. Just got that from Captain Murphy, who's with Colonel Sternberg. Word is they're going to hold back until 1645 now before they cut their tanks and Panzer grenadiers loose again."

"Great news," Bob shot back, and when Horn stared at him he saw Bob was smirking like he did most of the time when things got tense.

"Oh shit, you're not going to believe this one guys," Sergeant Horn suddenly barked out. Now he was smirking. "God damn, you gotta' love Terry Allen. He just put a message out on the German battle net a few minutes ago."

Then, with a broad grin, Sergeant Horn added, "Boy, has he got balls; our general taunted the bastards. Unbelievable. Here's what he said: 'What the hell are you waiting for? We've been ready since 4:00 p.m. Signed First Division.'"

~THIRTY-ONE~

AT PRECISELY FIFTEEN MINUTES BEFORE five the steady drone of airplane engines was heard over the valley again. They were not American aircraft. The Stukas and Bf-109s tore over their own troops, dove, and all Bob heard next was screeching whistles and then explosions echoing through the hills. The attack went on for ten long minutes. Division's big anti-aircraft guns blazed away but missed downing any of the German planes; their bomb explosions blew some of Courtney Brown's men two feet into the air.

"Then the battlefield was ominously silent," an officer in the valley that afternoon said for anyone not there to witness what was happening.

But not for long. German artillery fire started anew in an attempt to provide an umbrella of cover while Panzer grenadiers crept steadily forward. At ten minutes past five Colonel Greer reported to division: "Three German companies in front of 3rd Battalion. Heavy tanks have started forward," followed ten minutes later with "3rd Battalion now surrounded."

Just how much depth the Germans had for this new attack came into clearer focus at about the same time. Bob York reported, "Several hundred German troops are moving in." Ben Sternberg was also watching this through his field glasses, and he let regiment know soon afterwards that the "enemy infantry is slipping through gap between you and the 16th Infantry."

Greer, not having seen any of this and uncertain of what affect the German troop massing could have on the men isolated on the south side of the valley, nevertheless put out to York's and Bob's battalion: "Stop anything that comes at you. Fight it out."

But it turned out that the American tank destroyer battalion protecting the Gabes Road fought it out for them. York had sized the German force right; they were actually two battalions of Panzer grenadiers, but what he hadn't seen was their tank support; the mostly Mark IVs were nearby but out of sight, milling about, creating dust and confusion. When the dead tired German foot soldiers finally lined up in extended formation and attacked, division artillery pieces first fired back using variable time fuse shells that rained high-explosive fragments all over them. Then the tank destroyer crews had a field day. They let those Germans that still could close in, and as the commander of the battalion bragged later, "We cut them down at fifteen hundred yards. It was like mowing hay."

When the Mark IV's finally rolled out, the three-inch guns of a yet another tank destroyer battalion General Allen had ordered up to help out was there to greet them. The new destroyer commanders performed like veterans; it was their very first time in combat. They drew the German tanks into the minefield by the sparkling salt lake south of Hill 336, then destroyed ten of them, plus two German anti-tank guns, and left three more Panzers damaged enough to be useless.

Between this just-arrived battalion and the tank destroyer battalion that had stood firm during the morning, over forty German tanks were destroyed, the vast majority of them by the tank destroyers' thinly armored, open-topped half-tracks with World War One-vintage 75mm guns. But they traded about thirty of their halftracks and many casualties for their victory. Some of their crews were killed by high explosive hits and chests being crushed; one died from a fractured skull. Others suffered arm, leg wounds and lacerations, eye and head wounds, injuries from shrapnel in their feet and arms, and compound fractures; one man had to have his leg amputated.

Total victory that day came about when Courtney Brown's men made another brave stand. After being surrounded again, his executive officer later explained, "With the first move of the enemy armor, the shells of our remaining artillery pieces began to erupt on the valley floor. These artillery pieces, previously ranged in, smothered the attackers with time and point detonating fire. What had been a well-organized attack became the movement of a disorganized mob."

One rifle company captain admitted he had more fun than he'd had in a long time with what was left of the disorganized mob. For others it wasn't nearly as much fun. The captain of Brown's K Company later told a correspondent for *The Stars and Stripes*, "At about 1730 hours we saw ten German halftracks and three light tanks moving against our 1st Platoon. They were running their halftracks over our entire position and shooting down into our foxholes again." Many in this platoon were casualties; after close hand-to-hand fighting all but eight were either killed or taken prisoner.

But the remaining men fought on with the help of the regiment's Cannon Company; together they knocked out two halftracks loaded with German reinforcements using their 105mm tubes, rifle grenades, .30-caliber armor-piercing ammunition and rocket launchers. Mortar sections like Bob's lobbed their 81mm rounds again and again on the Panzer grenadiers who managed to dismount their destroyed vehicles. American soldiers rushed to plug gaps; two died in the resultant melee but the Germans were stopped in these places. One soldier snuck up alone on an enemy machinegun position and blew it to bits with his hand grenades. Others spotted Germans cowered in a wadi and finished them off.

"It was the sweetest thing I'd ever seen," a proud Cliff Raymer, the K Company captain, told *The Stars and Stripes* reporter. "Morale was almost feverish. The boys had only one thing in mind—to keep the enemy away."

And they did while Raymer was suffering the last of what would amount to sixty percent casualties. The Germans suffered a far worse fate. A lieutenant in Raymer's weapons platoon found fifty of them dead in front of the position his men had defended. A rifleman counted 200 bodies. "One was a young, impeccably-uniformed German officer, still frozen on his knees with his PK pistol in his right hand," Courtney Brown's intelligence officer later told others. Another soldier—fined by Patton back at Bou Chebka—hadn't had time to straighten up his tie but remembered, "I looked down from the hill I was on the next morning, and below me were tanks lined up ten feet apart. They were burnt out wrecks, and there were bodies hanging on the tracks, some wedged in the tracks, but all dead."

It was just before midnight when Brown's men withdrew from the horseshoe-shaped ridge; they filed away silently, exhausted but proud. Regiment had even sent out a message to all units saying, "Congrats and appreciation for fine job well done."

The sounds of war had quieted; most of Brown's men only heard the shuffling of their worn service shoes and the soft crying of once haughty Germans when they passed the POW cages they were captive in.

"We knew we were beat," one said. "Our defeat was a disgrace."

While the Germans had indeed been stopped north of the Gabes Road, they still managed to recover thirty-six of their disabled tanks that night and into the morning of Wednesday March 24th. But plagued by heavy tank and infantry casualties, the 10th Panzer Division had to abandon its major offensive towards El Guettar, attacking only when a suitable opportunity presented itself. The German division was ordered to just conduct spoiling attacks along the ridges of the valley to keep the Americans off balance.

Bob York and Ben Sternberg knew that their battalions were still at risk. Bob, like everyone else, remained isolated and as he and the other Bearer Boys looked out through the moonlight at some still-smoldering tanks in the valley during the early hours that morning, they just knew their 2nd Battalion position could be the next target for attack.

Their instincts were dead on.

Sam Carter remembered the only thing his 1st Battalion did the day before was knock out a troop carrier that appeared lost and him ordering his mortar sections to fire at a small group of German infantry. "March 24 was also a quiet day for our battalion," he later wrote before sharing what Bob experienced. "However, the 2nd Battalion was getting direct fire from assault guns and tanks all day."

It started after first light, about the time the sun was rising over the valley, and the first victims were amongst Captain Randall's E Company. Ben Sternberg wasted little time and let Colonel Greer know that his 2nd Battalion was under attack, but he didn't raise sufficient alarm to cause a great deal of worry; when Greer informed division of the attack Allen echoed Sternberg's assessment and quickly told Patton, "We think we can handle it." His confidence was admirable; shortly after Sternberg reported the situation Randall's men were actually getting clobbered by artillery fire up and down the ridgeline they were on.

But General Ted Roosevelt was surveying the situation from a different command post, closer to the front. He called the division's operations officer when he heard Sternberg reporting the attack over the battle net and informed him, "I plan to send two companies of Rangers to reinforce the 1st and 2nd Battalions of the 18th."

The headquarters man asked, "Is the situation that bad?"

"They don't report much to their front, but they are counter battering," Roosevelt answered, counter battering meaning getting friendly artillery support. "The Germans are now working up to the hills; Sternberg and York are where they always have been. They want to clear the hilltop with the Rangers."

There was good cause for this request; Germans had already

been spotted on the bald thousand-foot up crown of Djebel Berda; Sternberg and York feared they might be hit from here, as well as possibly getting hit even harder from the plain.

Some negotiation between the headquarters officer and Roosevelt followed before the Rangers were ordered to move out just before noontime. But General Allen questioned the move; he was on Hill 336—where it all started for Sternberg and York two days earlier—and he was still planning on relieving the 1st and 2nd Battalions at the time. Allen was on the phone shortly afterwards with the same headquarters man Roosevelt had talked with when more artillery fire exploded on the south side of the valley. Looking through his binoculars, Allen said, "The Rangers are where they belong," before warning it would take them several hours to cross the valley. "We are having some light artillery fire over there and I think a battalion moving would draw more attention. So hold on until I call you."

It wasn't until close to dark before Darby's Rangers finally started to cross the valley. This was prompted by an urgent call from Colonel Greer: "There is a wedge in the line over there in front of Company E now, but the rest of the group is presently holding."

But barely. By now the 2nd Battalion really needed help. Even Colonel Greer knew this was abundantly clear. He was on the phone with division early that night, the situation was different, and when asked how everything was going, the regimental commander this time said, "The German's have occupied G Company's position. We are going to move our CP across the valley."

Captain Jeffrey's G Company certainly took the brunt of the German attack, but Randall's E Company was also clobbered with artillery and mortar fire most of the afternoon. The barrages even cut the communication wire between the CPs of Sternberg and Randall. The distance was difficult to cover in the best of circumstances; runners from the battalion command post had to climb over a hill, then crawl through a wadi before clawing over a second hill to Randall's location, just to get messages and orders back and forth.

Germans had occupied the very base of the hill beneath Company G during this time. "Shells from field guns and rifles suddenly began to splatter on their slope," *United Press* correspondent Phil Ault wrote. "The ridge they were on was bare rock. Snipers on a higher ridge could see them. Every time a doughboy raised his head, a bullet pinged past. They were pinned down to the ground so tightly that they couldn't even leave their foxholes to make a latrine. They were trapped, cut off from all help."

Some German snipers were wearing American field jackets, at first leaving some G Company men to think their own Company E was shooting at them. But the Germans were firing green tracers, and not the American red. They were hauling up ammunition in captured American trucks and half-tracks; 88mm shells and concussion grenades were now hitting foxholes, and as one survivor later told Phil Ault, "We just had to lie there and take it."

By now the battalion's ammunition situation was so bad that Sternberg had to risk sending four jeeps through the German defenses back to El Guettar to get more ammo from the regimental supply dump. Miraculously, the jeeps' drivers weaved through the enemy line so close to their Panzers that the German commanders couldn't fire their guns at the jeeps without the risk of hitting their own tanks. One jeep ran over a mine, but its two crew members survived and the three other jeeps even managed to return through the gauntlet of fires with the badly needed ammo.

But it was awful for Company G. One rifleman later told his brothers-in-arms, "They had dropped mortars on us all day long." The company's own 60mm mortar crews were targeted; well-placed barrages killed ammo servers, non-coms, and shrapnel even wounded Captain Jeffrey. He had to be evacuated, and after this his replacement bitterly complained, "The shelling got worse and then we could see German infantry getting ready to attack."

Volleys of enemy mortars started crashing onto the plateau Company G was on again; machinegun fire tore into any standing man. Then, early that night when the bright moon was low over the horizon the whine of numerous BMW R75 motorcycles was heard and about 300 grenadiers shot flares into the air, started whooping, and attacked. Artillery shells rained in first, and even more mortar shells pounded into G Company's position.

"Then we saw infantry swarming up the hill at us from three sides," Captain Jeffrey's replacement explained later. "They outnumbered us three-to-one. We were still in our foxholes and had nothing left to fight with except rifles and grenades. The barrages had knocked out our last mortar and last machinegun."

"Those guys wore black uniforms," one of the survivors later added. "Some had helmets on and some just field caps. They were all firing machine guns or throwing grenades. We threw grenades back. Searing flashes illuminated the hillside. The Germans rushed ahead, screaming like Indians and yelling show no mercy, kill all."

The Germans caught some of the men in their foxholes and ran their bayonets through them. One man recalled he saw one of his fellow soldiers who was trapped come out of his foxhole to surrender. "The Germans shot him and he dived back into his hole with an agonized cry to die." Other shivering death cries kept filling the air. One machine gun crew had been sliced in half by a direct shell hit.

Another man recalled how one of his buddies also tried to surrender; as soon as his hands went up a German shot him. "I was firing my rifle and hit some of them," one of the few survivors of that melee told others. This soldier got some gratification because he also remembered, "It tickled the hell out of me when I heard those sons a bitches give their own death screams." But after seeing that his remaining men were totally overwhelmed the replacement officer ordered the company to withdraw to save useless loss of more lives. "There was nothing else to do," he told Ben Sternberg later. "We were completely overwhelmed."

The lieutenant barely escaped being captured during that withdrawal; he and others jumped off a cliff to not be taken prisoner. Just thirty-six of the G Company men survived the attack. Their day began with about 130 other men, now either dead, wounded or captured. "We wanted to get reinforcements and go back up there," one private remembered. "We did not want to leave our comrades behind to die or become prisoners of war, but there wasn't enough of us left to do anything."

The Germans also captured several of the company's light machineguns, six 60mm mortars, two antitank guns and their five jeeps.

Company G had disintegrated.

March 24th was also the worse day Bob personally experienced during his combat time in North Africa. Tragedy struck his mortar section when G Company was attacked before darkness set in. Slugger, Gentle John and the Bearer Boys had been supporting F Company for most of the day, but when the action shifted to the shoulders of the long spur on the west side of Djebel Kreroua, Lieutenant Hobratschk had them register their mortar on the machinegun positions supporting the Germans coming towards Captain Jeffrey's men.

The Bearer Boys only had the 81mm shells they man-packed across the valley two nights earlier; they were heavy explosive and almost gone by this time. But one of their rounds found an entrenched heavy machine gun behind the Germans. Slugger destroyed it. The Germans answered back with artillery fire, and the high velocity rounds of two 75mm self-propelled guns; these weapons quickly found the Bearer Boy's mortar emplacement and that of another mortar crew close-by.

Bob had just handed Gentle John another round for Slugger to use to go after the German 75s when an artillery shell hit. It missed the mortar tube, but not by much. Everyone dove for cover as dust, splintering shale and shell fragments burst up into the air— everyone but Slugger.

He stayed at the mortar; Slugger was quickly heard calling Lieutenant Hobratschk for firing data and then he could be seen bending over to pick up another mortar and dropping it into the tube. Slugger yelled for everyone to stay away; he said that was an order. He got off two more rounds before Sergeant Horn—sensing the accuracy of the German return fires—screamed for the mortar to be moved. Bob and the other Bearer Boys rushed up to help, then a shell from a German self-propelled gun hit their mortar; this time it was knocked over. Slugger screamed for everyone to leave again, but Gentle John and Bob first helped get the mortar righted.

"Go, go, go!!!" was the next thing they heard Slugger bark out. And then they saw him—totally disregarding his own safety—resume firing; it was later confirmed he destroyed another machine gun before yet another German shell hunted for his mortar.

The last thing Bob saw was Slugger with an 81mm shell clenched tightly in his hands, ready to drop it into the tube. Then Slugger's blood was suddenly everywhere. What could be seen of him in no way resembled the man he had been; his body parts were scattered on the rocks around the now completely destroyed mortar. Slugger had taken a direct hit.

Sergeant Horn was the only one with the presence of mind to get everyone to dive deeper for cover. Slugger's radio was still working; Lieutenant Hobratschk's plaintiff voice could be heard calling out to him.

Horn jumped for it and answered with, "Lieutenant, we lost him."

Hobratschk yelled back, "Get the rest of the squad the hell out of there. Now!"

The Bearer Boys and Gentle John didn't want to leave what there was of Slugger behind, but an order was an order.

Slugger's remains were never recovered.

And there was another of their own they never saw again. Ralph Sproull, the Bearer Boy from Georgia, had made the run down to meet the jeeps carrying ammo back from the regimental supply dump, hoping he could refresh the squad's supply with a few more mortars. He never got back.

~THIRTY-TWO~

GENERAL PATTON'S HEADQUARTERS ORDERED THE withdrawal of Bob's battalion, and together with York's men they departed from Djebel Kreroua and Djebel Berda the following night. Their first stop followed a dejected march across the valley over to Hill 336, and then trucks took everyone back to Gafsa. It was far from pleasant here; parachute flares dropped by German bombers lit up the sky that night and butterfly bombs ignited. Even bigger bombs were falling nearby.

Darby's Rangers stayed and held the bald hilltop on Djebel Berda for three more days and were then relieved by a regiment of the 9th Infantry Division. Retaking the positions the Rangers, Bob's battalion and the 1st Battalion had stubbornly defended was very costly for the newcomers. They sustained 1,800 casualties; 430 were killed, nearly 900 were seriously wounded. The rest fell victim to exhaustion, disease, lesser wounds or were taken prisoner. Every battalion commander was a casualty.

The south side of the El Guettar valley would be remembered as the location of one of the largest casualty counts for U.S. infantry forces in North Africa. Bob was damned lucky to get away from here in one piece.

The First Division continued to operate through the funnel to the northeast during the first week of April. Units fought along dry shale wadis and extracted Germans who had taken refuge in the crevasses and rocky escarpments along the ridgelines in the hills; mortars weren't used. The rugged hills were too steep to manhandle them. "The action was very slow, due to strong enemy resistance, very difficult country and the fatigue of our troops," Patton even confessed to his diary.

Bob's 2nd Battalion was sent into action on the 7th; he was trucked to Sakket, a village several miles up the valley in the shadows of another high djebel. After leaving its shrines and light brown houses behind, Bob made a night march towards the soft sands of the Maizila Pass, near where the second phase of the El Guettar offensive finally ended after American forces made contact with their British counterparts.

It was far from an uneventful period for Bob; the Germans were making daily bombing runs and friendly air support was nowhere to be seen. Junker 88s dropped 500 pound bombs with instant fuses all too frequently. One officer even remarked, "So frequent was the bombing and strafing that it became possible to shave only between dives into a trench. This was a frightful day, as they seemed to have us entirely at their mercy—not an Allied plane all day."

After Bob was relieved on April 8th and trucked back through El Guettar to Gafsa again, he was handed a missive from George Patton's headquarters.

HEADQUARTERS II CORPS
APO 302
In the Field
8 April 1943
  GENERAL ORDER
  NUMBER 25

Soldiers of the II Corps:

After 22 days of relentless combat in mountains whose ruggedness beggars description, you have won the battle of El Guettar. Not alone on the front line, where death never ended his gruesome harvest, but everywhere else all of you have demonstrated your valor and constancy.

Over countless miles of dusty wind-swept roads, often under fire from the air, or from artillery, the men of supply services have ensured our food and ammunition. Under the most rigorous field conditions the maintenance units have collected and repaired your vehicles and weapons.

In small, isolated groups, or as individuals, men of the Signal Corps have constructed and maintained your communications. Except for the unceasing efforts of our Engineers, the roads could not have been used, or the lurking hazards of minefields overcome. In the air, the 12th Air Support Command gave us, as ever, proof of their untiring devotion and splendid courage. The Medical Corps has proven outstanding in its prompt and effective care of our wounded.

Due to your united efforts and to the manifest assistance of Almighty God, the splendid record of the American Army has attained added luster.

G. S. PATTON, JR.,
Lieutenant General   Commanding

Bob's immediate reaction was pure confusion. What air support, he wondered? Where was this untiring devotion and splendid courage while his mortar squad and the rifle companies were fighting for their lives on Djebel Kreroua? Just where the hell were these guys when Slugger was killed? Would he still be alive if 12th Air Support Command flew a damn mission before the motorcycle battalion hit back on March 24th?

Bob resigned himself to the probability he would never know, but his interest piqued when Sergeant Horn told him a few days later that he and the rest of the Bearer Boys were being summoned to Captain Murphy's command post for a meeting. This was quite unusual, so much so that Gentle John was the first to ask, "What's up, Sarge?"

"The captain may want to talk to us about Slugger," Horn speculated. "Maybe there will be some news about Ralph. I don't know. Lieutenant Hobratschk will be there, too. I doubt we're going to get chewed out. So let's get the boys together, and just get going."

Murphy's command post was in a large grove outside of the small Gafsa central village, away from its glaring sun and dried out mud houses. Shade for Captain Murphy's CP was provided by palm trees, and Bob's tent—like others—was under another palm tree about fifty yards away. Sergeant Horn said he had a good story he'd heard that he wanted to share with them while they walked over to meet with their commanders.

"It went something like this," Horn started saying. "Source is the S-2 in Colonel Brown's battalion, Captain Ed Kuehn. He's a straight shooter, and guys in intelligence usually get it right. Happened just before the Germans hit us a couple of weeks ago."

"We're all ears Sarge," Gentle John said for everyone.

"Well, Kuehn was at General Allen's CP waiting for a meeting to start. He was dozing under a palm tree when he heard sirens start blaring, and when he looked up there were four motorcycles coming in his direction. Directly behind the motorcycles was a command car, and Kuehn said he saw General Patton standing up in it looking like he was Mussolini, all decked out with twin pearl handled pistols on his hips and wearing a varnished helmet liner, but no helmet."

"No helmet?" Bob asked. "We'd 'a been fined big time for that."

"Wait, it gets better," Horn laughed. "There were jeeps behind Patton, all loaded with press people. Colonel Mason, our division operation's officer, came out of his big tent to see what the sirens were all about, and he wasn't wearing his helmet. So Patton started chewing his ass out. Mason's shirt was also unbuttoned, and his tie was loose. Patton really let him have it, right in front of junior officers and a bunch of enlisted men like you guys."

"I suppose high rank does have its privileges," Gentle John offered. "But from what I remember about training, chewing out someone as high up as a colonel in front of his subordinates, never mind lowly guys like us, is a big violation of military protocol."

"Let's put it this way men," Horn responded. "We've never seen anything like that in the First Division and I can assure you none of you ever will."

Captain Murphy looked dead serious when they arrived at his CP. He and Lieutenant Hobratschk were absorbed in conversation; Murphy was actually evincing the side of him that the Bearer Boys had come to know as the "no bullshit" part of his personality, which contrasted from his usual congenial way of getting everything he needed from his men.

When Murphy stood up as the tanned Bearer Boys started to salute, there was a noticeable limp in his step. Still, he started with, "At ease. This will be an informal briefing. Sit over there on those ammo crates. Lieutenant Hobratschk and I are going to go over something we know is very important to you personally.

"But first I want to read to you what General Allen wrote about the battles we fought over the past two weeks," Murphy said before looking down and continuing with, "You have met and defeated the toughest units in the German army with great credit to yourselves, the division, and to your country. I attribute your success to the loyalty and cooperation of every man of this division, to your cheerful discipline under great hardships and to your determination to get the job done. The German army has learned to fear the First Division, just as it did in the last war."

Murphy then looked up without any mention of just why he appeared pained. "I want to personally thank you for the way you men performed. We didn't get it as bad as the rifle companies did, but we got our share of casualties.

"Half of our 1st Machinegun Platoon men were killed or wounded; others were captured. Lieutenant Butkiewicz was even evacuated. We lost two heavy machineguns. Company H lost more men on the 24th of March than all of our combined days of fighting here in North Africa. And I'm well aware of the casualties we suffered in your mortar platoon. I'm sorry to say Private Sproull was very likely captured by the Germans; we had him down as missing before my executive officer verified he saw him being taken prisoner. But I wanted you to know that Lieutenant Hobratschk and I are in agreement that one of your squad members deserves special recognition.

"We are going to put Corporal Szelugoski in for the Distinguished Service Cross. This medal is awarded for extreme gallantry and it's the second highest the Army offers. Wally and I believe Slugger exhibited extraordinary heroism back there on Djebel Kreroua. We believe you would agree with us."

Captain Murphy let that hang and just stared at the Bearer Boys and Gentle John. No one spoke. What he did see were tears streaming down the faces of three of the hardened soldiers of Slugger's mortar squad. Lieutenant Hobratschk just stared off into nowhere, fearing he might tear up too. Bob was not one to tear up easily, but he did. He was actually thinking more about getting even with the Germans for killing Slugger than any thing else at that moment.

Then Murphy continued and said, "Men, I'm not going to pretend I know how you feel. Frankly, it's not about any of us now. We survived; we got out. We can fight another day. You may feel you owe this to Slugger, and if he were here I'm sure he'd be the first to say knock this sentimental stuff off and get back to work.

"OK, so let's honor that," Murphy said.

"Now I'm sure you're wondering about where we're going next. Here's what I know, and it is only big picture right now. We accomplished our mission during the last offensive; our job was to take pressure off the British flank while they went after the Mareth Line. It took several attempts and the Brits suffered thousands of casualties before we finally linked up the same day we were relieved and sent back here to Gafsa.

"Where we go next is likely going to put us in a place where we protect the Brits' flank again." Then Murphy shifted gears and added, "At the moment the Germans are slowly being squeezed into a pocket around Tunis. But we don't know when we'll get an order to move out yet. Here's what we have to do in the meantime. Your barrack bags arrived from Algeria, but don't get attached to them. Take exactly what you need and turn the rest in. Keep a change of underwear and socks, maybe extra handkerchiefs and any spare wool clothing you've got. That, plus your bedrolls. We're stripping down to bare essentials.

"Any questions?"

"Does this mean we don't have to take our neckties with us, Sir?" Bob smirked. His timing was priceless. Everyone cracked up.

"I'll do you one better Baummer," Captain Murphy shot back with his familiar grin; this time he also had that wry Irish look in his eyes. "General Patton is leaving us. Omar Bradley will be taking over II Corps. General Bradley hasn't issued any orders about wearing neckties. Use 'em to start a fire tonight. Actually, don't do that. That would be destroying Army property. But if you're short on toilet paper…

"Alright," a now chuckling Murphy added. "You're dismissed."

Lieutenant Hobratschk walked back to the tent camp the Bearer Boys were in about ten minutes later; he was carrying a canvas bag with him. Everyone was hoping he had something good in it, but first up was a question put forth by Gentle John.

"What happened to the Captain's leg, Lieutenant? He didn't mention anything about that, but it was obvious he was hurting some."

"Remember back when we left Djebel Mcheltat to cross over to the other side of the valley, the day we first got hit with artillery fire? Well, our captain almost got it; he jumped out of harms way just in time. Tore his leg up; he probably got a hernia. He refuses to get it looked at, and says he won't until we get this Tunisian fighting over with."

No one said anything about that. This was the captain they had come to know. Never complained about anything having to do with himself. His men always came first.

"OK, now I've got a couple of things I need to go over with you," Hobratschk continued. "Sergeant Horn has made recommendations that I've approved. It was actually his call, but we decided this together for a reason. Murga, you're moving up to gunner. You have demonstrated you know what you're doing; you were Slugger's assistant. I'm sure he'd approve of this, too."

Gentle John was speechless, but underneath all that he was damn proud.

"And Baummer, you're going to be Murga's assistant gunner. We're going to move Billy Uhouse from another section into your squad to round out your team. But we're going to have to wait for replacements before we can get someone to try to fill Ralph's boots. Any questions?"

There were none. They already knew who Uhouse was; he was competent and had success written all over him. He was from Pennsylvania, and would fit right in. But finding someone like Ralphie, with his southern roots, would likely be a tougher fit.

"OK then. I have one more thing," Hobratschk added. He reached into his canvas bag, and out came an 81mm mortar shell.

"This was the shell Slugger was getting ready to put down the barrel of the tube when he got it. Me and Captain Murphy found it lying near his radio. Amazing it didn't go off. Baummer, I know the two of you were very close. So I'm giving it to you so you can get even with the Germans next time we have the privilege of killing the bastards. Any further questions?"

There were none.

~THIRTY-THREE~

BOB RECEIVED THE ORDER TO MOVE out of Gafsa on April 14th. To where he didn't know, but what he did know was the ten-day rest period and frolicking in the oasis's nearby warm bath waters were almost over. A few days later he climbed into the back of a deuce and a half, and left the sandy desert country and the sad memories of Djebel Kreroua behind.

The First Division convoy eventually stretched into a seventy-five-mile line; there were so many trucks, big prime movers, jeeps and other vehicles churning up dust that Bob had to wear goggles to avoid getting it into his eyes, plus just to see what was going on around him. The wide flats he traveled through in the spring sunshine were absent vegetation, except for knee-high brush. The valleys were wide open with no cover, but for small olive groves and the ever-present cactus plants. Bob constantly worried the convey would be easy prey for German dive-bombers.

Otherwise conditions were perfect. The winter rains were over, the cold nights were a thing of the past and the days were getting longer. Bob, like everyone else, settled in and used his bedroll as a cushion to make the ride more comfortable as he traveled over the pitted roadways and played poker with the Bearer Boys to pass the time. He was through Feriana and Bou Chebka by this time; Morsott was next before he bounced through Clairefontaine and Souk Ahras. Here the convoy turned northeastward and eventually passed by the busted up white-stucco homes in the ancient

Roman city of Beja, where he spent too little time before being called to the Sbiba Pass back in February. Bob's face was caked with dust by now, but he could see more green shrubs and pine trees as he got farther north. The convoy finally weaved through Qued Zarga and by midnight Bob was up three dollars and ten miles north of well-remembered Longstop Hill, where his regiment had received their first German lesson during Christmas week four months earlier.

Bob marched away from here—Roum os Souk—on the night of the 19th, traversed narrow, rocky and rutted cart tracks in pitched-darkness while in two column formation, and at four the next morning his battalion relieved a battalion of the Black Watch that was attached to the Royal Scotland Regiment.

When daylight came he found he was in hilly country; the entire landscape above the valley was bald and rocky. The area was largely devoid of cover. The rolling ground around the chain of over thousand foot hills in front of him was deceptively filled with inviting bright red poppies, olive groves and whitewashed farm buildings, together making what was to Bob's immediate view look like a picture postcard. But the rock-infested ridges behind the mysterious hills that dominated the area were populated with Germans hell-bent on stopping the Americans from punching through to Tunis or Bizerte.

If the mines the Germans had planted in the hillsides, their accurately-sited machineguns and mortars or their heavy artillery pieces didn't stop the Americans, they would be helped by plenty of poisonous horned viper and cobra snakes that slithered in the grasslands which reached up to their well-dug in trenches. Straw-colored sac spiders, spiny tailed lizards, scorpions, centipedes, reddish-orange chiggers and man-eating red ants would find the wounded, wherever they lay.

But what made the area particularly dangerous was evidenced when Bob looked up into the sky that morning and saw a German plane approaching. It flew by so low that he could see the pilot waving to him. The German airman was on a reconnaissance mission. Bob swore at him, and after looking around he swore even more. There were no American planes he could see anywhere in the clear blue skies above him.

Allied fortunes in Tunisia had changed dramatically since the fighting at El Guettar ended. Axis forces were slowly being squeezed into a pocket around Tunis, just as Captain Murphy had told Bob's squad back at Gafsa. The British would put on the main show to finish the Germans off; their opening act would commence on April 22nd and the Brit's final objective was to take Tunis. The Americans were tasked with closing in on Bizerte in order to protect the flank of the two huge British Armies. To accomplish this, the four divisions that comprised General Bradley's II Corps would operate in two zones.

Bob's First Division was to clear the ten-mile line of hills north of the Tine River, in the southernmost zone. The division's area of operation was on the very edge of the Tine Valley and ran parallel to the river. It had already been dubbed the "mousetrap" because clearing the hills had to be done by the infantry before armored mobile units could use the flat valley floor to reach II Corps' first objective—Mateur—after which the American tanks could roll into Bizerte.

Unknown to Bob, the "mousetrap" was just one of the ways to get to Mateur; other routes to the north had been evaluated, and were still being decided on by General Bradley's staff. But the approach through the Tine Valley had gotten the attention of General Eisenhower, and it was he who decided the matter; he told Bradley "the southern portion of your sector appears to be reasonably suited for tank employment and it is in that area you will be expected to make your main effort, at least in the initial stages."

And Bob was about to learn that his 2nd Battalion was going to be tasked with taking the first hill in the highest chain of elevations that guarded the very neck of the area Eisenhower was referring to. His was the right-most unit on the First Division front and closest to the valley floor; ahead of Bob was Djebel Rmel. On Captain Murphy's map it was marked as Hill 350 and it was probably populated by fanatical units of the elite Barenthin Regiment. As General Bradley later wrote, "In esprit, intelligence, and tenacity, it surpassed every other Axis unit on our front."

The attack was set to go off on Good Friday, two days before Easter Sunday.

"Alright, listen up," Lieutenant Hobratschk yelled out at assembly the day before that Friday. "I want to go over the plan of attack with you all."

Bob, Gentle John and the Bearer Boys were gathered with the rest of their mortar platoon on a knoll under one of the few trees in the 2nd Battalion assembly area. They had just finished inspecting their new mortar.

"First off, is the plan for the attack," Hobratschk started. "We just got this yesterday afternoon from Colonel Sternberg. Your section sergeants each have maps that Captain Murphy gave them. Gather around and stay with me while I explain the plan.

"Alright, see where Pimple Hill is marked? That's the first rise along the battalion's line of advance. On the bottom of the page. Don't let the name fool ya'. It's a mountain; it's gentle rising, but 1,200 feet high. Captain Jeffrey—he's patched up now from the wound he took at El Guettar—is going to send a platoon from his G Company out ahead of us to take that hill. The regiment's recon platoon snuck up that way last night, and they came back with word it's lightly defended. The Germans may not consider this terrain that important to their defense.

"But beyond Pimple Hill things will be different. Hill 350 is where the Germans are strongly organized. It's a little under a mile from Pimple Hill, but in front of it is Windmill Farm and the recon guys said the Germans were outposted in force here last night. Gordon—I mean Captain Jeffrey—is expecting one of his platoons to take these Germans out.

"OK, any questions yet?" Hobratschk bellowed.

There was one. Sergeant Horn asked, "Do we know if the Hun bastards have any reserve forces behind Hill 350?"

"Yes, they do," Lieutenant Hobratschk answered. "The size we don't know but Hill 303, about a quarter of a mile past 350, was reported to be swarming with more Germans. What we do know is the Germans are using delaying actions. So it might be that the Hun bastards—as you so aptly call them Sergeant Horn—have sacrificial forces on 350.

"Any more questions?" Hobratschk added as he stared at the forty-five men gathered around him.

This time there were none.

"OK, now comes the main attack. Captain Randall's E Company will come in from the bare valley just off to the west. See where I'm talking about? Look at your maps. Our battalion command post is close to here. Randall's men will attack and hit the backside of 350, knock out the Germans, and the hill will be ours. His men will be supported by a half dozen light tanks

"Now are there any questions?"

Again there were none, but there were a lot of tentative looking soldiers staring at Lieutenant Hobratschk. Bob was one of them. He knew it was certainly not his place to question an assault plan, but what he hadn't heard yet was just where his mortar platoon fit into this scheme of operations. And he was smart enough not to ask; Hobratschk would get to that when he was ready.

"OK, if all goes according to plan G Company will help Randall's men with Hill 350 after they clear Windmill Farm. And the tanks will continue to assist both companies. Colonel Sternberg is keeping Captain Spinney's F Company in reserve, just in case they're needed. And here's what we're doing to help."

Now all eyes were fixed on Lieutenant Hobratschk. What his men had been waiting for was about to get revealed.

"OK, we are following G Company up to Pimple Hill. I was with Captain Murphy when we surveyed the terrain at noontime. It's excellent ground. The backside of the hill has enough defile for us not to be seen by the Germans. There's dirt roads that will allow us to get our weapons carriers and jeeps close enough to make carrying our mortars and shells as painless as possible. I want plenty of spacing between the mortar emplacements, at least a hundred yards. We'll be registering on Windmill Farm first, then when we get word it's been taken we'll shift our fires up onto the backside of 350 and do our part to clean it out before E Company gets there. Start figuring the initial data you need using your maps; there will be no way to get any adjustments until Captain Randall's men get closer to Hill 350. Let's just hope it's to lift fires because we've done our jobs and theirs becomes easier.

"Any questions?'

Again, there were none.

"OK, then," Hobratschk started again. "Here's the good news. At 0300 in the morning you all are going to witness the biggest artillery strike you've ever seen. We finally are at an advantage. Finally. This isn't El Guettar where we were on the defense; it isn't Sbiba where we knew Rommel had all his tanks coming for us and we were playing defense again.

"No, this time we're all going to kill the German 'sumbitches out in front of us in large numbers. The ones our artillery don't get, we'll all get with our mortars. The bastards we might miss will die at the end of a bayonet."

Yelps rang out; men started cheering wildly. Bob slapped Gentle John on the back of his head. Gentle John slapped him back and pulled his helmet down over his face before barking, "You better fasten your chin strap when we get into this fight, Pal. We're going to be working our asses off."

"OK, then," Lieutenant Hobratschk bellowed out to try to calm everyone down. "Again, we attack behind G Company, thirty minutes before the artillery show goes off. That's 0230 in the morning."

More cheering followed before Sergeant Horn started yelling for everyone to shut up and salute their lieutenant.

No one had to. Some tried, but by this time Lieutenant Hobratschk's fist was sky high; he had joined the rally.

There just wasn't a lot of saluting that went on in the First Division, especially before a fight.

~THIRTY-FOUR~

THE REGIMENT'S 3RD BATTALION ON Bob's left had a very bad start when they attacked the hill they were after the following morning; it was Hill 407 and it was just to the west of Hill 350. "We watched the soldiers of Company L straggle to the summit until they silhouetted against the sunrise," Lieutenant Franklyn Johnson of the Antitank platoon told other officers later. "And then, too quickly, it happened. After Arab huts spit their machine-gun fire, mortar rounds crashed down and bayonets slashed. The enemy caught the platoon in that moment of disorganization when an objective is reached— that minute or two when control over squads and teams is weakest."

It turned out there were far more Germans here than the Americans expected; they were holed up in other thatch huts, and when these Germans emerged they tore more holes into the ranks of the L Company men. Captain Fogg, commanding the company, was killed by a burst of machinegun fire; his number two was ripped apart by a mortar shell's blast. Forty percent of the platoon's men were killed, severely wounded, or taken prisoner within the first hour of the attack.

The entire battalion was still pinned down at noontime. Attempts to evacuate the wounded and bring up badly needed ammo and supplies had been thwarted, despite the attempts of the M Company mortar squads to lay smoke screens down so the ambulances and trucks wouldn't be seen. And it only got worse. By mid-afternoon the hill was littered with the blood-soaked bodies of too many Americans.

When Courtney Brown got the initial casualty count for the

day, the numbers were staggering. He suffered seventeen men killed, twenty-five seriously wounded and another forty-eight received lesser wounds. The same number were reported missing.

When he learned the next morning that those forty-eight missing men were dead, the rugged battalion commander wept.

Good Friday started the same way for Bob's battalion, but it ended much differently. Gordon Jeffrey's G Company platoon jumped off at two-fifteen, and within a half hour his men had Pimple Hill in the bag. Bob's mortar platoon followed Jeffrey's men, per the plan. His squad's mortar was emplaced high on the hill, but just far enough down its backside for the tube's location to be masked from German observation when first light came. Using his map coordinates, Sergeant Horn then helped Gentle John get the initial settings dialed in so their fire would directly hit the buildings that made up Windmill Farm.

At three, the First Division's big 155mm Long Toms and the regiment's own artillery batteries began its ear-splitting preparatory fires. Low hanging clouds eclipsed the near full moon, but not the explosions of light at the end of the artillerymen's tubes. After Windmill Farm was plastered with Roman candle-like arrays of sparks and explosions, the backside of Hill 350 was worked over by the artillery's gunners for a good forty-five minutes. Then Hill 303, where the German reserves were hiding a quarter of a mile farther back, was doused with multiple rounds of white phosphorous artillery shells.

But Captain Murphy had decided not to use H Company's smoke shells to join in the barrages on Windmill Farm, for fear the riflemen's charge would go well enough to have them on top of the Germans when the artillery fires lifted; stinging white phosphorous was no way to support your own men. Bob's squad instead coughed up nearly a hundred rounds of heavy explosive.

At just after three-thirty Sergeant Horn told Bob and Gentle John to hold their firing, and the suspense of waiting to hear about G Company's attack on Windmill Farm instead filled the air. The wait was short; a half hour later, after a spirited bayonet charge, Jeffrey's platoon took the farm, leaving the dead and wounded Germans where they fell.

Then all hell broke loose; minutes later more Germans came charging into both of G Company's flanks. Captain Jeffrey's men held, but casualties started mounting, and Ben Sternberg—quickly realizing Windmill Farm was not merely a lightly defended outpost—directed Jeffrey to fall back to Pimple Hill. Captain Murphy wasted little time, radioed Lieutenant Hobratsch, and ordered him to now lay his platoon's lethal white phosphorous shells onto the Germans around the farm. Bob and Gentle John's response was instant; more than twenty rounds flew into the now leaden sky in a matter of minutes, smothering the visibility of their opposite numbers so they wouldn't see Captain Randall's men dashing towards Hill 350.

Randall had worked his men through other outposts by this time, and they were closing in on the west side of the hill. But there had been enough time for Bob and Gentle John to also lay a dozen of their high explosive shells on the backside of the important hill mass before Randall's men fixed their bayonets and charged.

Thirty-five Germans were taken prisoner and an untold number killed. But other enemy forces had hidden in trenches carved into the hill, and when first light came their artillery and mortar fires rained down on Randall's men. Then came the counterattack. The company suffered forty percent casualties over the next hour and was ordered to withdraw; Randall was shot in the thigh but he remained on the hill with his wounded men for the rest of the day.

Ben Sternberg wasted little time planning a new attack. This time the six light tanks he still had at his disposal would go after Windmill Farm. Captain Spinney's F Company got the mission to come out of reserve and clean out the Germans on the backside of Hill 350. An additional ten Stuarts with 37mm guns would follow Spinney's men.

Bob's mortar platoon would repeat what they did during the first attack; Lieutenant Hobratschk wanted white phosphorous rounds first this time, followed by what he called the mother of all high explosive barrages. The white phosphorous rounds would be leveled on Windmill Farm since the tanks attacking it were closed up. Then, upon Hobratschk's order, the firing of the white phosphorous would shift. First, Bob and Gentle John would concentrate on the high ground north and east of Hill 350, then they would switch over to heavy explosive rounds and adjust their fires onto the backside of the hill; this firing would be lifted as soon as word came back saying Spinney's men were closing in for the kill.

Captain Murphy was paying close attention to the H Company machinegun platoons this time; one Bob could see, and these men were in slight defilade on the high ground closer to the crest of Pimple Hill. They would spray thousands of their .50-caliber rounds on the eastern side of 350 to keep the Germans here pinned down. The other platoon was positioned to deliver its deadly fire on three objectives: the crest of the hill, its western side before Spinney's men charged, and then out onto Hill 303 to help keep any German reserves from interfering with the attack.

Captain Spinney's plan of attack was unknown to Bob; all he knew was he had the shell that had been in Slugger's hand when he was killed and had painted on it 'You Die."

There was another thing Bob didn't know about, even though there were rumors going around about it. His supporting artillery battalion now had three American Indians in their ranks; they were Garfield Brown, Anthony Omaha Boy and John Smith. A novel suggestion had been made to their commander, a bald no-nonsense colonel named Percy Thompson. To reduce the time it took to code and decode firing commands in order to keep their positions secret from the Germans, one of the Indians in Percy's headquarter battery had suggested he and his forward observer party fellow Indian send fire direction adjustments back and forth in their native tongue, something they said "would baffle the Germans."

It was about to do just that.

At 11:15 the American Indian forward observer called in fire to smother the German positions with smoke shells. Thirty-six 105mm howitzers followed and covered Hill 350 with a virtual hell of ground-shifting blasts. Bob and Gentle John did their part, and fired forty rounds of smothering white phosphorous on Windmill Farm. When Lieutenant Hobratschk called for the firing to shift to Hill 350, the Bearer Boys were hardly able to keep their breath as they rushed over a hundred shells to Bob, who fed them into their section's red hot barrel time and again.

When the order came to cease firing, Bob pretended he didn't hear it and instead fed the last round in for Slugger and yelled, "Screw every one of you Germans!" Seconds later the mortar blasted out of the tube and then the entire squad watched it angle for the Germans on the backside of Hill 350.

Spinney's men had already fixed their bayonets. German return fire was heavy at first; it was mainly their own mortars that were trying to stop Spinney's company, but this never slowed the forward progress of his 1st Platoon. But it did stop the Stuart tanks that were supporting them; they got bogged down before they could reach Hill 350, and never got into the fight. Another of Spinney's platoons nevertheless charged up to follow the leading men; a third F Company platoon skirted to the left to bypass the others, and dashed for the backside of the hill, circling in from the west.

Bob could see some of this early movement from where he was perched. But he heard very little nor could he see a damn thing as the F Company men disappeared behind Hill 350 while German artillery and mortar fire poured in from Hill 303 onto the American attackers.

It was a different story at Colonel Greer's command post. He had visitors from Allied Headquarters in Algeria with him who had come to observe the attack. One was Eisenhower's assistant chief of staff, Major General Harold R. Bull, and he had wandered away from Greer's small blacked-out tent in a shallow wadi to a forward outpost to get a better view of the action.

Hobratschk's friend Lieutenant Downing was in Greer's CP when Bull returned; Downing later told Hobratschk that Bull had said, "F Company's attack was one of the bravest things he had ever seen." Colonel Greer also saw the attack and later added to that in a letter he sent to Captain Spinney's mother; he wrote: "There is one thing I shall always remember about your son. It was during this Battle of Mateur when he led a counterattack against Hill 350. Two major generals and myself watched the attack. The generals said it was the finest action they had seen in this war—or in the last one. All of his officers were wounded, but your son carried on and took the hill; it was a splendid job."

Lieutenant Downing was still in the regiment's command post when the gloomy reports of casualties started trickling in. "Spinney had been wounded, but he remained with the company the whole time," Downing later told Lieutenant Hobratschk. "Labombarde was shot in the heel; Hinchliffe was shot through the mouth; Fanning was wounded; Hart was the luckiest of 'em all, but had to be evacuated because he got an acute appendicitis attack."

Downing then went on to describe what had happened to one of the most well-thought of sergeants in the regiment; he was an old timer who revered Army life and especially combat. In fact, the more miserable conditions were, the more this past fifty- year old World War One veteran loved it. Bob also knew who he was; he was the stuff of legends.

"Sergeant Herbie Merrill was hit in the head with a mortar fragment and had practically been scalped," Downing said. "The wound had also paralyzed him from the waist down. He was all through with the war, but he had gone out with a wisecrack. He told the battalion surgeon 'As long as they keep hitting me in the head, they can't hurt me.'"

Another officer told Lieutenant Hobratschk, "First Sergeant Herbie Merrill was outstanding that day, as were the rest of the sergeants in F Company: Ben Worsham, Harry Hyatt, Cleveland Rhinehart and George Mauorga," all names familiar to Bob because his mortar section had supported the company many times in North Africa.

But casualties were widespread when an Army chaplain picked his way through the still mine-infested backside of Hill 350 the next day. "In some cases soldiers had lain on the battlefield to avoid drawing enemy fire. Some were badly knocked about and others were still severely shaken," Chaplain Ed Rogers told everyone later. "We were able to get a few of the dead off the field, but not the majority of them. We tried to get more bodies off that night, but it was very black and the terrain was not familiar. We gave up until morning—Easter Morning. All that day I worked the detail collecting the dead. I hope I never spend another Easter like that one."

The cost for taking Hill 350 had indeed been high. Forty-three men were killed that day, 160 received wounds and twenty went missing. Even the tanks supporting the regiment suffered. A total of eighteen, including five mediums, were lost.

But it was General Bull who had the most to say about that Good Friday in April of 1943. He was sufficiently impressed with what he observed to tell General Allen's chief of staff, Colonel Mason, to "write it up." Bob knew something was going down because Lieutenant Hobratschk had tallied the total number of mortars his platoon had expended to support the rifle companies. It would be some time before Bob got to see what actually got written up, but he did learn it was something called a Presidential Unit Citation. Rumor had it that very few had been previously awarded during the entire Northern African campaign, so it was indeed big news.

CITATION OF UNIT

At H-Hour on 23 April 1943, in the vicinity of Beja, Tunisia, the 2nd Battalion, 18th Infantry, launched its attack on Hill 350, a strongly fortified position blocking the neck of the Tine Valley. It was vitally important to the entire offensive that this hill be taken, to provide a route to the plains of Mateur for the armored forces.

The hills on either side of the valley were to be seized in simultaneous attacks by adjoining units, while the 2nd Battalion conducted a double envelopment strategy. Each assaulting force suffered forty percent casualties during this attack. Adjoining units had failed to take the hills on the flanks, thus imperiling this battalion's overall security. Under an umbrella of heavy artillery fire, superior enemy forces launched a powerful and determined counterattack, driving the 2nd Battalion from its newly won objective.

Undaunted by this initial setback, this task force, although greatly weakened by severe losses, displayed unexcelled courage and prowess in arms by regrouping and again assaulting the important hill. Moving steadily over rugged terrain entirely devoid of cover, through an inferno of artillery, mortar, and machine-gun fire, the attackers never wavered in their purpose. The battle raged fiercely, but ultimately the enemy was driven from his position and Hill 350 was again occupied by this organization.

Despite desperate measures by the enemy to retake his critical position, the personnel of this battalion steadfastly held their ground. The 2nd Battalion was the only one in the entire sector to take its objective on that day.

The conspicuous aggressiveness, valor, extraordinary heroism, and profound devotion to duty displayed by this battalion, insured the successful occupation of this vital terrain feature. The eminently significant accomplishment of this gallant and cohesive fighting force was instrumental in breaching the entire defense system in this sector, enabling II Corps to advance uninterruptedly until the capitulation of the Axis forces in Tunisia was achieved.

Captain Murphy later told the men in his company that they had expended 92,000 rounds of machinegun ammunition and 1,200 rounds of 81mm mortars to support the attack. Bob undoubtedly would have relished the recognition his battalion received that infamous day, had he been able to read the citation then, but he would not have agreed with the part about the entire II Corps being able to advance uninterruptedly until the Germans surrendered in North Africa.

It simply had not gone that smoothly.

~THIRTY-FIVE~

BOB YORK'S 1ST BATTALION TOOK Hill 407 the next morning and then patrols went forward to investigate the immediate hill to its north. Here his men found a battery of 88mm guns, two tanks and numerous German infantry in a draw. York called for artillery fire, it was laid in, and those not killed cut and ran.

York pressed on to determine just how far the Germans had pulled back. When night fell his battalion was in defensive positions on Hill 347, a good two miles north of where his men had started their day, and they found no Germans here.

Bob's 2nd Battalion was in reserve during these moves, but on the Monday following Easter Sunday Greer ordered Ben Sternberg forward, and his companies eventually spread out on Djebel Zerais and Hill 346; both were just to the north of Hill 303.

The most excitement Bob had during this time occurred when his mortar squad tried to settle in on the backside of Djebel Zerais; he first saw long fangs, then he quickly used his Colt 45 to kill a thick, six-foot long snake before he, Gentle John and the Bearer Boys laid down to get some sleep.

But there were other dangers around them when they woke up the following foggy morning.

"As the First Division advanced, it found itself raked with artillery fire from a range of hills to the north," General Bradley explained. "Before pushing on it became necessary for us to drive the enemy out of those higher hills and deny him artillery observation of our movements. On the northern rim of the valley, the bald face of a djebel soared into the African sky. It was known as Hill 609.

"By April 26, after only three days of attack, it had become clear that until 609 was taken and the enemy driven off its summit the First Division could not advance any further down the rim of the valley," Bradley further explained. "Just as soon as 609 was cleared, we could speed up Allen's advance and set the stage for Harmon's breakthrough."

Major General Ernest Harmon was the gravely voiced commander of the armored division that was to make the bold sweep down the Tine Valley to seize Mateur. But Bradley was fully aware of the First Division's plight. "Later that day I met with [British commander] Anderson in Terry Allen's CP," he wrote after the war. "Artillery fire from Hill 609 and its neighboring hills had splashed into the spines of the djebels on which Allen had advanced, showering his troops with shell fragments and sharp slivers of stone."

Colonel Greer's executive officer explained the situation Bob was in far more bluntly. "We were holding until other units could catch up with us," Jack Williamson noted in his diary that very day. "The problem was to keep us from being sent out on a limb and chewed up by artillery fire."

Thus all Bob could do was wait. Luckily his squad found an abandoned German cave carved into the hillside he was on where, on occasion, he could make out what looked like a crude Indian arrowhead that was facing towards him from Hill 609's 2,000-foot peak.

The next several days were a nightmare for the other regiments in the First Division. Two lesser hills had to be seized before Hill 609 was taken and Bob's 18th Infantry could move up to its next objective, Djebel Badjar.

A battalion of the 16th Infantry paid a heavy price taking the terrain protecting one of the approaches to Hill 609. Attacking due north at night using their compasses, these men managed to get through fields of short wheat to the base of the first hill they were to take before climbing to its crest and trying to overpower their opposite numbers with hand grenades and knives. But when the Germans counterattacked all of the battalion's wire lines were broken, their radios were shot out, and communication to their regimental commander ceased. An even larger enemy force came at the battalion the following morning and surrounded the men. A desperate hand-to-hand fight around the summit of the hill followed, but when it was over the battalion commander and roughly 150 of his men were captured; the rest were killed or wounded.

Bob York's 1st Battalion still moved closer to Djebel Badjar while Colonel Greer waited for Hill 609 to fall. There were clear indications that there was trouble ahead; this became evident after one of York's companies occupied Djebel Sidi Meftah, a ridge just before Badjar's rise up to nearly a thousand feet; a patrol captured some Germans who said the hill was still strongly defended.

Hill 609 finally fell on April 30th, and this allowed Bob's 2nd Battalion to also move up onto the same ridge York's companies were on; Bob and Gentle John set up their mortar and the Bearer Boys piled shells up while the rifle companies consolidated their positions, fully expecting the attack order on Djebel Badjar would come down soon.

But Bob instead spent more time looking at red and orange poppies in the Tine Valley than he did loading rounds into his mortar. Reconnaissance patrols had found it appeared the Germans were withdrawing. Then, heavy motor traffic could be heard during the night of May 2nd; when patrols went out to investigate this the next morning the men found that the Germans had indeed vacated Djebel Badjar, and headed eastward towards the blue turquois waters of the Mediterranean Sea where they would presumably be afforded safe passage out of Africa.

But it was far from over for Bob. Terry Allen's headquarters men had no sooner set up a new command post in a battered farm yard, which had been a former German supply dump, before word came down from General Bradley that same morning to keep moving.

The II Corps commander was now ready to cut General Harmon's tanks loose for their foray down the Tine Valley into Mateur. Bradley knew the First Division was exhausted from its fighting over hills in the most inhospitable terrain in Northern Tunisia, but "to lighten its load in the closing phase of the attack" he assigned a sector of the Chouigui Pass to Terry Allen "to contain the enemy between that vital passage and Mateur." The pertinent part of the order read: "Division will push out reconnaissance (foot and motor). Gain contact. Advance 18th Infantry into zone MATEUR road at which point it will be considered that Phase Line 1 has been reached." The remainder of the message carried instructions for the continuation of the attack with the ultimate mission of driving the Germans from Tunisia.

General Harmon's tanks swept up the Tine Valley Monday morning May the 3rd, and his reconnaissance platoon was knocking on doors in Mateur by noontime. Several armored vehicles fanned out amongst the buildings during the afternoon to punctuate for the Germans the arrival of American forces, but many of them had already fled and left demolished bridges behind.

Mateur was still a bad place to be. Fresh German infantry, armor and artillery pieces were rushed into the area to prevent Harmon's tanks from reaching their next objective—Ferryville. Bf-109s added to the German effort. They dive-bombed bridges as fast as American engineers could rebuild them.

But Harmon's tanks rolled out two days later and advanced over the nine miles of road to Ferryville that were defended by Germans now determined to fight to the last man. Anti-tank guns to support them populated the hills to either side of the roadway, and artillery pieces added to their effort to halt Harmon's tanks.

By this time Colonel Greer had set up his new command post in a few tents along a wadi to the west of Qued Tine, which was really a stream roughly ten miles due south of Mateur. The move to this area was well-remembered by Bob. When his 2nd Battalion crossed the road the tankers had used to first get up into Mateur, everything from trucks carrying armored infantry to prime movers towing artillery pieces still clogged the roadway. The air was full of dust, but there was what one soldier with Bob remembered as a "festive air," leaving this man to wonder whether the campaign was all over and they just forgot to tell the First Division.

But the distant rumbling of guns and shellfire on the road Harmon's tanks were now using to reach Ferryville were unmistakable; columns of black smoke from burning vehicles also filled the air. To Bob it meant the Germans were indeed going to make a last stand. He was now moving closer to the smashing echoes of 88s. Orders had come down; more hills had to be taken. The first one for Bob's 2nd Battalion was marked as Hill 232 on Captain Murphy's map.

It was now May 5th. Djebel Douimiss stood just to the south of this hill; intelligence had determined forces of the Barenthin Regiment were still in the area, but no one knew for sure who was on Hill 232, or what their strength might be.

The Qued Tine would have to be crossed by tanks in order for their weight to be added to the attack, and engineers had to build a bridge over the stream for that to happen. Ben Sternberg's orders were for Bob's 2nd Battalion to occupy and hold the large northern slope of Hill 232; Sternberg knew the Germans definitely had it under observation. Bob York and Courtney Brown also had their assignments; York was tasked with taking two nearby smaller hills while Brown took the eastern half of Hill 232. H-hour was set for 0300 the next morning.

The atmosphere at Colonel Greer's command post was unusually tense when the attack went off, but Ben Sternberg sent word forty-five minutes later reporting Bob's 2nd Battalion was advancing steadily towards Hill 232. So far so good. Greer was somewhat concerned when an officer in a forward outpost reported seeing red flares to the east five minutes later; it could mean the Germans were marking the area for their artillery to fire on.

But tensions eased after word came back saying Brown's 3rd Battalion was approaching the lower heights on the east side of Hill 232 and they were not encountering any opposition. This was followed minutes later with the news Bob York's 1st Battalion was on Hill 121, just to the south. Greer even breathed a sigh of relief when another outpost radioed in and reported the observer here saw another red flare, but it was about five miles further to the east.

Everything still looked good. Sternberg soon reported he was getting closer to Hill 232. But Greer started evincing real concern when word came back saying a hidden enemy 88 emplacement had been found, yet it did not trouble him enough to hold back on ordering the tanks to get ready to move forward so they could support the rifle companies as they attacked their hills.

It was still plenty dark when Bob's 2nd Battalion finally reached the base of Hill 232; Captain Murphy was with Ben Sternberg, and together they had determined that the mortar platoon would set their tubes up in a wadi just to the northwest. Lieutenant Ho-bratschk wasted little time and relayed the order to Sergeant Horn; minutes later, using their crude map, Bob and Gentle John had their mortar registered on the top of Hill 232 and were ready to fire on command when F Company began their attack.

They did not have to wait long. Captain Spinney, having quickly recovered from the wounds he received back on Hill 350, person-ally led his men forward, just as first light was appearing over the hill. All of the H Company mortars poured their 81mm high ex-plosive shells on the crest, then their gunners made adjustments to work their fires down the backside of the hill. Bob and Gentle John ceased firing just ahead of six; by now Spinney's men were nearing the top of the hill. The heavy machinegun platoons were about to weigh in with murderous cross firing that would cut down any German who dare pop up while Brown's 3rd Battalion made their attack on its eastern slope.

For Colonel Greer, the next hour was one of his worst in North Africa. The first indication of trouble came just before six-thirty. It turned out the Germans had both 88s and artillery pieces on nearby Djebel Douimiss. Bob York reported that his C Company was getting clobbered by them. Greer questioned if it really was artillery fire coming from Djebel Douimiss. York answered it was, and he also said German tanks had appeared; they came from the backside of Hill 232.

This was precisely where Bob's mortar was now placing its rounds, but their shells had little impact on the tanks. Before too long his entire battalion was pinned down by the 88s and German machinegun fire. Captain Spinney's men had neared the top of Hill 232 by this time, and they found that it was covered with mines and other booby traps. Spinney had no good options now; all he could do is have his men lay flat where they were, and hope for the best.

At six-thirty-five Colonel Greer learned two more things. Bob York was withdrawing his men onto the backside of Hill 121. Greer responded by finally ordering the tanks forward, only to have three Shermans hit mines on the same side of the Qued Tine his CP was on. This still did not deter Colonel Greer; he ordered the rest of the tankers to keep moving. The engineers searched for another route they could advance on, and luckily found one. They put in a bridge, but by now three hours had elapsed.

The delay was costly. Three more tanks were hit by artillery fire before they could cross over. It was just after nine when Greer learned that just one platoon of tanks did get across the bridge before it collapsed, but now it was too late.

Everything had turned bad. One of York's companies still on the southwest slope of Hill 232 was pinned down by German machinegun fire. Sternberg was reporting to Greer that he could go nowhere; worse, one of his outposts reported seeing about a hundred 3rd Battalion men being taken prisoner.

Just thirty-five men attached to Courtney Brown's three rifle companies and his heavy weapons company came off the eastern side of Hill 232 later that day. The dead and wounded lay where they fell. Amongst them was the body of Captain Cliff Raymer, the K Company commander who had led his men so gallantly at El Guettar.

It was almost as bad elsewhere. While Bob, Gentle John, the Bearer Boys and the rest of the 2nd Battalion were hopelessly pinned down, York's men were still in the fight. But all of York's light machineguns had been knocked out; Company A, being commanded by Captain McGregor, was unaccounted for; Greer didn't know it but they were pinned down by the same machinegun fire that was keeping Sternberg's men flat on their stomachs in shallow foxholes, and most of McGregor's men were eventually taken prisoners by the Germans; McGregor was one of them.

Colonel Greer ordered his ambulance drivers to find every medic who was still in the rear and go out after dark to evacuate the casualties. The number was gruesome. Numerous dead bodies were loaded up. Eighty wounded soldiers were finally given treatment. A hundred and ninety-three others were counted missing, and presumed captured.

"All officers, except one in I and K Companies were killed, missing or captured," Jack Williamson, Greer's executive officer, wrote in his diary that day about Courtney Brown's 3rd Battalion losses.

Bob had been very lucky again; no one in his squad had been hit, or taken prisoner, although a few of his Company H heavy machine gunners were captured. Spinney's men atop Hill 232 were pinned down until noontime before the firing let up; his casualties were fortunately light, but some of his F Company men were also missing. No one except the dead and captured actually left Hill

232 until the following morning, and not until a massive German artillery barrage covered the withdrawal of the Barenthin Regiment.

It was an ignominious way for Colonel Greer and all of his men to end their fighting in North Africa.

~THIRTY-SIX~

THE GERMAN SOLDIERS OF THE Barenthin Regiment marched into prisoner of war enclosures in formation and in-step two days later. "They were the only German unit to do so according to the reports I saw," General Allen's chief of staff told others. Word of the collapse of the entire German army in North Africa had already started trickling down within Bob's regiment, and to him it was as startling as it was to everyone else.

After 184 days, the North African campaign was suddenly over. "For miles and miles, farther than the eye could see, the Germans came under swinging white flags, often guarded only by one foot-sore GI," wrote Jack Thompson, the bearded war correspondent for the *Chicago Tribune*. "They came by battalions and regiments, singing their battle songs, with full equipment, the cocky Africa Korps, finally taken in defeat, in what up to that time had been the greatest defeat of Axis arms since the start of the war."

When the British mopped up the Cape Bon Peninsula the 18th Infantry soldiers captured during the fighting a few days earlier were freed. A rumor even got started about how Captain McGregor took the surrender of the commander of the 15th Panzer Division; it turned out to be true. After sending a farewell message to his homeland, Generalleutnant Willibald Borowitz had ordered a cease fire in his sector, and he then turned himself in to the former American prisoner of war McGregor. In all, 157,000 Germans and 86,700 Italians marched into captivity when Tunisia fell.

"There was a strong unofficial sentiment again that divisions that had fought in Tunisia would be returned to the states to impart combat information to the divisions preparing for overseas duty," Lieutenant Downing—still serving as a liaison between the regiment and division headquarters—told Lieutenant Hobratschk the day after the cease fire was ordered. "And there was an uneasy let-down feeling around regiment headquarters. The Tunisian war was over at last; the future was the big question."

Bob had already been in the line for more time than his predecessors in the First Division had been during all of World War One. His immediate reward was two days of loafing and resting up in a bivouac area west of the Qued Tine for what he hoped would be some more time off to go into Tunis and celebrate the Allied victory. Some officers did, but two days later word came down about Bob's fate; the regiment was going back to Algeria, and Bob soon learned he was headed for Oran, where he first landed in North Africa. Speculation was rampant about what that meant, but unknown to Bob was General Patton had already decided his fate.

There would be no going back to the states. Weeks earlier, Patton had met with Eisenhower to go over the plan for the upcoming invasion of Sicily. Patton would be in command of the American effort. He and Ike had been discussing the wide zone of beach area his newly-formed Seventh Army was tasked with taking and holding when the invasion began. Patton was reluctant to go ashore here with two of the green divisions already assigned to him.

"I want those First Division sons 'a bitches," Patton pleaded during that meeting. "I won't go on without them." Eisenhower acceded, and what it meant to Bob was more amphibious training was eventually going to consume his time for the foreseeable future.

Bob jumped into the back of a deuce and a half at dawn on Tuesday the 11th of May and immediately started playing cards to pass the time. The regiment's long convoy of trucks first passed through Beja, where Arabs—not pretty French girls—were waving wildly and throwing flowers and fruit to everyone; they were also begging for cigarettes, candy and chewing gum. During mid-afternoon the convoy went through the crossroads of ancient Roman and Berber civilizations at Souk Ahras, and then the trucks ground to a halt at Guelma, where Bob spent the night in his pup tent with Gentle John.

Morning brought more travel, this time on a better road through Constantine where signs indicated the town was off limits to regular troops; Bob, nor anyone else, was allowed to even venture away from the convoy during the brief halt here. Then, without a worry in the world about finding a German 88 placed in the hills, or a Stuka diving out of the skies, Bob rode in the pleasant sunshine through Setif before the convoy reached the tiny village of Maillot where he spent his second night; the next night found him in familiar L'Arba, twenty miles south of Algiers, where he bivouacked again near the same grove of large cork trees where he had encamped on his way to Tunisia back in December.

Hundreds cheered wildly when he passed through Blida, Affreville and Orleansville, then Oggaz, before Bob saw the distant specks of the spires that marked Oran on the bright Algerian horizon the next afternoon. By now the Bearer Boys were the ones cheering wildly; visions of its friendly bistros and pretty French women danced in their heads. But that was not to be, not right away. The convoy stopped next to a smelly, saucer-shaped pasture outside of Mangin, twelve miles short of Oran. The first order of business was setting up camp.

Lieutenant Hobratschk and Captain Murphy had come by train, and had shared more than a few drinks with other hoot-hollering officers along the way. One was the colorful Sam Carter, the heavy weapons company commander in Bob York's battalion. Hobratschk later shared what Sam had noticed when they got to Oran.

"As our train pulled into Oran we passed large pyramidal tents to either side of the tracks. Inside we could see rows of cots, all nicely made up with sheets, pillow cases and blankets. We imagined this was where we were going to put up," Captain Carter had said. "But when we got to the station, no one was there to greet us; no one at all. The train waited for about a half hour, then it started to back up past those nice tents where we thought we'd be let off, but the train kept going backwards until we were let off near an open field. From here we marched into what was to be our bivouac area."

It was the same smelly depression where Bob was. "We pitched our tents and set up our kitchens," Carter lamented. "Then we settled in as best we could. There were fifty-five-gallon drums filled with 100-octane fuel stored on the grounds, and we were told we could wash our uniforms in these drums, and then set them out to dry.

"We soon learned we were not going to be issued new uniforms to replace our woolen olive drabs, even though we had been living in them for six months. Most of us had only had two baths during the entire Tunisian campaign, the last one in the warm waters of the Roman baths at Gafsa a month ago. We were not happy. We had no bathing facilities in Mangin."

Bob, like everyone else, knew there was no further need for wool uniforms. The weather was already hot, and the bitter North African cold and rains of the previous winter were a thing of the past. General Allen also knew the First Division was going to Sicily, where the heat and humidity of summer there would be unbearable. The invasion was top secret, and plans for the division were known to very few, but Allen had made repeated attempts to obtain new khaki uniforms through normal channels, only to be rebuffed each time he tried; it would overburden the supply people, he was told. He finally took the matter up directly with George Patton, just as the two were sitting down to dinner one night in late May.

The rumormongering about that meeting only got down to officer levels; even they regarded Patton's treatment of General

Allen and the division to be despicable, and they didn't want soldiers like Bob to hear what was said. Colonel Mason, Allen's Chief of Staff, who witnessed the conversation, described it this way: "General Patton listened with increasing impatience during the two or three minutes it took General Allen to make the request, then his attitude changed abruptly.

"He told General Allen that he wouldn't need khaki uniforms because most of the division was going to get killed trying to invade Sicily, that he didn't think the First Division had enough guts to fight its way inland against the better-quality German troops we could be meeting, but that if General Allen got a foothold on Sicily and still had as much as a third of his division left, he would then see to it that our troops got khaki uniforms."

To a commanding general whose troops had given Patton his first victory as a corps commander back at El Guettar, this was beyond the pale. Mason captured what happened next. "This was a trademark Patton slur of the First Division. And it provided the customary Allen reaction. While Patton was still raging, he turned his head sideways to me and said, 'Let's go.' With that, and no amenities whatsoever, General Allen walked away with me in tow."

There was a brief moratorium on training after Bob settled in at Mangin. He played cards and shot craps with other men in his mortar platoon, and he even managed to send a brief note home to his mother, telling her he was OK, getting along fine, and for her not to worry about him. Then, word came down saying unrestricted passes were going to be granted so the long awaited trip he wanted to make into Oran could happen. But he had to wait his turn, which proved to be a rather lousy hand of cards when word starting filtering back about others' visits to the town the First Division had liberated during their very first fight of the war.

Lieutenant Johnson in Anti-tank was friendly with many of Ben Sternberg's men, so word traveled fast about his experience. "Trucks carried full loads of us into the city which has been our post-campaign goal for so long," Johnson told some officers. "However, there were unexpected complications in changed Oran. It seems that the occupation soldiers and base section commandos, having had their pick of goods, liquor, and women in the plush, fur-lined foxholes of Oran, deeply resented this 'muscling in' by combat troops.

"Besides, their neatly pressed slacks and new style summer sport shirts contrasted with our muddy boots, patched olive drabs and combat helmets," Johnson added mischievously. "Then, too, each Texas 36th Division man was proudly wearing a green and brown ribbon, which we had never seen. When we asked what it was, their reply was, 'Oh, don't you know? This is the European Theater Ribbon for occupying North Africa.'

"The First Division's next question was short," Johnson added with relish. "Were you at Longstop. . .Kasserine. . .Sbiba. . .El Guettar. . .?"

Lieutenant Johnson then turned to the subsequent hell raising during his visit to the city. "Gun-toting GIs and cocky junior officers took over Oran and a few First Division tommy-guns and pistols let fly into the air, scaring civilians indoors and bringing out the M.P.s. By evening the picture was simple: a bottle of vino, a French street-walker—*Lesh go shumplaysh*—an alley or an apartment room, a soldier out cold. Or maybe a street corner brawl raging between the 'recruits,' meaning the Texas boys, M.P.s and the exuberant intoxicated veterans. The latter usually shellacked their opponents, but the M.P.s grabbed so many that the next morning General Allen went to the jail and bailed out his boys, to the comfiture of the local authorities."

Bob had gotten wind of this story, but an even better one made the rounds two days later. An artillery man had gone into Oran in his jeep to get his watch fixed. The Frenchman who owned the shop told him he was busy with other work, and it would be weeks before he could get to his watch. The shop was small, and the door opened towards the street; the radioman in the jeep overheard what became a heated argument. The jeep the pair came to Oran in sported a pedestal-mounted .50-caliber machine gun with plenty of traverse. The radioman turned it and leveled the barrel towards the door. The shopkeeper quickly capitulated and repaired the watch while the artilleryman waited.

By now orders had been handed down from on high forbidding First Division soldiers from even patronizing Oran's bars and bistros because they were not wearing "proper" uniforms. This infuriated every soldier and officer in the regiment. Ed Kuehn, who had taken over Company K after Captain Raymer was killed, was one of those who took this order and his deep resentment of it to another level.

"Two jeep-loads of us officers went into Oran for a little R&R," Kuehn explained with no apologies offered. "It was our turn. Lieutenant Colonel York, together with Captain Brad Bacon, myself, Lieutenants Moore and Frank Leaman, were all involved. When we got to Oran everything was off-limits, except to the Mediterranean Base Section, the MBS personnel. Military police were posted in front of all the bars, but we still went into the only decent one there—the Golden Rooster. We brushed past the M.P.s over their protest and went inside where we saw smartly-dressed officers around a circular table drinking beer. We asked the bartender to pour us our own beers, but he said he could not serve us any beer."

This aroused the fighters in the group. "Colonel York then said to give us some wine, but the bartender said no to that too," Kuehn said. "That did it. Bob York jumped over the bar and started handing out bottles of beer to all of us. I jumped over the bar to help out. The occupation officers yelled for the M.P.s who soon started blowing their whistles at us. But we were already in a beautiful fight, and I can still remember the feeling I had when I landed a punch to some fat major's belly. Then we ran outside, got in our jeeps and headed for Mangin, singing and drinking beer all the way back."

Rumors even spread about how General Allen helped some 18th Infantry soldiers in front of the Alletti Hotel. Apparently some of the occupation forces had disparaged them; Allen first tried to break up the ensuing fight, but when he heard the Texas boys had indeed trashed his men, a well-sourced witness—Colonel Mason— later said Allen joined in the fun and had "beaten up some of the rear-area M.P.s."

"I was in the midst of that, right where this supposedly happened," Captain Murphy told Bob, Gentle John and the Bearer Boys the next day. "I'm leaving soon to have this damn hernia worked on, but I want you to know I saw this matter with General Allen differently. I didn't see him hitting any M.P.s, but I did see him look the other way when our soldiers beat up those Texas boys." Then he jokingly added, "I had to tell Wally to remember whose side he was on, your lieutenant being from Texas, and he looked the other way too! If I could I would have promoted him on the spot."

Every rank and file soldier of the First Division was proud as hell about what they joked was "the second taking of Oran." Others were not a bit amused. "When the rioting got out of hand Theater sternly directed me to order Allen to get his troops promptly out of town," General Bradley recalled. "While the episode resulted partly from our failure to prepare a rest area for troops back from the front, it also indicated a serious breakdown in discipline within the division. Allen's troops had strut their toughness while ignoring regulations that applied to all other units.

"While the Oran outbreak demonstrated the need for tightening discipline within the division, it also indicated how we had woefully overlooked a soldier's need for relaxation once he emerges from combat," Bradley confessed. "We could have probably prevented the rioting in Oran. Instead, we rushed the First into a dreary tent bivouac for the resumption of rigorous field training."

Terry Allen saw this much differently. He was fiercely loyal to his men; that is why he got so much out of them in combat. He resented Bradley; he had never even commanded a battalion in combat before he soared up the ranks. And when Patton weighed in on the "second taking of Oran" Allen didn't mince his words; he told his friend, "The troops have been in the line for six god-damn months. Let them celebrate getting back alive. It will stop soon!"

And it did. That, and General Patton had already settled the controversy between Bob's First Division and the 36th Division rather handily. The Texas boys would stay in Oran. Patton had evidenced weeks ago to Eisenhower that he preferred more experienced troops for the invasion of Sicily. Even if they had a supposed problem with discipline, Patton wanted men who won fights.

~THIRTY-SEVEN~

BOB WAS SITTING ON THE BEACH at Plage Beau Sejour following a swim in the warm Mediterranean a few days later when Lieutenant Hobratschk came up to him and introduced Lieutenant Richard Lindo. Bob recognized him; he knew Lindo was an artillery officer who had been a forward observer with his battalion back at El Guettar, but he had no idea why his platoon commander was here, of all places, introducing the artillery lieutenant to him.

Bob had company with him when the officers arrived; he was a replacement who had just arrived in Oran. His name was Paul Stegall, and he was from a tiny community in Anderson County South Carolina, near Pendleton, way up in the northwest corner of the state about as far away from beaches as was possible in the Palmetto State. The pair had taken an instant liking to one another. Paul had four brothers; he was the second oldest. He had plowed fields when he was a young teenager, been a stock boy at a grocery store, and was working in a textile mill when he got drafted. He was fair-skinned and handsome, about Bob's height, less outgoing than Bob, but it was his eagerness to help him learn the way a mortar squad worked together that Paul appreciated the most about his new friend.

Paul also liked the way Bob joked around; he had first warned Paul that the locals were always out to loot something a soldier had, and if he didn't want to loose his boots he'd better keep them on. Paul especially admired Bob's ability to be a good listener, and never judgmental of others. A deeply religious Baptist, Paul never heard Bob talk about someone behind their back; he just wasn't that way and Paul saw that as honorable. Paul was a quick study of a man's character. He didn't swear. He didn't even drink liquor or smoke cigarettes, but he seemed to fit right in. They were the same age, although Bob joked he had seniority on him because he was born in February of '21, whereas Paul had waited until September that year to come into this world.

Gentle John and the other Bearer Boys were frolicking in the water and throwing a colorful beach ball around. It was a lazy Friday afternoon, the sun was bright, there was a gentle wind and little to do other than relax.

Lieutenant Hobratschk and Lindo were also supposed to be relaxing that day, but for some strange reason they were wearing their uniforms. They weren't wearing helmets or ties, so Bob figured George Patton was no where to be seen. He was just starting to stand up to salute them, and Paul was following Bob's lead, when Lieutenant Hobratschk told both of them to stay put.

"We need to talk with you privately Bob," his commander started. Paul took this as his cue to leave, and after seeing that confirmed in Lieutenant Hobratschk's gestures, he said he was going to go for a swim; he headed for the water.

"Bob, I'm Lieutenant Lindo, 32nd Field," he began when they all sat together in the soft sand. "I'm afraid I have some bad news for you. Wally and I have known each other for some time, and he told me you were from that town in Connecticut where they make Peter Paul Mounds candy bars. He told me how your Grandmother had sent a box full of them to you last Christmas, and how you shared them with everybody in your mortar platoon. Bob, it's about Technical Sergeant George Walker…"

"Is George alright?" Bob interrupted; there was a look of deep worry on his face that Lindo could clearly see.

"Bob, I'm sorry to have to be the bearer of this news, but George was killed during the second week of May," Lindo said sadly. "He was attached to a 155mm artillery battalion we work with—7th

Field. He was a fine soldier, and I'm told liked by everyone. His family back in Naugatuck should have received a telegram from the Army notifying them of George's death by now, and I just felt I needed to come and find you, so I could personally tell you he was gone."

With this Bob stood up. Lindo and Hobratschk joined him. Bob turned to Lieutenant Lindo, and said, "Thank you, sir. And thank you Lieutenant Hobratschk. That was very thoughtful of you to mention to Lieutenant Lindo that I was from Naugatuck, and especially kind of you to come all the way here to tell me about George. He was a close boyhood friend of mine, and his family lives on the same street just down the hill from my mother. The war has now hit very close to home. I'll have to send word that I've heard about George. And now I'm going to have to settle the matter of his getting killed with the Germans by evening the score for George."

Lindo came over to Bob and shook his hand; Lieutenant Hobratschk did the same, and then they left. There was no saluting necessary.

The Bearer Boys—Paul was now one of them—and Gentle John happened to witness the gathering and when they saw Bob sit back down and lower his head into his hands, they all got out of the water, came up the beach, and gathered around him.

No one said anything. When Bob looked up, they saw tears in his eyes. At first Bob didn't say anything, but he eventually whispered, "I just heard my best boyhood friend from back home was killed."

It was Paul who found the right words to say. "Blessed are the dead," he prayed softly. "Yea, saith the Spirit, they that may rest from their labors; and their works do follow them."

"Thank you, Paul," Bob said to his new best friend.

Later that month Bob's letter arrived. Viola was happy. Her son had made it through the entire African war. He was safe. Where he would go to next there was no telling, and Bob hadn't even speculated about coming home. She called Sonny to share the news; it was the happiest either of them had been in weeks. Viola also called her sisters and Nellie; they were all overjoyed.

Then darkness came. In early June word spread like wildfire through Naugatuck. Mrs. Walker had received the Western-Union telegram from the Army. She was beyond consoling; her son George was dead.

"This is our war," Ernie Pyle later wrote for moments like this. "And we will carry it with us as far as we go from one battleground to another until it is all over, leaving some behind on every beach, in every field. We are just beginning with the ones who lie in back of us here in Tunisia. I don't know whether it was their good fortune or their misfortune to get out of it so early in the game.

"I guess it doesn't make any difference, once a man is gone. They died so others lived and nobody knows why it's so. They died and thereby the rest of us can go on. When we leave here for the next shore, there is nothing we can do for the ones beneath the wooden crosses, except to pause and murmur, 'Thanks, pal.'"

~THIRTY-EIGHT~

BOB GOT SOME BIG NEWS later that month. Colonel Greer bade farewell to the regiment; he was promoted to brigadier general and was going back to the states. In his parting address he heaped praise on every one of his men and officers, then his replacement was introduced. He came from Allied Headquarters; his name was Colonel George A. Smith, Jr. He had a high forehead, looked more pleasant and smiled more often than the always stern-faced Greer, but the reaction amongst the rank and file was mixed. Most were happy for Colonel Greer, but Bob was the first to tell Paul that having a new commander named right away was a sure sign they were going to be in a real fight again somewhere, and soon.

General Allen gave a very frank talk a few days later. "We love and respect Terry Allen even more after he talked to us at Mangin," an officer remembered. "Without a word regarding the Oran troubles, our division commander praised the men in the ranks for their work in Tunisia, and stated that them—not him or any other officer—must be rewarded for the main accomplishments of the Red One division now being so highly praised in stateside newspapers.

"He gave us his credo: 'Do your job. We don't want heroes—dead heroes. We're not out for glory—we're here to do a dirty, stinking job.'"

After Allen's talk Bob turned to Paul and, with his trademark smirk said, "Well that settles that. Told you we were going fighting. Where we're headed nobody knows, except the higher ups, and they are keeping a tight lid on it. Bets are on it's either Italy, Turkey, Greece, or maybe even France."

Their African vacation was terminated in late May. The entire regiment, with all of its attachments—from artillery batteries to medics—moved into the brushy LaMacta Forest; it was on the edge of the blue Mediterranean clear across the Gulf of Arzew, a safe fifty or so miles from the Texas boys back in Oran. Training started anew; for three weeks Bob found himself repeating landing after landing on the beaches opposite the forest and in the vicinity of Mers el Hadjada, where coastal dunes gave way to the cliffs and hills at Sidi Mansour.

It took just a day or two for George Patton to make his initial appearance, and he had in his company a virtual who's who in the United States Army, including General Eisenhower, General Bradley and the man at the very top of the organization chart, General George C. Marshall, who was visiting from Washington. The group, which also included senior African Headquarters officials, had been watching from a distance a practice landing by Bob's 18th Infantry.

For Paul it was not an exercise where he was baptized by fire; there was no loud fire, but it was still stressful for him since it was his very first landing practice with his new company. Down came the ramps from the LCI they were on, and together with Bob and the rest of their mortar squad, they all sloshed ashore, bent low and fanned out as if they were actually storming a hostile beach.

They were. The generals were close by, and one was particularly demonstrative. Patton broke out from the group when he saw a nearby squad of riflemen, ran towards them and screamed, "And just where in the hell are your goddamn bayonets?"

The answer was a full display of First Division cockiness. As the story got told later, a rifleman just stared hard at Patton and said casually, "Well, we didn't expect the beach to be defended by a three-star general." That brought out the best ire in George Patton's makeup; he swore loudly some more, and harangued every private and corporal in the squad, telling them "a fighting man needs steel at the end of his rifle."

Bob and Paul saw the show from a safe distance, but everyone nearby stood in embarrassed silence as Patton kept delivering volley after volley of obscenities. One of them was General Bull, who had witnessed F Company's attack on Hill 350 a little over a month earlier. This time he just stared at General Marshall, and said nothing before pivoting towards General Bradley and whispering, "Well, there goes Georgie's chance for a crack at higher command. That temper of his is going to finish him yet."

Not quite yet, for the next day Patton accompanied Marshall to Colonel Smith's CP where the Army's top commander "made a fine talk to the men," according to Patton's diary entry that night. The duo had actually spoken just to the officers and some non-coms of the 18th, so Bob nor Paul got to hear any words of inspiration that may have been offered.

It was a matter of just a few more days before Patton made another appearance. "Sirens screamed and a command car carrying three flags appeared, followed by a covey of lesser vehicles," Lieutenant Johnson in the Antitank Company told a group of officers the following Thursday. "An aid ran over and bid Jones to line up the company, which he hastily did, as Patton and a staff of colonels majestically swept into view. Aside from the amount of brass, what impressed us most was 'Old Blood and Guts' in his costume, from his shined and spurred boots, pink breeches, tailored shirt, and silver buckled belt—minus six-shooters—to his shellacked helmet."

But the visit was short. "We barely had the time to take this all in when, with only a word to Jones and a glance at the rest of us, 'God' moved on."

He moved next to the 32nd Field Artillery's location. "Up comes Patton with a group of generals, British, French and American,"

Battery A's commander John Whittemore told Lieutenant Lindo, who retold the story to Lieutenant Hobratschk. "They stood alongside me, observed the infantry landing and then Patton came up to me and asked, 'Who's outfit is that?'

"I told him whose it was, then he asked why they hadn't reduced the pressure in their tires," Whittemore explained. "So I told him, 'Sir, I don't know. It's not my outfit. I don't have anything to do with them.'

"Then Patton chewed me out! Up one leg and down the other. He took me for a fare-thee-well. With that foul language burning in my ears, General Patton and his group then left."

In this case there was cause for Patton to be angered. A packet of instructions had languished in General Allen's command post, one of which had been issued by General Patton himself. Tire pressure on jeeps was to be reduced to improve traction when they made beach landings.

But on June 18th Patton was the happiest general in North Africa. It was the day Bob and Paul, along with the rest of the regiment, made a practice beach landing at night.

"The troops came in firing a smoke screen which was as effective on water as on shore," Patton wrote in his diary. "They also fired Harpoon and Bangalore shells. The 18th, making the initial landing, performed as perfectly as I have ever seen troops do. They came ashore very fast, spread out at once, and proceeded with speed and determination to their objectives—the high hills two miles from the shore—and occupied their summits in about two hours. On the whole it was the most satisfactory night operation I have seen. I am delighted with the whole thing."

Six days later Patton found himself not quite as pleased. "The Navy was fifty minutes late in getting the left combat team ashore and missed the beach by distances varying from one mile to three and three-quarters miles," he told his diary. "Terry Allen is in a poor mental state."

And who could blame him? If it were the real thing a disaster could have unfolded. On June 30th Patton came back for another visit to the First Division, but Allen and Roosevelt were off decorating some soldiers. Patton stuck around and did nothing until three the next afternoon. He wanted to go swimming so he went with his entourage to General Allen's villa to undress. "It was rough and dirty," he recalled. "Teddy Roosevelt and Terry went in with us. Lots of First Division men were in and all saluted. The First Division is back on its feet and so is Terry."

Bob and Paul were two of the soldiers that did the saluting on that fine first Thursday in July. To them it was actually amusing. Except for General Allen, none of the other higher ups looked all that fit.

General Patton went swimming again the next day. "I saw Allen and told him how good he is," Patton recorded in his diary. "He is a good battle leader. The water was perfect."

On July 5th Patton paid his final respects to Eisenhower; the date for disembarking to Sicily was very close. "Ike started out by giving me a long lecture on the bad discipline of the First Division," Patton wrote that night. By now he was quite satisfied with the division's preparedness for the important assignment he had given to General Allen, and his final response to Eisenhower was brusque.

"I told Ike he was mistaken and that, anyhow, no one whips a dog before putting them into a fight."

By now Bob was back in Tunisia in an assembly area codenamed KENTUCKY near the ancient city of Carthage, where Hannibal was defeated by the Romans during the Second Punic War. The day before Patton bid farewell to Eisenhower was Independence Day in America, but Bob was unable to celebrate it; he was staging for the next operation. Speculators by now had narrowed the likely locations for this combat tour to Italy, Greece or maybe even Sicily. Many reasoned if it were France, why would the Army have moved them closer to Tunis when Oran would have been a better jumping off point to invade the French shores?

The hardened training marches every day for the past six days were now a thing of the past, as were the evenings swimming in the Mediterranean Sea. Bob washed his wool uniform in gasoline for the last time; he was packed up and ready to go wherever it was the Army in its infinite wisdom was sending him. His company's jeeps had been waterproofed and his squad's mortar was cleaned, inspected and test fired. Sailing lists were made up; on July 5th Bob learned that he would be marching to the dock area beside the nearby picturesque village of LaGoulette, which was located at the entrance of the channel leading into Tunis. This port had been chosen because the Germans had used the area to house oil storage and repair facilities, thus it was a perfect staging area for American destroyers, transports and other vessels that were about to embark upon the largest amphibious undertaking of the war.

Bob's squad was billeted on a brand new 441-foot cargo ship, the *Robert Rowan*, when the invasion fleet sailed out into the Gulf of Tunis at seven-thirty that night. The vessel had made its maiden voyage from Hampton Roads Virginia, across the Atlantic and into Oran Harbor just three weeks earlier; it was now loaded with 150 trucks of various tonnages, four new towed 57mm guns, some older 37s, three ambulances, numerous jeeps and about 310 enlisted men. Lieutenant Hobratschk was not aboard; Captain Jeffrey of G Company was the detachment commander. All Bob could make of why he was sailing with this company was Jeffrey's riflemen could very well need his mortar squad's immediate support wherever it was they would be landing.

For some strange reason that turned out to be Sousse, still on the Tunisian coast; the *Robert Rowan* had rounded Cap Bon, then made hard southward for about one hundred miles to drop anchor here. This is where Bob got his first indication that the big show—wherever it was the Navy was taking him—would be going off soon. It came from General Eisenhower himself, and was read by Captain Jeffrey:

We are about to engage in the second phase of the operation which began with the invasion of North Africa. We have defeated our enemies' forces on the south shore of the Mediterranean and captured his army intact. The French in North Africa, for whom the yoke of Axis domination has been lifted, are now our loyal allies.

However, this is not enough. Our untiring pressure on the enemy must be maintained, and as this book falls into your hands we are about to pursue the invasion and occupation of enemy territory. The successful conclusion of these operations will not only strike closer to the heart of the Axis, but also will remove the last threat to the sea lanes of the Mediterranean.

Remember that this time it is indeed enemy territory which we are attacking, and as such we must expect extremely difficult fighting. But we have learned to work smoothly alongside one another as a team, and many of you who will be in the first ranks of this force know full well the power of our Allied air and naval superiority. The task is difficult but your skill, courage, and devotion to duty will be successful in driving our enemies closer to disaster and leading us towards victory and the liberation of Europe and Asia.

It was now the morning of July 8th, and orders came down to get ready to disembark and go to shore. Paul turned to Bob and said, "Why in the world are we doing this?"

"Damned if I know," Bob answered. "But look around us. There's ships all over the place; our rifle battalions and the rest of our Company H are packed up on those LCIs and the *Lawton Evans* and the *Joseph Pulitzer*. See them over there? Looks like the boys are getting ready to load up into landing craft and put to shore, too."

"OK, I suppose we'll know more soon," Paul ventured. "Got another question, maybe a harder one. What 'book' was Eisenhower referring to that was going to fall into our hands?"

'If it's anything like it was when we first landed back in Oran, we'll probably be receiving booklets telling us about the cultures of the people whose country we will be invading, and a bunch of to-dos and not-to-dos. Maybe there will be more inspiring instructions, too."

"Well, all in time I s'pose," Paul guessed.

They were simply sent ashore to stretch their legs and go on a short hike; that was that. Then the British fed them their noon meal. They were back aboard the *Robert Rowan* later that afternoon, and by dusk it weighed anchor, joined hundreds of other ships and headed out into the deep, turquoise waters of the Mediterranean Sea.

The ship was backlit during the final moments of the setting sun; the *Robert Rowan* was far from the vessels at the head of the convoy when Bob turned to Paul and asked, "Are you scared?"

"Not a bit," he quickly answered. "I'm with you."

COMBAT:
SICILY

Journey of the Purple Heart

~THIRTY-NINE~

BOB, GENTLE JOHN, PAUL AND the rest of the Bearer Boys were watching the massive fleet of ships pushing through the water that night when Captain Jeffrey came up to them.

"Men, we're sure glad to have you with us," the well-liked officer started. "First, I want you to know that I got a chance to see your Captain Murphy before we left Oran. He's in the new hospital at Mers el Kerbir on the coast just southwest of the city and recovering from his hernia operation. He's doing well; he was even complaining about having to stay back. As you know, Lieutenant Rosenberg has command of H Company until your fine captain returns. I want you to know I asked Colonel Sternberg for permission to have you aboard with us, rather than a machine gun squad. You gave us tremendous support back when my company got hit at El Guettar, and we're confident if we need you again we can count on you.

"Now, follow me down into the hold. I'm going to brief you and the rest of the company about our next mission."

Captain Jeffrey had a case full of papers, and when everyone got to the dimly lit meeting room he started shuffling through them. Bob, like everyone else, sat down to listen as Jeffrey first read aloud General Patton's Order of the Day:

S-E-C-R-E-T
HEADQUARTERS SEVENTH UNITED STATE ARMY
A.P.O. No. 758, U.S. Army
At sea

Soldiers of the 7th American Army:

We are indeed honored to have been selected by General Eisenhower as the American component of this new and greater attack against the Axis. We are teamed with the justly famous British 8th Army, which attacks on our right, and we have for the Army Group Commander that veteran and distinguished soldier, Sir Harold Alexander.

In addition to the two armies, our attack will be supported by the annihilating might of the Allied Navies and Air Forces.

Owing to the necessity for secrecy, I am unable to put in writing the location of our impending battle. However, I hereby direct the officers who will read you this after you are at sea to tell you where you are going and why.

When we land we will meet German and Italian soldiers whom it is our honor and privilege to attack and destroy.

Many of you have in your veins German and Italian blood, but remember that these ancestors of yours so loved freedom that they gave up home and country to cross the ocean in search of liberty. The ancestors of the people we shall kill lacked the courage to make such a sacrifice and remain as slaves.

During the last year we Americans have met and defeated the best troops Germany, Italy and Japan possess. Many of us have shared in these glorious victories. Those of you who have not been so fortunate, now have your opportunity to gain equal fame.

In landing operations retreat is impossible. To surrender is as ignoble as it is foolish. Due to our Air Force and our Navy the enemy is unable to evacuate prisoners. Therefore, our soldiers who are taken prisoner, will remain to starve and run the added risk of being bombed or shelled by their own comrades who will be unable to tell prisoners from the enemy.

Above all else remember that we as the attackers have initiative. We know exactly what we are going to do, while the enemy is ignorant of our intentions and can only parry our blows. We must retain this tremendous advantage by always attacking; rapidly, ruthlessly, viciously, and without rest. However tired and hungry you may be, the enemy will be more tired and hungry—keep punching! No man is beaten until he thinks he is. Our enemy knows that his cause is hopeless.

The fact that we are operating in enemy country does not permit us to forget our American tradition of respect for private property, non-combatants, and women. Civilians who have the stupidity to fight us we will kill. Those who remain passive will not be harmed but will be required to rigidly conform to such rules as we shall publish for their control and guidance.

The glory of American arms, the honor our country, the future of the whole world rests in your individual hands. See to it that you are worthy of great trust.

God is with us. We shall win.

/s/ G.S. Patton, Jr
Lieut. General, U.S. Army
Commanding

"OK, now let me see a show of hands," Captain Jeffrey continued. "How many of you believe it's Sicily where we'll be landing?"

About one hundred and fifty of the two hundred men in the briefing stuck their hands up.

"Well, so much for preserving the top secrets of the United States Army," Jeffrey laughed. "Indeed we are invading Sicily, and you'll be getting your freshly printed *Soldier's Guide to Sicily* when this meeting is over. But first, let me brief you on our mission."

All eyes were fixed on Captain Jeffrey as he shuffled through his papers while overlay maps were passed around. Beaches were marked with numbers. The town of Gela was on the left side of the map; Scoglitti was on the right.

"Alright, men, let's start with the big picture," Jeffrey began. "We're one of eight divisions landing along a hundred-mile front in southeastern Sicily. The Brits will be landing four divisions, an independent brigade and a commando force along a forty-mile front that's not on your maps, but it's well east of where we'll be coming ashore.

"Our Seventh Army will land three infantry divisions and an armored division over a wider front; it's fifty miles long. The 45th Division will be landing on five numbered beaches to our right that extend from the highway at Scoglitti halfway back to Gela. The 1st and 4th Ranger Battalions will be landing directly in front of Gela; their job is to take this fishing village and divert the Italians defending the area from our main assault, which will be in the center and spread out over four numbered beaches. The 3rd Division will be landing to the left of the Rangers on four beaches straddling the port of Licata

"OK, now here's more about what you really need to know," Captain Jeffrey continued in a clipped manner. "First, we're part of Kool Force, which includes the 2nd Armored Division. We don't go in right away; we go after the 16th and 26th. They will be making the main assault; their mission is to establish a beachhead. We'll likely be ordered in within twenty-four hours, if not sooner.

"We land on Beach 67. Look at your maps; it's marked. What you can't see easily is it's 5,200 yards long, but just ten to 30 yards deep. The beach is backed by low sand dunes for one to two miles before the main coastal roads. We don't know the actual gradient of the beach; I'm told it's not too steep but there are sandbars anywhere from fifty to a hundred yards offshore. Word is the beach we land on is suitable for our LCVPs to bring us ashore, meaning they can get over any sandbars we might encounter. The beach itself has fine hard sand. There are no exit roads for vehicles. They will come in on a beach to our right.

"We'll assemble initially with the rest of the companies just off the beach," Captain Jeffrey added. "We'll also have artillery support; the 32nd Field will be landing near us, also to our right.

"OK, our mission is to then move up to an assembly area that's a little less than a mile inland. It's on higher ground. Bob York's battalion will be on our right. Colonel Brown will come in behind us, and assist as needed. Our initial objective is to hold this higher ground while Combat Command B of the 2nd Armored lands their tanks. We'll stay here until we receive further orders, which will eventually come from division, and according to what I've read may include providing assistance to the 26th Infantry in seizing an airport about five miles north of Gela. It's on you maps, marked as the Ponte Olivo airfield.

"Any questions?"

No one spoke up; Bob, like most others, was just taking it all in but he and Paul were already starting to look at each other. Bob knew just what he was thinking—what do we know about the Italians defending the beach they were going to land on?

"Alright," Captain Jeffrey started back in, right on queue. "Here's what we know about the strength of our enemy. First, Sicily's coast is defended mainly by the Italian Sixth Army. In our landing area we'll be up against the 206th Coastal Division. What we know is there's about 3,600 men in our area. They are armed with rifles, machineguns and mortars, and are backed up by medium artillery batteries. Recently the Italians raised their battalion strength from 400 to 600 men, and they may have mobile reserves further inland.

"The Ponte Olivo airport is guarded by a garrison of 1,300 or so more men. They have a natural line of defense in the line of hills north, northeast and northwest of Gela. Aerial photographs revealed that these defensive locations have been well prepared, and the airport has been especially well-fortified. Thirty-six-caliber anti-aircraft guns strengthen this position. Another Italian regiment, the 54th, is operating in the Gela area.

"On the German side we know less. First, we think they have positioned their main troop strength elsewhere, expecting we'll be landing on Corsica or Sardinia in preparation for invading the Italian mainland. That said, our most recent intelligence indicates German armored units may be positioned as mobile reserves somewhere inland on Sicily. When the Germans knew it was about over back in Tunisia, they stopped sending reinforcements; we believe these units are on the island and started out with about four battalions—all in strength—but now they are three Panzer-grenadier regiments.

"There are other recent indications the Italians are welcoming more help from the Germans, just in case," Jeffrey added. "G-2 on that is the Herman Goering Division, which was busted up pretty badly back in April and May, is also on Sicily somewhere and is being reconstituted as a Panzer division.

"So, there you have it," Captain Jeffrey concluded. "That's all the dope we've got. H-hour is 0245 on Saturday morning. That leaves tomorrow to get rested up, and by nightfall we need to be ready to go ashore if there's problems on the beach. That means we all have to be combat loaded. Our jeeps will come in later. It will be a night landing for the first waves, and there are promises we can expect quite a show to be put on by the Navy's big guns to support the landings, the likes of which they say none of us have ever seen before.

"So go to your bunks and get some rest. Oh, and don't forget to take your *Soldier's Guide to Sicily* handbooks with you and read them."

And with that the G Company commander simply said, "Thank you, men, and may God be with us."

The Bearer Boys settled into their bunks well before lights out and started reading their handbooks. They learned that Sicily was the largest island in the Mediterranean and its importance was two-fold. First, the Axis powers controlled its sea lanes from the island. Second, its dozen-odd larger aerodromes gave the Axis air support capabilities during the North Africa fight. In fact, Sicily was thought to still be the headquarters of Air Marshall Kesselring's Luftwaffe.

The booklet also pointed out that Sicily's northern tip was separated from Italy by just two miles of water, and once the Allies controlled the island it would pose a vital threat to the Italian mainland; it would indeed put the Army's air forces within two hours flight time of Rome itself once Sicily's airdromes were seized.

Bob read that the island had a long and unhappy history that left it primitive and undeveloped. A score of ancient rulers had controlled Sicily for ages, and it never even had a constitution until the Napoleonic period before falling again into tyranny. "Many of the old evils still remain," Bob was told. "Absentee landlords, poverty, sickness (particularly malaria) and bad government prevail. General poverty and poor living conditions forced up the rate of emigration—to the United States in particular."

Then, all of a sudden Louie the Rub piped up and laughed, "Did you read the part about Sicily being 'viciously Cinderella' yet?"

"Yea, I'm just seeing that now," Bob answered. "Says Mussolini promised all these public works programs and..."

"He didn't come through with any of them," Louie interrupted.

"Says forty-percent of Sicilians are still illiterate," Gentle John added. "Two houses out of three are without drinking water, and about half need to use outhouses because there is no running water."

Everyone then quieted down and started reading about the topography of the island, its irregular mass of mountains, some with sheer drops into the sea. But there were broad and fertile areas along the Plain of Gela where they would be landing. Roads wound along the coastal strip here, just as Captain Jeffrey had told them, and the booklet even described the narrow roadways that went inland over foothills, some precariously following the precipitous sides of mountains.

"Main centers of civilization are by the sea while many smaller towns nestle in the mountains," Bob continued to read. "In view of the troubled history of the island these latter tend to be in naturally strong positions—particularly the older ones, some of which are on veritable pinnacles of rock."

"Sounds like we'll be climbing lots of hills before the fighting is over," Paul offered. "But the good news is some are covered with terraced vines and orchards of lemons, oranges and even almonds and olives. We'll eat well at least."

"Guys, did you read about Mount Etna still being active?" Gentle John asked. "It's 11,000 feet high. Sure hope the ash doesn't blow at us while we conquer the island."

"I'm ahead of you all," Bob quipped. "Says here Sicily is the land of sunshine this time of year. I'm wondering what the women will be like."

"Don't get your hopes up," Louie the Rub shot back. "Generally they are pretty ugly, so I learned growing up in an Italian family, and besides that they are strict Catholics."

"Well, Southern Baptist girls are far from ugly Louie," Paul kidded. "Maybe when this war is over you can come visit me in South Carolina and I'll show you the ropes."

Bob started smirking then added to that, "Careful Paul. I wouldn't risk my reputation trying to fix Louie up with anyone."

Everyone shared a good laugh at that, then they went back to reading their guide booklets. The next two pages were full of statistics about Sicily's provinces and communes, their average square miles and populations.

Suddenly Louie piped up again and said, "Let me read this to you guys, just so you know I'm right to tell ya' to stay away from the broads. Says the Sicilian is well known for being the jealous type and I quote—so far as his womenfolk are concerned, in a crisis he still resorts to the dagger."

The Bearer Boys were now laughing so hard that if they were on a smaller boat they very well might have tipped it over.

This didn't stop Louie. "In this what do they eat section it says my favorite dish is theirs, too. Pasta! With tomato sauce, even meat, sardines, fish, cheese and olive oil. Yummee! Just add fresh bread, and we'll be eating far better than we did in North Africa. Fruits and nuts are plentiful. Lemons, almonds and pistachios. Grapes, too. Add lemon peel and candied oranges, and what a dessert. What more could we ask for!"

"Women to have dinner with," Bob quipped.

"Funny, Bob," Louie fired back. "We already look like shit in these wool uniforms. Imagine how those swaggering Roman gigolos will be dressed, with their daggers swaying at their sides. Forget about the women!"

"Hey, I'm looking at the list of towns here, and Gela—where we land—isn't even in the book," Paul informed everyone.

"So what?" Gentle John said. "We'll be through it before the Roman gigolos get up from their siestas tomorrow."

"See where all these diseases we could get are listed?" Bob asked. "Malaria, as usual. We need to sleep under mosquito nets to avoid getting that. Yea, right. Now here's a new one. Sandfly fever. It's transmitted by small midget-like insects. They can be found anywhere there's moisture, shade or—get this—even food. Lying in foxholes could be a danger to our health, too. Says these critters are in the soil and in the sides of banks and culverts, but if attacked the book says apply the scorched earth policy. Use something called Flysol."

"Says typhoid is also a fly-borne disease," Paul added. "I was inoculated for that back at Fort Jackson before I came overseas. It's good for a year, I was told. You guys gotten shots in the past year?"

Everyone looked at each other, wondering if they did. Most couldn't remember.

"Look here," Louie suddenly yelled out. "Told ya' to stay away from the Sicilian broads. Says VD thrives on the island. Also says contact with the civilian population can bring on the other diseases, too. Stick with me boys."

The currency, weights and measures sections were interesting, but the guide booklet said the U.S. soldier would carry no money other than yellow seal dollars and United States coins. Even francs from French North Africa had to be converted. But Italian lira would remain legal tender, leaving everyone thinking they better know the conversion rates for that. They would undoubtedly loot Italian soldiers of their money when they killed them, and it would come in handy when the poker playing got hot.

"Good luck learning some of the useful words and phrases," Louie laughed. "The part I can't figure out is who we'll use them on."

"What's the Italian word for surrender?" Bob smirked. "That's all we'll need to know, Louie."

"Arrendersi!"

"Between the leaves of this guide there's a list of to dos and not-to-does," Gentle John offered. "Two things hit me. One, don't talk politics or religion with the Sicilians, and two—remember that the Sicilians are not Germans and many of them hate the Germans as much as we do."

"Think the Germans will show up right away?" Paul asked Bob.

"It's hard telling, not knowing, but I'll bet they do; they certainly did surprise us back in North Africa, especially at El Guettar."

"Hey you all," Sergeant Horn broke in. He had been saying nothing, and had just finished looking at the pictures of the bigger cities in Sicily that were in his booklet. "We need to get some sleep. So it's time to shut up."

So everyone shut up and started falling asleep one by one to the sounds of the wind whipping through the rigging of the *Robert Rowan*. Then the rocking of the vessel finished off those still awake, and before too long it was dead quiet down below.

The last thing Bob heard was Paul asking him if he was scared.

And the last thing Paul remembered Bob saying was, "No, I'm not scared. I'm with you, but I am worried about getting air support from our own Army air forces when we need it."

~FORTY~

BAD WEATHER ROARED IN AT midnight after the leading edge of a vicious southwester struck the fleet. By the time the convoy passed Malta the wind had picked up to nearly forty knots. "The flat-bottomed LCIs rose in the waves, shivered, plunged, and shook sideways like frightened mustangs," Lieutenant Downing remembered. "It was almost impossible to remain on deck, since the rain and spray drenched everything, making footing slippery. The spray beating down on the decks, the slithering motion of the ship, the height of the waves, and the way the ship seemed about to snap as it reached the crest of each wave made me almost seasick."

"It was the roughest damn patch of water I ever did see," an artilleryman recalled. "We were in columns of boats and the waves were so big you'd see bows, then sterns of ships lift completely out of the seas. Before long we saw every part of the boats' bottoms."

The heavy seas took a toll on many of the LCTs carrying tanks and heavier trucks. "The sea was so rough that the anchor that was in the rear of our LCT broke loose, and kept banging the rear of the LCT until it caused a large hole and water started coming in," another participant in the rough crossing remembered. "We finally got it plugged up with a mattress and got the anchor tied down."

With her twenty-seven-foot draft stabilizing the 441-foot *Robert Rowan*, the ride to Sicily was slowed to six knots, but it was far less uncomfortable for Bob and Paul. They, along with Gentle John and the other Bearer Boys, pretty much slept through the whole thing. What finally woke them up was the crash of the ship's stern-mounted deck gun after it broke loose from its base and telegraphed a massive clang into the hold.

But the seas abated and by the time they got on deck that morning the big waves had started to give way to long rollers that were helping carry the first soldiers ashore. The air was damp and chilly. First light at twenty minutes before five revealed hundreds of transports biting hard at their anchors, waiting to be ordered into the beach. "The great panorama of naval might, its American ensigns flapping wildly before the wind, stretched the horizon and beyond," one observer remembered. "Silver barrage balloons tugged violently at captive cables from each vessel."

The *Robert Rowan* was still well off shore, but Bob and Paul could see the hazy plain of Gela in the distance. Smoke that followed brilliant, bursting arcs of shell fire from the guns on the big American destroyers was rising in the air. "Some were solid flame, some were intermittent, but all were dynamic and graceful as they laced the sky," Lieutenant Johnson wrote aboard his LCT. "Each of the fiery projectiles from the battlewagons' cannons expanded in an orange explosion, signaling destruction of a shoreline emplacement."

Other landing crafts were plowing up and down the coastline waiting to land. But the most visible evidence that the Axis forces were not going to give up Sicily without a fight came too soon. A pair of Stukas dove out of the sky just before sunrise—Bob and Paul barely saw them—then the German fighters went quiet as the pilots cut off their engines and swept towards the stern of the USS *Maddox*, only to pull up to about a hundred feet and drop their bombs. All Bob and Paul could make out next was a great blob of light which reddened the sky. One bomb had exploded about twenty-five yards off the *Maddox's* stern, another off the starboard propeller guard, but a third jarred the ship after it scored a direct hit.

What Bob and Paul couldn't see was the *Maddox* was awash in her stern minutes later. Now near-dead in the water, she listed to port and then rolled onto her starboard side. What they could see was her bow standing vertically before it disappeared below the surface of the water, taking eight officers and 203 hands with her to the bottom of the sea.

The *Maddox* had been too close for comfort, and as the mountains of Sicily became plainly outlined when the sun rose all Bob and Paul could do was pray they'd get off the *Robert Rowan* alive and get to shore to fight like infantry soldiers should.

Closer to shore off Licata was another show being put on by German aircraft. Although it was miles away, Bob and Paul could make out faint flickers of flares against the smoking Sicilian coast as bombs burst near the USS *Sentinel*. One bomb opened an eight-foot long hole in her aft engine compartment. She was quickly hit again four times by German bombers; her crew was able to thwart two of these attacks with their anti-aircraft guns, but one three-inch gun was put out of action. Another bomb put the forward engine out of commission.

By six-fifteen the *Sentinel* had lost all power and was badly listing. "We lost a destroyer," General Patton wrote in his diary that morning. "The Germans dropped a number of flares of considerable power, evidently with the purpose of silhouetting our ships against them, but the dropping of flares was not followed by an air attack in considerable force."

More planes weren't necessary in the case of the *Sentinel*; she capsized and went under a few hours later. But what Bob had feared about air support thankfully was answered by Army air force fighters when they started roaring across the skies in pursuit of German planes that were spotting targets for more of their bombers. Some of the Nazi planes were blown out of the sky. American destroyers were still hitting enemy shore batteries and other emplacements, sending more black smoke swirling into the now very sunny skies.

Then, at about ten-thirty, Bob and Paul felt the throbbing of the *Robert Rowan*'s triple-expansion steam engines as her oil-fired boilers fed more power to her single screw; she started towards shore. "Something's not right," Bob said to Paul. "We weren't supposed to land this quickly."

Bob was correct. Patton had suddenly ordered Kool Force, his reserve, to come closer to shore and anchor in the Dime area off Gela. It wasn't even noontime yet, and as the *Robert Rowan* made its way towards the beach the German air show went on. Bf-109s strafed the shoreline where he and Paul were to land. Higher level bombing targeted the transport area where their *Robert Rowan* was anchored. Enemy bombers dove at the beach through the afternoon in desperate attempts to stop more American landing craft from reaching shore. Then just before nightfall a lone Bf-109 got through the Allied air cover and struck a nearby LST trying to land that was heavily loaded with fully fueled vehicles and ammunition.

Massive explosions rose into the sky as the LST started sinking; another nearby was damaged. Yet another was rushing to save the men trapped on the stern of the flaming transport. Beach operations had to be temporarily halted due to the continued showering of shrapnel set off by the explosions of ammunition, and trucks breaking apart on the doomed LST.

Things ashore were so bad that General Allen, after being subjected to hours of what he claimed was "continuous dive-bombing," requested more American fighter cover. Another LST was burning from yet another "hit and run" raid, and these strikes continued into the night. The German planes were still targeting the transport area, and Bob and Paul were now anxious as hell to get away from here and onto shore.

The Germans had been far closer to the Gela beaches than intelligence reports had estimated. After the American landings were reported to Paul Conrath, the commander of the Herman

Goering Division, he started planning an immediate counterattack. Two *kampfgruppens* were assembled that morning in Caltagirone, a hilltop town twenty miles inland between the plain of Gela and Catania; one was infantry-heavy and the other was tank-heavy.

Conrath wanted his strike to begin early enough to avoid attacking directly into the morning sun; it was his tank-heavy *kampfgruppen* that set out first for Niscemi, with orders to continue down a secondary road to the south which joined the Gela highway at Piano Lupo, one of the objectives Captain Jeffrey had told Bob was the First Division's on the day of the landings.

But two things slowed the move. Allied aircraft harassed Conrath's tanks, and Italian troops fleeing pell-mell northward for the mountains got in the way. The narrow, twisting roads also didn't help matters. By nine that morning, the German tanks were far short of the road junction at Piano Lupo; at ten the attack still hadn't begun, the sun was much higher, and an enraged Conrath relieved his task force commander and personally stepped into the leadership void.

Conrath finally attacked five hours later than his plan called for and he met a similar fate. Vicious naval gunfire deluged his tanks as they crawled through the inhospitable Sicilian terrain. He had no choice but to turn back towards Niscemi, leaving a staff officer at Terry Allen's CP northeast of Gela breathlessly stating, "Tanks are withdrawing; it seems we are too much for them!"

But Allen's G-2, Colonel Bob Porter, was far more realistic in his assessment of the day's events. "Our section told the commanders if they met tanks the first day, they would be able to stay on the beaches because there would be no infantry with the Panzers," he explained that night. "If they met tanks the second day, there would really be a bad fight unless they got in tank-proof terrain. It would be very difficult for us since our anti-tank weapons were not due to land until the middle of the second day. We estimated that by daylight on the second day, the German artillery, tanks and infantry could mount a coordinated attack."

By now there were some artillery pieces that had made it to shore; that was it insofar as any weaponry that could support the American rifle companies. But Patton still wanted more infantry on the beach. The transport *Orizaba* had been host to Lieutenant Colonel Sternberg and the other battalion commanders that afternoon and was already close to shore. They had orders to land with their men as soon as possible. Colonel Smith and his S-3 were already ashore making a reconnaissance for an assembly area when the 18th Infantry hit the beach.

"Alright men, listen up," Captain Jeffrey bellowed out early that evening. "There's been a change in plans. There's trouble brewing on the beach. We're going to shore on LCIs, and not our LCVPs. Yes, we are going to board the LCVPs first, but then we're going to be transferred over to. . .wait a second. . .here it is. . .LCI 316."

A mix of cheers and groans followed, prompting Captain Jeffrey to add, "I don't know what the screw up is, but here's the good news. We'll be with our own when we land. Aboard LCI 316 is Colonel Sternberg, a platoon of Company F, the headquarters detachment of the 32nd Field, and one of my G company platoons. You there in the mortar squad of H Company. Know Lieutenant Rosenberg is also aboard with another 72 men from your company."

Unknown to Captain Jeffrey was General Hugh Gaffey, who commanded the 2nd Armored Division and Kool Force, had ordered debarkation from the deeper draft LCIs, rather than the near flat-bottomed LCVPs, which would have been able to get over the sandbars and more easily onto the beach. And it would only get worse. The beachmaster was expecting LCVPs to land the men, and he would be as surprised as everyone else when the 18th Infantry arrived on Beach 67 aboard thirty-five-ton, 160-foot long LCIs.

"They're bigger targets," Bob murmured to Paul. "But have faith. The Army in its infinite wisdom has our best interests in mind."

"Alright guys," Sergeant Horn started. "Let's get our combat loads together. Put your vests on and. . ."

"How we going to wear ammo aprons and these inflatable life vests under our armpits at the same time, Sarge?" Gentle John interrupted.

"Well, I see it like this," Horn shot back. "First we practiced this, but supposing we don't need to blow up our life jackets? All you ammo bearers will be better off wearing your aprons with your 81s when we unload. If for some reason we have to use the inflatables, we're going to have to carry the mortars and its pieces up over our heads."

"And paddle in with our feet?" Bob smirked.

"Yes, smart ass. We are the First Division, and that means we will be amphibious if we have to. I'll even be giving it my all for our country by carrying the mortar tube, so John gets the lighter load with the bipod. Anything to help you guys."

Paul was just taking this all in when Bob turned to him and said, "OK, let's go and get made up for the big show."

Bob knew he'd get stuck carrying the baseplate to shore, but since this was Paul's first landing and he would be carrying his mortars, Bob wanted to be sure when he fitted his vest over his shoulders Paul got it tight enough so it wouldn't cause any chafing before he put his life jacket on.

After Paul demonstrated he knew what he was doing, Bob messed with him a little by jiggling his helmet. "Better tighten that up a tad before we land Paul," he kidded. "You're a handsome guy, and we wouldn't want you to get your face scratched if your helmet pulled back when some Wop or German hits you in the head with a bullet."

"Funny, Bob," Paul laughed. "How do I keep my money dry if we end up having to swim to shore?"

"That's easy," Bob shot back. "Hey Louie, you've got the most unused rubbers in the United States Army. Can you spare one so Paul can put his money in it?"

"Sergeant Horn got it right when he called you a smart ass, Bob," Louie answered. Then reaching in his pocket, he fished out a rubber and handed it to Paul.

"Never saw one of these things before," Paul joked.

That got everyone laughing, even the more serious Billy Uhouse. Then Sergeant Horn got them all lined up so he could inspect their loads. Satisfied, he then said, "Alright now, get ready to line your sorry asses up in a single file so I can lead you to the aft cargo compartment where our LCVPs will meet us and take us over to LCI 316.

So they lined up one behind the other with Paul right behind Bob. Then, turning to look at him, Bob wisecracked, "I'm gonna' loot you when you get it."

A half hour later they were aboard the LCI. By now it was dark and when both Lieutenant Rosenberg and their own Lieutenant Hobratschk greeted them, they first offered everyone their evening meal and then told them they would be debarking for the beach soon. The seas were still heavy, but a faint moon would be rising just ahead of midnight. No one was hungry. Most of the soldiers were sitting around smoking cigarettes, so everyone but Paul lit up and waited for the LCI to start for shore.

~FORTY-ONE~

IT WAS JUST AFTER MDNIGHT when they departed for the beach. Bob could make out still-swelling waves as the LCI got closer in, and he could see some men ashore waving their arms; he figured they had to be the beach control party that would tell him where to go after he landed.

Paul was staring straight ahead when the LCI jerked to a stop; Bob felt a rough jar, then there was silence, followed by the sounds of waves slapping against the side of the landing craft and Lieutenant Hobratschk calmly saying, "Alright men, line up. We depart on the left-hand ramp. Let's go."

As Bob and Paul got closer to the ramp they could see men inflating their life vests; this meant the LCI was not close enough to shore to wade in, and the water could be deep. No one in their mortar squad swore; they just calmly removed their life vests, took off their ammo aprons, put their vests back on, and pressed the valve arms, immediately filling them with air.

"God, that's tight," Paul said as his vest squeezed against his chest. Bob just nodded, and suggested he get off first because he'd done this before when he landed in North Africa.

When they got to the ramp and started down using its rope railing they could see men already in the water up to their necks. When Bob reached the bottom of the ramp he just plunged into the water and started moving ever so slowly. He was holding the baseplate over his head and Paul thought he looked like Charles Atlas in one of his cartoon advertisements.

The beach was seventy-five yards away and it was plenty dark out now; the moon had set. When Paul jumped into the water his life vest kept him afloat but water gushed into his pants and boots, sinking him lower. Ahead he saw Bob's dim figure, and other men grasping a rope; it was guiding them into shore. Paul shifted his ammo vest onto his right shoulder, and then leaned in and grabbed the rope with his left hand. His feet thankfully were touching the bottom.

They were ashore within minutes, but some others had let go of the rope and were paddling madly to reach the beach; a few went into shock. A couple of men and an officer drowned. The first thing Bob and Paul did was look around to see if the rest of the Bearer Boys, Gentle John and Sergeant Horn had made it in; they had, and no one had lost any of their loads.

So far so good; no German planes were in the air near them. Instead they spotted a man in a raincoat. He was with the beach control party and he told them the beach hadn't been completely cleared of mines, and to head to the right where they would see two strips of white tape that would lead them safely off the beach.

Bob and Paul were both shivering; Paul's teeth were chattering, but they took off their life vests, left them in the sand, moved steadily inside the white tape and eventually reached an inland road before marching to an assembly area in an amphitheater-like depression surrounded by olive groves a mile inland. First light was now filling the skies, and with it anti-aircraft fire could be heard; red tracer bullets started streaking through the air. Then a German fighter zoomed in with its guns rattling, and both Bob and Paul dove for cover in a plowed field just off the roadway that brought them this far. The plane kept going, with its guns still blazing.

Then Lieutenant Hobratschk came upon them and yelled, "Let's go guys. We just got word that the 16th Infantry is in a fight for their lives, and we have to get farther forward to help them out."

Getting further away from the beach was fortunate. Just after six that morning a dozen German dive bombers again attacked the transport area. Patton's command ship, the *Monrovia* was hit this time; she suffered some damage to her engine room after a Stuka made two passes over her.

The *Orizaba* was also damaged; she received six holes in her hull above the waterline, and her electric and gyro cables leading to the bridge were cut. It was a bad morning to be offshore. The transport *Joseph T. Dickman* was also slightly damaged. By midmorning the German shelling on the beach where Bob and Paul had landed became so accurate that it had to be closed for twenty minutes. Salvage operations were even suspended.

But it was far worse inland for the 16th Infantry. The German attack had jumped off just after six that morning; the air strikes on the landing area, and heavy artillery fire aimed at the beaches were to prevent Conrath from having to tangle with more American forces as he mounted his second attack.

And this time it was going to start better for Paul Conrath.

The column that was headed for Gela met naval gunfire but escaped from it without loosing many tanks, then the tanks headed east towards the Piano Lupo road junction where a battalion of the 16th Infantry had taken up defensive positions. A second column also converged on Abbio Priolo, a couple of miles north of Piano Lupo, where the other two battalions of the 16th lay in wait; Conrath intended to annihilate these American forces and then push his tank battalions across the Gela plain towards Route 115, all the way down to the beaches where Bob and Paul had landed.

The odds were far from even when the German tanks came in from the west towards Abbio Priolo and started firing their machineguns and cannons at any American within point-blank range.

The overall situation as relayed to General Allen's CP was bleak. "We are being overrun by tanks," Colonel George Taylor, the 16th's commander reported. "In our 2nd Battalion area, the enemy has ten tanks in front of the battalion and has ringed them with an additional thirty."

Taylor had also ordered his men to hold their ground. "Everyone stays put just where he is. . .under no circumstances will anyone be pulled back. Take cover from the tanks. Don't let anything else get through!"

Despite the gallant stand of the 16th's rifle companies and its regiment's Cannon Company, the Gela plain became the most horrific location of the two-day old battle for Sicily, "a raging inferno of exploding shells, smoke and fire," as one observer saw it. An outpost of the 18th's A Company was testimony to this when it reported to Bob York an estimated thirty enemy tanks coming down the plain from the north at ten-thirty that morning.

From his position on Route 115 near where the road from Niscemi intersected at Piano Lupo, Antitank Company's Lieutenant Johnson first saw several tanks coming his way at about the same time. Thinking they could be American, he wisely looked through his field glasses for confirmation, only to tell everyone later, "Those tanks were the enemy's and they came our way, and fast. And here we were, with nothing larger than a rifle. At 12:30 a dozen German Mark IV and Italian tanks approached, firing every few hundred feet. By 1:00, there were twenty-two, only a thousand yards away; by 1:30 the number is fifty, and we were witnessing the greatest attack by German armor since El Guettar."

And there was not a single friendly Allied plane in sight.

Bob and Paul, along with Gentle John and the rest of the Bearer Boys, were behind the 1st Battalion when the tanks came. They were in a shallow ditch beside a few scraggly olive trees, off the roadway because it was being shelled by naval gunfire from the destroyers in the Bay of Gela. The hot sun was beating down, and everyone was drenched in sweat. On the open plain they could see some burning tanks. Back towards the beach the anti-aircraft fire was very loud. Then Bob saw puffs of smoke in the sky and red tracers streaking in every direction.

"Paul, look behind you," Bob yelled.

So they both did; incoming was a Stuka, and tracers were chasing it.

"It's smoking," Paul suddenly cheered. "Look at that! It's drifting and. . .wow. . .it's going down. See those flames coming out of it?"

They both watched as the Stuka swept over their heads and get lower before it plunged to the earth; then there was nothing but black smoke. Minutes later another bomber came in. This one was just two-hundred feet off the ground, and it was headed towards Courtney Brown's 3rd Battalion, which was located on the southern slope of a nearby hill along the Niscemi road. Seconds later Bob and Paul could see more German fighters heading for 3rd Bat's position, all of them also flying low.

"I don't know what those German pilots are thinking Paul," Bob yelled out. "They're at tree top level, and their bombs won't have time to straighten out and hit on their fuses. Our guys should be lucky."

"So what are we going to do?" Paul asked. His question was timely, for minutes later Sergeant Horn appeared and told them, "I just got word from Lieutenant Hobratschk. Rosenberg told him our mortars wouldn't do a damn thing to stop the tanks, so he wants us to help the 32nd Field artillerymen get their howitzers into positions to fire at 'em."

Bob started to say something but he was drowned out by the echoes of the big guns on the naval destroyers that were still pounding the area. Then one huge shell roared overhead, and to their left everyone watched a German tank get blown to bits.

But by now others had gotten through and were coming at Bob and Paul's position. All hell was breaking loose.

There was no German infantry that could be seen following the tanks, but the attack was so threatening it prompted Colonel

Smith to relocate his command post. "The appearance was quite ludicrous, they were leaving a dug-in position in a mad rush and they were carrying arm-loads of blankets, shovels, binoculars and weapons in what looked like complete disorder," an eye-witness to the event relayed later. "And the tanks were still nearly eight hundred and fifty yards away."

At less than a quarter mile from where they were, the tanks sure looked real close to Bob and Paul. Some of the Panzers had already smashed through the 1st Battalion's lines, but York's men—even though they were limited to using their grenades and small arms—got help from a 33rd Field Artillery battery concealed in a wooded area, the 16th Infantry's Cannon Company, and four 2nd Armored American tanks that had made it to shore. Together they got their fair share of German tank kills, prompting one officer to later boast, "It was a beautiful exhibition of direct fire."

But other enemy tanks had also broken through Courtney Brown's 3rd Battalion's positions, and were now shelling Bob and Paul's 2nd Battalion. The firing was close enough for the supporting naval gunfire to be temporarily silenced for fear its shells would hit friendly troops. One did. Captain Kuehn, the K Company commander, later told everyone, "One five-inch shell hit our forward battalion communications section. It made a big hole and you couldn't find a fingernail anywhere because we scratched for cover wherever we could find it. I was close when it hit and covered with dirt. I only had a nosebleed, but I was deaf with a concussion for days."

It had already been a long day for General Terry Allen, who wished he could have found cover from his friend George Patton. The Seventh Army commander had come ashore at nine-thirty that morning "to the whir of Signal Corps cameras in an immaculate uniform complete with necktie, knee-length polished black leather boots and twin ivory-handled revolvers," according to one account.

To his credit Patton did make a difference. After having pictures taken of him that would appear in many stateside papers, he saw tanks that were separately heading down the Ponte Olivo road towards Gela. When he came upon a naval officer with a radio he ordered, "If you can connect with your Goddamn Navy, tell them for God's sake to drop some shell fire on the road." Shells from the cruiser *Boise* answered and hammered the advancing tanks. Patton at that time was near Gela, and before he departed the Ranger command post, he told a captain to "kill everyone of the goddam bastards."

At about the time Bob and Paul were seeing the approaching tanks Patton had arrived at Terry Allen's command post. Allen was away, but when he returned he found Patton sitting in his chair enjoying a cigar with his legs propped up on his field desk.

"How is the division doing?" Patton nonchalantly asked Allen.

"It's no tea party but we're doing OK. We need additional artillery support," the First Division commander answered.

But Patton just waved his hand and said, "I'm now an Army commander; take this up with Keyes."

General Keyes was Patton's deputy commander, but all that was on Terry Allen's mind at the time was saving his division from the tank attack. Dogged tired, with red eyes and disheveled hair, Allen left his command post again, this time in his jeep with General Roosevelt, and made out for the front lines. When they got there the pair climbed to the top of a sand dune about a half mile from where Bob and Paul were, took in the situation and returned to the division's CP. Here Allen first studied his maps, then a staff officer came up to him and asked whether he would order a withdrawal down to the beaches.

General Allen simply looked at him and roared back, "Retreat? Hell no! We haven't begun to fight!"

What Allen and Roosevelt had seen was a battery of the 32nd Field Artillery in a series of sand dunes and gulches at a bend on the tree-lined road that ran up to Piano Lupo; the howitzers had just been set up near a 200-foot-high plateau to meet the German tanks.

Change orders came down when Lieutenant Rosenberg got word from Ben Sternberg that he wanted all the mortar fire he had at his disposal laid in behind the tanks so any harder to see infantry support the Germans had would be nullified. Sternberg also ordered his rifle company commanders to send men over to help the artillerymen get their pieces into place.

"There was no room to maneuver the section trucks," Lieutenant Marshall explained later. "It took strong arms and backs to turn the trails of the two and a quarter ton guns into place."

Lieutenant Johnson, with his Antitank men in gullies and ditches near a bamboo grove—but still without weapons—witnessed firsthand what Bob and Paul could barely see. "One small howitzer, unnoticed in a corner of the olive orchard in front of me, began to bang away point blank at the leading tank. At first the other tanks could not find their leader's assailant, but soon shells and machinegun slugs were spraying the landscape around us. The outfit's back is to the Mediterranean, and that leading German tank, followed by tens of others, is about to cut off all lateral communications and stab through to the sandy beach itself.

"But just at the darkest moment the 105 gets lucky and hits on three of the tanks. As they flame brightly the last round of 105 ammo is slammed into the breach and the gunner desperately aims at the leader's tank, now starting to cross the road. He sets the ambitious monster afire, and we breath again, for this action is followed by two others; other tanks, apparently not knowing how near victory they are, take fright and turn clumsily about, then scuttle back up the plain to their mountain hideout."

The near thirty rounds of 81mm mortars that the Bearer Boys, Bob and Gentle John were able to team together and fire at the hapless German infantry had certainly helped stir up smoke and a lot of dust, maybe even killing some Germans they couldn't see. But they need not have worried.

Lieutenant Marshall confirmed that when he revealed, "All the artillery that could be brought to bear, with tubes leveled, kept firing at the incoming tanks. With all that artillery fire, mortars fired by our infantry on the flanks and fire from a couple of our tanks that got ashore, the German tank attack was stopped. The Panzers did not even reach the tree-lined Gela highway."

"The German tank commander was killed early in the action," Ben Sternberg pointed out. "From then on the tanks seemed lost. After loosing fourteen, they withdrew. A water-filled wadi also helped keep the tanks from overrunning us. Our mortars stopped the progress of the enemy infantry following the tanks; they also withdrew to their own lines."

General Allen later said naval gunfire support "was tremendously effective" during the fighting. He even wrote in his summary of the invasion, "One of the destroyers, the USS *Edson*, thereafter sported thirteen miniature German tanks painted on the forward smoke stack."

An untold number of Germans were killed, many others had been wounded or injured, and some lost Nazi tankers who had watched their Panzers burn eventually came into the regimental command post to surrender.

General Bradley, who claimed that of the sixty Panzers committed to the counterattack directed at the First Division, more than half were destroyed. "Though overrun, Allen's infantry did not fall back," he added. "Allen had barely squeaked through, for those tanks had advanced to within 2,000 yards of the beach before they turned.

"I question whether any other U.S. division could have repelled that charge in time to save the beach from tank penetration. Only the perverse Big Red One with its no less perverse commander was both hard and experienced enough to take that assault in stride."

~FORTY-TWO~

BOB AND PAUL WERE AWAITING further orders when the ominous roar from eighteen or so enemy bombers filled their ears. Bob told Paul that they looked like Focke-Wulfs and Heinkels; they were being followed by a half-dozen Stukas, and all were approaching the transport area just off the beach they had landed on earlier that morning. It was now getting on towards four and there was plenty of daylight left, but the beach and the bay off Gela suddenly were so dark it looked like midnight had arrived.

Dust clouds rose up; fires started. Even General Patton, returning to Gela from the front, was mesmerized. "From a Liberty freight ship smoke was rising," he told his diary that night. "Before our eyes a tremendous explosion threw white and black clouds several thousand feet into the air."

The Liberty ship was loaded with ammunition; the tremendous explosions had split her in two, and salvage ships were racing to rescue those aboard and try to save what equipment and transports they could. Complicating matters was radio transmission aboard the USS *Samuel Chase* was delayed after its antenna was shot away; the *Chase* was the flagship of Rear Admiral Hall, commander of the invasion fleet in the Dime area. After another seventeen German planes bombed the bay, terrified men jumped into the water as abandon ship orders were yelled out aboard the Liberty ship.

Three 1,000-pound bombs had already hit it. All vessels nearby were ordered to stand clear. Then, at five o'clock the ship literally blew up and flames became more visible for miles. She burned brightly into the night; attempts to lay smoke screens around the ship to remove glare on other transports so the Germans couldn't target them were ineffectual; the wind blew the smoke away, revealing the still blazing Liberty ship and the brilliant beacon of light she had become.

And, again there were no friendly strikes by the Army air forces in the Bay of Gela that Bob or anyone else could see.

But many of the Army's men that were still aboard the Liberty ship, fourteen U.S. Navy personnel, plus thirty-two armed guards and forty-one crewmen, were safe. They all got out alive and were picked up by PT boats and transferred to nearby destroyers. The USS *McLanahan* then tried to sink the doomed vessel so she couldn't be seen by German planes, but this failed because the Liberty ship was in shallow water. She came to rest on her keel and burned for two more days.

Amongst the survivors were Captain William "Soup" Campbell and his men of the 18th's Service Company. They were rescued from what could have been their watery graves when a cruiser approached and lowered a rope gang-net. Gone, however, was about a third of the combat team's transports. Bob's 2nd Battalion was particularly hard hit. Sixty of its trucks and jeeps, plus his mortar platoon's weapons carriers, were on the bottom of the Gulf of Gela.

But there was little time to think about that; orders had already come down to meet up with the 26th Infantry and capture the Ponte Olivo aerodrome. German planes were still using it as a springboard to launch airstrikes on the beaches and the transport area; it had to be taken.

It was plenty dark by this time, but two pieces of news filtered in. Lieutenant Hobratschk was the source for both.

"Just got word that Axis Sally, the German propaganda gal, was heard over the radio," he told Bob's mortar squad. "She was telling her listeners that we were driven off the beaches."

This brought hearty laughter, but stunned silence followed when Lieutenant Hobratschk revealed the second piece of news.

"That ship that blew up off shore, the one with all our jeeps on it. . .it was the Liberty ship you guys crossed on. Yep, it was the *Robert Rowan*. Now, aren't you happy to be where you all are?"

Where Bob and his squad were two hours later was at the start of an eight-mile march that would put his battalion just off the road that ran straight northward from Gela towards the Ponte Olivo aerodrome. E Company and Jeffrey's G Company were lined up first, with Bob's H Company next, then Ben Sternberg's Headquarters Company, followed by Captain Spinney's F Company men. Together, they formed the battalion column, and it was just after midnight when the almond groves and the Plain of Gela were left behind.

Naval vessels offshore were still firing at targets inland; Bob hoped the aerodrome was one of them. But shells were also whistling overhead in the opposite direction; German and Italian artillery batteries inland were answering back with more salvos aimed down onto the beach and out into the bay.

Then, for some unknown reason, it seemed like every anti-aircraft gun in the Bay of Gela suddenly opened up. Bob and Paul looked skyward to try to find out why, and they saw several small specks of what appeared to be two-motored planes in formations coming towards the beach. There was no way to tell if they were friendly, or not. But a flare had gone up, followed by more loud firing of anti-aircraft guns. Billowing parachutes, backlit by the dim moon but bearing easily visible paratroopers of some nationality, suddenly filled the skies.

It soon became clear something was horribly wrong.

The sky literally lit up with crossing ack-ack fire while Bob and Paul watched the horror show unfold; the still-burning fire on the *Robert Rowan* added more light that reflected both the shoreline, and other planes flying in over the bay. Someone in Captain

Jeffrey's company in front of Bob's squad was the first to yell out, "It could be a German attack!"

"We could hear the roar of planes coming toward us from the direction of the sea," another officer remembered. "Their navigation lights could be seen. But we knew they were troop carriers."

Colonel Sternberg was amongst the first to realize the flak rising like fountains sprouting fire was hitting American paratroopers. One was even drifting downward with his parachute fully blossomed towards the 2nd Battalion's column, and his jump uniform looked very similar to German coveralls.

"Do not fire!" Ben Sternberg screamed into his radio.

No one did, but every pair of eyes in the battalion was looking skyward by this time; it was gut-wrenching watching the hapless columns of slow-flying C-47s literally getting blown out of the sky.

"Planes dropped out of formation and crashed into the sea," one eyewitness remembered. "Others, like clumsy whales, wheeled and attempted to get beyond the flak. More planes dived into the sea, and those that escaped raced like a covey of quail for what they thought was the protection of the beach. They were hit again, and this time by American ground units, believing the planes to be German. Some lucky men jumped and escaped alive; the less fortunate were riddled by flak before reaching the ground. Planes forced down into the water were machine gunned by shore parties as paratroopers attempted to launch rubber boats."

"The whole world just opened up on them," an officer who was aboard a destroyer in the bay recalled. "It was raining bodies and body parts. Shrapnel from shells literally ripped open those C-47s like a tin can, spilling the paratroopers out over the ocean."

Although Bob and Paul had no way of knowing this as they watched the sad, draconian scene from their position just off the Gela-Ponte Olivo road, twenty-three aircraft were lost; later reports revealed thirty-seven others were severely damaged. Sixty pilots and crewmen died; many were never recovered from the sea. Eighty-one expensively trained paratroopers were needlessly killed; one hundred and thirty-two others were wounded, and another sixteen went missing.

Everyone suffered. The assistant division commander of the 82nd Airborne was amongst them. One of the planes lost was carrying him as an official observer. Even the chaplain of the suffering regimental combat team—the 504th—who managed to land against a stone wall in a vineyard over in the 45th Division area was fired upon; after he loudly identified himself as an American the firing did not cease, but the chaplain miraculously escaped death after he screamed a curse word in plain English, and started shooting into the air to prove he wasn't a German.

Later word filtered down that the combat team's commander, Colonel Rueben Tucker, barely escaped death. The C-47 he was aboard survived, but it had over 1,000 shell holes in its fuselage.

Ben Sternberg had been fortunate enough to receive word in enough time to keep his men from adding to the carnage. Colonel Mason, General Allen's G-3, had thirty-minutes advanced notice of the airborne drop and had issued instructions to all of the First Division battalion commanders to hold their fire.

Bob and Paul nevertheless watched the weird disaster unfold with a feeling of hopeless frustration; it was over in what seemed to them to be a matter of minutes. The paratrooper that had landed near them was rolling up his chute, swearing like a madman when Lieutenant Hobratschk yelled, "Let's go. We have to get up to that hill ahead of us. The damage has been done. We can't fix that, but we can kill every bastard up at that airdrome."

It was 1:30 when Bob's battalion lined up to follow the 26th Infantry's 2nd Battalion northward along a draw paralleling the Gela-Ponte Olivo road. An Italian roadblock just to the north was quickly cleared. The quarter moon was still up and the explosion of light at the end of the Italian artillery tubes closer to the aerodrome also helped cast intermittent brilliance on the landscape.

Bob could see that above the next hill's scrub-bushed slopes the most prominent feature was an old castle. The Roman candle-like array of sparks that dotted the sky also permitted him to see it was topped with the ruins of a Medieval tower, prompting him to joke with Paul about Dracula maybe being on the Italian's side that night.

"I can see barbed wire around the place," Paul kidded back. "With any luck Bela Lugosi is up there sucking the blood out of the Wops shooting at us."

"You two are really funny," Carmen the Charmer Giello laughed, followed by Louie the Rub Rubato carping, "Didn't take Paul too long to become a smart ass like Bob and start picking on us brave and patriotic Italian-Americans."

A steely stare by Sergeant Horn ceased that kidding around, and after Italian artillery and mortar fire came at them minutes later everything stopped being funny; their spotters had found the battalion, and were now laying concentrations directly into the draw ahead of them. Then tanks appeared out of nowhere.

The only cover in the area were ditches and ravines at the base of the hill. Ben Sternberg ordered everyone to withdraw here.

"This really sucks," Bob smirked. "Where is Dracula when we need him?"

First light proved to be far better to have on their side, for when it came four of their own tanks showed up. Equally advantageous was the early rays of the sun allowed American artillery observers the opportunity to call for observed fires. Even more heartening was the lobbing of shells from a cruiser offshore; later records revealed it was the USS *Bosie*, and 255 of her rounds had been effectively aimed at the castle on the hill, permitting the 26th's battalion to surge forward, gain the crest, kill or capture what was left of the Italian rifle battalion, and even occupy the medieval tower. From here, more friendly artillery was called in, and with the firing of the *Bosie* still adding to the crescendo American soldiers of the 26th were able to swing left and take Monte della Guardia, another rocky hill nearer the aerodrome.

This made it easier for Bob's battalion to dash towards the aerodrome itself, especially after the friendly tanks that had showed up pounded the Italians. Nine hundred eventually surrendered, but as Ben Sternberg told everyone later, "They had surrendered unnecessarily, as they had wonderful prepared positions with numerous automatic weapons; however, this was only the beginning of wholesale surrender by the Italians."

"We were damned lucky," Lieutenant Hobratschk told Sergeant Horn. "There were concrete pillboxes and plenty of barbed-wire entanglements around the airport, and that battery of Italian artillery at the head of the draw we came through could have caused real damage to us. Tell your men we appreciated the mortar rounds they laid on those bastards."

"Yesterday, Ponte Olivo sent aloft fighters and light bombers to strafe our troops and sink our ships," another officer added. "Now it is a mass of shredded aircraft and crazily swaying hangers."

Two days later the aerodrome was free of explosives and booby traps and back in use, this time for American planes to fly in supplies and to finally support further movement inland.

General Allen punctuated the importance of seizing the aerodrome when he noted, "It's quick capture resulted in nullifying the overwhelming air superiority which the Germans had previously maintained in the II Corp beach area."

There had been no resting on its laurels for Bob's battalion, however. "We were ordered to occupy Hill 200 outside of the airport which was accomplished without resistance," Sternberg explained. "But enemy artillery fire was used both against our personnel and also to set fields afire in order to slow the advance of our infantry."

Although a large portion of the division's lines had been moved forward five miles further inland due to the capture of the Ponte Olivo airfield, General Patton was not satisfied. "I am not too pleased with the progress of the First Division," he wrote in his diary that night. Then referring to where Bob and Paul spent a cold evening, despite the fires burning near them, Patton added "They had halted just north of the Ponte Olivo airport, waiting for the 16th Infantry to catch up. I ordered them to keep moving."

~FORTY-THREE~

VIOLA HAD FIRST HEARD ABOUT the landings while she was still at work on Saturday, the 10th Of July. The announcement came over a loud speaker, and she was simply told the invasion of Europe had begun, that Allied troops landed in Sicily. Naugatuck was sweltering in the heat and humidity summer brought to the industrial Connecticut Valley, but when her shift ended Viola was especially eager to get to the newsstand at the foot of the hill on Oak Street.

After she picked up the *New York Times*, she gave the familiar newsboy the three cents it cost, read the headline ALLIED TROOPS START INVASION OF SICILY; NAVAL ESCORTS BOMBARDED SHORE DEFENSES; LANDINGS PRECEDED BY A SEVERE AIR AT-TACK, and started up the hill. Mrs. Walker was not on her porch, but Viola called out to her anyway, knowing George's mother would likely hear her through her open windows and be grateful for the greeting.

After checking her mail, Viola went inside and put her heavy embroidered purse on her cluttered coffee table in the living room. Disappointed there was no letter from Bob, she then headed for the kitchen and spread the paper out to read. The first thing she noticed was a map of Sicily, underneath which it noted, "General Eisenhower announced that his troops had debarked at various points on Sicily early today. The landings were preceded by furious air assaults and warships accompanying the transports shelled the coastal defenses. Troops got ashore at the western tip of the island, according to Algiers radio. Strong forces of tanks were reported being used. The invasion had been preceded by heavy bombings of a variety of targets."

Viola read down the right side of the front page that "Allied infantry landed at a number of places on the rocky Sicilian coast under a canopy of naval gunfire early this morning as the long-awaited invasion began. General Dwight D. Eisenhower, Allied Commander in Chief, speaking to the people of France, called the attack 'the first page to the liberation of the European Continent,' and promised 'there will be others.'

"In the early hours of yesterday morning another announcement from General Eisenhower's headquarters brought the news for which free people everywhere have been waiting eagerly and hopefully ever since the conquest of Tunisia."

Viola continued reading, thinking she would find that Bob's First Division was amongst the troops that landed on Sicily's western shore, but the news didn't mention any of the units that had participated in the invasion.

That night she nevertheless said a prayer for Bob before she fell asleep, exhausted but happy she had the next day off.

Over coffee in the morning she opened her world atlas and looked at Sicily's western shore. If Bob did land during the invasion she figured he must have come ashore at either Trapani, or Marsala, maybe even Palermo.

Sonny called that night and told her that was likely not the case. "Mother, American forces landed along the southern shore of Sicily. The British came in on the southeastern shoreline."

"Then why would the *Times* say our troops landed on the western shore of Sicily?" Viola wondered.

"It may have been that Eisenhower was still in Algiers when the invasion began, and the radio reported landings on Sicily's western shores at his direction to throw the Italians and any Germans in the area off," Sonny ventured. "Perhaps Eisenhower hoped they'd send forces there to lessen the resistance when our own forces came ashore where they actually did."

"I just know Bob landed on Sicily," Viola suddenly said.

"It's likely true Mother, but we simply have no way of knowing for sure. We're just going to have to wait for further reports."

"Wait. That's all I do Sonny. Wait, wait, wait!"

"I know," Sonny offered as sympathetically as he could. "But we must have faith. We know Bob has able commanders, and as he's said to you every time he's written he can take care of himself when he needs to."

"Yea, Mrs. Walker thought that about George, too," Viola said back.

"How is Mrs. Walker, Mother?"

"She's devastated Sonny. God help me if I ever had to deal with Bob getting killed."

"He'll be alright, Mother. Have faith."

When Monday came the *Times* headline read: ALLIES CAPTURE THREE AIRDROMES IN SICILY; WARSHIPS SMASH TANKS TO LET AMERICANS GAIN; OUR CASUALTIES LIGHT; 2,000 SHIPS IN ARMADA.

And this time Viola learned, "Allied troops, swiftly overrunning Italian defenses in the greatest combined operation in history, have captured three Sicilian airfields and the city of Pachino near the southeast coast, it was announced tonight. The Americans seized two aerodromes, one at Gela on the southern coast and the other slightly inland, after having smashed a heavy Axis tank counter-attack..."

But further reading still didn't tell Viola if the First Division was in Sicily, even though this time the paper got it right about where Bob actually was when the Ponte Olivo aerodrome fell.

Where Bob was actually heading became clearer to his commanders on that same Monday. General Bradley explained it to them in a way that made Patton's impatience better understood. With the Ponte Olivo and other airdromes taken, II Corps' next objective was a good twenty-five more miles inland; it was a road-way that ran parallel to the northwest coast of Sicily.

On Ben Sternberg's map it was marked as the Yellow Line; over-lays also showed him that his 2nd Battalion's line of advance would be to the west of the main roadway which bisected the island and ran from Sicily's southern shores up through Enna and then to Nicosia.

It soon became apparent that the 18th Infantry, along with the rest of II Corps, had gotten the raw end of the deal, the deal being the boundary lines drawn by the British and forced upon Patton's Seventh Army. Once again, like it was in North Africa, the British were treating the Americans as if they were their blocking force as they advanced up to Messina, just like they had towards Tunis at the end of the North African campaign, thus attaining the mil-itary objective of the Sicilian invasion and all the glory that came with it.

Paul would remember the job he was assigned to as the most difficult twenty-something days of the Sicilian campaign, where the marching was endless and over terrain so rugged that every-thing had to be hand-carried, from mortars to lousy C and D ration meals. Bob, on the other hand, saw everything through the lens of irony and his usual good natured way of shrugging things off. When Lieutenant Hobratschk and Sergeant Horn tried to make some sense of just what it was they would be doing, Bob did his best to keep a straight face, but that failed.

"So General Patton says brave Germans like my ancestors left Germany to come to America, and so we're killing the ones that didn't," Bob smirked. "I get that. But the part I don't get is this. The other side of my family is British, as in my grandmother came from London and still has a heavy Brit accent. But knowing her I suspect she'd be happy being here with us if she could kill a few Brits."

"Smart ass," Sergeant Horn laughed.

"That about sums it up, men," Lieutenant Hobratschk added.

The drive northward found Bob's 2nd Battalion first seizing two high hills near Mazzarino. "A reconnaissance patrol previously found the objective to be unoccupied," Ben Sternberg later recalled.

But the next day initially looked like there could be trouble ahead. "Lieutenant Lindo just spotted a bunch of Italian trucks and guns in the woods just east of here," Sergeant Horn yelled out while Bob and Paul were eating their breakfast ration. "Let's set up and get ready to provide supporting fires. Our artillery is first going to clobber the area, and then E Company is going in to finish the job. Our orders are to use heavy explosive shells. Go, go, go!"

A half hour later it was all over. Two hundred Italians surrendered; thirty trucks and eleven 100mm guns were also confiscated.

By the time Bob's battalion moved up into Barrafranca the Italians there had fled. "All that remained of this key military installation were the familiar heaps of wrecked and abandoned trucks, guns and other equipment, and the dead," Lieutenant Johnson of the regiment's Antitank Company noted in his diary. Gone, too, by this time was the 16th Infantry; General Allen had already ordered its men to leapfrog past the 26th and push towards Pietraperzia, the First Division's next objective. Allen never let his men rest on their laurels.

Pietraperzia had been conquered by the Normans in the 16th Century and this time it was also easily cleared by the First Division. "Then we spent the following day in an assembly area just to the north of Pietraperzia," Ben Sternberg remembered. "We received some hostile artillery fire which caused a few casualties. We were supposed to assist the 16th Infantry in attacking the next hill, Mt. Copovarso, but orders were changed placing our battalion in reserve after we made another six-mile shuttle and approach march towards Villarosa.

"Turned out the Italians had also withdrawn from their defensive position at Villarosa to a new line on a ridge south of Alimena," Sternberg later explained. "A patrol was sent out while permission was being awaited to move our battalion in the same direction. This was refused and we instead went into division reserve and moved to another bivouac just outside of Villapriolo."

The respite was short, but it gave Bob and Paul time to reflect on the progress of the second phase of their Sicilian campaign thus far.

The latest *Stars and Stripes* started making the rounds; the headline screamed about the fact Sicily had been invaded, and how "radios warn French people to wait for the right moment." But the most interesting thing to Bob was reading "Il Duce on the spot; pleads for support." Louie the Rub said that meant he was going down soon.

There were dead, rotting cows and mules in the nearby fields, but the wind was carrying the stench away from them. Lieutenant Johnson had also come by to talk with Ben Sternberg and he said he was amazed at "the vast supply of trucks, bicycles, motorcycles, rifles and medium howitzers, all strewn in the wildest disarray among the bodies of Sicily's defenders."

There were also plenty of British bodies on the Plain of Catania, east of where Bob was, by this time; about 400 officers and another 5,400 other ranks were already casualties. The British, having encountered unexpected heavy fighting in their zone, had left the important hub at Enna unmolested, and in General Bradley's view this meant the great walled city was his for the taking. Protected by hills, the ancient citadel was supposedly impregnable, but General Allen nevertheless sent the 16th Infantry up the steep hill mass into Enna on July 20th. The fighting was over so quickly that Bradley's G-2 remarked, "Not bad, not bad at all. It took the Saracens twenty years in their siege of Enna. Our boys did it in five hours."

After Enna fell Bob's battalion moved to yet another bivouac area south of Alimena where Ben Sternberg established a new command post in a scrubby olive orchard just off the road that led to Bompietro. Bob, Paul, Gentle John and the rest of the Bearer Boys spent a sleepless night near this orchard; the sounds of war were up ahead.

Filthy Bompietro was of little military value, but Sternberg was ordered to seize a hill just to its north on July 22nd so the regiment's trucks and supplies could move through unimpeded. This time tragedy struck; the retreating enemy forces sent several 105 mm howitzer shells to greet the battalion's arrival, and after Sternberg's companies de-trucked a single explosion killed twelve men in E Company and left eleven wounded.

Bob's squad was more fortunate, even though they were less than a hundred yards from where the shells hit. The well over thousand-foot hill was seized by the rifle companies that morning, but there were no enemy forces to exact revenge on. They had again withdrawn in force, and only a few were taken prisoner.

Sternberg wasted little time and sent a patrol forward to secure a road junction two miles ahead that was closer to Petralia. Few shots were fired back in anger; the decadent town had also been abandoned.

That night Bob learned that his battalion had once again reverted to division reserve. There were three other things that made him happy: mail from home came up from the beach and the jeep that brought it had Captain Murphy riding in its right seat. He was back from his stay at the hospital near Arzew in North Africa. New U rations also arrived; they fed three meals to five men and contained canned fruit, cheese, crackers, sugar, bacon, vegetables, cereal, coffee, plus cigarettes and matches—even toilet paper.

There was also one letter for Bob; it was a brief note from his Gram Nellie along with a late June Sunday edition of the *Naugatuck Daily News*. After reading it from front to back, he got in his bedroll and settled down on some straw Paul had picked up in a nearby wheat field to make sleeping on the ground more comfortable that night.

Then Bob decided it was time to write a letter home to his mother.

> *July 26, 1943*
> *Dear Mom;*
> *I guess it's about time that I wrote to you so you'll know that I am still all right. We are on an island called Sicily and I suppose that you know by now that it has been invaded by the British and us. By the time you get this letter it should be all over and I expect to be here when it does end, if you know what I mean.*
> *I hope that you are getting along all right and that you will be a good girl until I get home. Don't work too hard, and please don't forget to write. Let me know how everything is going around town and I shall be hoping to see you soon.*
> *Love,*
> * Bob*
> *PS: Give everyone my love.*

Bob was about to set the letter aside, but then he decided he should share what his letter from Gram Nellie had said about George Walker. So he turned the V-Mail sheet over, and started writing again. He wanted his mother to know he had the news, but he didn't want to tell her he had been carrying the burden of that news with him since he landed in Sicily.

> *I received a letter from Gram today, and she informed me that George Walker was killed in North Africa, and of course it didn't sound very good to hear that so I'll have to settle the score for him when I get the chance. I never did see much of him after he joined the army, but I did meet him in England when we were there and it was the same old Walker, still crazy as ever. I am sorry to hear what happened to him, and please let his mother know this.*

And please don't worry about me, Mom. I can take care of myself when I have to. Worry about Sonny and his girl troubles instead, and tell him to write me, OK?

~FORTY-FOUR~

WHEN A TIRED VIOLA GOT HOME from work back in Naugatuck that same day she found the latest *Life* magazine waiting in her mailbox. She was anxious to see if anything had been written about the Sicily invasion.

She wasn't disappointed.

It would be the first time she learned more; reports from Sicily had been delayed due to what had been previously reported as "transmission problems." But Sonny later told her that likely translated into the delays being attributable to censorship, and not releasing any information too soon that could be useful to Hitler or Mussolini.

"After seven days of fighting the invasion was going well," Viola was told before she read the obvious. "To the people at home, however, the pattern and strategy was not clear. Because it was necessary to keep movements of the Allied armies secret, the fighting was reported only in isolated fragments."

Viola then read, "By week's end certain things were obvious. The Allies had caught the Italians and Germans by surprise. The movement of 2,000 invasion ships and barges from North Africa had been a big logistical success. The Italian fleet had been unwilling to come out and fight, and the Axis air force, though a pesky nuisance, had been unable to slow up the landing operations.

"In Washington, military authorities reported the invasion ahead of schedule," Viola now read. "But they warned of hard fighting to come. Apparently the Axis had 300,000 experienced troops in Sicily and many mountain positions, from which it will be tough to drive them."

Viola read on, hoping to see some mention of the First Division, but there was none. Instead there were stories about where the British had landed and how "such a scene would be impossible without complete command of the air and sea."

A piece entitled "Troop Landings at Gela in Sicily" by war correspondent Jack Belden filled the following page. Viola quickly scanned it, again looking for any mention of the First Division. Seeing nothing, she flipped to the last page that covered the invasion, and saw that it was headlined "OUR ARMY."

Life magazine wasted no effort in putting the best word ruffles and flourishes into every paragraph of this piece. "With its Allies our Army achieved in the Sicilian landing a new high in military science," the editorial began beneath the words "Gargantuan Timetable." This followed with, "The attack on Sicily is a landmark—like Alexander's long march into India, or Hannibal's use of double envelopment at Cannae.

"The Army has produced officers that rank with any in the world, whether strategically or tactically," Viola was assured. "Destiny is pointing her finger at us, and through the smoke of battle we are beginning to gather, dimly, that she has a job for us to do. It is somehow like reading the Book of Revelation to find boys from the Mississippi Valley storming the legendary shores of civilization, to hear Joe Sciavoni of Brooklyn is crouching in a large barge, miserably seasick, on the waters that carried Ulysses safely out of the whirlpools of Scylla and Charybdis (which lie in the ancient world between Messina and the Italian mainland), or that Ole Carlson, the big Minnesota Swede, is advancing on Agrigento, where they buried Archimedes, the great Greek scientist who terrified the Romans with the engines of war."

For Viola this piece was a pretty tall drink of water, for she wasn't well-educated in the classics. But seeing there was just one paragraph left, she took it in.

"For about 450 years the New World has been allowed to grow up behind the rim of San Salvador, which Columbus discovered in 1492. And now here we are back again, with jeeps and parachutes, to break the grip of northern barbarians upon the Homeric lands from which our civilization sprang. We seek no empire. But we bring with us out of the New World this demand: that henceforth, on our planet, men shall be free from tyranny and murder, that they shall have the right to life, liberty and the pursuit of happiness; and there shall be opened up before them the simple truths that we have practiced on the Kansas plains."

Viola put the magazine down on her coffee table after she read these words, still not knowing whether the First Division had landed in Sicily, or if her son Bob was still alive.

Her sister Katherine came by for dinner that Saturday night.

"I'm just a first grade school teacher, Viola," she laughed after reading the *Life* editorial. "We haven't even taught the children about Columbus discovering America yet."

When Viola talked to Sonny on Sunday she expected his Ivy League education would have permitted him to appreciate *Life's* towering words.

"Mother," he reminded her, "I majored in psychology. Roosevelt's speech writers couldn't have said it better. We're all very proud of our Army. *Life* was doing everything it could to keep our spirits high, and its editors did a great job at that. We simply cannot wage war without the full support of us here on the home front.

"So we just have to keep working hard, try not too worry too much about Bob, and keep hoping for the best."

August came and so did the oppressive heat that began the dog days of summer. Viola was on her way home that first Friday of the month, and as was her custom she stopped at the newsstand at the foot of Oak Street before heading up the hill. The news boy, knowing Bob was with the First Division, greeted her with a copy of that week's *Time*, and this time Viola's heart really raced.

She reached into her purse to pay for it, but the news boy said, "It's on me Mrs. Baummer."

The cover had a picture of Bob's handsome, slightly grinning top commander spread across it, with an inscription beneath it that read: "Major General Terry Allen of the First Division," followed with, "The infantry, the infantry, with dirt behind their ears."

Inside, a delighted Viola read:

Last week, somewhere along the German's last line in Sicily, General Allen and his men were very busy. Also in the line were at least four other U.S. divisions. All of them fought well. But upon Terry Allen and his First Division, as upon no other commander or unit in Sicily, there has fallen a special mark on war and history, a mark reserved for front line fighting men, and esteemed by them.

It is a mark of the greatest division in being and of a great division commander in the making. These inseparable reputations—the reputation of the division and that of its commander—are the first to be publically recognized in the U.S. Army of World War II. To all soldiers there is food for thought, and to many there is satisfaction in the fact that the joint reputation was won by a division of infantrymen, the men on foot and who, up until now, have finally had to win the battles and the wars.

The infantry, the infantry, with dirt behind their ears ..... when Allen took over the First, the division had no superior in the Army and in the opinion of its men, no equal. Its boast, when Allen was ready to take it to England last year, was that all but six of its 16,000-odd men were volunteers. They were already calling themselves "the first team." They drilled, they maneuvered, played under their soldier patch (the figure "1" in red) with a special swagger and they roared the infantry's song with special gusto:

The infantry, the infantry
With dirt behind their ears.
They can whip their weight in wildcats,
And drink their weight in beers.
The cavalry, artillery
And the goddamn engineers
They'll never catch the infantry
In a hundred thousand years.

With the division sobered and hardened Terry Allen was gaining a personal luster but he would certainly point to his stars and fame and say: "You know who is responsible for that? The enlisted men, that's who."

By the time Viola finished reading the piece she had reached her front door and her heart was beating with pride. Only one thing could have made her happier.

But when she checked her mail there was no letter from Bob.

~FORTY-FIVE~

THE SITUATION IN SICILY HAD changed by this time. At the end of July, the 45th Division was positioned on the north coastal road and could mount a continued drive towards Messina. The British were facing different circumstances; they were still having problems advancing up the narrow Catania road on Sicily's eastern shore.

General Bradley had been under new orders for several days. "Army Group stiffened its original directive for the U.S. attack towards Messina," he noted. "We were ordered to thrust eastward along the north coast road and the road Nicosia-Troina-Cesaro and employ the maximum strength we could maintain. After starting the 45th Division toward Messina on the north coast road, I pivoted the First Division east on the Nicosia-Troina route. Twenty miles of brush-covered mountains separated these parallel roads and there were few connecting paths between them."

The Germans had established a new defensive line in anticipation of the American's changed plans—what they called the Etna stellung. It ran from the Catania road, starting roughly twenty miles north of Catania, and then moved away from the flat, swampy Catania plain westward along the base of Mt. Etna before veering northward past the hilltop town of Troina—the highest on Sicily—and finally up to San Fratello, which the 45th Division was now heading for along the north coastal road.

The Germans had also strengthened their defenses. The stubborn Herman Goering Division would continue to hold up the

British. The 15th Panzer Grenadier Division would defend Troina. Four artillery battalions from the Italian Aosta Division even came under German control to support them. Troina would be where they would make their final bold stand on Sicily and fight to the last cartridge.

But the Americans had misread the German's plans. All information pointed to heavy troop and materiel movements merely passing through—but not stopping at—Troina. Bradley's intelligence section wrongly estimated the Germans would make their final stand on the high ground five mile east of Troina, closer to Randazzo and Cesaro.

The intelligence at the end of July even said the Germans were "offering slight resistance to our advancing force; they are fighting delaying actions; bulk of force withdrawing; delaying forces in small groups; indications are Troina lightly held."

Late July found Bob and Paul on a ridge three miles north of Nicosia close to Gangi, still in First Division reserve, but expecting to get into the easy fight forecasted by II Corps that would finally push the Germans off Sicily.

Although the Germans had left the immediate area near the ridge Bob and Paul were on, heavy and accurate artillery fire hit it with frequency. But Captain Murphy had demonstrated that he was back in full command of Company H, and once their bivouac area was consolidated near a field of tomatoes Bob and Paul found they had some time on their hands, enough to actually wonder just when they would get back to chasing Germans down.

Rumors added to the waiting, and one that seemed too good to be true quickly made the rounds of artillery shells landing nearby less threatening. Mussolini was no longer in power, leaving everyone to speculate that all of Sicily, including what was left of the Italian army would soon surrender. Word also came down about Nicosia falling, and this raised hopes that the Germans would also leave soon. The other battalions of the 18th were chasing them down on Highway 120, the main road that led to Troina, and routing them out of the big hills to the north.

All, from where Bob and Paul could see it, was going well.

Other big news reached Bob's 2nd Battalion after a heavy rain left the area on the 1st of August. General Allen had received word that the entire First Division was going to be relieved ahead of the fight for Troina, and word of this traveled fast. A regiment of the 9th Division had already arrived in the area, with the rest of this division expected in a matter of a few more days.

"What's not to like about this?" Bob deadpanned to Paul when they got that news.

Troina, home to 12,000 Sicilians, lay atop a high, dominating ridge. In order to give the 9th Division's regiment knowledge of the sector before it was officially turned over, Terry Allen committed its commander, the colorful Colonel Harry "Paddy" Flint, for the initial assault on Troina on the first day of August.

The attack did not go well. Flint's men were greeted by heavy machinegun and mortar fire when they jumped off; First Division artillery responded in anger, but Flint's regiment was still forced to halt for the night in the hills off Highway 120 and wait until morning to give taking Troina another try.

That effort again met resistance far greater than was expected; the Germans were still thought to have just covering forces in Troina for their withdrawing troops. But two of their battalions were actually positioned in the hills north of Highway 120; another was nearby in reserve; yet two more battalions were also dug in atop a two-kilometer-long ridgeline south of the stronghold. The stone buildings in the town itself were being used by the Germans for their protection and to observe the American movements; they had excellent views over the entire area and significant positioning from which to direct artillery fire.

When Flint's men made their next try to take the hilltop away from the Germans, they were stopped again.

Terry Allen was now faced with a dilemma. He could wait for the rest of the 9th Division to arrive, or he could renew the attack with his own tired men and hopefully turn over the sector absent resistance. Allen was one of the most attack-minded general officers of World War II, and never one to shy away from a fight. He quickly concluded that it was the First Division's moral obligation to capture Troina, and his Field Order #20 that night spelled out how it would be done.

All Bob and Paul knew was an alert order had been issued earlier that day for movement by truck around to the south flank of the Troina position, and that the role of their regiment was to back up the attack of the 16th Infantry that was slated to begin at three the next morning. But the sounds of war were already present. Both hostile and friendly air activity became increasingly active when Bob and Paul started boarding their duce and a half later that afternoon to depart from the ridge near Gangi and head into battle.

Six German planes were soon flying overhead, and they both watched in awe when they dove to strafe the road that would first take them through Nicosia. Thankfully, the German pilots caused no damage, and it was immensely gratifying for Bob and Paul to watch four of these planes crash into hillsides after being hit by their own anti-aircraft fire.

It was early evening when Bob and Paul bounced over the narrow cobblestone streets in Nicosia to the cheers of its grateful citizenry. A few threw bottles of wine and flowers into the back of their deuce and a half. After a priest blessed the convoy they left the village behind and it was nearing eight o'clock when they reached their assembly area just to the south of Gagliano.

The town had been the scene of a bitterly fought pitch battle just days earlier, but had fallen after it was hit by a squadron of American A-20 Havoc bombers. Bob and Paul were still eight miles from Troina, the about to be blanketed in darkness landscape beyond the big castle in Gagliano looked plenty inhospitable, and it was clear the trails forward couldn't support anything on wheels.

It just didn't feel right. How were they going to get their mortar and ammo through this Godforsaken terrain?

The answer came quickly. Help was on the way and it arrived an hour later. The reinforcements weren't much to look at and they had bridles fashioned from cut up ammo bags, yet the mules would be able to carry their blankets, rations and mortar shells, plus their squad's mortar tube, pod and baseplate through the steep hills and deep ravines that lay ahead.

Bob wanted nothing to do with leading the pack on this mission, so once the first mule was loaded up Billy Uhouse stepped up and pulled on its reins to get it moving. Carmen the Charmer got behind the animal and gave it a push, only to be thrown a kick that almost hit him in the crotch. But Louie the Rub saved the night by whispering in the mule's ear, and off it started, ever so slowly, with the other Bearer Boys, Gentle John, Bob and Paul following. Bob wisecracked that Louie must have said something to the stubborn beast in Italian.

H Company was in the very back of the column when the battalion finally moved out in force at ten that night. The rifle companies went first because they were hand carrying lighter loads and Ben Sternberg didn't want a pack of mules slowing their advance up. In fact, Sternberg didn't believe he'd need H Company's mortar support right away, but after his headquarters company set up a temporary command post in a wadi a few miles into the move while everyone caught their breath and gulped down some water, he started to do some more thinking; he actually grew strangely suspicious—something Captain Murphy also sensed.

The column moved on. Occasional shell explosions were the only thing lighting up the night when the battalion reached what Sternberg believed was a hill that overlooked Monte Bianco just after four the next morning. Then, when daylight came, his reasons for being suspicious were confirmed.

"We were surprised to discover that the battalion's actual objective—Monte Bianco—was really a very small hill, hardly big enough for a platoon to fit on," Captain Murphy told Lieutenant Hobratschk when he arrived with the mortar platoon and its pack of mules. "Ben feels that in light of the fact that its also dominated by high ground to the south and east it's not the place to be. Instead he sees opportunity in the position we're in. So we're going to set up right here on this hill because we can not only see Monte Bianco, we can also watch the whole left flank of the damn Germans around Troina and start hitting them when the attack goes off."

The Germans were also watching them by this time. They had even sent out combat patrols from Mt. Pellegrino, which was just off to the east, and these forces wasted little time before they started harassing the flank of the just-arrived Americans. This changed everything, and Colonel Smith reluctantly called off Sternberg's attack towards Troina until the situation could be better evaluated.

Ben Sternberg was nevertheless anxious to do something. He asked Colonel Smith for permission to fire on targets that were stopping the adjacent 16th Infantry, which was attacking Troina from the west at the time. But another problem came up. It was discovered that every one of the rifle company commanders, plus Captain Murphy, were having a hell of a time locating their actual positions on the maps that had been given to them. Smith had no choice now but to refuse permission to fire on enemy targets for fear any coordinates that would be used to register artillery or mortar fire could instead land on the friendly troops of the 16th.

"Dammit," Sternberg told Colonel Smith over his radio. "We've got excellent observation here, and we'd sure like to use it."

"Well, you damn well may Ben," Smith answered in his southern drawl. "I just got a call from division and was told General Allen will be up here tomorrow to make a personal reconnaissance of your position. I'll be with him. And make sure Lucky Lindo and Murph are there."

"Yes, sir," Sternberg said back before clicking off his radio. Others nearby then heard him swear again.

Ben Sternberg's disappointment with the decision to wait was justified. He had heard fragmentary reports on his radio during the morning that revealed just how bad it had gone for the 16th's battalion that he wanted to support.

But Colonel Smith's thinking was sound at the time. He was very concerned about the 2nd Battalion's open flank; Smith also knew that one of the companies of the 16th had also had trouble reading their maps and, after they went down a wrong road, walked right into an ambush; 60 men from their E Company were overwhelmed by a staggering volume of hostile fire. And it only got worse. A glum message from their battalion commander during mid-morning read, "E now has two platoons missing; F has only one and a half platoons fighting strength." Then just before noontime an update revealed, "We now have what's left of F Company—thirty-five men and one officer. G has about forty men left."

That night in his small farmhouse that was his command post—always codenamed Danger Forward—General Allen was giving out orders for the next day when he suddenly asked to be excused. His immediate reports wondered what this could be about and they had no choice but to wait. Two war correspondents nevertheless elected to follow Allen into the olive grove he was suddenly headed for. They found him kneeling under the star-lit sky in prayer. One eventually asked if he was praying for the success of the operation.

"No," the First Division commander responded. "I'm praying there will be no unnecessary casualties tomorrow; I'm praying that no man's life will be wasted."

The First Division had four infantry regiments poised to make the coordinated attack on August 4th. It jumped off late that afternoon. Eight artillery battalions first unleased their fury; two flights of P-51 fighters, modified for dive bombing, dropped 500-pound bombs. But despite the shattering preparatory effort the combined American forces attempting to encircle Troina only made slight gains before the Germans responded with their own artillery fire and progress again ground to a halt.

The best gains were made on the southern salient, despite the stubbornness of the Germans here; Bob York's 1st Battalion ran into a German force that was entrenched on a ridge in front of nearby Mount Pellegrino, engaged them in hand-to-hand fighting, and beat them off the ridge.

This secured Ben Sternberg's position from attack into his flank that had so worried Colonel Smith; the timing was fortuitous. It was later that afternoon when General Allen made his appearance with Smith. Captain Murphy and Lieutenant Lindo joined the meeting. It was brief. Seeing that the 2nd Battalion's position was indeed the best there was for striking at the stubborn German defenders on the ridges south of Troina, Allen gave the go ahead to hit them.

For Bob and Paul it meant they were going to get into the action in a big way. When Captain Murphy got back to their position on a rock outcropping he went from section to section and wished everyone well. He also told them they'd have plenty of mortars; General Allen had made sure of that, and Colonel Smith had in turn ordered Lieutenant Johnson's Antitank Company platoon to procure at least fifty more mules and press them into formation as pack trains.

"We took the dumb, emaciated animals from their impoverished peasant owners," Johnson told everyone later. "Then we took them up to our rendezvous and supply dump. We loaded each mule with 250 pounds of mortar shells. That was fairly easy; working them that night over the skyline crags and precipitous cliffs up to our hilltop CP near the battalion commanders was one of those times, as the British say 'we'd had it!'"

"We repeatedly stumbled in the dark into the wrong ravines trying to keep hold of our only guide, a thin phone wire laid along the ground from our rendezvous point to the CP, but after many trips we eventually got enough supplies for the troops and ammo for the mortars, our only support weapons up there."

Everyone in Bob's squad joined with the other mortar sections that night and carried the just-delivered shells up closer to their mortar locations for what was to be a noon attack the next day.

Unknown to anyone, General Allen had made his appearance at the 18th Infantry CP that day after leaving a briefing back at his farmhouse command post just outside of Cerami where he had received orders that he told his wife in a letter that night "came as a great surprise and the actual meaning of which I do not exactly know."

The order had inadvertently come via a routine mail delivery. When one of Allen's aides opened the letter and read what it said, he rushed it over to Colonel Mason, the division's chief of staff. Shocked when he read it, Mason went to General Allen's G-2, Colonel Porter, let him read it, and then asked for his advice on what to do with it. Together they discussed whether they should show it to their commander, and after some hushed discussion they concluded because it was likely others knew about the order they had to show it to their boss.

Allen was briefing other subordinates on the next day's attack when he was handed the order. He read it, then turned to Porter and whispered, "Bob, what do I do with this?"

There were tears in his eyes, but Allen continued the briefing and delivered more instructions to his staff, all of whom were wondering just what was going on. The briefing came to an end a few minutes later, then General Allen called Bradley. The II Corps commander was evasive, and simply told him, "Carry on, we'll sort this out later."

Not long afterwards the phone rang. It was George Patton.

Bradley had called Patton to let him know Allen had the news. But, pretending he didn't know, Patton asked his friend of twenty-five years if the order for his relief had arrived.

"Yes," was the answer.

"Well, you're not relieved," Patton shot back. "I say you're not relieved until you've taken Troina and the First Division has completed its job in Sicily!"

General Allen had chosen not to tell anyone about the order when he was up with Ben Sternberg and the other 18th Infantry officers later that day, for he feared the news might have an impact on their moral. He was correct; that would come later.

But Allen was especially touched when he saw his old friend George Patton was waiting to console him after he got back to his command post in Cerami.

~FORTY-SIX~

"THIS IS GOING TO BE DIFFERENT than it was at El Guettar," Sergeant Horn told the Bearer Boys the next morning. "We'll have air support. We don't have a definitive time it will come, but it's as good as guaranteed because General Allen said so.

"OK, the attack goes off at noontime. The rifle companies are going to try to advance. F Company will be heading towards that hill up there to our left; its marked as Hill 570 on my map. Unfortunately, it's wide open to German observation. Lieutenant Lindo is going to register the mother of all artillery strikes on the hill first, and then we could very well get called on to fire some mortars that way.

"Monte Pellegrino, over there to the right, still has Germans on it, probably good-sized in numbers, and they have been sending patrols in this direction to feel us out," Sergeant Horn added. "We captured a few of the Hun bastards last night, and we got them to tell us their plan was to try to get around our position here and come in at us from the rear. We aren't going to let that happen. G and E Companies are headed that way to cut them off."

About that time Lieutenant Hobratschk showed up; he wanted to inspect the area Bob's mortar was in. He was impressed.

"You did good men. I like the way you stacked up the mortars. Two distinct locations, close enough, but separated from each other so if the Germans hit one it won't take out the other.

"Now listen to me carefully. We don't want any unnecessary bravado. If the Germans zero in on your mortar, and I call for you to abandon the position, do it. No questions. We don't want to lose any of you. Bad enough we lost Slugger back at El Guettar. Sure, he was a hero, but he's gone. Stegall, you got any questions? You're still the new guy."

Paul had no questions; he just had a determined look on his face, made confident because he and Bob had practiced handing off mortars earlier that morning. Bob wanted them to be handed to him at chest height, so he could pivot quickly and shove them down into the tube. He told Paul he planned to turn the barrel red by feeding it as fast as he could hand mortars to him. They were ready.

"Alright then," Lieutenant Hobratschk said. "I am going to stay in the area; Captain Murphy is up with the command group, and will be awaiting Colonel Sternberg's orders to commence firing. You're registered in on covering F Company first, but I have a feeling Lindo will get the Krauts running for cover when he lays artillery on them and we'll be focusing more on Monte Pellegrino. You have the coordinates for that, and despite the lousy maps Bradley's headquarters gave us, we also now have that registered in, right John?

"Yes, sir," Gentle John shot back. "We're ready."

"I'm fully expecting we'll be using heavy explosive," Hobratschk assured them. "You've got about 250 rounds. Took the mules forever to get them up here, but we've got 'em now. Use every one of them if we're called on to do that, OK?

"But get the hell out if I tell you to. Usual order on firing commands. Sergeant Roof is up with Captain Murphy. He'll call them down to me, and then Sergeant Horn will get the word to fire and make adjustments as requested. Any questions?"

There were none.

At precisely twelve o'clock Lieutenant Lindo began to have what he would later call a field day laying artillery on the Germans around Hill 570. Bob and Paul watched as F Company's riflemen started swarming the hill a half hour later. It wasn't long before they could make out some men on the very top of the hill mass. Then they heard the roaring of two squads of sleek Apache A-36 dive bombers overhead. Everyone watched to see if they were going to hit the hill, fearful if they did so their own would be clobbered.

But both squads kept going northward; some of the planes broke off towards the west, dove, and apparently dropped their bombs in areas where the other American battalions were fighting.

Harder to see now because of the dust and smoke Lindo had arranged on Hill 570, there was no way Bob and Paul could know that F Company was being counterattacked.

Then an unexpected call came down to lay mortar fire on the east side of the hill to cover the riflemen's withdrawal. Paul handed the first round to Bob. He dropped it into the tube, then yelled "screw you and die" at the Germans before stepping back behind the tube because the pressure wave was less here.

Seconds later Paul handed him another round. Same procedure. Then eight more. Now the tube was heating up. Chances for searing hot pieces of propellant from the mortar to hit Bob or Gentle John increased. They definitely didn't want to get any of it in their eyes. But Bob ducked behind the tube every time, dropped to his knees, covered his ears, then stood back up and took another round from Paul.

"Hang it, Bob. I'm ready. Let's go!" Gentle John yelled.

Paul screamed back to the other Bearer Boys, "Go, go, go. Get me more mortars. We're just getting started."

Bob barked at Paul, "Tighten up your damn helmet."

"I'm fine; you're sweating. Take this from me and fire away."

The tip of their mortar tube grew to a brighter red as Bob laid in round after round. Gentle John kept crouching down to check the bubble on his sight as each flew off. All was good. The tip of the tube was hot as hell now, but Bob was trained to slide his hands down the tube where it was cooler as he slithered into his usual crotch position as each muzzle blast roared out.

"Quit jerking off, Bob!" Carmen the Charmer yelled, bringing moral to a fever pitch.

"Screw you," Bob yelled back. "Give me another round, Paul."

"Shut up," Sergeant Horn screamed, laughing his ass off as he did.

They learned later that their covering fires had allowed F Company's men to withdraw to a safer position. Then the call came down to shift their firing. A near platoon of Germans was trying to infiltrate their flank and coming in fast. Machineguns roared. Now it was Bob's mortar squad's turn to add to the mayhem.

Theirs and the other sections' tubes got the ones the machine gunners didn't cut down, which was fortunate. The men of E and G Companies were already past this enemy platoon and heading for Monte Pelligrino. Together they had held off what could have been a direct attack on Bob and Paul's position.

And they hadn't been spotted yet by any German counterbattery fire. Lieutenant Lindo was still going crazy calling in artillery fire. Before it was over 705 of his rounds landed on the Germans.

"Lindo kept having a grand time knocking out enemy batteries and shelling hostile defensive positions, all of which were in plain view," Ben Sternberg boasted later. "Reports eventually showed that there were at least fourteen German guns and many of their prime movers that had been destroyed. Because of the excellent work of our machine guns and mortars, this also proved quite costly to the Germans. It allowed Bob York to move up and finally clear Monte Pellegrino. This is what had permitted me to use E and G Companies in a direct drive towards Troina."

And to support that move Bob's squad fired another 150 rounds, repeatedly as called for. G Company had a platoon on Mount Bianco by late afternoon and were holding the southern half of the small hill. But the fighting to stay there was so close, no more than fifty yards apart at any time, that Sternberg had to call off mortar support. Captain Jeffrey's men held, but his casualties were heavy.

They were heavier for the Germans.

"At dusk E Company sent a platoon to relieve G Company," Sternberg noted later. "This move was completed after they, too, suffered numerous casualties. But the next morning it was quite evident that the enemy had withdrawn from Troina."

"The continuing progress of the 18th Infantry proved to be the the decisive factor for this," Terry Allen later wrote in his factual summary of the battle. "The enemy's loss of the commanding high ground on the deep south flank had a telling effect, and completely demoralized their defenses."

A patrol from the 16th Infantry entered Troina unopposed on August 6th and found it buried in rubble. Combat reporter Don Whitehead was with these men; he saw first hand what the citizens of the hilltop town had endured. "One room of the cathedral contained the stench of human excrement and hundreds of sweating bodies, which was sickening," he later wrote. The battalion commander who was with the patrol was equally affected. "I never wanted to capture a town more in my life," he told Whitehead, before gesturing helplessly. "But now. . ."

The Germans had not allowed the citizens to leave once the battle opened, but when the Germans left many of the townspeople also fled out of fear of more strikes. One hundred and fifty still lay dead—some Germans and Italian soldiers—on the streets, in demolished houses, even in the round feudal tower that the Germans had used as an observation post.

"Plaster and dust and the stench of death filled the air," another tired American soldier remembered. "Rubble completely blocked one street. The water mains were broken. The main street, where it made a right angle turn on the northeast face of the cliff, was completely blown away. A 200-pound aerial bomb lay unexploded in the center of the church."

Bob's entire battalion moved to a bivouac area closer to Troina and remained here for another week. Beneath the constant spirals of steam rising lazily from the apex of Mt. Etna, Bob and Paul rested, did all they could to get the grimy sweat and stench out of their wool uniforms, took a helmet bath, cleaned their equipment and help zero their mortar.

The area was full of dust most days, black powdery lava dust. The daytime Sicilian sun was hot; the nights were chilly. And the rumors about why General Allen was relieved—word had gotten out—were everywhere; word had also come down that Ted Roosevelt was also leaving the First Division.

"We idolized these two outspoken officers," Lieutenant Johnson said for everyone. "We were shocked to learn that their inspiring leadership would no longer be with us. No one announced the reason, but we angrily recalled the clashes between Allen, Bradley and Patton over the spirited high-jinks of our units in Oran after the Tunisian campaign. Tough old Terry Allen was strict on discipline, but he would go to bat for any man of his, colonel or private.

"The talk went something like this: The three men disagreed on training, for Patton and Bradley stressed parade-ground spit and polish and close-order drill, while Terry and Teddy insisted for a fighting outfit, battle training was most important. This was because they were always trying to save their men's lives, never using them to gain glory and make reputations as have some generals. All these reasons have contributed to this peremptory sacking of our leaders at the climax of their Sicilian victory.

"However, no reasons are enough to those who bid them farewell on the battlefield at Troina. Even shaggy old Regular Army sergeants weep unashamedly as the two men who led us across the beach at Arzew and night-fought us through Tunisia and Sicily drove off."

Bob and Paul were equally saddened, especially Bob who had been with the beloved generals for well over a year. Both sent official word; General Allen's came on the day he and Roosevelt were both relieved. And, as usual, Terry Allen heaped praise on his men, rather than draw attention to himself.

TO ALL MEMBERS OF THE FIGHTING FIRST

In compliance with recent orders, Major General Clarence Huebner, who fought in this division with great distinction during the last war, has been designated as Division Commander. I feel most fortunate to have been your commander during the preceding year. You should all be proud of your combat record.

Following the successful landing at Oran on November 8, 1942, detached elements of the Division fought effectively at Medjez-el-bab, Ousseltia, Kasserine Valley and Sbiba. In the Ousseltia valley, you steadied a critical sector in the Kasserine counterattack of February 22 and you effectively restored a critical situation. In the seizure of Gafsa on March 17th, followed by the grueling battle of El Guettar, you out-maneuvered and completely outfought the enemy; you virtually destroyed the Italian Centuaro Division and completely defeated the German 10th Panzer Division. Immediately thereafter, you took over a critical sector in the final drive for Tunis. In this post of honor, you drove through the best German combat units, over difficult terrain, and broke the hinge of German resistance in front of Tunis.

In the invasion of Sicily, you have fought unceasingly for 28 days as the spear point of the American Seventh Army. After landing against enemy opposition at Gela, you fought off a determined German and Italian counterattack, heavily reinforced by tanks. You then fought your way across Sicily by fatiguing marches, hard fighting and maneuvering at Niscemi, Ponti Olivo airport, Villa Rosa, Alimena, Bompietro, Petralia, Gangi and at Nicosia. During this drive you destroyed at least 74 German tanks. The drive culminated in your hard-fought victory at Troina, where you again broke the hinge of the German resistance and decisively defeated the 15th Panzer Division.

You have lived up to your battle slogan: "NOTHING IN HELL MUST STOP OR DELAY THE FIRST DIVISION."

In taking leave of you, I extend my sincere personal thanks to all for your unselfish devotion to duty and your unfailing loyal support.

Ted Roosevelt's open letter to the officers and men of the division was brief, but it was clear he was also very saddened to be leaving.

More than 26 years ago the First Division was formed, and I joined it at the time. I have served with it in two wars and have served with no other unit.

We have been together in combat; we know each other as men do only when they have been battle comrades. I do not have to tell you what I think of you, for you know. You will always be in my heart.

I have been ordered away. It was a great grief for me, and my hope is that sometime I may return, for it is with you that I belong.

Your record is splendid. You are known as assault troops the world over. You will add in the future new honors to our history.

May luck go with your battle worn colors as glory always has.

Paul noticed that Bob was tearing up after reading Roosevelt's letter; he would miss the bellowing, bull-frogged-voiced and extremely brave second in command.

At first Paul said nothing, but after a minute or two he decided to sit down next to his friend and talk.

"They were something else, weren't they Bob?" Paul started. "I've only been with you guys since June, so I can only begin to imagine how you must feel."

"It's like loosing a father Paul," Bob explained. "And I mean that. I'm not being a sentimental old fool. They took care of us. Patton's in all of this for personal glory, and men dying is just the cost of that to him. Terry Allen and Teddy Roosevelt never wasted a man. We took it on the chin plenty, but that was our job and we were damn proud to do it."

Bob couldn't talk about losing Slugger; it still pained him too much. Nor George Walker, although his thoughts were more with his mother back in Naugatuck now.

"Rumors are going around again that the entire division may be relieved and sent back to the states," Paul offered. "You believe any of this?"

"Hell no. No damn way," Bob quickly answered. "Why would we be assigned a brand new commander if we were going home? That's a bad omen. God knows where we'll go next, but we'll probably be fighting somewhere until this damn war is over."

~FORTY-SEVEN~

LIEUTENANT DOWNING SHOWED UP AT the regiment's command post a few days later; he had still been working as a liaison between the regiment and division, but with hostilities ended at Troina he was returning to his regular duties under Colonel Smith. Downing was carrying orders with him that had been issued by the new First Division commander, General Clarence Huebner.

When Colonel Smith read them he just nodded and told Downing to carry the new orders over to Ben Sternberg's CP and show them to him. It happened that there was a company commanders' meeting going on when Downing arrived, and after welcoming him back Sternberg asked what he had for him.

"Orders, sir, from division," Downing quickly answered. But the look on his face told Sternberg something unusual was up.

"Read them to us John."

So Lieutenant Downing did.

"I communicated the instructions as directed," Downing remembered. "And like good loyal officers they were first received without comment. But the reaction of the company grade officers and sergeants, when the orders were passed on, were violent and blasphemous."

The orders called for an immediate resumption of training, to include conditioning hikes, close order drill and other by the book refreshers like learning how and when to salute.

"You've got to be shitting me," was all Sergeant Horn said when the order trickled down to him. "After climbing hills for the past four weeks, fighting mules, Germans and Italians, taking hikes is simply gross. Just who the hell is this new general?"

It turned out General Huebner had enlisted with the 18th Infantry before the First War and was recognized to be one of its most efficient soldiers, its best rifle shooter, and on top of that the most neatly dressed. He soon caught the attention of higher ups, was commissioned in 1916, and had advanced to the rank of lieutenant colonel before the First War ended.

By the time World War II started the talented Huebner was serving as the Army Field Forces Director of Training. Back in March of 1943, while Bob was fighting at El Guettar, Huebner had been reassigned to North Africa as the Theater G-3. He was not particularly diplomatic by nature, but he nevertheless ended up as Deputy Chief of Staff for the combined Eighteenth Army Group under the mercurial British General Sir Harold Alexander.

At the personal direction of General Eisenhower, Huebner's mission was to assure that American forces were not disparaged against when it came to combat assignments. He was to "erode further favoritism based on nationality and lobby for a genuinely allied approach in future battles." And Huebner gained quite a reputation while he was in this duty position.

In fact, he rankled Alexander's staff so much with his crisp, abrasive style that he was fired while the First Division was fighting in Nicosia a week before Troina fell. It was rumored that he had even called Bernard Montgomery "a really obnoxious bastard," and this along with what was perceived as his genuine dislike of the British is what General Bradley had to weigh before assigning him command of the Big Red One.

But Bradley wanted him because he was a stern disciplinarian and an excellent trainer.

It didn't take long for General Huebner to show up with Colonel Smith to observe how Bob and Paul were doing with their training. It happened on a day when they were practicing shooting their freshly inspected mortar on a makeshift range near Monte Pelligrino. They knew Huebner was in the area; they had been warned by Captain Murphy. Lieutenant Johnson's antitank platoon was nearby, resting in the grass after testing their 57mm guns.

Bob could see Huebner getting out of his jeep and going in their direction; he was actually close enough to watch him come up behind Johnson and even heard him loudly snap, "Get up, lieutenant!"

As Johnson told it later, "I called my men to attention, and then the general reprimanded me for allowing my men to relax and for not spending time between firing in close order drill. General Huebner then ordered the men to fall in at left dress instead of the ordinary right dress. A new replacement happened to be the man on our squad's left end, and with the command 'Dress left, dress,' instead of holding fast so that all the men could line up even with him, the new man stepped to the left and the whole platoon started sidestepping down the hill. To the general this gross error was infuriating, but to me it was hilarious and I could not hold back a smile."

Bob could see Huebner was not looking particularly amused, and then he heard the general bark "Let's see if your men know how to salute, Johnson!"

"Having done no saluting while campaigning, the platoon was extremely ragged," Johnson noted. "General Huebner just watched us while we tried and yelled 'Terrible!'"

The next thing Bob heard was Huebner shouting, "Johnson, how long will it take you to teach these men how to salute?"

Bob didn't hear Johnson answer with "twenty-four hours, Sir," but he never forgot Huebner shooting back with, "I'll give you three minutes!" before he simply turned and left with his staff and Colonel Smith in tow.

Modified orders came down the next day: "It is emphasized that future training schedules must include intensive close order and saluting practice," it read.

General Huebner also made a profound impression on his own

headquarters staff back in Cerami. "The mood at the command post was formal," Colonel Mason remembered. "Those of us who had been plebes at West Point acted like plebes again, saluting "Yes, Sir," "No, Sir," "No excuse, Sir," when we interacted with anyone.

"This went on day after day. We were addressed by title, and we responded in kind, formal and military, and secretly mad as hell at this new commanding general. Gradually, very gradually, my dull brain began to analyze what was going on, though. Orders were being obeyed, not questioned. All ranks were saluting like soldiers. When we were chewed out, we ended up mad as hell but not humiliated.

"Then, one by one, the old man got us in his pocket. He got us together, and brought in all the officers and NCOs for a short talk one day when we were still near Troina. His talk was simple, straight from the heart, utterly sincere, and was on the heritage of the First Division, its World War One accomplishments, covering his own involvement, what it had accomplished so far in World War II, and what still had to be done.

"He knew we were spearheading the Normandy Invasion, but the rest of the division of course did not know that at the time."

Bob's gut had been right when he talked to Paul about the assignment of a brand new general being a bad omen. But as he and Paul spent that long, hot August week on the hills south of Troina doing long marches and enduring Sergeant Horn's watchful eye as they practiced drilling and saluting, it even began to dawn on them that this new general just might know what the hell he was doing after all.

Everyone was waiting to get official word that the Sicilian campaign was over. But when Colonel Sternberg disappeared with a quartering party on the morning of August 13th and alert orders came down for movement that night, Bob bet Paul they'd be back in the action soon.

The battalion boarded trucks just before dark and traveled through the darkness for a destination unknown to any of the men. Bob doubled the bet; if they were going to a rest area they would have known that by now. First light instead found them in a grassy field surrounded by cactus patches off a road on the other side of Mt. Etna, about a kilometer west of Randazzo. Breakfast was served right after the sun came up, and then the companies lined up and moved out at 8:30, the men in single file to either side of the road.

The move was slow, with many halts; the road was covered with dust, and black lava boulders lined it on both sides. Bob and Paul just grunted most of the time, still wondering where this was all going to lead to; the convoy had been making frequent stops. It wasn't long before word filtered back that the constant delays were due to problems the engineers were having removing mines the Germans had left behind. At least that started to explain things.

It turned out the holdup was really due to the lava beds outside of Randazzo. Being magnetic, the engineers were unable to use their mine detectors to remove them; there were both teller and personnel mines blocking the way. Bob and Paul, marching one behind the other with spacing that would have made General Huebner happy, were successful in avoiding the treacherous foot mines, but the battalion's truck drivers had to trust their movement to luck.

Bob and Paul saw one three-quarter ton truck that wasn't lucky as they got closer to Randazzo; it was rolled over on its side. It was now getting to be late afternoon, and the journey was not over. But when they entered the town they couldn't wait to get through it and keep going.

"I never saw such a devastated city," Lieutenant Downing remembered for everyone. "Our artillery, British artillery and planes had really dispensed destruction with a lavish hand. The streets were choked with debris from toppled houses. Bulldozers had cleared a narrow path through the side streets, through which the traffic painfully inched its way. The streets through the main part of town were absolutely impassible. Not a single house appeared untouched, and already the stench of the rotting bodies of trapped civilians mingled with smoke from smoldering fires in the hot evening air."

It was later that night when the battalion bivouacked two more miles eastward at Francavilla, near a junction in the road that went northward towards Novara, another ten miles away. Finally, the mission became better understood.

"We were ordered to pass through our 3rd Battalion up at Mt. Novara, and to keep going until we contacted the 3rd Division on the north coastal road," Ben Sternberg explained. "They were still fighting towards Messina at the time."

After the action that followed, Bob called off his bet with Paul about getting into the fight because they never left the bivouac area. F Company did and marched up to another assembly area just to the west of Novara; the men were richly rewarded for their efforts when they entered the town the next morning. A great deal of military equipment and stores were found; 150 Italians were taken prisoner.

"We sent a patrol under an officer out to contact the 3rd Division as ordered," Sternberg added to his account. "This was accomplished, thus ending the Sicilian Campaign for the First Division."

~FORTY-EIGHT~

THIS TIME THE BATTALION BIVOUACKED north of Mojo, just to the east of Randazzo, and it wasn't all that bad here. The immediate area was loaded with cornfields, tomato patches and vineyards; streams even flowed through a series of rocky pools. A fifteen-foot waterfall offered perfect showers. Bob and Paul took in the surroundings, ate well, and got their best bath and shave of the entire campaign. They had even been issued summer khaki uniforms to wear. Mail arrived; two months of back pay were given out by the paymaster in lira notes. It was too good to last.

Officers from the regimental motor transportation pool were in the final stages of organizing serials two days later. Then, on the 20th Bob and Paul loaded into their deuce and a half for wherever it was the Army was now going to send them. This time Bob was pretty certain it would be to another rest area, but training would undoubtedly resume.

The long line of trucks had barely started out when there was a loud blast, what at first Bob thought to be a bomb. There was a deafening report that followed, and he could see stone and dirt suddenly pouring through some tree branches off the road ahead. Men were yelling, and then a column of black smoke started rising up.

It turned out that some engineers were trying to clear a bypass to a bridge so the convoy could get through, and a mine went off. A large rock was thrown up and it landed on one of Ben Sternberg's headquarters company men, killing him instantly.

"This kind of death, after the campaign was over, was more un-nerving than those which occurred during the actual period of combat," Sternberg lamented. "There were so useless."

When the convoy finally got started again it was very hot out, but things settled down. Hours passed as Bob and Paul went back through Randazzo, passed Troina, then went by Nicosia, Enna and Barrafranca. Night came, truck lights went on, and then just before the sun rose Bob and Paul were dropped off at an almond orchard near Licata on the shores of the Mediterranean.

The next two days were spent organizing the camp, setting up tents, digging latrines and blasting sump holes for garbage. Then, big news came that the Army, in its infinite wisdom, had decided its brave soldiers were entitled to an outing; the next night found them in an amphitheater-like setting a mile from the camp.

For a few hours it was almost like being at home. Bob Hope and Frances Langford, a comely blonde with a beautiful contralto voice, plus their troupe, were there to entertain them.

"It was the same old Hope, throwing out the same old corn," Lieutenant Johnson remembered. "And did we love it! Hope said he never left home, and he sure brought a bit of it to us. Then he kicked in with his old gag routine. 'Get ready to sweep up the eye-balls, men.' He introduced the scantily-clad Langford. The audi-ence went wild; it was the first pretty American girl we'd seen in a long time. She sang, she swayed, she joked...she just was...and our eyes not only popped but our tongues hung out."

Frances Langford, wearing white slacks and just a white brassiere, sang her memorable hits, warming up with "Once in a While," before filling the air with "I'm in the Mood for Love." Hardened soldiers became misty; they temporarily forgot ever being shot at. Bob and Paul were mesmerized. Louie the Rub went crazy with lust. Carmen the Charmer couldn't stop talking about her sweet voice.

But everyone was soon reminded that there was a war still

going. A few days later Johnson's platoon was visited again by General Huebner; the Red One's CO remembered them. "He came stalking to us, signaling the rest of us to halt," Johnson told others who weren't there later. "He still had saluting on his mind; he ordered Hank to have the First Platoon perform a hand salute."

"But, Sir, the men are carrying rifles," Hank protested.

"Do as I say!" Huebner fired back.

"So the First performed what the drill regulations forbade; each man fumbled his rifle in his left hand and raised his right in salute! We watched in astonishment, but the general seemed satisfied as he climbed back into his waiting command car, then left us."

Big changes in the 2nd Battalion command had already occurred. Ben Sternberg, protective of his men during the fighting and always competent, was reassigned to Colonel Smith's staff; he swapped being the battalion's commander with Jack Williamson, who had been Smith's executive officer. A Brooklyn New Yorker born on the 4th of July, Williamson had graduated from West Point, where he was characterized in the academy's 1935 *Howitzer* as a "straight shooter in rifle, pistol and life." He joined the 18th Infantry while it was still in training stateside. Like General Huebner, the stern-faced and high fore-headed Williamson was a tough disciplinarian, no nonsense to the core.

When Bob got the news about Williamson taking over he just turned to Paul and said, "Well that settles that. No way we're going home!"

There was another change in H Company; Lieutenant Hobratschk had been evacuated. No one got the whole story, but he was rumored to have gotten sick with something back in Randazzo. He'd be back, but none other than Lieutenant Downing showed up the Sunday after the USO show to take over Bob and Paul's mortar platoon.

"I was suddenly in good company," Downing said. "I was with congenial officers. Besides Captain Murphy and Rosie, there was

Lieutenant Farrar who commanded the machine gun platoon. I had not gained a great deal of favor with Colonel Williamson, and he had lectured me on the necessity for my working hard to rehabilitate myself with this new assignment. I looked forward to doing this."

And Downing most certainly did start rehabilitating himself. Eight hour days started for the mortar platoon with vigorous exercises and ended with close order drill. Then word came down a week into this that everyone had to shine their boots, for none other than Gorgeous Georgie Patton was going to make an appearance the following day.

When it went off in a bowl-shaped hillside setting, Patton started off with, "First I thought I'd stand up here and let you soldiers see I'm as big a son of a bitch as you think I am." Then he talked at some length about the importance of replacements, saying words that were barely heard like "divisions are not animated tables of organization but have souls just as human beings have, and that in order to get the best results they must be maintained at strength with men who have been in them long enough to acquire the unit soul."

Unknown to Bob or Paul, Patton had been ordered to apologize to units whose soldiers he had slapped around in evacuation tents earlier that month; there had been two incidents, both involving First Division soldiers. Apologizing was not something General Patton was accustomed to, but he tried. He mumbled a half-hearted mea culpa, and said he was sorry for something no one seemed to get. Was it for sacking Allen and Roosevelt many wondered?

"His message was confused and not well-received," one officer remembered. "We remained slightly mystified as he hastily concluded by thanking the division for its part in the campaign just completed." Later, a biographer of the famous general wrote, "Patton's speech to the men of the Big Red One was greeted with stony silence, although one eye-witness recalled hearing a few scattered boos."

There was no love lost between George Patton and the men of the First Division. "He sure had an amazing legend in World War II," D Company's Captain Sam Carter wrote after the war. "But Patton was disliked by many of us in the 18th Infantry. It started back in North Africa at El Guettar when a lieutenant who had made three separate attacks on a hill and who should have been decorated, was fined by Patton for not wearing his leggings tucked in and his tie straight. Word of this spread throughout the First Division that night, and we had no use for him after this."

Training started again the next day. Colonel Williamson, who did have a dry sense of humor, described the protocol: "Our emphasis was on marksmanship, training lieutenants, and watching out for General Huebner."

At this Bob and Paul succeeded. In fact, this time Lieutenant Downing made their training interesting.

"I signed up for large amounts of salvaged ammunition from division ordinance, and we fired as often as possible on a range located on a nearby barren hillside," Downing told an approving Captain Murphy. "Firing the weapons added interest for the boys, and it showed us any deficiencies in our training much better than dry-running could in the company area."

Training had to go back to the fundamentals to please Colonel Williamson. "We progressed from basic recruit training to a point where we could do close order drill like garrison soldiers," Downing boasted.

But there was time off, too. Bob and Paul used that to tour the area on day passes Captain Murphy generously allowed. It seemed to him like a fair deal. Murphy was plenty occupied in the new Officer's Club that had been set up in a captured Italian wall tent, replete with picnic tables, a crap table and a well-stocked bar—everything from red and white wine, to banana gin, cognac, orange gin, vermouth and anisette—constructed from old ration boxes and boards.

What Bob and Paul saw while their officers drank, played poker and shot craps was far more sobering. One day they went down to the beach area where the 3rd Division had landed when the invasion began. Natives were there selling grapes at three times the price they were when U.S. forces landed. But the bodies of Americans who had died coming ashore were gone; the landing crafts that brought them into the beach were starting to rust. Out in the bay masts protruded where ships sank. Bob and Paul milled about for hours, and thanked their lucky stars for having survived that awful day when the German tanks attacked them.

They were heading back to camp when they saw a grim sight that made their day. A crushed tank was lying in a hillside just off the road they were on, its machine gun split up and its huge muzzle pointing into the ground.

"You don't look good," Paul told Bob the next morning.

"Oh, it's nothing," Bob tried to explain. "Maybe I just look a little pale because of all the dust we've been breathing, that black lava around Mt. Etna, that white chalky stuff in the middle of this God-forsaken country, and now the sand dust we inhaled at the beach yesterday."

"You look like you're going to puke, Bob," Paul answered back.

And he was right. It came on quickly. Bob's head started spinning and then he vomited. Paul looked for Lieutenant Downing to ask him what he should do; their lieutenant was not anywhere to be seen. Paul took Bob over to the infirmary. The medic took his temperature; his teeth were chattering and by now he was starting to shake all over.

He had malaria.

The medic sent him over to the 1st Medical Battalion, which was by now a collection station for others who were sick. An orderly took Bob into their large hospital tent and assigned him to a stretcher that was lying on the dirt floor. Bob noticed there was no separation of patients by rank; there were even some civilians in his midst. Then, looking at an opening in the tent wall, in came Lieutenant Downing. He had already been there for two days. They nodded.

Then Bob started to salute him, but Downing waved him off.

Together they stayed at the hospital tent for two more days. Orderlies came by to take their temperatures, and hand out atabrine tablets. When either had to relieve themselves, they used a canvas-enclosed latrine; washing their faces required drawing water from a five-gallon bucket and then using their helmets for a sink.

Both were loaded into an ambulance three days later and driven to the 15th Evacuation Hospital a few miles away. But things got better for both Bob and Lieutenant Downing. This time they got beds with sheets to sleep on. And after a couple more weeks the yellow hue that the atabrine tablets gave them began to disappear and the ward doctor decided they could both return to duty.

Together they left the hospital and walked out to the main road. The first jeep that came along picked them up, and took them to regimental headquarters. They reported back in, and then went over to the H Company camp to start training again.

~FORTY-NINE~

BOB QUICKLY LEARNED THAT THE battalion was actually about to get ready to make another move, this time over to an aerodrome near Licata. Even though the 45th Division had secured it shortly after the landings, the higher ups were concerned about it being retaken; it was being used by Allied aircraft to bomb locations in Italy. The assignment seemed a bit ridiculous to some, but no one dared question orders. Fortunately, the stay in the bivouac area on the edge of the field was short—just a couple of days—before yet another movement order came down; this time the battalion was returning to Mazzarino.

It was an uneventful trip for Bob and Paul, unlike their time fighting for the area in July. There were curious sights to take in, from watching Sicilians in mule-drawn colorful carts finally going about their normal daily routines, to annoying "Off Limits to Troops" signs that were posted outside every filthy village they passed by.

The convoy finally pulled into an olive grove that was behind a sports arena on the outskirts of Mazzarino and set up camp. It became a festive place to be. After Bob and Paul pitched their pup tent lots of visitors arrived. They included the mayor of Mazzarino, a delegation of parish priests, and even all the members of the local carabinieri.

"The men also received visits from local women who were interested in bettering their standard of living through gifts of money, cigarettes, or food," Lieutenant Downing sheepishly noted.

"We officers, like gold fish in a bowl, under the watchful observation of the men of our company and the local visitors, were necessarily living on a high moral plane."

Which meant Captain Murphy and everyone else with rank were simply looking the other way so their men could finally unwind. Murphy even solemnly declared that the goings on were just an application of the lessons learned after the Tunisian campaign: the men needed and deserved unsupervised time off.

Trips were even allowed into Mazzarino under the premise that patrolling was necessary, another clever idea Murphy came up with. "The company was forbidden to loiter in the town, but the patrols were sent through and every soldier, even the cooks, were given an opportunity to go," Downing pointed out. "If the patrols stopped at wine or souvenir shops, it was obviously in the line of duty."

There were days when Captain Murphy would even disappear with just about every officer in the company, except Lieutenant Downing; he had to stay back and keep an eye on things because he was the least senior in time with H Company. Downing was the friendly type when in rest areas, even around the men who reported to him. But when Murphy headed off one morning, Downing looked glum; Bob was nearby and overheard him say, "All you men get to go into town a lot more than I do, by God. Now look at this. I'm stuck here while the rest of the officers have their fun again."

"Sir," Bob offered to get Downing's attention, then when he looked at him quipped, "this is what we so admire about Captain Murphy, Lieutenant; he wouldn't ask a soldier to do a task he wasn't willing to take on himself."

Everybody thought that was pretty damn funny but Lieutenant Downing.

This setup was too good to last and it wasn't long before trucks arrived to take the battalion back to their old training area, this time closer to Palma. The mood amongst the men grew more pensive. Rumors had been going around that something had to come down in the way of orders soon so they could finally leave Sicily. Many thought Italy would be next.

But the training grind instead went on. Lieutenant Downing started off with black board lectures that were followed by firing practices on a range General Huebner frequented. Then there was the day a demonstration was put on, per order of division headquarters, to compare foreign mortars with Bob's 81mm tube.

"We already had two Italian mortar tubes that we had used late in the campaign," Downing explained after the demonstration was over. It turned out that Bob's section had been trained in the nomenclature of the weapon, and had been selected by Downing to put on the demonstration of how it fired for a group of officers Huebner had sent to observe the affair.

"They did a good job and were promised a letter of commendation," a proud Lieutenant Downing told Captain Murphy that night. Bob's lieutenant was certainly making progress redeeming himself in the eyes of both Murphy and Colonel Williamson.

Redemption was carried to the next level after General Huebner, following a few personal visits during drill periods over the next week, determined officers needed to demonstrate they were proficient in understanding the newly published *Manual of Small Arms*. Lieutenant Downing captured how that went.

This blast resounded from division headquarters brought forth all the officers of the regiment onto the drill field, each equipped with an M-1 rifle and cartridge belt. Colonel Smith acted as platoon sergeant, the field officers acted as squad leaders, and all company grade officers like Captain Murphy transitioned to the rank of private. We were given detailed instructions on the position of the right thumb at "Present Arms" and the angle of the bore at "Port Arms." We ran through the manual with the field officers walking around making corrections. A few unfortunate individuals—I was one of them—were called out to demonstrate the different movements and it was painful to see us officers and even some company commanders trying to recall the detailed descriptions of the movements of the Manual of Arms. The enlisted men hovering inconspicuously around the edges of the field were, no doubt, amused, but at the same time were probably anticipating their own grief when this recruit training would descend on them the next morning.

When Lieutenant Downing returned to the platoon area that night Bob and Paul were there to greet him. They had been amongst the curious hanging around the field that day.

"Good evening, Lieutenant," Bob started.

"Don't even go there Baummer," Downing fired back.

Bob didn't; he just smirked while Paul looked the other way, fearing he'd break out laughing.

Disease was taking a bigger toll than training by now; it was getting to be well into September, nights were still balmy and humid, and sanitation measures did little to stifle the spread of germs. The diet Bob and Paul were on was the best the Army could provide, but they were mainly "B" rations which consisted of dehydrated potatoes, carrots, cabbage, eggs, luncheon meats, occasional Vienna sausages, chili con carne, crackers and greasy butter. The best thing that could be said about it was it was a steady diet.

Others thought it was nauseating; add the cathartic effect of the daily atabrine tablets, open latrines, constant flies, plus the always glaring sun, and all too many got sick. Dysentery, malaria, yellow jaundice, sand-fly fever—everything the *Soldiers Guide to Sicily* warned about—reduced some platoons to half strength. Too many men caught impetigo, a skin infection that started with small water blisters that broke out and flies swarmed to; this caused the sores to spread and before too long those with the bacteria in their systems had to be swathed in bandages to cover up the white, powdery ointment used to dry the sores and keep the flies off them.

Captain Merriam, the battalion surgeon, made regular rounds to pass out pills and isolate those who got sick, but there was a lot of resistance to that. No one wanted to be left behind if a move order suddenly came down. Nobody wanted to end up in a strange outfit if the First Division left Sicily. There were plenty of rumors still going around; Allied forces had already landed in Salerno, and the regiment was on twenty-four-hour alert in case reinforcements were needed. Virtually no one in H Company wanted any part of that unless they went there with every one of their brothers-in-arms, so everyone did what they could to stay out of the hospital, including finding places to hide when Doc Merriam came into their tent area.

Even though everyone from Bob to Captain Murphy were beginning to feel that if they didn't get out of this disease-ridden country they'd rot away, training went on. Most days it was made up of drill and conditioning marches, but this was broken up one time when Bob's platoon was designated to perform a twenty-four-hour guard assignment at a prisoner of war camp. They went there and back in jeeps and there wasn't much work involved.

When Lieutenant Downing reported back to Captain Murphy the next day his captain was in a very grim mood. By now it was pretty well certain the division would leave Sicily soon, and just about every bet was wagered on going back to England.

"The projected move brought forth an order which was the toughest I ever saw our captain have to comply with," Downing told Sergeant Horn. "He had to select a quota of men from the company to be sent to the 3rd Division in Italy, and these men would miss the trip ahead."

Captain Murphy decided the best way to fulfill the order was to ask for volunteers; he called a company meeting for this purpose; there were none. He next asked his company officers to put a list together of men they'd be willing to transfer out, and this was done mainly to get rid of those that the officers disliked, or were considered to be "eight-balls."

But Murphy, after giving this some additional thought, decided he didn't like that method, and changed his mind about what to do. He got pragmatic this time. A list was compiled of the last men to come in as replacements; in other words, had the least time in service with H Company. This was fairly easy to accomplish, and when the list was produced Captain Murphy reviewed it, but did not announce anything until the actual move orders were issued by battalion for the unfortunate men to transfer out; he didn't want them to go AWOL.

A full field inspection of the division and its equipment was made a few days later by none other than General John Lucas, a corn cob pipe-smoker who had taken over temporary command of II Corps from General Bradley. Something big was up. The inspection came across more like it was a check list of things to do; shortly afterwards equipment started getting turned in. Only personal weapons and clothes would go along with the men departing Sicily; they would be re-equipped in England for their next assignment, wherever that was that the Army in its infinite wisdom would be sending them into combat.

Sailing lists were soon made up, and a drive started to make everyone's uniform look respectable. New Red One patches were issued to replace any that were tattered, or missing on anyone's shirt or overcoat. Dulled markings of the division's patch on helmets were repainted; some of the helmets themselves had to be freshened up first with olive drab paint to make them presentable.

"We look smart enough to make a triumphal march up Piccadilly Square," Captain Murphy jokingly told everyone in the company when he performed an inspection after the paint dried and everyone looked crisp and military-like in their uniforms. He also had an important announcement.

"Men of the mortar platoon," he bellowed mischievously. "Your vacation is over. Lieutenant Downing has been reassigned to battalion headquarters and he's leaving us. We'll miss him; he did a fine job while he was here with the company, but Colonel Williamson wants him back. Now turn around."

Everyone followed that order; there stood Lieutenant Hobratschk.

Captain Murphy then yelled over the cheers of every man in the mortar platoon, "Welcome back Wally."

The big moment everyone had been waiting for came just days later. It was pouring out; bad weather seemed to still accompany every major move the First Division made. Bob and Paul were under orders to pack up and move out, but they waited in their tent until the last minute to stay as dry as they could before the trucks arrived.

After they boarded up they were driven to the Augusta port where LCTs were waiting to take them from the dock area out to the familiar *Reina del Pacifico*, the same transport Bob had made practice landings from back in Scotland before the regiment went to North Africa. It was Monday, October 25th 1943 and Sicily, with all of its treacherous hills and Mt. Etna, was about to fade behind the wake of the sturdy old troop transport.

General Huebner was on the ship when Bob and Paul boarded, so everyone tried to stay out of his sight. Some had to. There were many officers and men that had been sick who didn't want to be left behind; they headed for the ship's infirmary. H Company was assigned an unusual task; Bob and Paul learned that they would be manning the anti-aircraft guns and the rocket launchers on the big ship, just in case they were attacked from the air. They heartily looked forward to this duty position, as it would keep them plenty busy, away from training, and removed from Huebner's watchful eyes.

Bob's and Paul's berths were assigned to them after they made a brief stop in Algiers; they were well below deck. Destroyers—

some Italian whose naval commanders would have been pleased to sink any Allied ship that was invading Sicily back in July, had they been allowed to—were now providing escort services and dropping depth charges to drive away German U-boats. Bob and Paul's watches made for long days but being tasked with the ship's security was actually thrilling to them; sleep, however, was made difficult when the recurring thuds of the destroyers' depth charges echoed inside the hull of the ship.

There was plenty of time to reflect. Bob and Paul would talk often about what they had been through in Sicily and speculate endlessly about the war, how long it would last, and where they'd next be fighting. Neither harbored any fantasies they'd be going home soon.

But they talked often about home, family and God.

They accepted that they were no longer civilians, that what they were really doing as soldiers was not just about killing their enemy; it was more about preserving life as they had known it, democracy, their memories about home and family, knowing God was on their side.

They were not naïve; they had seen death. But they had been lucky; just how long their luck would hold out neither knew.

"Hey, remember that Rudyard Kipling-like poem that was posted on the back of the *Daily Bulletin* the other day?" Paul asked to break things up one night.

"Sure do," Bob answered.

"Now all you young soldiers, who are sailing the sea," the poem began. "Just drop what you're doing and listen to me. And I'll tell of a soldier, the kind you should be. A soldier that's fit for a soldier."

Thinking more about this brought both humor and melancholy to Paul and Bob, and to pass the time they tried to remember the rest of the poem.

"Now this place that we're going, there's plenty to drink. Just remember your stomach ain't coated with zinc. If you're smart you won't mix with the ladies too bold. . .you're sure to find some wherever you look, who are out to get husbands by hook or by crook. And they'll tie you up fast by the ring and the book, if you don't watch your step as a soldier.

"When the next big push comes off, and it will be pretty quick, and when you're up toward the front with the shells falling thick, here's some points to remember; I hope that they stick. For they will help you behave as a soldier."

The days grew foggy as the *Reina del Pacifico* got closer to the British Isles. Then, another order came down. When Captain Murphy read it he just shook his head and handed it to Lieutenant Hobratschk.

The order called for the removal of all traces of Bob and Paul's affiliation with the First Division.

They had to rip the patches off their shirts and overcoats; the Red One insignia on their helmets had to go, too. Lieutenant Hobratschk also had the unfortunate task of telling them they could mention nothing to anyone about having come from the Mediterranean, specifically having seen combat in North Africa and Sicily.

Instead, they were told they had to look like fresh replacements, and if asked when they arrived in England where they were from, they were to say that they had just arrived from training in the States.

NORMANDY

Journey of the Purple Heart

~FIFTY~

BOB AND PAUL WERE TOPSIDE leaning on the starboard rail during the afternoon the *Reina del Pacifico* ghosted through the River Mersey into barrage balloon-filled Liverpool harbor. Fisherman aboard their small bobbing boats saluted them as they headed to the city's floating docks. There were no bands to greet them, but they did manage to see a few British ATS girls strolling along a pier. Being with the British army, Bob expected they would welcome the cheers, yells and even the few whistles the men were regaling them with, but the women ran for it, and were gone before the *Reina* tied up.

Instead, American military police in white helmet liners, white leggins and white belts were their main greeting party; there were a few civilian workers milling about, but otherwise the dock was abandoned. Everyone was kept aboard the *Reina* until it got dark, but it wasn't long after this when Bob and Paul joined the rest of their mortar platoon in the drizzling rain and started down their assigned gangplank to the dock platform.

They quickly lined up and marched in columns of twos onto a street. Few people were out and about, so there was little in their way as Bob and Paul started clipping along under the watchful eyes of Sergeant Horn. But up ahead, the move bore no resemblance to a smart victory march through Piccadilly Square; in fact, the tired First Division soldiers were slipping and stumbling, bumping into each other and swearing like soldiers shouldn't because they were sleepy and irritable.

Dim lights further ahead marked the gates of a railroad yard. Then things picked up; when Bob and Paul reached the platform to board the train, waiting for them were women in Red Cross uniforms handing out coffee and doughnuts. They even had cigarettes, so Bob bought a pack before they boarded their assigned car, sat down and waited to head off to wherever it was the Army was now sending him.

A few warning whistles were heard a half hour later, and then their train car jerked, stopped, jerked again, and then started rolling away from Liverpool.

They spent the night first playing cards and rolling up the blackout curtain next to their seat so they could try to get a glimpse of the English countryside, but there was nothing to see; the night was inky black and rain was still coming down. Station signs along the way were gone. Highway direction signs had also been removed to keep German spies from being able to relay the locations of any troop movements. Bob and Paul spent a fitful night slumped shoulder-to-shoulder attempting to sleep, waking up all too frequently wondering where they were going.

When daylight came they were rolling by quaint country houses, compact farms with beautiful green fields bordered by low hedges, and endless haystacks with peaked tops. Bob and Paul took in this tranquil beauty of the countryside, dined on their K Ration, and forgot for a while about where they were going. When they pulled into one station, they wanted to forget everything else but the women of the Volunteer Services who jumped up into their car, filled up their cups with tea and gave them small paper bags with cakes in them.

"This is not how I remember England," Bob laughed. "Those women weren't all that much to look at, but I never had this kind of treatment before; the damn Army was in too much of a rush to get us up to Scotland for training, and then we went from there right to North Africa."

"Shush up, Bob," Paul warned quickly. "You were supposedly

never in North Africa. Careful what you say; say it in the wrong place and somebody overhears. . .and I'm gonna' loot you before you get hauled off to the brig."

"Funny. OK, but do you know what day it is?" Bob asked.

"Monday?" Paul guessed.

It was, but it was also November 8th and the first anniversary of Bob's landing in North Africa.

Later that afternoon, the train arrived in Dorchester, a town about ten miles inland from Weymouth, the big port city on the English Channel. There was no time for sightseeing; trucks were waiting to take them somewhere else. But Bob and Paul could see that Dorchester had prepared itself for an invasion; large concrete blocks shaped like dragon's teeth were planted in the ground; an-titank ditches had been dug, tall poles were sticking up in fields to thwart glider landings, and barbed wire was strung up everywhere.

"Although the German invasion did not materialise, we did get a friendly invasion from the U.S. Army," one resident of Dorchester recalled with some humor years later. "Their main force arrived in town on 8 November 1943. We didn't know it then but it was the First Infantry Division, the Big Red One. They were very polite, addressed everyone as 'sir' or 'madam' and had a language all their own."

It was the 3rd Battalion and Service Company from Bob's regi-ment that remained in an encampment outside of Dorchester; these were the men the people remembered. When Bob and Paul boarded their truck the journey for them continued further south along a narrow, twisty road that went to the southeast for roughly five miles and eventually into the village of Broadmayne. After they passed by a big stone church that was up on a hill, a few farmhouses with outbuildings, several stores, and some quaint 18th Century cottages that were all built close to the road, it wasn't long before their truck turned into a small camp and stopped.

Bob and Paul could hear the driver say to Lieutenant Hobratschk, who was riding up front with him, "Sir, my truck will be leaving. This is your destination."

The camp was full of Nissen Huts, plus a half dozen frame buildings—one which was a kitchen—a double orderly room, two latrines and a day room where training lectures could start again.

The inside of a Nissen Hut was a familiar setting to Bob; he had stayed in a couple back when he was in the British Isles the first time. The beds looked inviting; they were steel hospital cots with straw mattresses. A blanket and a pillow was on each bed.

It didn't take long to settle in. Bob lit the small cast iron stove, opened the draft so the smoke would draw up the pipe into the chilly outside air, and the dampness in the hut went away in no time. The other Bearer Boys settled in while this was happening. Gentle John said they should play cards; everyone thought that was great idea, so he turned on the single bulb hanging from the round ceiling, and then they all sat down in a circle on the concrete floor and started playing poker.

After spending the next few days organizing the camp grounds, formal training began again. It started out with just one hour of exercising every morning, and eventually expanded to full conditioning marches, during which Bob and Paul had to cover sixteen miles in less than four hours. There were even night exercises where they shuffled through the wet English countryside near Broadmayne and simulated attacks on imaginary enemy lines.

"Training during the day was onerous but bearable," one of the battalion officers pointed out. "Training at night when the pubs were open was a different matter. But we kept reminding ourselves that one of these days we wouldn't be able to return to warm barracks, good food and coffee, and we'd be back to the miserable routine of sleeping where we stopped."

The food was, in fact, quite good; the Army was all too aware that a big adjustment was being made from the tropical warmth of Sicily to the cold, damp English climate. There were extra allotments of fresh meat and vegetables; the Army was indeed trying to enrich the soldiers blood and bring them to the peak of fitness for what lay ahead.

But the emphasis remained on training. Night and street fighting were practiced, the latter by tangling with fellow soldier "opponents" in shattered houses and stores, up rubble-strewn streets and alleys; Bob and Paul participated in these exercises in Weymouth. Lectures back at the camp in Broadmayne even covered a lot of ground, including German aircraft and tank identification.

When December came another phase of training began, unlike anything Bob and Paul had experienced to date; it was practice assaulting dummy pillboxes. Army intelligence was well aware of the real concrete emplacements that the Germans had already built around major harbors in France and were now siting on the bluffs across the English Channel. Some were in clusters linked together by communication trenches; ammo bunkers were below ground and nearby. Many of the pillboxes even had living quarters capable of billeting up to forty men.

But what would make them deadly for any U.S. soldier daring to try to take a pillbox in a bluff above a beach was many had multiple firing embrasures where more than a handful of Germans in each one shared interlocking fields of fire with the nearest pillbox, creating a virtual wall of steel for any invader to get by.

And the Germans were making preparations to add more troop strength to their shoreline defenses. That same December Bob and Paul started attacking simulated pillboxes saw a new German division being formed that it would be their destiny to face. Units with combat experience that had fought the Russians at Stalingrad, and the previous summer during the Kursk Offensive, were reinforced by men who had come from hospitals in Italy and North Africa. Dirty, brown cattle carts were also delivering new recruits, many just seventeen years old and fresh from three-week training courses.

But, unlike American soldiers, the young Germans were not fed well; wartime rationing in Germany prevented that before they were conscripted. After they arrived at St. Lo, twenty-five miles from the Normandy coast, most could not even finish six-mile forced marches. Steps were taken to correct this; milk, butter and fresh meat were taken from local farmers. The cobbled together units were soon declared fully formed and ready for combat, actually two full months before Bob and Paul would meet them on a beach in Normandy that Erwin Rommel, Bob's nemesis back at Sbiba in North Africa, had eerily predicted would be where the Allies landed when the invasion came.

German officers would brag that their men were so well trained that they could shoot their weapons in their sleep; two were omniscient and planned for various landing scenarios centered right on Colleville sur Mer and St. Laurent, about a mile away. Both villages were planned landing locations when the invasion came. A large percentage of the machine guns in the German pillboxes were captured weapons, but sufficient ammunition would be found for them; barbed wire would surround the concrete forts and trenches joining them would be dug. Dependable, rapid fire 88mm flak guns were going to be ready; they would be backed up by an artillery regiment with their trails on the ground inland, and their forward spotters in the pillboxes looking down on any Americans that dared rise out of the sea and try to land there.

Preparations would result in the forces manning the area being called the best trained of the infantry divisions along the entire Normandy coast. A veteran *feldwebel*—a technical sergeant in the German army—even told his superior officer that he had enough ammunition in his pillbox to stop the first, second, third, fourth and maybe even the fifth waves of whatever force came at them.

Thus it was fortuitous that the Army was training Bob and Paul in combat techniques to destroy pillboxes; in fact, training was directed almost exclusively at this over time.

"We rigged up dummy pillboxes at first, but then we found a real one nearby belonging to a British air base," Lieutenant Downing explained; he was now commanding F Company and Bob's mortar section was training at the time with his men. "The pillbox had been built along with other pillboxes and road blocks at crossroads all over England shortly after Dunkirk, but wasn't being manned. We strung barbed wire around it and used it as a realistic training aid."

Then things got far more realistic. "We also worked out problems we had at first in a narrow valley not far from Broadmayne using live ammunition and assaulting solid concrete blocks representing pillboxes," Downing added. "They were all out attacks utilizing mortars, machineguns and rifles."

It was during this exercise that Bob's squad clearly saw how they would fit in when the real thing came. They would first hit the pillbox with heavy explosive shells while the company's machine gunners leveled fire at the embrasures the Germans were manning; these combined actions would hopefully kill them, or force them to cower inside and be unable to return fire. Then when the riflemen started bursting for the box Bob's squad would lay down smoke shells to screen their advance.

All hell would then break loose; the riflemen would emerge from the screen, charge the pillbox, lob hand grenades into the embrasures, even climb on top of it and drop a couple down the air vent.

The haughty Germans not already dead, who thought they could survive multiple waves of attacks, would either die right then from suffocation, or rifle and machinegun fire if they tried to run.

~FIFTY-ONE~

WHEN CHRISTMAS CAME THE ARMY provided a delicious turkey dinner with all the trimmings to make the celebration as homelike as possible. Some of the men in Bob's company went to private homes to celebrate the day; others brought guests to the camp and took their meals in the officer's mess, which Captain Murphy had made open to all ranks. Bob and Paul pretty much stayed at the camp through the holidays, but on New Years Eve they ventured over to the Black Dog, a local watering hole in Broadmayne.

They were two men on a special mission.

The company officers were welcoming the new year on the outskirts of Weymouth in a small establishment called the Old Borough Arms. The proprietor was an elderly, white haired gentleman that Captain Murphy had taken special care to befriend over the past few weeks. The establishment's owner in turn made sure that enough whiskey was always on hand for Murphy and his fellow officers; whiskey was scarce after all in England, he told them, because it was being exported to the States.

Captain Murphy was planning ahead on this New Years Eve, however. Bob and Paul had even been assigned one of the company's jeeps and a galvanized bucket to assist them in performing their critical mission. Their job was simply to fill the five-gallon pail up with beer and bring it back to the camp so when the Old Borough Arms' proprietor ended the night by announcing, "Time, gentlemen, please; act of Parliament," there was more to drink at the officer's mess.

The new year was far less festive; it brought a resumption of training, and with it some changes in Bob's mortar squad. The Army was planning ahead, and with the expectation that casualties would be substantial during the upcoming invasion, plenty of replacements had started to arrive.

"Most of them had been sent over from the States," Lieutenant Hobratschk pointed out. "A few were ship jumpers who came in under guard, and they tried to give us the impression that they were hard characters when they arrived at H Company. But no one treated them with the awed regard they expected.

"They were made to understand that they now belonged to a combat outfit, and until they had been shot at they were about as formidable as a group of starry-eyed finishing school students. Most of them fit into the company well after their orientation had given them the proper perspective."

In order to provide a good mix of experienced and new men, Lieutenant Hobratschk made new squad assignments in each section. Sergeant Horn was replaced by Stan Kroener; he was from Brooklyn New York. Bob nor Paul liked that change; Horn was a known to them and joked around, whereas Sergeant Kroener seemed more mercurial and too demanding.

Carmen the Charmer and Louie the Rub were also transferred. Two new guys took their place; one was an outgoing type named Ralph J. Spinosi from a South Philadelphia suburb, who went by "Smiling Jack." The other was from Warren Ohio, a steel town in the northeastern part of the state about fourteen miles north of Youngstown; his name was Eugene Sproull.

Neither were ship jumpers; along with Paul, Billy Uhouse and Willy Driscoll the five would easily blend together as Bearer Boys.

January passed quickly; the most remembered event by Bob happened on the 16th when none other than Bernard Montgomery arrived at Bridport, about twenty miles west of Dorchester, to inspect the First Division. Although much of his talk was drowned out by a defective public address system, Montgomery did send a letter to General Huebner a few days later which included his expressing "how greatly impressed I was by the soldierly bearing and obvious efficiency of the officers and men" and how appreciative he was to have such a fine division under his command.

One officer also remembered "visits and praise from generals as prominent as Montgomery were sure signs that we were not destined for passive garrison assignments for much longer." And he was right. Orders arrived shortly afterwards for a move to the Assault Training Center in Braunton, a hundred miles away on England's west coast.

It was the hardest time during training that Bob and Paul experienced before the invasion. They stayed in a tent with cots; at least there was a Sibley stove in it to help ward off the cold chill that never left the sandy expanse, where they mainly practiced assaulting pillboxes with the rifle companies.

"The terrain was a collection of rolling sand dunes, broken by rutted sandy roads," Lieutenant Downing described. "The weather was cold, wintery, windy and bleak. Although we were well aware of the fact that we were going to get an unhealthy job to do in the European landing, everyone got bored with this continual assaulting of dummy emplacements.

"The Assault Training Center officer supervising the exercises, a lieutenant who had never seen combat, was snowed under by our voluble veteran's Sicilian experiences and was completely subdued. The projected campaign was too remote to arouse any enthusiasm to overcome the cold weather and the depressing terrain."

After Bob and Paul returned to Broadmayne training continued through cold and rainy February and into March. Then, when April came, orders were received sending them to Blanford, twenty-five miles to the northeast, for what was billed as a practice river crossing.

They moved out in trucks on a rainy Wednesday to an open area next to the River Stour, then waited around for the exercise to begin under the cover of darkness that night. Bob and Paul were assembled with the rifle companies near the water's edge by this time, and when the exercise began guides with luminous buttons on the back of their helmets led them to the elongated doughnut-shaped raft they were to cross the river on. Both got plenty soaked by the awkward paddlers who propelled the raft when they crossed over; they were engineers more accustomed to removing obstacles from roads.

But the mission was accomplished. Bob and Paul landed on the far shore, and then stumbled through a muddy, swampy field and finally emerged on a piece of high ground where they were greeted by signal flashlights. Here they found their trucks waiting, and after they boarded up they were driven back to Broadmayne. Another phase of their training was completed.

The tempo of training picked up later that month with a full dress rehearsal for the invasion at Slapton Sands on the Devon coast. Bob and Paul boarded an LCT at Weymouth this time and on April 28th proceeded westward; they had been issued life jackets and were alerted by Captain Murphy to "expect anything," since word had spread that the landing convoy of the 16th Infantry had already been attacked by German E-boats.

The Slapton Sands area had been cleared of civilians; so vital was the dress rehearsal that the commanders had ordered the use of live naval and artillery ammunition to make the exercise as real as possible. On the morning of the 29th Bob and Paul started into shore on an LCI; it was raining and naval shells were indeed soaring over their heads towards the shoreline. The beach was supposed to resemble the terrain where they would be landing in Normandy; it was flat and gravely before it gave way to a swamp and then to a sharply sloping hill. Beyond here were plowed fields, broken into small squares by low hedges, and a few narrow and sunken roads.

They landed with a platoon of F Company men; it was uneventful. Bob's squad then struggled up the slippery hill, reached their pre-designated assembly area, and then started out for what became a miserable single-file hike where they stumbled through endless fields, up and down hills, into the afternoon. The Navy fired shells the whole time, but they were high and landed too far away to arouse anyone's interest.

They reached a small village later that afternoon; some of the houses here had been hit by naval gunfire and were slightly damaged. The maneuver was declared over. Orin Rosenberg, who had commanded H Company back in Sicily, hosted an after action party for the 2nd Battalion officers that night; it was held in the large house of a British Royal Navy officer who was away and had pinned a note on the door asking that his house be treated kindly. It was; no one spilled any beer out of the five-gallon buckets they dipped into before the officers laid out their bed rolls on the floor and fell out in front of the fireplaces for a good night's rest.

Bob and Paul slept on the damp, cold ground under a tent in their assigned bivouac area, were loaded up on trucks the next morning, brought to the train station up in Totnes, and eventually driven back to the camp at Broadmayne.

Spring had arrived, and with it came thoughts that something was going to happen soon. Colonel Smith already knew big things were in the works; back on March 23rd the regiment was placed on "short notice alert" for movement to marshalling areas in Weymouth. The men in the line could even see signs portending the big show was getting closer.

Dorchester and Broadmayne were filling up with troops and equipment from new units. Hedges and trees were being cut down to create parking areas for more trucks and other vehicles; dumps for the endless arrival of new equipment were populating wooded areas around Bob's camp. The roads outside of Broadmayne were even being widened, but convoys were still tying up traffic, forcing military police to detour anyone trying to get to the local pubs, theaters and dance halls.

"Our nightly recreation trips became fruitless," Lieutenant Downing shared. "One night I spent four hours in Weymouth trying to buy a drink of Scotch and couldn't even get a glass of beer. The British populace still outwardly retained its quiet, courteous demeanor, but we could sense that they wished we would be gone soon. They were being crowded out of their own pubs by hordes of American soldiers and this annoyance was another burden added to rationing restrictions on food, clothing, liquor and tobacco. I was surprised that they took the discomforts as good-naturedly as they did."

Important visitors started showing up to help ease any discomfort those in the First Division had about the upcoming invasion. On a Sunday in mid-May General Eisenhower visited each battalion in Bob's regiment, and spoke individually to some of the officers and men. Ike preferred small groups where he could talk personally with his soldiers; it was an informal visit. Bob nor Paul were close enough to hear anything he said, and some were not even paying the attention they should have; they were more smitten by the appearance of their Supreme Commander's chauffeur, the very attractive former Irish model Kay Summersby.

General Bradley paid a more extensive visit shortly afterwards. This time the regiment lined up in battalion formation. Following inspection, Bradley asked the officers to assemble so he could talk personally with them.

"We lined up by rank, but when he came to address us, he was standing by his jeep and he beckoned all of us to group closely around him," Lieutenant Downing told some non-coms later.

"His speech was logical and inspirational in its simplicity. He used no fiery rhetoric, but told us that although we would have an unpleasant job, we would be supported by every resource the Allies had. This would be no side-show like Africa or Sicily; this was an all-out effort. The invasion would not fail because too much was at stake. Divisions would pour in behind us at a rate we could not dream of. It would be no four division war, like Tunisia.

On D-Day plus thirty, over forty divisions would be ashore. He stated figures to prove that the number of people killed in the upcoming battle would be small compared to the number engaged. He said, 'I wouldn't miss this show for anything in the world. Some of you will be killed, but any person who lives through this invasion will be proud for the rest of his life for having been a part of it.'"

For Bob and Paul just waiting was taking a toll. They were sleeping in their Nissen hut one night after Bradley's visit when bombs started exploding; fifty-caliber machineguns and anti-aircraft fire were suddenly heard outside, increasing in intensity after every round. Then, all of a sudden, two bombs hit close by and the windows in their hut blew out; the door flew open. They went outside to see what was happening, but all they could see were tracer bullets racing up into the sky and flashes of light from the exploding anti-aircraft shells.

Searchlights were probing and trying to find the German planes responsible for all the commotion. But soon the night quieted, and Bob and Paul went back to bed.

In the morning they found out that the bombers had hit their former H Company barracks area, killing two and wounding thirteen others; they had moved out just a week or so earlier.

"Captain Murphy was at the bombed area and gave me most of the information I needed to fill out my report," Lieutenant Downing, now with the battalion's headquarters company, told Colonel Williamson. "One bomb was unexploded, and he asked me if I cared to look at it. Nobody knew exactly when or if it might go off. It could have been a time bomb, or it just could have been a dud. I felt no compulsion to see it myself. Here's the report."

Williamson read it quickly, put it down on his field desk, then turned back to Downing and said, "John, you need to go back and get the personal effects of our headquarters man who was killed. We need to send these home to his family."

So Downing went back to perform this unpleasant task, consumed with the thought that casualty reporting was starting off a little ahead of schedule.

Bob and Paul, like everyone else, had been speculating about just when the big show would go off.

"Those 5th Ranger Battalion men showing up in our area was a sure sign we'll be moving out soon," Bob told Paul. "That was the case before we invaded North Africa. After the Rangers showed up then, it was just a matter of days before we got alert orders to be ready to pack up."

"I'm thinking this has got to go off soon too," Paul ventured. "The tension is getting to be too much. Especially between me and Sergeant Kroener. Remember that time during training a week or so ago when he ordered me to fall to the ground, do a roll, and then get into a prone position and fire my rifle? When I asked him to first show me how that was done, and he refused? He's still pretty sore about that."

"I remember that all too well," Bob answered. "So much for never asking a man to do what he wasn't willing to do himself."

"There's other things happening too, troublesome stuff," Paul added. "That guy who shot himself between his thumb and fore-finger, thinking he could avoid the upcoming fight. He's good for nothing; he wouldn't fit into our squad. Then there was that other guy, a new replacement, who threw his rifle somewhere; he just hid it, thinking he'd get out of fighting. He also had too much of a mouth; he's just sorry to look at now."

"Yea, I love the way Captain Murphy handled those two," Bob said. "The old man is making them both get ready for what's ahead, and I heard our good captain is sending the one who hid his rifle into the next fight without one. Gotta' love that."

"We're running out of room here in England, even with the bar-rage balloons keeping her afloat," Paul laughed. "I'm afraid this island will sink with all the troops and material weighing things down. We gotta' be moving out soon."

"I'm guessing you're right Paul. And the reason I'm thinking it's so is up in the sky above those barrage balloons. There's going to be a full-moon period in early June."

~FIFTY-TWO~

LATE MAY FOUND BOB AND PAUL under movement restrictions. All the exits to their camp were sealed off with concertina wire and the camp itself was surrounded by barbed-wire fences. Soldiers patrolled the entire area's perimeter to keep them in. They weren't going anywhere; no loose lips would let anyone know the invasion was indeed going to happen soon.

But their officers were going somewhere when they marched out of the camp one sunny morning in columns of twos. They were all headed to a former staff officer's quarters, disclosure as to exactly where was TOP SECRET. When they arrived here they were assembled in the dining room, the doors were closed and guards barred anyone else from getting in.

"Maps, charts, sketches of the beach area, and a gully marked E-1, our exit from the sand, hung on the secret room's walls," Lieutenant Johnson told his non-coms later. "Recent photos outlined the steep and bare cliffs in Normandy along our sector—Omaha, Easy Red."

Pictures of known, and suspected underwater obstacles also hung from the walls, but what got everyone's full attention was what sat on a table in the center of the room.

"It was a ten-foot square rubber scale model of the coast, and approximately twenty-five miles inland," Johnson remembered. "It possessed detail in color down to individual trees and fences so that by gazing at it horizontally we could determine if our 57s could fire across the ridges."

Colonel Smith gave a few introductory remarks when everyone finally sat down, and then he turned the meeting over to Major Colacicco, his operations officer. Somehow Colacicco had to summarize the over one hundred pages of instructions that had come down to the regiment from General Huebner's staff. At this he excelled, first describing the big picture by pointing at the huge map in the front of the room and letting the officers know that the primary military objectives when the invasion went off were to secure a beachhead on the Normandy coast between Port-en-Bessin and the Vire River, and then push twenty-five miles inland where the Army's V Corps would link up with the British Second Army.

Then, still staying focused on the big picture, Frank Colacicco explained how V Corps would arrive in Normandy in three echelons; the first would come in at H-hour when the landings began, and this would include the Red One's veteran 16th Infantry and the green 116th Infantry that was attached to the 29th Division, a National Guard unit that would see its very first combat on D-Day.

The 18th, Colacicco quickly added, would reinforce these assault echelons three hours after the initial landings; another regiment of the 29th would land next to them when they did. Lieutenant Downing clearly spoke for others when this information came down.

"We were surprised," he revealed. "We hadn't expected to be the division making the initial assault. It would be our third in as many invasions since we came overseas. However, we cannot choose our missions, and our regimental task was not as hazardous as that of the 16th Infantry, who would be going first. This made us feel a lot better. It was a matter of relativity. Going in behind another regiment gave us a little better chance of coming through in one piece."

But it became clear that the 18th was to land squarely in the center of Omaha Beach, and having a better chance of getting through in one piece was largely dependent on the 16th's success in opening the key draw—E1—in the area. This draw was really a cart track used by farmers, so it would have to be bulldozed to make it passable when tanks, H Company's and other's jeeps, trucks, artillery pieces, Johnson's 57s and hundreds more vehicles were put ashore to add weight to the infantry's beachhead and support the drive further inland.

Colacicco pointed out that the job of opening the draw was expected to be done by the time the 18th landed, thus the remainder of their mission could be focused on. The regiment would pass through the 16th, he told everyone, and first secure the east-west road stretch about a mile and a half behind Colleville-sur-Mer that connected the port city of Cherbourg with Caen.

Second, the regiment was also to seize two pieces of high ground north of Trevieres, another good mile further inland, from where observation would be afforded into the adjacent Ruquet valley.

"In summary, let me read you our formal order," Major Colacicco said. "The 18th Infantry, reinforced, will land on Beach Omaha beginning at H plus 195 minutes on D-Day. The 18th will pass through the 16th Infantry and/or the 116th Infantry with the mission of securing the high ground south of the Aure River before dark on D-Day. It will take up defensive positions on the captured high ground prior to the expected coordinated attack on D plus one.

"There you have it, gentlemen," Colacicco then solemnly announced. "By accomplishing our mission we will help establish a solid defensive perimeter along the entire V Corps front and be able to observe from Mont Cauvin any German counterattacks coming our way. Now Major Middleworth will brief you on our order of battle."

Captain Murphy's attention was immediately piqued. His 2nd Battalion was going to land first, go through the 16th's 2nd Battalion, secure the high ground behind Colleville-sur-Mer, set up the roadblock on the road behind the village, and then establish a defensive position near Mosles, approximately five miles to the southeast, plus set up yet another road block here.

It was clearly an ambitious plan; the 2nd Battalion would have to get through the beachhead and then almost seven miles of German occupied France in order to accomplish its D-Day mission.

All Murphy could wonder was would the 16th's assault units succeed in neutralizing the beach strongpoints before they landed, or would this hold his battalion up? Was there a secondary enemy defensive line along the Colleville-St. Laurent road where the battalion would have to put the first roadblock in? Had the Germans mined the road? Were there minefields inland off the roads? Was the high ground south of the Aure River occupied, and if so in what strength? Could they be counterattacked right away?

Captain Murphy's attention turned back to the briefing when Middleworth started explaining the other battalion's missions. The 3rd Battalion would land thirty-minutes behind Murphy and have Trevieres as their final objective; Bob York's 1st Battalion would land at the same time, advance on the right flank of the regiment, and angle towards the Foret de Cerisy, a good fifteen miles inland between Bayeux and St. Lo.

Support would pour in behind all three battalions. Cannon Company would land at ten-thirty, the 32nd Field Artillery a half hour later; Anti-tank would come in next, then Service Company would follow and establish supply and ammunition dumps.

"The diagrams clearly showed us what units would proceed shoreward in what order," Lieutenant Johnson remembered. "The pictures of known and suspected underwater and beach obstacles that would aid an eighteen-foot tide to hamper us, intricate machine gun positions, artillery emplacements, ammo dumps, observation points, and bristling concrete pillboxes all graphically portrayed the deadly impediments we would face before Normandy might become a beachhead."

Rolls of maps were handed out as the meeting drew to a close. "These maps were clear and accurate," Captain Murphy would remember later. "They even marked enemy installations, brought up to date. We also got a silhouette of the shoreline that was photographed from a submarine, which gave us a view of the coast as it would look from an assault craft. This silhouette was tied in with the map and prominent terrain features were even marked. We were optimistic about getting the job we were given done."

"When each man stepped away from that secret meeting he knew where he would land, what units were to his right and left, where he would proceed, and much of what he had to capture or destroy," Lieutenant Johnson added. "Then only experience, guts and sacrifice would carry him on."

By now Bob and Paul were as ready as they were going to be for the invasion. Their British money had been converted into French francs, and their overseas caps and neckties had been turned in. Personal items were handed over to the regimental S-4 and put in indefinite storage. Only what was essential for combat duty was in their immediate future, and the Army had issued plenty of new gear to them for this purpose.

Gas masks with a snout canister was one of the early items they both received; it had to be carried in a black rubber case. Bob and Paul were also given a small folded package containing cans of anti-gas shoe impregnate, eye ointment, transparent plastic eye shields and plastic gas covers; when unfolded the latter would completely shield a squatting man from mustard gas that invasion planners were worried could be sprayed from a German plane. A new type of water purification tablet was even given to them; it was Halozone and came with their C-Rations.

One of their more recent issues was an assault jacket; this was to replace the packs they had carried in Sicily. It was Army olive drab in color, made of canvas, sleeveless, and had pockets for their mortars in the front, on the sides, and in the back. Adding to their protection against gas attack, the Army even provided gas-proof underwear to Bob and Paul; their new shirts, trousers, socks and leggins were also supposedly gas-proof. They had been treated with a chemical which made them airtight, and unfortunately made them sweat more during the now warmer spring days.

Small one-quarter pound blocks of TNT with a fuse and igniter were also issued; the Army believed these could be used to blast out fox holes far quicker than having to dig them. All kinds of waterproof plastic bags were handed out so Bob and Paul's personal side arms, its bullets, their compasses, their personal identification papers, even their money, cigarettes, candy, toilet paper and other loose gear could be kept dry.

They were also given a paratrooper's first aid kit, which contained a syringe of morphine; the needle was plenty big, but the battalion surgeon had shown them how to use it to kill pain if they were wounded, first warning that the sulfa tablets they also received in the kit had to be taken immediately to prevent infection.

Red One patches were also sewn back on their shirts. Green camouflaged nets were issued to cover their helmets. Maps of France, printed on pieces of linen about the size of a handkerchief, were distributed to the leaders of each mortar section. In order to see their officers, Captain Murphy and Lieutenant Hobratschk had painted white, perpendicular one-by-three-inch bars on the back of their helmets; non-coms like Sergeant Kroener bore horizontal bars across the backs of their helmets, near the brim.

Bob and Paul's hair was cut short; the barbers were trimming everyone's hair to a maximum one-inch length so their head wouldn't be a breeding ground for insects. A drive was on to make all the men carry ten thousand dollars worth of life insurance; Bob already had his policy but Paul signed up just in case he was killed.

Then the alert order came down on June 4th. Bob and Paul gathered up all of their equipment, then sat around waiting for transportation; trucks arrived just before dusk. They piled in, and then the convoy of 2nd Battalion soldiers was escorted by military police towards Weymouth; civilians lined the road giving them "V" for victory hand waves. On Weymouth's outskirts they detrucked, formed in columns of twos, and then Bob and Paul marched side-by-side down a concrete stairway, onto a sandy beach, and headed toward the port facility in the main part of town.

After they had gone about two hundred yards the column suddenly halted; Bob and Paul were told by Sergeant Kroener to get their canteen cups out. Next they passed under a huge tent and had their cups filled with hot coffee. Doughnuts, cigarettes and paperback books were given to them. They also received a printed booklet outlining the Allied war aims.

After they drank their coffee, Bob and Paul lined up again and marched towards the hard standings in the dock area. "As we passed along the beach in front of the seaside pubs and hotels, we took in farewell glances," Lieutenant Downing remembered. "People even called and waved to us from the windows and a few hung over the iron railings lining the street, watching us as we marched past. Some yelled good luck; we could certainly use some. It was beginning to sink in we were really leaving as we marched aboard our LCIs tied three to four deep at the dock."

There were air raid sirens wailing that night; bombs hit Weymouth but not the dock area. After things quieted down Bob and Paul slept well enough aboard their transport, the 492-foot USS *Anne Arundel*. After a short period of calisthenics on the docks the next morning, they went to religious services; it rained most of the day.

Near last light that night activity picked up all over Weymouth harbor. The *Anne Arundel's* crew tossed her lines, and before too long Bob and Paul were heading out into the harbor; they had managed to find space on deck near the transport's stern railing. Before too long Weymouth started to fade away, the *Anne Arundel* picked up speed and began to rock gently on the swells of the open water. Then darkness fell, and all Bob and Paul could make out were the dim outlines of hundreds of LCIs, LCTs and other assault transports in the huge convoy heading for Normandy.

They eventually went down below and tried to fall out. Bob's last thoughts were mixed with feelings of being homesick, but he knew he wouldn't be going home until the war ended.

~FIFTY-THREE~

BOB HAD WRITTEN HIS LAST LETTER to his brother Sonny at the end of April, but it was held up from being mailed because of the volume of letters his company executive officer, Lieutenant Lucas, had to deal with. Even though Bob was about to embark on the largest invasion of enemy-held country in modern history, any letter he wrote to the people back home obviously had to make no mention of this. Lieutenant Lucas had a cardboard ration box full of letters to read, sign, and then affix the censor stamp to, so Bob's letter was delayed before it was sent out. Sonny didn't get it until the Friday before Bob boarded the *Anne Arundel* to cross the English Channel and do his part to make the Invasion of Normandy a success.

> *Dear Brother,*
>
> *Received the letters that you sent and I am finally getting around to answering them. I even received a few more letters from your girl, and I still can't figure out how she thinks of so much to write about, and by the way she talks I think that she is after your scalp and will get you in the end.*
>
> *I haven't heard from mom now for a number of weeks, but I keep writing to her in hopes she will answer them. You can send me a package of something if you want to, and I don't care what you put in it. I still get plenty of letters from Gram and the other relatives, so I have plenty of people to write to.*
>
> *I am still on good terms with my blonde English girl, and*

have been seeing her every weekend I'm off, and it's sure a good way to pass the time away.

I shall close for now, but I shall write again soon. Take care of yourself, and I shall be hoping to see you soon.

As ever,

Bob

It was one of Bob's better kept secrets, this business of having met a blonde English girl. Her name was Lily, and he was smitten with her. All Paul, his best friend knew, was they had met in a shop back at Broadmayne sometime earlier that spring. Her family lived in Puddleton, and Lily's father was a driver for the Bere Regis Bus Company. He was the harden-bitten sort, generally mistrustful of the American GIs, but he had taken a liking to Bob. He especially admired the fact that he and Lily went to church on Sundays.

Sonny was still working at the synthetic rubber plant in Institute, West Virginia, and he was now living in nearby Charleston in a boarding house with other young men who worked at the nearby DuPont and Carbide plants. What Bob didn't know when he wrote his letter was that his brother had also met a new girl. Sonny had invited one of his roommates to go to a dance his plant in Institute was throwing a few weeks earlier, and this chap had brought a date with him.

She was stunning looking, and vivacious, but her date had a bad night; he was tired and drank too much. Sonny forgot about the girl after his scalp, seized on the opportunity to go after the attractive, bright-eyed brunette, and asked her to dance. They did, both took an instant liking to each other, and after waltzing the night away it was Sonny who drove Laura Jean Fox back to her home in Charleston in his new dark blue Chevy coupe.

The Friday Bob's letter arrived found the new pair getting ready to join some of Sonny's other roommates for an outing to a cottage south of Charleston that was off a dirt road on the Coal River; one of Laura Jean's friends and her husband owned it. He was with the Army in the Pacific but his wife, who worked for the telephone company in Charleston, frequently invited her friends so they could get away for the weekends and enjoy themselves. Sonny and his roommates had recently started renting it from her to help with expenses. Everyone had to work on Saturday mornings, but they would shop together for food during the afternoon—men included—then head for the cottage.

This weekend would be a delayed celebration of Memorial Day. He and Laura Jean, with three others in the back seat, were driving through Hansford, listening to the Belmont Stakes, when a newsman suddenly broke in and said, "Now, we have this special announcement."

Everyone stopped talking and started listening in silence.

"The *Associated Press* is reporting that the highly anticipated invasion of France has begun. We repeat, the *Associated Press* has reported that the invasion of France has begun. Stay tuned for further information."

It came three minutes later when the *Associated Press* killed the story.

Early that evening Sonny was pulling into the cottage's dirt drive when another announcement was made. This time his car radio was tuned into the Charleston NBC affiliate and *The People's War* was on the air.

"Good evening, and first as usual, folks, I want to bring you the late bulletins from the NBC studios here in New York," Harold Fleming began. "Less than two hours ago, the Associated Press flashed word that Allied troops landed in France. But, almost immediately, AP followed with the announcement 'kill flash, false report.' The Associated Press explains that the flash was sent in error by a new operator who was practicing without authorization."

It was later learned that the AP London Bureau's typist had accidently pushed the wrong button on her teletype transmitter. There was no further mention of the invasion after this most unfortunate incident.

Sunday came and everyone had fun sunbathing on the beach, swimming, and enjoying a big cookout before they went home that night. Sonny was back at work the next day, not knowing that his brother was already aboard a big transport heading for the Normandy coast. But the false AP announcement had made an impact, enough to motivate him to sit down and answer the letter he had received from Bob the previous Friday.

Dear Bob,

You can say this came after a long silence, and I'm afraid I have no real excuse to offer. I went up to Naugatuck a few weeks ago on a business trip and returned via Williamsport where I almost got roped into marrying Billie. She is still hot on my trail and has given me until the first week in July to make up my mind. She is coming down here to spend her vacation and she says that it has to be a yes or no then. I really don't know in my own mind about this whole affair even today.

Found Mom very well and still plugging away six days a week for the good old U.S. Rubber Company when I was up in Naugatuck. Did some work around the house, took the storm windows down, cut and trimmed the lawn and hedges, and generally tidied up. She was very well pleased with the whole business. Saw some people around town and quite a few asked about you, including all of the relatives who are hoping to hear from you soon.

Find the draft getting somewhat nearer. Received my papers to take the pre-induction physical examination in Naugatuck, but had it transferred down here. Heard from the local draft board and I am to go to Huntington to get the business done and over with. There has been no change in my draft status and I assume this is in line with getting all 26 year olds and younger processed. Can't get too excited over the whole business yet. Still plugging away at Institute with work piling up daily.

Will mail you the box that you asked for tomorrow and so far

I have some cigarettes, a lighter, cards, a pair of dice, some razor blades and other stuff in it. Let me know if there is anything more that you want, and I will get it to you much more promptly than I did this time.

Have been doing some playing around here. A few of us have rented a camp and will spend weekends there this summer. Has four bedrooms, no running water and an outhouse. Just getting ready for Army training in the future. Does have some fairly decent swimming, as the river is just in front of the house, and there's something that looks like a rowboat we use too.

Write and let me know how you are doing, Bob. I will be certain to get that box off tomorrow. Take care of yourself and continue to have as much fun as you can. Give those English gals my love, and keep your nose clean. You know what I mean.

Regards,

Ed

Sonny had chosen not to tell Bob about meeting Laura Jean yet, but he did decide that he should send Bob's last letter up to Naugatuck so his mother could read it. He turned it over, wrote a brief note, and mailed it the next day, Tuesday, June 6th, 1944.

~FIFTY-FOUR~

BOB ARRIVED OFF THE NORMANDY coast while his brother got ready to go to bed back in Charleston. It was just after one in the morning where Bob was when he and Paul heard their serial being called out over the *Anne Arundel's* loudspeakers. The first flight had already boarded their LCVPs; they were lucky. It consisted of F and E Company men, plus Williamson's command group. All were able to load at deck level, making their departure into the choppy sea orderly and without incident.

"We had to load using cargo nets hung over the side of the ship," Captain Murphy never forgot. "On a calm sea this was no big deal, but in rough water it is not only a big deal—it's damn dangerous. The LCVPs we were to board were pitching and rolling, rising and falling continuously—often all four at the same time."

Bob and Paul were on the same LCVP as Captain Murphy. When they got in line to go down the net, no one but the new guys were frightened. The usual wisecracks filled the air, and Bob didn't miss delivering one to Paul.

"Tighten up your chin strap," he kidded. Then, after Paul did Bob told him to start down the net first. Bob remembered all too well how his hand had been crushed going down a net off the shores of Virginia back in early 1942. He wasn't about to let the same thing happen to Paul.

When they landed in their LCVP, it was Captain Murphy who greeted them and made sure they didn't fall onto its slippery flat cargo area. The engine was going, and making enough noise to drown out near everything, but Bob heard Paul yell out a big thanks for making sure he went down the net first.

"No big deal Paul," Bob shouted back. Then the LCVP started rocking like crazy as it began making its way towards the shore. Both were leaning against the gunnel, grabbing anything they could to stay steady when Bob suddenly started smirking.

"You got all your money in one of those plastic bags, right?" he asked Paul.

"Sure do," was the answer.

"Good, because I'm gonna' loot you when you get it."

It was still plenty dark when they reached their designated assembly area; it was a good six miles from the beach.

"When we arrived here we began going in endless circles so we could hold our position behind the first wave in our battalion," Captain Murphy remembered. "By the time we completed four or five circles I was most unhappy."

Many of the men were already seasick, and puke was starting to flood the LCVP. Waves threw spray in, adding to the slipperiness of the cargo area; the seas were four to five feet high. It was just three in the morning, and if all went according to plan Bob and Paul would spend roughly five more hours going in circles.

When Major Colacicco gave his briefing before the regiment left England it was centered on what was known at the time; elements of the German 352nd Division were conducting training exercises in the area. What wasn't known was one battalion had rotated into the sector right in the middle of Omaha Beach where Bob and Paul were going to come ashore that morning.

Four full-strength companies were on alert for the American's arrival; they were lying in wait in five pillboxes on Easy Red beach and were backed up by at least forty-eight artillery tubes. Numerous obstacles were emplaced everywhere along the beach. Long stakes carved from tree trunks and drawn by horse wagons from the Foret de Cerisy were topped with mines and submerged at the water's edge.

Concrete walls had been constructed to bar tanks and other vehicles from advancing when they came ashore. Barbed wire fences, tangle-foot obstacles and concertina-wire barriers were set up just in front of the beach shingle to provide a second barrier of protection for the Germans defending Omaha Beach. Anti-tank ditches were dug to keep the American armor from even getting off the beach. And thousands of mines had been emplaced in the bluffs adjacent to the E-1 draw beach exit, the important objective for the forces of the Big Red One landing on Easy Red.

U.S. forces parachuting into Normandy in the early morning hours was the first indication to the Germans something big was going to happen. When British parachute troops landed in Caen, the threat was raised to Alert Stage II.

Within minutes German commanders in bunker after bunker were shaking their men, many screaming at the top of their lungs *"Raus! Raus!* Everybody up. Full combat gear. This is it. The invasion. All men report to your stations!" Ripped by the call to alarm, grenadiers hurried to get in place, loaded their guns, and got ready to fire.

They expected the Americans would arrive at dawn. It meant another long wait after weeks of waiting. But the 352nd's commander, General Dietrich Kraiss, waited only until three that morning to order his reserve unit up from St. Lo and through the Foret de Cerisy to St. Jean de Daye. The village was a little over twenty-miles inland from Colleville-sur-Mer, where Bob and Paul would be landing.

When darkness began to give way to early light the Germans got their first glimpses of the Allied armada. The initial sightings resulted in a frantic call from an observation post near Port-en-Bessen, less than four miles to the east of Colleville. Another German in his bunker saw through the early morning mist dim outlines of ships that appeared to be everywhere. He reached for his field glasses and when he peered through them he saw a more distinct shape; it was a masthead, then another, and another, until the sea was full of them.

He scribbled out a message and gave it to an orderly to pass on. It read: "Thousands of ships in front of us. The invasion is at our doorsteps!" Then he fixed his sight back on the mighty armada arrayed before him.

Then came noise from the air. "Waves of bombers are approaching us!" another German yelled. "Very quickly bombs landed in the sand and rocks, roaring and whizzing. Dust and smoke surrounded us. The earth trembled. Our eyes and noses got full of dust. Sand gritted between our teeth. We had no hope for help. Our planes stayed away, and we had no flak. Unhindered, the American bombers kept dropping their deadly cargoes. Wave after wave flew over. Debris buried much of our strongpoint. I saw bombs score a direct hit on a nearby bunker, throwing dirt, wire and part of it into the air."

This German was in a bunker closer to Port-en-Bessen, yet he worried about others. "For those men inland the situation was far worse. Several bombers had overshot their targets, but near Colleville the *stabskompanies* of Grenadier Regiment 916 had the good fortune to be missed by most of the planes. All sorts of bombers filled the sky; a couple were on fire. I could see black smoke belching out of the fiercely burning village of Treviers."

But the aerial bombardment was far from over. "More planes appeared, smaller single-engine ones," another German described. "They flew lower, bombing and shooting at us with machineguns. Even a single man was a target!" Later another German would say, "Despite the ferocity of the air bombardment, damage to the coastal defenses was minor. An apparent miscalculation caused most of the bombers to fly over their targets, a factor that would not bode well for the American GIs that had to cross the beaches."

"But the air bombardment was not enough," a German in a bunker close to where Bob and Paul would land remembered. "In the gray of the morning the fleet moved closer to us, bringing more trouble. As if on parade the ships stood before us, and with mighty flashes and deafening thunder they opened fire on us.

Throughout the bombardment the fleet moved closer to shore. We watched as the fleet grew bigger. The rain of shells seemed without end. Fountains of earth shot into the sky and fell back again. The anti-tank guns in some bunkers were already firing back, but for the rest of us the wait was still on."

"Throughout the time the fleet moved even closer to the beach," another grenadier recalled. "Now we could see all the ships clearly. The bombardment ended around six, and then it got quiet, but not for long. Once more the ships fired at us; this time they were apparently directed to blow a path through the obstacles on the beach. The mine stakes near us were torn apart as the steady wall of fire pushed nearer and nearer. A rolling pin of smoke, dust and flames came towards us, cutting everything in its path down with howls, whistling and hissing.

"We sat small and helpless at our weapons; here we took refuge and prayed. Then the first shells landed amongst us. Over and around us it drummed and pattered. Splinters shot through the air, clanging against the concrete of our bunker or hitting the ground. The sea was alive with activity. The landing crafts were starting to close in on the beach."

Another German felt the Naval bombardment was not very effective overall; he was a commander. "Although the ground shook violently and dust and sand were in the cloud covering and all over everything, so far we were unhurt. For an eternity of minutes the shelling continued, but the guns on those battleships reached more targets inland. The monstrous shells rained on vital road junctions. Then the barrages started to slacken, followed by another eerie silence. I ordered clear and concise instructions that every man was to hold their fire until the enemy infantry disembarked onto the beaches."

"We saw the landing craft coming," a terrified grenadier then remembered. "It seemed like hundreds of them. They rocked back and forth, and then they all suddenly turned and began coming straight in towards the beach. We jumped behind our machineguns. Our commander yelled to hold our fire until he gave the order. Sweat rolled down my brow as I watched the boats come closer and closer. My stomach was in knots."

A nearby *oberleutnant* also watched and waited. All of his men's guns were sighted in to pre-determined targets along Omaha Beach, anticipating they would soon hear the code word "DORA," which would mean they would target the low tide line with their opening salvos.

Every German still breathing rushed from cover to man his weapon. One brought his M.G. 42 to bear on the length of the beach. He tucked the butt of this machinegun into his shoulder, braced for the recoil, then recalled, "I checked the view down my sight but somehow I just couldn't watch what was happening. I closed my eyes and waited for the order to fire.

"Then the order "*Fuer*! *Fuer*! *Fuer*! came down. I pulled the trigger up tight, the machinegun roared, sending hot lead into the men running along the beach. I saw some go down. Others dove for whatever cover was out there while my bullets ripped up and down the sand."

Another opened fire nearby; the Americans in front of him were also pinned down. "When I stopped to reload or change the barrel, one or two brave GIs made for the cover under the seawall, but their survival was short-lived. Our mortars waited for this moment and laid down a terrible shelling on them, showering these men with splinters and rocks and inflicting heavy casualties."

Other PAK guns began pouring more direct fire into the landing crafts as they came into range. One manning his gun recalled, "GIs sprang forth from their boats, then sank in water up to their knees, sometimes even up to their chests. They headed for the seawall. We sprang into action. The Americans made their first steps in close formation but broke apart under the bursts from our dependable guns."

Sweat made tracks through the dirt on another German gunner's face while he kept pressure on the trigger of his M.G. 42. Wads of cotton stuck in his ears blunted the sharp reports, but his shoulder was practically numb from the many recoils of his constant firing.

But he was still clear-headed. "I fired as I had been trained to do—in short bursts fifteen to twenty-nine centimeters above the ground. When the gun jammed I cleared it quickly because every second counted. When I pulled the bolt back for what seemed the thousandth time, I paused for a good look down at the beach. I saw Amis everywhere. Some were dead and others quite alive. Landing boats were backing away from the beach now. Some were burning. I saw one hit a mine, sending shrapnel into the sea and into the men who had just landed. We straightened up. Another large group of boats was approaching. More *Amis*!

A *leutnant* at that moment thought the Americans were in complete disarray, even foolish. "We never thought the Allies would expose her men to such a folly as to land at low tide against our division," he later said. "At the water's edge near St. Laurent and Colleville the enemy was in search of coastal zone obstacles. Many motor vehicles, amongst these ten tanks, stood burning on the beach. The American obstacle demolition squads soon gave up.

"Debarkation from the landing boats then ceased. The fire from our battle positions and our artillery were well placed, and inflicted considerable casualties. A great many dead and wounded lay on the beach."

As of ten that morning no casualties had occurred to any of the German gun crews stationed inland; their guns were too well camouflaged. The commander here had all of the places where American troops would likely land pre-plotted before the invasion, and his howitzers were adding more firepower to the defender's blasts from their bunkers closer to the beaches.

And now the tide was rolling in, forcing the Americans who had taken cover under the sea obstacles to make for the beach shingle closer to the E-1 exit near St. Laurent. But for those landing in the next wave the dangers were even greater; the obstacles were disappearing under the rising tide, but they could still blow up a LCVP if it ran over one.

As it approached eleven that morning, the Germans made adjustments. Two artillery regiments would now shift their firing at the Americans who had a thin toehold beneath Colleville. All of the units in the bunkers looking down on the beach here had sustained casualties, but were still operational.

"The situation on the beach was fast approaching a breaking point, though it was a question of who would break first," a German commander noted. "It had been hours since the first GIs splashed ashore. Nothing seemed to be going right for these men. It was now up to the next individuals to act, or this would end up in a humiliating defeat for the *Amis*."

There was very little news about the progress of the men ashore, even aboard General Bradley's command ship. "As the morning lengthened, my worries deepened over the alarming and fragmentary reports we picked up over the Navy net," he remembered. "From these messages we could piece together only an incoherent account of sinkings, swampings, heavy enemy fire, and chaos on the beach. By 0830 hours, the two assault regiments had expected to break through the water's edge defenses and force their way inland, yet V Corps had not yet even confirmed news of the landings."

Correspondent Don Whitehead was on Omaha Beach with the 16th Infantry at that very moment, and all he wanted to do was burrow into the sand because he feared the invasion was going to become a failure. But then he remembered the words of Colonel George Taylor, the regiment's commander, that he had outlined for him in his battle plans.

"The first six hours will be the toughest. That is the period when we'll be weakest. But we've got to open the door. Somebody has to lead the way—and if we fail...well...then the troops behind us will do the job. They'll just keep throwing stuff onto the beaches until something breaks. That's the plan."

~FIFTY-FIVE~

COLONEL WILLIAMSON RECEIVED ONLY ONE message from shore during the morning that mattered; it came at ten minutes past nine from his reconnaissance platoon that was already on the beach. It read: "Orders from General Wyman for 2nd Battalion to push up the draw as planned and assist Combat Team 16 in overcoming opposition." Wyman was the division's Assistant Commander and he had landed right behind the first wave. He had been moving up and down the fire-swept beach trying to get his men reorganized for the past three hours.

But Williamson had to deal with another set of problems offshore just to get started into the beach. His LCVPs kept going around in circles, even after his order to head to the beach was issued. Confusion reigned and tempers started rising. Williamson made contact with a Naval officer who admitted he was in command, but that his boat group commander was "missing" and he simply did not know where to land.

This did not set well with Colonel Williamson, so he used his radio to make contact with his shore party; the answer came back: "Land on the right side of the valley by the Ruquet River."

Referring to a "valley" as a point of reference would cause some confusion before it was understood that it was a term used to describe the depression in the sky-line caused by the drainage of the tiny Ruquet River into the ocean. But there was no mistaking that this was near where the important E-1 exit off the beach was located.

Williamson immediately passed this order on to the Naval officer, but again he hesitated. This, too, did not set well with the 2nd Battalion commander, so he escalated the matter to the boat group commander who all of a sudden could be found. But the answer Williamson received about starting to shore nearly brought him to a breaking point.

"There are no channels marked and it is not safe to go in!" the Navy man protested.

Williamson refused to accept this excuse, and instead directed his ire at the officer he had been tangling with before his commander was suddenly found.

"I want you to order the boats in now, regardless of the channels!"

This time the naval officer complied, but forty-five valuable minutes had been lost before the first flight started towards the beach.

The delay was actually a mixed-blessing. Twenty-two men in a platoon of E Company attached to the 16th Regiment's 2nd Battalion had managed to get off the beach by this time.

"We found a construction shack near the strongpoint overlooking E-1," Lieutenant John Spalding, commander of this platoon, told others later. "One of my sergeants fired his bazooka into it, but no one came out. We were about to go on when I spied a stovepipe about seventy yards away sticking out of the ground."

After Spalding spread his men out around this inviting target, small arms fire started up. "We discovered an underground dugout when another sergeant went out to investigate this," he remembered. "We soon learned there was a mortar in it, a position for a 75mm antitank gun, and all this overlooked the E-1 draw. The dugout even had radios, excellent sleeping facilities, dogs."

Spaulding was able to describe all this because his sergeant had fired three shots into the stove pipe vent and the Germans had rushed out to surrender. His men were frisking the prisoners for hidden weapons when he took a look out into the Channel and what he saw was encouraging; Spaulding remembered, "I could make out the indistinct shapes of yet another wave of landing craft."

It was the first flight that Colonel Williamson had finally managed to get started for shore, and they were going to have the advantage of landing much closer to the beach edge because the tide was nearly full.

Bob and Paul's flight was right behind them. "About this time I looked over the bow of our LCVP, and the first wave was only small dots in the distance," Captain Murphy observed. "I turned towards the helmsman, and he said 'Here we go, Sir,' and after completing one last circle, he straightened the boat out, and signaled for the other four landing craft in our wave to form up on line with us. We were in the center of the flight, and there was about fifteen yards of spacing between our LCVPs. Shortly after we came abreast, the signal was flashed to go and we were off for the beach."

Murphy also remembered the sea was rough enough to take water over both the bow and the sides of the LCVP he, Bob, Paul and the other men were on, "not enough to endanger the boat, but enough to keep everyone soaked and miserable. Everyone that wasn't too sick was trying to get to the side of the craft to get a look at the shore, but we were still too far out and all we could see were shell bursts hitting the bluffs and down along the shoreline."

Then something incredible happened. "About twenty minutes after we started out I noticed a big battleship as she let go with a few salvos," Murphy rejoiced. "The roar of her guns was terrific, and it gave us a needed shot of encouragement!"

Technical Sergeant James Knight remembered this Godsend as a near miracle; he was on a dune near the E-1 exit at that moment. "The situation on the beach looked hopeless, but all of a sudden this destroyer loomed out amongst the dozens of landing craft and amphibious vehicles coming to shore," he remembered. "She was headed straight towards me. Even though she wasn't listing or smoking, my first thought was that she had either struck a mine or taken a torpedo hit and was damaged badly enough that she was being beached.

"But the destroyer started turning to the right, and even before she completed the turn to be parallel to the beach, all her guns opened fire. Then I saw smoke leave the gun barrels, and the first shells landed a few yards above my rock cover!"

Owen Keeler was the gunnery officer aboard the 348-foot Gleaves-class destroyer USS *Frankford* that was suddenly making her mark on the history of D-Day. She had been guided towards the beach by Lieutenant Commander James L. Semmes, a Naval Academy graduate from Memphis, Tennessee. His ship had expended its bombardment ammunition allowance earlier that morning, but when he received his new orders just before 10:00, he was reloaded and ready to go.

"Get on them, men!" came the urgent voice of Rear Admiral Carleton Bryant, another Naval Academy graduate, at that time. "Get on them! We must knock out those guns. They are raising hell with the men on the beach, and we can't have any more of that. We must stop it!"

So Semmes decided to take the *Frankford* in for a closer look and what he saw was not very encouraging. "In clear daylight I could see that things were going very poorly on Omaha Beach," he recalled. "All the soldiers were huddling low behind walls, and no movement up the hill and off the sand could be seen." Semmes then ordered his communications officer to make contact with any spotters he could find on the beach so he could line up the *Frankford's* firing at the strongpoints around the E-1 exit.

"With a sick feeling in my stomach that we were facing a total fiasco, I then moved the ship in as close to shore as I could without bumping the bottom," Semmes remembered. "This gave us closer distance to improve vision for picking up enemy movement and strong points. My gunnery officer, Lieutenant Keeler, found pill-boxes, machinegun nests, and other targets of opportunity."

Keeler recalled, "The tide was in our favor at that moment. Navigating by fathometer and his seamen's eye, Commander Semmes took us in close enough to put our optical range finder, ranging on the bluffs above Omaha Beach, against the stops. We were 300-400 yards away. But the camouflage on the beach was still good. We could not spot a target, and frankly we didn't know just how far our troops had advanced."

But luck was with Keeler. "Then one of our light tanks that was sitting on the water's edge with a broken track fired at something on the hill. We immediately followed with a five-inch salvo. The gunner then flipped open his hatch, looked around at us, waved, dropped back into the tank and fired at another target. For the next few minutes he was our fire control party. Our rangefinder optics could examine the spots where his shells hit."

The *Frankford's* Deck Log revealed she started firing at twenty minutes after ten that morning; the first salvo hit a pillbox in the River Ruquet valley, and "the target was destroyed." The next entry said, "Troops on Easy Red held up by battery located on a ridge. After closer observation the exact location of the battery was noted at 1032 hours. At 1036 commenced firing using direct fire, range about 400 yards. On the fifth salvo a direct hit was obtained, a large cloud of green smoke was noted and the battery ceased firing."

Minutes later, although the *Frankford* was now nearly bumping the bottom, she started firing again. "Two machinegun nests were spotted covering the road leading from the Ruquet River Valley to St. Laurent. Commenced firing. Ceased fire at 1057 hours, having effectively stopped all machine gun fire from the nests." Somehow, right in the middle of this, the crew of the *Frankford* managed to pull five wounded American soldiers out of the water.

Sometime during those forty minutes that the *Frankford* fired her salvos Lieutenant Spalding recalled, "We set off our last yellow smoke grenades to let the Navy know that we were Americans, since their time fire was getting pretty close." He also learned that General Wyman had ordered the 18th's 2nd Battalion to now take over the mission of his battered battalion. "So we never crossed the E-1 draw," Spalding later mentioned. "Instead we went along the trail towards Colleville-sur-Mer."

None of this was known to Bob or Paul as their LCVP drew closer to the beach. "The engines of the LCVPs were noisy enough, so much so that what was going on around us was nullified," Captain Murphy pointed out. "I moved over to the side of our boat for a look at the beach. We were still too far out to see any detail, but what I did see gave me a chill. There were still a lot of our men hugging the beach, and no equipment was moving."

But Murphy had little time to dwell on this. "All of a sudden I heard whistling, then explosions, then the pinging of lead along both sides of our landing craft. Everybody hit the deck, except the poor helmsman. We went through this wall of fire rapidly. About this time, I looked over the flight to see how badly our group had been hit. The far right boat seemed to be in trouble, but was limping along. I waved and someone waved back. Then I turned to the helmsman and said, "Let's go! Take me to shore!

"The boat moved forward until we came to a sudden stop, about which threw most of us against the ramp. The helmsman lowered it. I ran off first and jumped into the water; it was half way up to my knees and the shore looked to still be fifty to sixty yards away. Then a machine gunner ran past me and sank in water up to his hips. He raised his machine gun over his head, took another step, and then all I could see was the gun. But his head came out of the water. I watched Lieutenant Hester run down the right side of the ramp, then move farther to the right of us where he found shallow water all the way in. We followed him."

As did Bob and Paul. "There was some stray stuff still flying around and a mortar shell every now and then," Murphy remembered. "As I was wading through the water and got about ten feet from the first dry sand I came upon the body of a soldier. There was a lot of dropped equipment floating around, but I moved closer to make sure the body wasn't one of my men's. I was horrified to see his face waving back and forth like a Halloween mask. He had been decapitated, leaving only his face and part of his scalp attached to his neck."

Bob and Paul saw this, too. "Soldiers in battle are exposed to traumatic experiences, but we had a mission and an objective to take," Murphy told a curious questioner many years later. "So we had to keep going."

It was now just after eleven, and Bob and Paul took their first steps onto Omaha Beach; Bob went first when they rushed towards the seawall to get away from what were now larger artillery shells being directed towards the beach line by a German spotter in the tower atop the twelfth-century church in Colleville.

~FIFTY-SIX~

"THIS AIN'T SICILY," BOB YELLED out to Paul. "Look at all those tanks, those half-tracks and other vehicles, all shot up."

"There goes the old man," Paul yelled back. "And O'Grady is with F Company somewhere. Who's calling the shots?"

"We are," Bob quickly answered. "Ain't that right Sergeant Kroener?"

"I have no radio contact with anyone," he quickly answered. "But yea, we're not going to sit here and take this crap from the Germans. John, let's get your tube set up. Bob, get your sorry ass over here and get ready to feed the mortars. The rest of you start getting those shells out of your vests and piling them up. We're going to register on the backside of that big pillbox that's billowing out all that smoke, and a bit further in to keep any Germans out there from reinforcing the bastards in the pillboxes we can't see.

"And I don't want any shorts. We don't know exactly where our guys are. F and E have been ashore for about a half hour, and they could be going up the draw. Now let's start shooting. We've got thirty rounds. Then we're going to get the hell off this beach.

"Go! Go! Go!"

A couple of Sherman tanks joined the party and fired at the edge of the big pillbox. Two halftracks, still in the water, were letting go with their .50-caliber machine guns; 37mm guns were shelling targets to the right and left of the draw. One gunner had real aim; he fired a full clip and part of a second clip of his machinegun right at the embrasure of the big pillbox. He must have scored. Puffs of smoke and dust poured out of the bunker's slits.

All hell was breaking loose, this time on the Germans.

After Bob plunged the last 81mm mortar down his squad's tube he took one look at the mutilated bodies of the men who had landed before him and then heard Sergeant Kroener scream, "Let's go. There's a wooded area at the bottom of the draw. We're going to head there. Over the top. Now! Go! Go! Go!"

"Paul, stay the hell behind me," Bob yelled before the whole squad jumped over the shingle and started for the draw.

Captain Murphy had taken off with Lieutenant Hester right after they landed. "I told him to move the machine gunners up to the seawall since that was the only cover where we were," Murphy told others later. "Then I told him I was going to try to find our battalion commander, Colonel Williamson.

"And tell Hobratschk where I went, and for him to keep an eye out for me."

Murphy then charged off to his left, totally disregarding his own safety, and came upon a battalion command group, but the faces were unfamiliar. This group—with a regiment of the 29th—had landed right on top of Murphy's battalion; he asked the commander of this outfit if he had seen Colonel Williamson.

"He replied in the affirmative, and pointed in the direction from which I had come," Murphy recalled with some frustration. "So I thanked him, started back down the seawall, and found our commander near a bunker where some Germans were being taken as prisoners."

Murphy didn't know it, and Williamson didn't say anything about it, but his battalion commander had been running up and down the beach trying to get everyone organized, and had even led the daring assault on the pillbox the Germans were being hauled out of.

"Murph, Rosenberg's taken that big bunker protecting the draw and twenty Krauts who called it quits," Williamson informed him. "Charlie Penick's to Orin's right, mopping up. Thank God for that destroyer and those guys who kept shooting their 37s and machine guns at the damn thing. That bunker's done. We're now going to get Cannon Company, transportation and our field artillery ashore. We'll get the draw bulldozed, and then we're going to get off this damn beach, over the top, and secure that dirt road that runs from St. Laurent to Colleville.

"We're going to follow Charlie's E Company, and I want you with me, but first get your company organized, and if you can find Gordon Jeffrey tell him his G Company is to come up behind your men.

"We have to succeed. Some troops are getting off the beach in other places I'm being told, but all the draws are closed and still being strongly defended. We've got to clear E-1 to bust this thing open!"

"Our timing was sure off schedule," Captain Murphy knew at the time. "It was well past noon when E Company reached the top of the bluff before they deployed and attacked due south to cut the St. Laurent to Colleville road. They ran into sporadic rifle fire the whole way; often it was automatic weapons the Germans were using on them."

But by this time Orin Rosenberg's F Company had taken the surviving Germans in the big bunker just fifty-feet to the west of the E-1 draw as prisoners. Engineers were bulldozing their first gap through the dune line near here. For Bob's squad it was now do or die; they had to get off the beach, and the only way to do it was to get past the antitank ditch in front of them, then follow the narrow path marked by tape that led to the top of the bluffs.

Sergeant Kroener quickly lined them up after they broke down their mortar. Gentle John went first, Bob got right behind him, then Paul; he was followed by Smiling Jack from Philly, then Gene Sproull, Billy Uhouse and Willy Driscoll. Paul had the mortar barrel hoisted over his left shoulder; Bob was carrying the base plate; Billy Uhouse the bi-pod. Sergeant Kroener was the last in line; he wanted to keep an eye on everyone. He checked his watch; it was just minutes after high-noon.

Shells were still exploding on landing craft coming in behind them, so they took off fast and were surprised to find the reedy-bottomed antitank ditch had been filled in by a bulldozer; they crossed these ten yards without incident. Then they spread out, putting about five yards between each of them, and moved up to the area where the marked path started. But what they saw was not much of a path; it was narrow, and not a bit wider than Gentle John's big shoulders.

It was marked to either side by glossy white tape; olive drab colored toilet paper identified mines on both sides of the path. A steady stream of artillery and mortars was still coming from somewhere over the bluffs beyond the green, treeless hill line. Instinctively they bunched up, each now close enough to the man in front of him to reach out and touch his back.

Sergeant Kroener yelled, "OK, now let's move. And watch out for any patches of dead grass that aren't marked. Sure as hell the damn Krauts planted mines under them."

So off they went, ever so carefully, each matching the exact steps of the man in front of him. Staying balanced was essential; one slip and they could easily fall on a mine outside of the tape. But every time an artillery shell whistled over their heads, they tended to squat, causing Sergeant Kroener to bark, "Stay straight up or one of you are going to fall on your sorry ass, and the next thing you know you'll be dead. Now keep going!"

So they did, and one-by-one they soon passed by the strongpoint that Company F had taken the prisoners from. Trenches that were dug into the bluff above the big bunker were now empty of Germans; a smaller pillbox near it had some sort of a camouflaged gun in a pit, but its barrel was aimed downward into the dirt, no longer able to kill Americans.

Ahead there were the already dead, some covered with blankets, and the dying, most just comforted by prayers and morphine. Some had dismembered arms, or legs that had been blown off; too many were lying just off the path in their own blood with bandages covering their wounds.

One yelled, "Careful ahead. There's plenty more mines!"

Another screamed, "Stay away from me! There are mines every-where!"

Sergeant Kroener just said, "Keep going men."

Small puffs of smoke spurt up ahead, and there were indeed more mines, but they kept going until the path gave way to brush, then a long, flat reach that was pocked with ditches and bomb craters. Scattered rifle and burb gun fire could be heard in the distance, and then Bob started seeing lines of hedgerows further south that were grown higher than any one of them.

But they had all made it this far.

"OK, now let's find Lieutenant Hobratschk and see where he wants us next," Sergeant Kroener bellowed before he told everyone to turn around. "We got no mortars left, so I picked up three rifles and some ammo clips while we were coming up the path."

Bob and Paul each got a rifle before they started heading south on the narrow dirt road, still worrying about more mines.

"I was with the battalion command group when we started down this road," Captain Murphy remembered. "I had retrieved the mortar section that landed with F Company, and Lieutenant Francis O'Grady was with me. We were moving down the road following Company E. There was constant sporadic rifle and automatic weapons fire up ahead, but then I heard an incoming artillery shell. I hollered to O'Grady, and then dove into the ditch on one side of the road; O'Grady dived into a shell hole on the other side of the road.

"The shell hit very close, showering me with dirt. I looked across the road and my worst fears were confirmed. The shell had landed closer to O'Grady! I ran over to where he was laying and he looked up and asked, 'How bad am I hit, Captain?' I replied, 'I don't know, but it doesn't look too bad,' then I called for a medic. When he arrived I told O'Grady, 'I have to go, I'll see you when you get back from England.'"

When Bob went by O'Grady he had a raincoat over him; it would apparently be a while before they took him down to the beach. They never found Lieutenant Hobratschk. Murphy and the rest of the battalion command group were still closer to E Company, so Bob's squad kept going down the narrow dirt road for about two hundred more yards and then they came to the junction where it met the road eastward to Colleville.

The intersection where the two roads met was lined with wire fences; signs were hung on them reading "*Achtung! Mien!*"

Bob smirked and said to Paul, "How thoughtful of the bastards to warn us of those mines."

Paul laughed before Sergeant Kroener told them both to be quiet, and after the whole squad turned left he added, "See that line of hedgerows to both sides of the low spot in the road up ahead? All that shooting we heard was our guys flushing the Huns out of 'em, but when we go by the openings I want you all to pay attention just in case there's any snipers still hiding in there."

The hedges were well over six-feet high, and in some places much taller. One a bit farther down the road on the right was being hit by another mortar squad; they were flushing the Germans out with smoke shells. The command group was getting out ahead of them now, and it appeared this squad needed some additional help.

"What do you think, Bob?" Gentle John asked him.

"I'm thinking that white phosphorous is gonna' send some Krauts out of the opening to surrender, but that sure as hell doesn't mean all of the sons-a-bitches are flushed out. Hell, they could still be in any corner of that field, and all it would take is one with a spray gun to pop up and squeeze off some bursts, and any of our guys near the opening are goners."

Sergeant Kroener just looked at both of them and said, "We never got any training on how to deal with these damn hedgerows. Hell, back in England they were half this tall at best."

"Permission requested to go up to the side of that hedgerow, and see what I can do to help out, Sarge," Bob asked.

"Go ahead, we'll move up to try to get past the opening, expecting we might draw some fire," Kroener answered. "I can see our men frisking the Germans that are surrendering, but like you I suspect they're now bait for a sniper hoping to let go and kill more of our guys. We'll make some noise to try to get the Germans to reveal themselves. See what you can do Bob. Take Stegall with you."

So Bob took off with Paul and silently snuck up to the hedgerow and leaned against a spot near the front opening where the overgrowth hung out like a roof. Then Bob whispered for Paul to stick his helmet up on the barrel of his rifle and poke it through the overhang.

"Make some noise too, Paul."

So Paul screamed, "There he is!" as he raised his helmet up, and sure enough up popped a sniper who fell for the ruse.

Bob stepped back, got a bead on him, and let go with his rifle. The first round got him right in the head; he spun around and the next thing Bob saw was the big, black-mustached German fall into his own pool of blood.

Then another jumped out of a foxhole closer to the opening in front of the hedgerow, and started for the group that was surrendering. Paul quickly got the drop on him and three bullets later he was plenty dead.

"Well, that's the first time we've been close enough to actually see the Germans we killed," Bob smirked. "A lot different than shooting a mortar at them from hundreds of yards away, eh Paul? And you did damn good. I'm not even going to have to loot you, 'cause you got your guy before he could even come close to getting you. Good going."

"Nice job, men," Sergeant Kroener told them when they rejoined their squad. "No medals, though. We don't hand those out in the First Division for just doing our job. Now let's get going. We've got to make it to Colleville. Word is we now own the mission of the 2nd Battalion of the 16th. Just came in on my radio from Lieutenant Hobratschk. He needs us up there. The Germans are giving what's left of a couple 16th Infantry companies a real hard time. Now move."

"We continued our advance until we were a few hundred yards from Colleville," Captain Murphy noted. "It was here we set up a defensive position to cut off any Germans trying to escape from the village."

"We actually veered south at about 1500 hours to get here," Carl Randall, Murphy's good friend and now the battalion's S-3, later noted. "This area was in the objective boundaries of the 2nd Battalion of the 16th. Our E Company was put on the west flank of our new position to tie in with them later that afternoon."

It wasn't much earlier that afternoon when the 16th's Company G reached the western edge of Colleville. They quickly got into a hell of a fight for the village, were pretty much isolated, and fought stone house to stone house trying to gain the upper hand for the rest of the day. Naval gunfire pummeled Colleville, but missed the five-story church tower that was housing snipers and forward artillery observers; instead Americans were hit.

German reinforcements were even brought up late in the day from St. Jean De Daye to try to save the village; many rode bicycles to get there. Lieutenant Spalding's men spent several hours tangling with these newcomers in the adjacent woods while the confused fighting in the village went on.

"Quite probably the German attack would have swept G Company from the town, and the remnants from E and F from its environs if not for the timely arrival of the 2nd Battalion, 18th Infantry," an historian quite familiar with the fighting in Colleville later wrote. "Minute by minute, hour by hour, the Germans lost control of the village."

"We had constant small arms skirmishes with some enemy positions," Captain Randall pointed out. "Just before dark F Company was pulled back and put north of G Company. This move formed a three-sided box around the enemy in, and around Colleville. Small arms fire kept up through the night as the Germans attempted to escape. All three rifle companies worked on pockets of resistance, and by 0900 the next morning they had over 160 prisoners after killing about fifty more."

Bob's mortar section did not participate in the action because of the closeness of the Germans to his fellow Americans. They actually followed Lieutenant Downing, who remembered "scattered rifle and 'burp' gun fire was going on all the time" during their move to the assembly area.

~FIFTY-SEVEN~

THE OTHER 18TH INFANTRY UNITS were ashore by now. Cannon Company, which landed right behind Bob and Paul, experienced difficulties getting vehicles off their LCTs, but as one soldier aptly put it, "Eventually we winched our unit to shore." It took time, and the company commander was seriously wounded, but by nightfall Cannon Company's half-tracks were available to the rifle companies for support.

Bob York's men hit the beach a few hundred yards east of the Ruquet River after wading ashore in waist-deep water about the time Cannon Company landed. The almost bloodless success of the battalion in reaching the top of the bluffs overlooking Easy Red Beach was in large part attributable to the previous combat experience of its officers and men. But one stood out. "We just followed in Lieutenant Colonel York's footsteps," a man in his headquarters company remembered. "He made you feel that everything was what was expected, so everything was normal."

But it was far from normal for the 3rd Battalion when they landed a little after one-thirty. These men were subjected to steady rounds of artillery fire. The LCI carrying the riflemen of Captain Frank Fitch's Company L struck two mines when they came into the beach. Luck was not with these men. "The bow hit a mine, and as their LCI started to sink the stern hit another mine," Major Colacicco, who was working toward the shore at that moment recalled. "Most of the casualties were men on the bow."

Once the battalion got ashore, Company L's Captain Fitch

stepped on a mine and then was hit by a shell; he died. A sole sniper caused considerable casualties as the rest of the company worked its way far enough up the hill to outflank the culprit, and he was captured.

"Someone lying in the minefield said they should have killed the son of a bitch, not captured him," Pfc. Howard Johnson, an L Company rifleman, angrily remembered. "As they brought him through us he kept pointing and saying '*minen*,' smiling all the while. We wanted to get ahold of him we were so mad. We learned he had run out of ammo and surrendered after killing as many of us as he could, but it was his smiling that really set us off."

When Major Colacicco got to shore he scurried down the beach and ran into a 32nd Field Artillery observer who told him General Wyman wanted to see him. "Just about then a shell hit beside us," Frank Colacicco recalled. "The blast knocked me down, but I finally got up and found General Wyman under a wrecked half-track. He told me to take over the mission of the 1st Battalion of the 16th, so I left and went to find Joe Sisson, our 3rd Battalion commander."

That was not an easy task. Colacicco had to navigate up the taped path and around the dead and wounded to get to the top of the bluff, where he finally found Sisson. "We've been told to keep advancing until we hear firing," Colacicco informed him.

Later Colacicco said, "We did so on a small road where we later spent the night."

The regiment's Anti Tank Company experienced similar problems when they landed on Omaha Beach that afternoon. Lieutenant Johnson was commanding their 3rd Platoon and was assigned to Sisson's battalion. Two of his men were killed on the beach and all of his equipment, with the exception of one 57mm gun and a one-and-a-half-ton truck, was lost in the Channel.

But Johnson kept going, moved through the minefield, then through some scrubby brush near a smashed German pillbox, and eventually went by some concrete mixers that had been used to build the bunkers that were now destroyed. He recalled seeing discarded tools and "dead Germans all over the place" before he ran into Major Colacicco.

"I told him the situation and he was very alarmed to learn that our equipment was lost," Johnson explained. "Then he told me the G-2 on the antitank situation ahead." Major Colacicco didn't know much, but both he and Johnson had been on Sicily the day after the initial landings and neither forgot the German tank counterattacks. Both feared this could also happen the next day here in Normandy.

But all necessary jeeps and other equipment to support the regiment's drive further inland had also made it to shore. "Extensive waterproofing of all of the combat team's transportation, and the know how acquired from two previous assault landings, resulted in surprisingly few losses," remembered Major Frank Dupree. "And the services of our supply guys resulted in the fact that at no time was any battalion lacking in ammo, water, even rations. All our units continued to function throughout the day, despite the constant artillery and mortar barrages."

Captain John Brownlee, who commanded Colonel Smith's Headquarters Company, had equal reason to believe he earned his pay that day. "We actually came off the beach with more equipment than we landed with," Brownlee explained later.

As darkness settled in Bob and Paul dug their slit trench next to a hedgerow in an area south of Colleville "which on our maps was a ridge, but was perfectly flat and cut up by these thick hedgerows into small fields and orchards," according to Captain Randall.

"All during the night the trapped Germans sneaked up the hedgerows, poked their burp guns over the top and fired bursts into our area," Lieutenant Downing remembered. "Since Americans and Germans were so close together, we were not bothered by their artillery or mortar fire."

The moon was full that night; the air was cold. The sounds of war were ever-present. German planes finally responded to the invasion, and flew in over Bob and Paul; they were JU-88s with pilots more interested in bombing the ships off shore so more troops and supplies could be prevented from reaching the beaches. The constant rattling of guns still made it difficult for them to sleep. Occasional flares shot up, sent aloft by hopeful Germans who were still marking American infantry targets.

Sleep never really came to Bob or Paul. They talked a lot. They shared their anger at the Germans who got them into this mess. They agreed the real heroes were dead, that their own bravery couldn't even hold a candle up to those guys. They shared feelings of guilt because they had survived; anger blended with sadness most of the night, but there was no talk or even hints about self-pity. Neither saw the world this way. They were just glad to be alive. They knew they still had work to do.

There was simply no way for them to know that back home the Liberty Bell pealed for the first time in over a hundred years, or that millions of Americans heard this event on their radios. All to support them and their fellow soldiers.

No way they knew that all day long church bells tolled across the land, school bells rang, factories were repeatedly sounding their whistles, and foghorns were blasting away in seaside harbors back home.

In their half-sleep in the middle of that night, neither Bob nor Paul could begin to imagine that the Statue of Liberty had been lit up for the first time in years. Or that her torch was blinking sequences of flashes repeatedly for fifteen long minutes, proclaiming "V for Victory" at the end of a day the mayor of New York City called "the most exciting moment of our lives." It was an America where everyone knew their country was never more together, stronger and determined.

If either Bob or Paul wondered if what they helped do on that

June 6th of 1944 would ever be remembered, they would not have been disappointed had they read Carl Randall's *Record of Events* for their battalion which highlighted their actions that month.

"The fighting done by the 2nd Battalion during the month of June 1944 should go down in history, especially on D-Day and D+1," Randall wrote. "Individual deeds of valor were so commonplace as to be almost unnoticed. The battalion, by the fighting spirit of its officers and men, was the first to push through the beachhead maintenance line and get behind enemy positions, thus driving out the forces protecting the beach and forming the wedge that permitted other troops to get off the beach."

The official Army account of D-Day agreed with Randall. It stated: "At 1130 hours, the Germans, in the last organized defense of the E-1 draw, surrendered to the 2nd Battalion of the 18th Infantry. Thus in a little over an hour, concerted bold action brought the most substantial improvement on the beach since the start of the landings. Stubborn enemy resistance at strongpoints inland had held up movement around St. Laurent, but the 2nd Battalion of the 18th was more than a half-mile deep into enemy territory by the end of the day. Barely large enough to be called a foothold, this strip was nevertheless inside the planned beachhead maintenance area."

"Their position was indeed thin," well-regarded British historian Chester Wilmot wrote in *The Struggle for Europe*, first published in 1952. "But it was held by men who had been ashore before in North Africa and Sicily and could not be dismayed even by the most desperate situation. Had this sector of Omaha Beach been assigned to troops less experienced, less resolute, or less ably commanded, the assault might never have penetrated the beaches."

Nor could Bob or Paul ever imagine what Colonel Smith would say in a letter to his wife just two weeks after the Normandy landings. First revealing that he had spent the night of D-Day "in a German dugout that was twenty feet under the ground and smelled to high heaven," he wrote about his men: "Since then we have pushed steadily into Normandy. These lads of mine are fighting fools. They have marched, fought, and dug trenches day after day without complaint and with a wonderful spirit. Who says this modern generation is soft? Hitler has no more claim that he has all the supermen."

On June 17th of that historic month General Huebner approved a Presidential Unit Citation for the 18th Infantry, citing its D-Day achievements. Part of the citation read, "The individual calmness, endurance, superior efficiency, and devotion to duty exhibited by the Regiment was a direct contribution to the successful establishment of a firm beachhead on the ramparts of 'Fortress Europe' and will without doubt result in the successful conclusion to the war in Europe."

The cost to Colonel Smith was far less than it was to other regiments that landed in Normandy on D-Day. A later count showed the Big Red One suffered 184 killed, 713 wounded and 277 were recorded as missing, an untold number of whom were likely killed and whose bodies were never found. Forty-five enlisted men of the 18th Infantry were amongst the missing. Twelve officers and 136 enlisted men were wounded, but just one officer and eleven enlisted men died on D-Day. Many of the dead were buried in temporary graves near St. Laurent, above the bluffs Bob and Paul had crossed that morning.

Today it is the location of the permanent hallowed ground that is the Normandy American Cemetery and Memorial where the spirit of American youth rose from the waves on D-Day.

The cemetery is situated atop a cliff directly overlooking Omaha Beach. A small jut of land affords an excellent view of where Bob and Paul came ashore. From here, the whole action of the brave men who landed beneath the E-1 draw, scaled the escarpment and took their first steps on higher French soil to free Europe can be visualized.

It is a fitting tribute neither Bob nor Paul could ever have begun to imagine as they tried to sleep in their slit trench under the full moon in Normandy on that cold Tuesday night in 1944.

~FIFTY-EIGHT~

WHEN BOB AND PAUL WOKE up on June 7th the first thing they did was heat up some coffee, eat a ration, and wait for orders. Little did they know that they had already come down from regiment.

"During the night we received orders to attack southeastward, force a crossing of the Aure River, and then secure the high ground in the vicinity of Mosles," Captain Murphy explained. "Fortunate for us, Company H's weapons carriers had landed and they had been brought forward, relieving the men from having to carry their mortar and its ammo during the day's march."

"Mosles had been our D-Day objective," Captain Randall added. "As such, our artillery and Naval shore control parties had established an OP at Le Chau Rogue the previous afternoon and shelled the town with good results. The battalion moved out at 1000 hours in two columns abreast. F Company moved south off the Bellafontaine to Mosles road with two platoons of 57mm antitank guns following. G and H Companies, plus the battalion headquarters company, moved on a parallel road about 600 yards to the west. E Company followed to protect our rear and flanks as we advanced. Soon after starting we received a platoon of M4 tanks and we put these behind the antitank platoons."

"The advance seemed to go along quite smoothly," Lieutenant Downing remembered. His Headquarters Company was right behind where Bob and Paul were marching in column, with the usual ten yards of dispersion between the men.

"This advance was mostly down little roads and lanes," Downing added. "There was no mortar or artillery fire. The movement would go forward at a good rate for a while, and then stop, forward and stop again, but we were making progress all the time. We passed through a few French farmyards and went by little groups of scattered houses. The people stood aloof and undemonstrative, and looked at us as if we were from another world.

"In time, as we were moving along the edge of an open field, opposition developed up forward, made known to us by the annoying burp-burp of machine pistols. The riflemen ahead of my group deployed and advanced."

"This was G Company coming down the Houtteville road," Randall later noted. "They ran into German mortar and machine gun fire from south of the Aure River."

Bob's squad was ordered to set up their mortar, and register on the likely location of the Germans. For the next half-hour the Bearer Boys brought him rounds, and Bob and Gentle John did their part to help Captain Jeffrey's riflemen bust up their opposite numbers across the river.

Captain Rosenberg's F Company initially fared a bit better. "He rushed a platoon across a 300-yard stone causeway closer to Mosles," Carl Randall recorded. "But the enemy took the bridge under fire so we got ready to push the tanks out ahead of them."

"It was now sometime after 1430 hours," Captain Murphy recalled. "This causeway being the only way to cross the Aure, our men shifted here after our mortars helped G Company get things quieted down."

Lieutenant Downing, who joined this move with his Headquarters Company, remembered, "We arrived at a hill crest overlooking the river, on the far side of which were the gray stone buildings of Mosles. We could see scattered riflemen running across the causeway toward the town."

Bob and Paul were on the causeway by this time, and when Downing crossed he recalled with some chagrin, "We had progressed about fifty yards when some of the American tanks roared down the road behind us and started to cross over. As always, they drew concentrated fire from the Germans across the river. I cursed them heartily. Tanks are always a welcome sight to an infantry man except when they travel too close. They always draw fire, which does not ricochet off an unarmored foot soldier. I ran headlong across the causeway to the other side."

"The tanks were nevertheless pushed ahead," Captain Randall pointed out. "This enabled the rest of F Company to cross the river and fan out to the right, but a very heavy engagement took place immediately. G Company had the tanks with them, so they pushed forward and crossed the bridge to help out."

"We followed the tanks," Captain Murphy remembered.

"The tanks continued on up through the town," Downing added. "I was waiting behind a stone house for the rest of my group to cross. Jeeps came zipping behind them, and pulled up nearby. I noticed a couple of riflemen firing towards town. One of them came over and told me that he thought a sniper was in a church up the street. One of the jeep drivers asked me if he could fire his .50-caliber machine gun at it. I said that he could.

"The church had a row of curtained windows just under the eaves of the roof. The jeep driver fired his gun, traversing along the whole row of windows, shattering all of them. But an ambulance jeep went up through the town later, and returned fully loaded.

"One of them was a tank lieutenant who was unloaded on a stretcher. His hair was burned off, and his face, arms and chest were black. He was also bleeding from a wound on the thigh. He kept up a continuous stream of conversation and smoked a cigarette. He had run his tank against a hedgerow outside of the town and the muzzle of the tank's gun had gotten filled with dirt.

"He later fired the gun at an enemy position. The plugged muzzle had caused a flashback, burning him and setting fire to the tank. As he jumped out, the Germans shot him in the thigh. He looked a mess, but kept chatting away in high spirits. I guess it was the reaction from being so close to death and the elation at having cheated the old Grim Reaper."

"The town was taken by 1700 hours," Captain Randall entered in his report of the day's actions. "Then we got the companies organized for an all-around defense. F Company stayed in Mosles; G was next to them, then E Company which guarded a crossroad about one kilometer west of Mosles."

Company H bivouacked in an apple orchard bordered by hedgerows on the main highway just east of Mosles where Colonel Williamson set up his command post in a dugout that had been built by the occupants of the lone house here. "We lower-ranking officers fixed up a guard schedule so that we could supervise the defenses, and get a little sleep," Lieutenant Downing remembered this time.

Bob and Paul dug a slit trench so they could also settle down for another cold night. They ate their ration, but didn't say much. They were just grateful to have lived through another day. But the area was far from quiet; they could hear some firing of rifles closer to Mosles. German planes flew over on their way to the beach again after dark. At midnight they heard the ruffled reports of the Navy's big guns, and then the swishing of their shells as they passed overhead, hopefully at their next day's objective, which of course they didn't know anything about yet. It made sleep difficult and Bob couldn't even smoke to pass the time because of the blackout rules.

But the Germans knew where they were.

"They retaliated with mortar shelling, some of which fell in our area," Lieutenant Downing later related. "Two shells landed in the rear part of the orchard, the explosions followed by yells and excited cries. But the shelling ceased as suddenly as it started, and we settled back down to try to get a little rest.

Captain Murphy got the final word in about that day's action. "A few prisoners were taken and the Germans lost about thirty killed. The 2nd Battalion lost several men, but none of them were in H Company."

First Division intelligence intercepted a message warning that a strong counterattack by the 352nd Division was expected at daybreak on June 8th. Then, orders came down two hours later from Colonel Smith to have the 2nd Battalion make physical contact with the enemy "by sending patrols as far out as possible in all directions."

"We first organized the high ground just south of Mosles for the defense, and then patrols went out along the road to Tour-en-Bessen," Captain Murphy explained. "The patrol reported back that they were unable to make contact with the 16th Infantry and the Germans still held the village."

"But a battalion of the 26th passed to the east on the Bayeux road, and this gave our left flank, which had been exposed up to now, protection," Carl Randall pointed out. "Then orders were received during the afternoon to secure a ridge further south of Mosles."

It didn't take long for Bob and Paul to figure out that this ridge—it was only about a half mile away—was big enough for the whole regiment to assemble on.

"What gives?" Bob asked Sergeant Kroener.

"Damned if I know, but Lieutenant Hobratschk seems to be in the know. Apparently regiment is going to have the other battalions pick up the fight once we take that ridge, and we're going into reserve."

No one cheered because speculation was just speculation until final orders came down, no matter who was doing the guessing.

It was easy to see that the gravel road south was bounded on both sides by hedgerows. Jeffrey's G Company was on the left, and Rosenberg's men were marching in columns of twos on the other side of the road when the battalion finally jumped off just before six that night. Bob and Paul's squad was right behind F

Company, and their jeep carrier with all of their equipment and mortars was following them.

Intense firing broke out almost immediately. Lieutenant Downing, who was bringing up the battalion headquarters men, was right behind Company H again; he remembered, "There were reports of rifles, BARs, 'burp' guns, bazookas and intermittent 'crumps' of German mortar shells. The advance was slow and halting. It was getting quite dark when I saw the heavy weapons company men take their weapons off the jeeps and begin setting up in the fields to either side of the road."

What Downing didn't realize was the battalion, despite the starts and stops, had made it close to the ridge, close enough given it was now past last light.

They were just south of Moulagny.

"We dug in here for the night," Captain Murphy remembered. "Our mortars were set up for an all-around defense, just in case we needed them."

It was a good call.

"In the morning we straightened our line," Captain Randall noted. "All companies were in line; G, F, E, from left to right. The enemy was three hundred yards in front of us."

The skies were cloudy on Friday morning, June 9th. But not for long. A drizzling, cold rain filled the air at mid-morning; still, there was some good news. The attack further south would be spearheaded by Bob York's 1st Battalion and Sisson's 3rd Battalion companies.

Bob and Paul's 2nd Battalion would indeed be put in reserve, only to be called upon if the other battalions ran into trouble reaching their phase lines. The time of the attack was to be as near to noon as possible. The objective was Tronquay, six miles further south. Sisson's forces would take it, then the 2nd Battalion would move down and occupy the village.

By this time the entire defensive line of the 916th Grenadier

Regiment opposite the 18th Infantry was being pushed back on a wide front. An officer, just one of three left in his battalion of the 916th, later said, "Our tactics were now simple when we were attacked by infantry. We would hold with the aid of the hedgerows. If we saw them withdraw we then did so ourselves. Then their infantry would take over our old line, thinking we were destroyed. Afterwards they would advance casually and we would hit them from the next hedgerow. We lost ground, but it was all we could do."

On June 9th the 916th Grenadier Regiment was under new orders. They could only withdraw when their ammunition ran out.

Bob had a slow morning—hurrying up and waiting—as was always the case before he went into reserve with his battalion. He stayed in the bivouac area with Paul, and when they saw Captain Murphy go into a farmhouse off a side road where Colonel Williamson was preparing that day's orders, they figured it was just a matter of time before they'd hear something.

It was quiet to their front at the time, so they had little to do but keep waiting. Paul had just finished eating his C-ration when he turned to Bob.

"You thought much about what you're going to do when this war is over?" he asked him.

"Not too much," Bob answered before he revealed he really had put some thought into it. "Eisenhower says we'll be done by Christmas. I suppose that could mean we'll be back in England for New Years Day. I think I told you my grandmother's from London, Paul. Her husband, my grandfather, died last year. I'm thinking it's time for me to make a family. Hell, we're getting old. I'm almost twenty-four years old already. I'll have to start from scratch, find a job and someplace to live, of course. But I need to marry the right woman, so when this war does end I'm going to go back to England, come hell or high water, and figure out if Lily's the right one."

"Well, what if she's not?" Paul asked.

"Then I'm going to go home to Naugatuck, I'm gonna' buy me

an Indian Scout, and take a long ride somewhere. Maybe down south. I'll come see you in South Carolina! How's that?"

"That would be great," Paul said. "But I worry that when we do end the war here, the Army could ship us off to the Pacific to help end the war there."

"Hard telling not knowing where the Army, in its infinite wisdom, will send us," Bob lamented. "We'll have had enough of war by the time we're done here in Europe, so let's make a deal. They'll probably send us back to the States first, even if we get ordered to the Pacific. We'll take leave, you and me. We'll get two Indians, and then just go AWOL."

Paul laughed hard at that one. Then Gentle John came by; he'd been playing poker with some of the other Bearer Boys. They shot the bull. A rumor was getting around saying that the house Williamson was using for his CP had a bedroom in it with a big hole in the wall, and that it had been used by the Germans before their arrival.

"Don't even think about going to take a look," Sergeant Kroener, who overheard the talk about the CP, yelled sternly. "We need to stay put. There won't be any time to go sight-seeing till we get to Tronquay."

Kroener looked at his watch. It was going on two in the afternoon already.

Suddenly there was an increasing volume of small arms fire down the road. Then, the windows of Williamson's CP shattered.

Fire was coming into their camp.

The attack had jumped off a half-hour earlier. "The 3rd Battalion by-passed an enemy strongpoint that was off a narrow road close to Beaumont, just three-quarters of a mile away," Captain Randall remembered. "So our E and F Companies had to move down to clean it up."

"We set up our mortars right away to support the attack," Captain Murphy added. "These men got on the enemy positions."

Randall later recorded that "about thirty prisoners were taken and twenty Germans were killed," also noting friendly casualties were light here, but "two enemy shells landed on E Company. Several men were killed, and about seven were wounded."

Lieutenant Downing remembered hearing a "flurry of firing."

"I had directed Lieutenant Hobratschk to send a section of mortars south in order to provide closer support to the two rifle companies," Captain Murphy later explained. "As the companies were overrunning the enemy position, they received considerable artillery and mortar fire. The mortar section I sent down to help out was on the move, and it got hit."

"The trees in the vicinity caused the shells to burst overhead, making the casualty count higher," Captain Randall added. "No further enemy action was encountered that day; we bivouacked at Blay the night of June 9th."

"On this day Company H had casualties," Captain Murphy needed to add. "We lost four men; two were killed. Two others wounded."

~FIFTY-NINE~

SONNY HAD JUST PUT ANOTHER WEEK of work behind him. He last saw Laura Jean on Wednesday, the day after the invasion. He was getting a hay fever shot in Charleston, and Sonny told her he couldn't believe that it had finally happened.

They both admitted they were scared, scared mainly because all the news about the invasion was sketchy. And while Sonny was pretty sure Bob's First Division likely participated, there was no way to know for sure. He had just spent a full day at the plant that Saturday. He and Laura Jean weren't planning to go out to the cottage on the Coal River until the next morning, so he decided to sit down and write a letter to Bob.

June 10, 1944

Dear Bob;

Got that box off to you that I said I would in my last letter and it really had quite an assortment of stuff in it, including a cigarette lighter and other odds and ends, plus some food that would not spoil. Hope that you get it soon and that you like it.

Haven't heard from Mary Jane since she went into the Army, but suspect that she is much too busy to be doing some writing these days. From what Mother has said they are keeping the little girl hopping, and I guess that she is just the one to be doing such.

I very successfully passed my Army physical the other day and now find myself being healthy with a 2B deferment, meaning deferred because of my job here at the plant in Institute. This deferment expires on July 11th. Will be in a position to tell you more then.

Managed to push a fender in on the car the other day in the parking lot at work. Just wasn't awake when I went to park it that morning and found myself nosily cutting a corner much too close. Swerved a little bit and then I proceeded to really give myself hell for being so dumb to do such a thing. Of course I was accused of everything under the sun, even having some of my more "intimate" friends suggest that I stop drinking long enough so that I might get to work sober the next day. So goes life at work, rather dull and routine with the exception of some information that I was finally getting a raise.

Billie is coming down here for her vacation during the first week of July with marriage in her eyes. Halfway thinking that I will still be a single man when she leaves. I am having one hell of a time making my mind up, and today it looks this way. I am still trying to put marriage on a scientific basis, but find it increasingly difficult to do so, particularly with Billie being extremely insistent these days, as she tells me there is another waiting to marry her, and that I better make up my mind pretty soon if I am to have her. I am getting the squeeze play but good.

Hope that you fared well in the Invasion, and that you will continue to manage. Good luck.

Regards,

Ed

Billie did show up three weeks later. For Sonny, it was tougher for him to confess to Laura Jean that she was coming than it was for him to tell Billie no to marriage. Years later Sonny would simply remember he put her on a bus and she went back to her home in Williamsport Pennsylvania. Laura Jean also went home to see her friends in Ravenswood, where her family lived in West Virginia, and had a ball. Then Sonny called and asked her if he could pick her up and drive her back to Charleston. She agreed.

The 4th of July fell on the following Tuesday and they went to the cottage on the Coal River, and this time they had a ball together.

Then Thursday came, and when Sonny got home from work there were two U.S. V-Mail letters in his mailbox; the return address on both said WAR DEPARTMENT OFFICIAL BUSINESS.

The first one Sonny looked at had a hand stamped on it with its forefinger pointed to RETURN TO SENDER. At the bottom of the envelope were two penciled notations. One was crossed out. It read: KIA 6/9/44. The other read: MISSING, and it was initialed by a 1st Lieutenant of the Infantry.

Confused, and with a pit in his stomach, Sonny then looked at the other V-Mail. This one was postmarked a week earlier. This time the hand stamp read: DECEASED, although the same lieutenant had affixed his initials with MISSING on the bottom, beneath the window.

Inside each were the V-Mail letters Sonny had last sent to Bob.

He put them both down. He wondered—is my brother dead, or just missing? To Sonny, this was maddening; logic and order were two pillars that supported the way he thought.

And until he could figure out what was going on, he wasn't about to get his mother upset. He talked to no one about the matter, not even Laura Jean.

Sonny simply shut down.

Sonny's Uncle Rudy called the next day.

"We're here with your mother, Sonny," he told him. "Both me and your Uncle Arthur. A Western Union telegram just came. It said Bob was missing in action in France since June 9th."

Sonny's first impulse was to thank God Bob wasn't dead, like one of his returned V-Mails had said. He asked his Uncle Rudy to put his mother on the phone.

"Sonny, she's too distraught to talk to you."

"Should I come up?" Sonny asked.

"I'd wait a day or two. We might know more. Arthur and I are keeping an eye on her, and Nellie's on her way. I'll tell your mother you called. Can you call tomorrow?

"Of course," Sonny answered.

Two days later a letter arrived from the War Department.

Mrs. Viola Baummer
90 Oak Street
Naugatuck, Connecticut

Dear Mrs. Baummer,

This letter is to confirm my recent telegram in which you were informed that your son, Private First Class Robert A. Baummer, ASN 11-012-180—Infantry, has been reported missing in action in France since 9 June 1944.

I know that added distress is caused by failure to receive more details. Therefore, I wish to assure you that at any time more information is received, it will be transmitted to you without delay, and if in the meantime no additional information is received, I will communicate with you at the expiration of three months.

The term "missing in action" is used only to indicate the whereabouts or status of an individual is not immediately known. It is not intended to convey the impression that the case is closed. I wish to emphasize that every effort is exerted continuously to clear up the status of our personnel. Under war conditions, this is a difficult task as you must readily realize. Experience has shown that many persons reported as missing in action are subsequently reported as prisoners of war, but as information is furnished by countries with which we are at war, the War Department is helpless to expedite such reports. However, in order to relieve financial worry, Congress has enacted legislation which continues in force the pay, allowance and allotments to dependents of personnel carried as missing in action.

Permit me to extend my heartfelt sympathy during this time of uncertainty.

Sincerely,

J.A. Ulio
Major General
The Adjutant General

The *Waterbury Republican American* had picked up on the story, and it appeared in the paper the day after the Western Union Telegram arrived.

Pfc. Baummer Missing in French Battle

Naugatuck—Pfc. Robert A. Baummer, son of Mrs. Viola Baummer of 90 Oak Street, is missing in action in France, his mother has been notified. He is a member of an infantry division in the Army.

No details of the action after which Pfc. Baummer was reported missing were given in the notifying telegram, which stated only that it took place June 9. It is believed the local man had been in France since D-Day. He is a veteran of fighting in North Africa and Sicily, and escaped injury in both of those campaigns.

The last letter received from him was written on May 20, at which time he was feeling well. He is the first Naugatuck man not a member of an air force unit to be reported missing in well over a year. At the time of the North African Invasion, some Naugatuck infantrymen were reported missing and later listed as prisoners or safe. Pfc. Baummer has been in the Army since December, 1940 and has been overseas about two years.

No one knew during that first week of July that a Graves Registration unit had buried Bob's remains in the 1st American Cemetery near St. Laurent at 1700 hours on Tuesday, the 13th of June, and incorrectly marked the date of his death as D-Day, June 6th. One of his dog tags was nailed to his marker; the other, per regulation, was buried with his body in Grave 145, Plot F, Row 8. A man named Root was buried to one side of him; a Sternbank to the other. The only personal effects found before Bob was wrapped in an olive-drab blanket and put into the earth were his billfold and a pocket knife.

On July 6th, one day before Viola received the Western Union telegram telling her that her son was missing in action, Captain Murphy's executive officer, Lieutenant Lucas, changed Bob's status on that day's Company H Morning Report from MISSING to KILLED IN ACTION as of June 9, 1944.

When Viola came home from work on Tuesday, the 25th of July, as she climbed Oak Street she could see an old red pickup truck parked in her driveway; she immediately recognized it as Harold's, the Naugatuck cop who had helped her through her husband's death and written a letter of recommendation for Bob before he went off to the Connecticut Junior Republic to straighten his life out.

As she drew closer, Harold opened his door, placed his left foot down, then twisted out of the truck and stood up. He was facing Viola as she stepped closer, and the tears in her eyes told him she knew why he was there.

"Mrs. Baummer, I am so sorry."

Then he gave her the telegram.

Western Union
25 July 1944

NAUGWBY FROM: WASHINGTON D.C.
MRS. VIOLA K. BAUMMER
90 OAK STREET
NAUGATUCK, CONNECTICUT

THE SECRETARY OF WAR DESIRES THAT I TENDER
HIS DEEP SYMPATHY TO YOU IN THE LOSS OF YOUR
SON PRIVATE FIRST CLASS ROBERT A. BAUMMER
WHO WAS PREVIOUSLY REPORTED MISSING IN AC-
TION—REPORT NOW RECEIVED STATES HE WAS
KILLED IN ACTION 9 JUNE IN FRANCE—LETTER FOL-
LOWS

SIGNED;
ULIO, THE ADJUTANT GENERAL

Journey of the Purple Heart

COMING HOME

Journey of the Purple Heart

~SIXTY~

SONNY TOOK THE FIRST TRAIN OUT of Charleston that he could catch to go home and be with his mother; she had managed to call and tell him about receiving the telegram. No one had left her side since she got it. Gram Nellie came and Viola's sister Kathryn—the first grade school teacher—stayed with her for days. Sonny's uncles came by to pay their respects; neighbors also came and went. Mrs. Walker appeared at her door the morning after Viola got the telegram. Harold stopped by every night after he got off duty. By the time Sonny got to Oak Street, the whole town knew his brother was dead.

The Naugatuck paper had made that known.

Sonny was there to see the Army's promised letter when it arrived. Dated the 27th, it expressed "profound regret" to Viola, even promising "if additional information is received it will be transmitted to you promptly." The letter expressed empathy. "I realize the burden of anxiety that has been yours since he was first reported missing in action, and deeply regret the sorrow this later report brings you," the Adjutant General wrote. "May the knowledge that he made the supreme sacrifice for his home and country be a source of sustaining strength."

Sonny told his mother on several occasions that Bob's getting killed was his fault for convincing him to go into the Army.

It was a turning point for Viola. As deep as her grief was, she firmly reminded him that Bob had made his own decision to enlist.

"Sonny, we have to accept what happened. Actually, we'll likely never know what happened to Bob in France. But we need to get on with our lives. You have an important job, and I suppose I do too. I'm going to go back to work next week. Things will never be normal again, but routine is good."

Sonny accepted this, returned to Charleston during the first weekend in August, but never forgave himself for suggesting his brother join the Army.

His relationship with Laura Jean got serious. Her empathy for his grieving was evidenced by unspoken kindness; she never questioned him about how he really felt, nor did Sonny ever express this to her; he was compartmentalizing his feelings about his brother's death, and would for the rest of his life.

"I don't remember him ever talking about it," Laura Jean would say years later. "He always kept his feelings to himself."

When his friends at work brought Bob up, Sonny would say nothing. Pretty soon word got around to leave his brother's death out of the conversation when anyone talked to him.

Sonny and Laura Jean spent the late summer weekends they could at the Coal River. Then October came; they had known each other for going on seven months now.

They were in a corner drugstore in Charleston one night that month after they got off work. Sonny would later say, "When she started asking me to take her out seven days a week, I decided it was cheaper to get married."

"He made that up," Laura Jean laughed when she heard this. "But, out of the clear blue while we were enjoying chocolate milk shakes that were so thick we had to eat them with our spoons, he looked at me and said, 'Let's get married.' I told him I would have to think about it."

She didn't take long. They were married on November 11th in the historic brick two-story Baptist Temple in Charleston. Viola came with her sister Kathryn. It was the first time Laura Jean met

Viola. She and Sonny spent their wedding night in nearby Huntington but they had to get up at six the next morning so they could bring Viola and Kathryn to the airport. The incoming flight was late, so the newlyweds spent their first day of marriage waiting until they finally departed later that afternoon.

Sonny and Laura Jean settled into an apartment in Kawana, a river town just south of Charleston, and Sonny did his best to follow his mother's advice to get on with their lives.

Viola had to deal with the unpleasant business of Bob's final affairs when she got back to Naugatuck. The Army had already sent letters advising her that she would receive six months of Death Gratuity pay and any applicable life insurance proceeds because "the deceased named her as his beneficiary."

A letter even came from the Army Services Forces in Boston, first offering their sympathies, and then informing Viola that the Personal Affairs Division represented the Army's "sincere interest in providing any needed assistance or advice to those whose personal lives are affected by this total war in which we are all engaged."

"Feel free to call," the letter said, but Viola never did. She was more concerned about where her son was buried.

The only information she received about this came months later in a notice from the War Department. "The remains of our personnel who lost their lives while serving outside the continental limits of the United States cannot be returned to this country until after the cessation of hostilities," Viola was told.

But the letter did say, "The graves are properly marked and recorded to preserve their identity and everything possible is done by the military authorities to care for these graves until such time as the remains may be returned to the United States. As soon as military security will permit, the Quartermaster General will furnish the grave locations of these honored heroes to the next of kin in each case; and upon termination of the war will communicate with the families concerned relative to the return of the remains to this country."

It brought Viola to tears when she read, "Personal effects, when recoverable, will be sent to the next of kin as soon as practicable. Despite the most painstaking efforts to recover and identify remains some may never be located, particularly those of personnel first reported as missing in action and subsequently determined by the War Department to be deceased."

It was Sonny who persisted with the Quartermaster General on Bob's burial location and the disposition of his personal effects. One letter he wrote mentioned Bob had left a footlocker behind at Ft. Devens before he went overseas; a polite response came two weeks later, but Bob's footlocker was never found.

Still, Sonny persisted and the Army finally sent a letter in April of 1945 telling him Bob's property, "consisting of a few small items, is being sent to you." When they arrived in Naugatuck there were just two items; one was Bob's billfold, and it contained the picture of his mother he had carried with him throughout his war. The other item was a small pocket knife Sonny had given him before he went overseas.

In October of 1946, a year and a half after Bob's remains were buried, Viola finally received a letter telling her he was interred with "fitting dignity and solemnity" at the Military Cemetery in St. Laurent, twenty miles northeast of St. Lo, France."

An Army brigadier general followed this letter with his own, offering: "Enclosed, herewith, is a picture of the United States Military Cemetery St. Laurent, France, in which your son is buried. It is my sincere hope that you may gain some solace from this view of the surroundings in which your loved one rests. This cemetery will be maintained as a temporary resting place until, in accordance with your wishes, all remains are either placed in permanent American cemeteries overseas or returned to the Homeland for final burial."

In March of 1947 Viola received another letter, along with a pamphlet and the necessary forms that finally allowed her to express her wishes about the disposition of Bob's remains.

Her son was finally coming home.

~SIXTY-ONE~

PER VIOLA'S WISHES, BOB'S REMAINS were disinterred from his shallow grave in France in September of 1947 and placed in a metal casket. The casket was then loaded onto a deuce and a half, which carried it to the Port of Cherbourg. Here, the port unit commander signed for Bob's casket, and awaited the arrival of others.

On November 15th Viola received a telegram informing her that the remains of her son would "arrive New York aboard the USAT *Robert F. Burns* on November 24," that debarkation and moving of the remains "would be under military guard," and "transportation by rail to final destination will take a few additional days."

Viola had already designated her wishes to have Bob's casket delivered to the Alderson Funeral Home on Meadow Street in Naugatuck. Thus she was also asked "to instruct the funeral director to make arrangements to accept remains at railroad station upon arrival."

It was Sonny who had to do this for his mother; she was too distraught to even begin to focus on the details of her son's funeral. But the Naugatuck paper took charge and on the front page of the December 15th edition notified the town that the funeral of Pfc. Robert A. Baummer would be held that Wednesday.

The body will be met at the train station by a delegation from the Naugatuck Veterans council, and will be escorted to the Alderson Funeral Home," the piece informed its readers and then added, "Friends may call at the funeral home tomorrow evening from 7 to 9 o'clock. Funeral services will take place Wednesday afternoon at 2 o'clock from the St. Michael's church. Reburial will be in Grove Cemetery. Full military rites will be conducted at the grave. Friends are asked to omit flowers.

Another front page piece evidencing how Bob's hometown greeted him the next night appeared the morning of his funeral.

Veterans Pay Touching Tribute to Pfc. Baummer

The body of Pfc. Robert A. Baummer arrived in Naugatuck last night and was met at the railroad station by 43 delegates from various veterans organizations.

The uniformed veterans of World War I and II stood quietly at attention and saluted as the casket was lowered from the train and carried to a waiting hearse.

The men fell in line and escorted the body to the Alderson Funeral Home.

An honor guard, under the direction of the commander of the All American Veterans, stood at parade rest, one man on each side of the casket, during the hours the funeral home was open. Every 15 minutes the two-man guard was relieved and two new men took their place.

The entire veterans delegation filed through the home, and as each man reached the casket he turned and saluted his departed comrade. It was a touching tribute.

Well over a hundred others also came to pay their respects. Many were boyhood friends of Bob's. All of his relatives, of course, were there. Some were Sonny's boyhood classmates. A few no one knew also came, but one stood out.

"He never spoke unless he was spoken to," Laura Jean remembered. "But for some reason I never forgot his dignified manner."

He was Sergeant Billy Ramsey, who was with the Headquarters

Company, 504th Parachute Infantry Regiment, the very 82nd Airborne Division unit that had made their ill-fated jump into Sicily the first night Bob had come ashore here. Ramsey had met Bob's flag-draped coffin when it arrived in Brooklyn and was unloaded by stevedores from the *Robert F. Burns* at the Army terminal pier shed, and then eventually placed in a mortuary car, a converted Pullman with the windows covered out of dignity and respect for the fallen.

Military Police stood by when the mortuary car was pulled out of the terminal's East Yard and taken to Grand Central Station, where Bob's coffin was placed on Train Number 20 to New Haven, after which it was transferred to the line that brought his remains to Naugatuck, arriving at six-twenty-seven that night at the elaborately ornamented train station.

Sergeant Ramsey stood beside Bob's coffin the entire way, and he would remain with him until he was lowered into the ground the next day.

The hearse bearing Bob's coffin left the Alderson Funeral Home at a quarter to two on the dreary, lead-gray and cloudy 17th of December; the temperature was in the mid-twenties, and the wind from the north was brisk. Two limousines carrying Bob's immediate family and friends serving as pall bearers followed, and within a matter of minutes the procession—which again included a delegation from the Veterans Council—reached the St. Michael's Episcopal Church on the town green.

Under the watchful eye of Sergeant Ramsey, the six pall bearers received Bob's coffin from the hearse, followed the color guard up the church's half-dozen steps, and then through the gabled entrance porch into the vaulted-arched nave where the assembled mourners were seated in the pews.

Viola, Sonny and a now two-month pregnant Laura Jean, as well as Bob's other immediate relatives occupied the first row of pews.

The service was brief, per Viola's wishes. Laura Jean would later say that the church service was not particularly special. Sonny only remembered one thing about the day of Bob's service; he buried everything else about the funeral with his brother.

What Sonny remembered happened following the church service after the police-escorted funeral procession crossed the Naugatuck River and met Route 8 before going down South Main Street to the cemetery.

The driver of a big interstate truck, upon recognizing he was viewing a military funeral, stopped, stepped out of his cab onto the pavement, removed his cap, stood at attention and saluted.

The cars proceeded down South Main Street towards Grove Cemetery, turned right and went through its stone wall-bordered entrance, and passed by the Tuttle Memorial Chapel. Then the long line bore left, then right where the cars had to slow considerably to traverse the rutted non-paved surface through its tranquil acreage before making a final left turn and going down into a cold hollow where the Baummer family plot was located amongst several tall pine trees.

The pall bearers removed Bob's casket and carried their hometown hero to his grave. The committal service was also brief, but pageant. His Uncle Arthur had offered a fitting tribute for Bob to St. Michael's Reverend Langhorst, one Arthur remembered from an impressive service where he had been a color bearer years earlier during the burial of a Naugatuck World War One veteran.

"This service is doubly sacred," Langhorst began, "We are not only laying to rest a loved one, but placing in an honored grave the body of a patriot. The fact that he was a soldier demands that tribute of love and respect to be laid in his grave, and this we gladly do because he had a part in the great sacrifice which meant so much to us all.

"We commit Private First Class Robert Arthur Baummer to thy care, O God our Father, beseeching Thee through Christ our Lord to keep alive Thy grace in our hearts," the good reverent continued. "Watch Thou, O Heavenly Father, over those who watch or weep today, and give better angels over those who sleep. Through Christ our Lord, Amen."

The honor guard then briskly lifted the American flag that covered Bob's casket and held it tautly over him. Everyone in uniform snapped to attention. The firing squad heard "Present Arms!" and quickly fired three volleys. Austin Phillips, a veteran of both world wars, had already emerged from the hearse where he had gone to fetch his bugle so its valves would be warm.

He was now standing at attention directly across the dirt road that had brought Bob to his final resting place, with his bugle pointed towards his casket as the third haunting volley rang out.

Laura Jean squeezed Sonny's hand while he held Viola tightly with his other arm; they were seated close to the casket. Then all became quiet as Austin Phillips sounded the beautiful drone of Taps, followed by him tucking his bugle into his left side while he rendered a final sharp hand salute to Bob.

The honor guard then folded his flag into the traditional tri-cornered shape for military funerals; no stripes were visible, just blue and upward pointing stars. The flag was handed to Sergeant Billy Ramsey, who stepped up and stood before Viola with Bob's flag at waist height, the longer straight edge facing her.

He then leaned down and said softly, so quietly that few heard, "As a representative of the United States Army it is my high privilege to present this flag to you. Let it be a symbol of the grateful appreciation this nation feels for the distinguished service rendered to our country by your son."

"Thank you," Viola somehow managed to get out. "I shall hold this flag as dear to me as Bob's Purple Heart, which I will carry with me wherever I go until the day I'm buried next to my son."

~AFTERWORD~

I FINALLY LEARNED WHAT HAPPENED to my uncle Bob fifty years later. It was the night I talked with Paul Stegall for the first time back in 1997.

"On June 9th we were moving from one hedgerow to another," he told me. "Your uncle was in mortars, you know. He was the assistant gunner in our section. They were 81mm shells we used. We were going up a wagon trail—that's the way the farmers would get in and out of these hedgerows. We didn't think that the Germans would pick us up, but they must have seen us coming because they let go with shells and rifle fire that was unbelievable.

"Bob took a direct hit from a shell. He never knew what hit him. It happened so fast, But, when it was over there were bodies everywhere. So many were just lying there; heads were gone, as were arms and legs. It was just awful. I had your uncle's blood and flesh all over my uniform. I was lucky; I was on my way to get more mortars from the weapons carrier. I only got hit by some shrapnel from the shell that killed Bob. Please let your family know he didn't suffer. They had no evacuation tents that far inland, so they took me down to the beach, then back to England.

"Ralph Spinosi was killed the day your uncle got it. All they found was his field jacket. It had "Smiling Jack from South Philly" written on the back. That's how they identified his remains. Corporal Eugene Sproull died, too. Four others were badly wounded. One was Private Billy Uhouse, who had the flesh stripped from the outside of his thigh on his right leg. I'll never forget that day for as long as I live."

I moved to Florida in 2010. Sonny had died a year earlier at ninety-one-years of age. He never talked about his brother; not ever, even at the end of his life. Laura Jean passed that same fall.

Colonel Robert E. Murphy died in 2011. He was one of the finest human beings I ever had the privilege to know. He served in Vietnam after War Two, and had been a state representative, serving his Manchester New Hampshire district after he retired from the military. Part of his obituary read: "In later years, as his memory failed him, he became a quiet listener. But his passion and delight was and remained his grandchildren, and he was happiest when surrounded by his family. After more than sixty years of service to his nation and to his state, and two wars on three continents, he died quietly and in peace."

The years flew by and then, out of no where, in July of 2017, I received an email from the publisher of *American Iliad*, the official history of the 18th Infantry Regiment during World War II that I had written with the help of military historian Mark J. Reardon back in 2004. The email said a Kay Stegall wanted to reach me. I was informed that her father, who's health was starting to fail at ninety-five grand years, wanted to finally meet me in person. Could I come to Greenville South Carolina, where he still lived?

I was going to give the keynote address at the Old Hickory 30th Division Hundredth Anniversary Reunion in August, so I made arrangements to get to Greenville before I went up to Raleigh North Carolina to give my little talk. I was on Interstate 385 near Laurens, about forty miles from Greenville, when my cell phone rang. It was August 4th, another memorable day during the journey of my uncle Bob's Purple Heart.

The caller identified herself as Jane Robelot, and she told me she was a news anchor at WYFF in Greenville. A film crew was going to be at the Stegall home; they wanted to record Paul Stegall and me when we met, and a segment about this would likely air that night. Was I OK with this?

"I'm fine with anything the Stegall family wants," I told her.

The Stegall's tidy home, nestled in a stand of tall trees, was set back a hundred and fifty yards or so down a dirt driveway. As I got closer I saw Kay; she was standing on the porch. I got out of my car, and walked into the house with her. A cameraman was standing next to Paul, and he was sitting on a stool by his kitchen. I didn't count them, but there were about fifteen other people there, all his children and grandchildren. Paul's wife Jean was sitting across from him. Jane Robelot, who I later learned had been a co-anchor of CBS's *This Morning* back in the late 1990s, gave me a big smile as the camera started rolling.

Paul and I locked eyes, and seconds later we were hugging each other. We exchanged some words of greeting, and then the general conversation was about finally meeting after all these years. Paul looked frail, and we both had tears in our eyes. I happened to look over at Jane Robelot, and she too was tearing up.

But the cameraman's hands were steady when I reached into my pocket and pulled out my uncle Bob's Purple Heart.

"I want you to have this," I told Paul. "I want you to have this while you continue to fight the good fight, and beat back old age. I am sure that if Bob were here, this is exactly what he would have wanted."

The room went quiet as Paul stared at his best friend from the war's Purple Heart. Then he looked up at me with gratitude I never forgot.

Jane Robelot interviewed both of us. When I told her about Paul's experiences on D-Day, her eyes welled up again. Paul was a favorite citizen of Greenville. He had been the owner/operator of three service stations, and during his thirty-three years of operation he had built up quite a reputation. Paul was generous, honest and fundamentally one of the most decent men of his time. He had helped a lot of poor people, color not meaning a thing to him, even personally lending them the money they needed to buy cars from him.

His family could not have been kinder to me. Kay had bought a few copies of *American Iliad*, and Paul asked me to sign them so he could give them to his friends. It was a grand day, and Jane Robelot led in that night before a short segment was broadcasted on WYFF that memorialized my finally meeting my uncle Bob's best friend.

A month and a half later, on September 22nd, I called Paul; it was his 96th birthday. "I made it," he first told me.

Then Paul wanted to talk about the war. "I remember having to walk all but twelve of the hundred or so miles up Sicily. . .carrying mortars. . .mules helped some in the hills. Remember getting packages from home at Christmas and sharing what was in them. D-Day. . .had to constantly adjust my head to keep from swallowing water when we were coming ashore. When Bob was killed it was awful. Everybody loved him; he was gentle; he made us laugh; he always joked around; he listened to other people's problems; he comforted us. It was never the same after he died."

Kay had told me privately that her father lived all of his life with survivor's guilt, and for some reason I tried to help him with that on his birthday.

"Paul," I started. "You have so much to celebrate. Bob would be so proud of you. Listen, I want to read you something. It's right off a framed piece President Roosevelt sent to Bob's mother.

"He stands in the unbroken line of patriots who have dared to die, that freedom may live, and grow, and increase its blessings. Freedom lives, and through it he lives, in a way that would humble the undertakings of most men."

"That's very nice, Bob," Paul managed to say. "I really wanted to stay after your uncle Bob got hit, and get even with the Germans, but they made me go to the hospital back in England."

"Paul, think about this." I struggled to say what was on my

mind; it came out awkwardly, as usual, but went something like this. "I met your family; you did so many things to help people after the war. You increased freedom's blessings; you gave, you did not take freedom, nor its cost, for granted. It's exactly what Bob would have wanted. He would be so proud of you, the decent family you have raised. . ."

And then I gave up. Paul listened politely, but didn't say a thing.

Kay emailed me a little over a month later. "Daddy slid down to the floor and in the tub twice in the last two weeks. His body is just getting weaker. Last night Daddy was saying what a good man your uncle was, and how they'd been talking about lots of different things before that terrible moment when the shell hit. It's been an eventful day today, too. He slid in the tub again, and couldn't pull himself up. He was in that predicament for probably forty-five minutes until my Mom and I heard him call out."

Three days later—it was now October 19th—Kay emailed me with an update. "Daddy said your uncle was a career man, and he thought they were both born in 1921. Daddy thought Bob was a machine gunner, and he was an artillery guy."

Paul was slipping fast, and his memory seemed to be fading. Then another email came.

"This week when I asked Daddy about that unfortunate day your uncle was killed, I just knew that it impacted my dad so much. Bob, getting Daddy to eat is becoming more and more of a challenge. So many things are going against him. . .no taste or smell. Difficulty swallowing food. He weighs only 117 pounds now, but he mowed the field yesterday, and a little today too. I don't know how he goes on!"

I got another update as it got closer to Thanksgiving. "I just got to Greenville, and as we were talking Daddy said he'd like to talk with you. Please let me know if you have time to talk to Daddy," Kay wrote.

We talked on Thanksgiving Day; it was the last time Paul and I would talk on the phone.

Later that month Kay emailed me again. "I'm writing from the ER. We took Daddy here today. He has pneumonia and it's not looking good for him. He fell in the tub again, and he's not bouncing back. I just wanted you to know. He's a true hero."

I wrote her back, then later that night Kay told me, "After more than ten hours in the ER, Daddy was FINALLY taken to a room tonight in the coronary care unit. He's in a nice room and hopefully he'll be able to get some rest."

The next day Kay said in another email, "Daddy is more stable than he was yesterday, but he is a little weaker than he was this morning. He can't eat the food they are giving to him. Likely not going to be fun decisions in the coming days, but Daddy's mind is still good. He's a fighter for sure."

But by December 2nd the news wasn't good. "Daddy much worse," Kay wrote. "I've been with him constantly. Pneumonia is a horrible thing. Praying for sleep for him now. Bob, the news is very bleak. My mother is managing as best she can. They celebrated 69 years of marriage on November 20. Tonight was the most difficult thing of my life so far, watching my dad go through this."

But the way her emailed closed sent a shiver down my spine. "Know that Daddy has told quite a few people in the hospital about his friend Bob Baumer."

I thought about that; it was pretty special for Kay to mention this. But, my thoughts were more along the line—what would my uncle Bob want me to do right now?

I hopped on my Indian motorcycle at four o'clock the next morning, rode through cold mist from Jacksonville to the Georgia border, and continued up Interstate 95 to I-26, took it west past Columbia South Carolina, then got on the Veteran's Memorial Highway that brought me into Greenville. It was maybe two or so that afternoon when I walked into Paul's room.

He was hooked up to so many things I hardly could find him.

But there he was, and Paul knew it was me. I sat in a chair and just watched Paul in silence, respecting Kay and her husband, plus her brothers were there. Family came first.

But then Kay signaled it was OK to try to talk to her father, and I did in my ever so awkward way.

"So, you're still fighting the good fight, I see."

Paul managed to mumble some words that effectively told me he was losing the fight.

"So you'll be with Bob soon. Will you save a place for me when you get up there?" Paul smiled; it was his way of saying yes.

He was very weak; the end was near. I had a short time to talk with Kay and her brothers, and I told them how great it was to see them there with their father. Then, I left, and got back on my Indian and rode all the way back to Florida, freezing as it got past midnight, but I didn't care.

My heart warmed me; I had done the right thing for both Paul and my uncle Bob.

Kay emailed me the next day, and thanked me for coming. "He's continuing to decline," she told me. "I don't know how much time we have now, not much at all...days at the most."

Paul died two days later. "The last living soul who knew my uncle Bob is gone," I told my journal that night.

A couple months went by before I heard from Kay again. "I was worried about you," she started. "I sent an email a few weeks back and thought maybe it ended up in your junk mail. I want to get your uncle Robert's Purple Heart safely back in your hands. Things are not the same without Daddy here; miss him terribly."

I rode up to Greenville again that summer, and visited with Kay and her mother. I received my uncle Bob's Purple Heart from them, and started a new chapter in its journey, one with no ending until the day I see Paul and Bob in heaven.

It happens every Memorial Day. My uncle Bob's Purple Heart is now back safely with his flag in its mahogany box, but it comes out after I get home from the local remembrance the town I live in puts on.

When I get back to my little house, the real ceremony begins. I bring out Bob's flag and his Purple Heart from the special place I keep it in for this solemn day when we are supposed to remember those who died in foreign wars. I open up my personal copy of *American Iliad*, and turn to the Honor Roll, where the names are listed of the 1,513 soldiers of the 18th Infantry Regiment who made the ultimate sacrifice during World War II.

They were all Bob's brothers. I say every name out loud while I hold his Purple Heart in the palm of my hand, stare at his flag, and am forever humbled by these words that were written by an 18th Infantry soldier who made it through his war but had to come back home in a wheel chair:

> *Do not stand at my grave and weep.*
> *I am here. I do not sleep.*
> *I'm in the wind that lifts the leaves,*
> *Then let's them rest beneath the trees.*
> *I have moved on, my friend.*
> *Duty first! Follow me!*

Pfc. Robert A. Baummer

Journey of the Purple Heart

~A NOTE ON SOURCES AND ACKNOWLEDGMENTS~

MILITARY OPERATIONS DESCRIBED IN THIS book were based on pertinent World War II First Division and 18th Infantry Regiment General and Field Orders, to include Intelligence Annex Summaries; Official Memorandums; Battle and After Action reports; G-2 Periodic Reports; S-3 Operations Reports and Summaries of Battalion Operations. All were retrieved at either the National Archives in College Park Maryland; the Center of Military History in Washington DC; the Military History Institute Archives and Library at the Army War College at Carlisle Barracks in Carlisle Pennsylvania; the Microfilm Collections in the Combined Arms Research Center in Fort Leavenworth Kansas; the Fort Hood Texas Tank Destroyer School; the Robert R. McCormick Research Center at the Cantigny First Infantry Division Museum in Wheaton Illinois, and the Dwight D. Eisenhower Library in Abilene Kansas.

The National Personnel Records Center in St. Louis Missouri provided key Morning Reports that pertained to Pfc. Robert A. Baummer's Company H, as well as his being missing and then killed-in-action in France. Correspondence and battle descriptions provided by Lt. General Robert H. York and others were found at the United States Military Academy at West Point New York. 18th Infantry Regiment and 2nd Battalion S-1 Journal entries, which were actual minute-to-minute order changes, records of personnel involved, radio messages, and other actions taken at both battalion and regimental levels, also materially contributed to the battles you read about in this book.

Personal diaries of the individual combatants were provided to the author mainly by family members; attribution to their fathers in every case appeared in this book. Several officers wrote important post war unpublished memoirs, salient parts of which also appeared with attribution on the pages you have read. In the early 1950s many 18th Infantry officer veterans wrote monographs about their personal battle experiences during World War II; they were invaluable to this writer and were retrieved at the Donovan Research Library at Ft. Benning, Georgia.

It is fair to say that this book would not have been possible to write without the voluminous letters and personal papers that were provided to me by Colonel Robert E. Murphy. An extraordinary man, to whom I owe so much.

I was able to gain further insight into the mortar platoon's role in combat from a senior historian at the Camp Blanding Museum in Starke, Florida; his name is Dr. George B. Cressman, Jr. He provided to me the World War II era *Department of the Army Technical Field Manual*, which governed field maintenance of the 81mm mortar; the *Infantry Field Manual* that provided weapon, ammunition and technical information; *Training the Soldier –Mechanical Manual*, and the *Heavy Weapons Company Infantry Regiment Manual* which detailed doctrine tactical movements of the mortar sections and squads, organization of the mortar platoon and its role in both offensive actions and the defense, to include the 81mm mortar's emplacement and relative training schedules and exercises. Extremely helpful to the author was seeing the 81mm mortar display at the Camp Blanding Museum. Thank you very much, Dr. Cressman, as well as all at the Camp Blanding Museum who assisted me.

It was Mary Jane Kamerzel, my grandmother Viola Baummer's youngest sister, who helped me the most in the early 1990s with starting to piece together Pfc. Robert A. Baummer's short life. My mother Laura Jean was the one who always encouraged me to keep going, and never give up trying to find out what happened to him. Oddly, it was my father Sonny's reluctance to talk about his brother that motivated me more than anything to learn as much as I could about his war. They are all gone now. The least I can do is thank each and every one of them immensely.

Had it not been for Judith Clark, I would have never found Paul Stegall. Judy, with her research back in 1997, was key in continuing the journey of my uncle Bob's Purple Heart and allowing it to fall into Paul Stegall's hands twenty years later. Thank you again Judy.

I still choke up every time I think of Paul. An elegant and humble man, it is difficult to put into words my thanks for his friendship and contributions to this book. His legacy was carried forward by his courageous daughter Kay as she relayed to me Paul's last weeks and the days before he passed away; this was followed with more friendship, and her offers to help me during the proof reads of this book. Kay's brother Alan Stegall took the time to read the entire manuscript, and helped add to it by relating to me incidents he remembered his father telling him about the war. The word thanks cannot be said often enough to both Alan and Kay.

Others were kind enough to read the manuscript, offering both encouragement and valuable suggestions along the way. My thanks to Jill Mautner, Barry Konet, Carol Maleska, Florence C. Eaton and Kurt Marhoefer.

Writing about military history is not easy. Those of us who do it get better at it with the support of others with the same obsession. It is hard to believe that it is going on twenty years since my first book was published with the help of Mark J. Reardon. To Mark I owe a special gratitude, for he has remained at my side through every book I've written since then, and he's already giving me tremendous support with the next book I've got planned. Thank you, my friend.

Steven F. Underwood is another author I was fortunate to recently befriend, and it was he who introduced me to Hellgate Press. I am indebted to you Steven because Harley Patrick and his team are real professionals.

And last but far from least, my gratitude to Melissa Clark for her work in creating my Website, *www.robertwbaumer.com,* as well as both my personal and business Facebook pages.

~BIBLIOGRAPHY~

Astor, Gerald, *Terrible Terry Allen: Combat General of World War II – The Life of an American Soldier*, Novato, CA: Presidio Press, 2003.

Ault, Phil, Parris, Jr., John A., Russell, Ned, Disher, Leo, *Springboard to Berlin*, New York, NY, Thomas Y. Crowell Company, 1943.

Austin, A.B., *Birth of an Army, The Story of the Tunisian Campaign,* London, Victor Gollancz LTD, 1943.

Barron, Leo, *Patton's First Victory*, Guilford, CT: Stackpole Books, 2018.

Baumer, Robert W., with Mark J. Reardon, *American Iliad: The 18th Infantry Regiment in World War II.* Bedford, PA: Aberjona Press, 2004.

Blum, John N., *V was for Victory, Politics and American Culture during World War II,* New York and London, Harcourt Brace Jovanovich, 1976

Bradley, Omar N., *A Soldier's Story*, New York, NY: Henry Holt and Company, Inc., 1951.

Bradley, Omar N., and Blair, Clay, *A General's Life*, New York, Simon & Schuster, 1983.

Butcher, Harry C., *My Three Years with Eisenhower,* New York, Simon and Schuster, 1946.

Center of Military History, *Omaha Beachhead – American Forces in Action*, Historical Division War Department, Washington DC, 1945.

Davis, Kenneth S., *Soldier of Democracy: A Biography of Dwight D. Eisenhower,* New York, Bantam Books, 1952.

D'Este, Carlo, *Bitter Victory: The Battle for Sicily, 1943*, New York NY: E.P. Dutton, 1988.

D'Este, Carlo, *Patton: A Genius for War*, New York NY: HarperCollins Publishers,

Downing, John P., *At War with the British*, Daytona Beach FL, self-published by John P. Downing, circa 1980.

Downing, John P., *No Promotion*, Daytona Beach, FL, a non-published memoir by John P. Downing, 1980.

Eisenhower, David, *Eisenhower at War 1943-1945*, New York, Random House, 1986.

Goldstein, Richard, *America at D-Day: A Book of Remembrance*, New York, NY: Dell Publishing, 1994.

Goodwin, Doris Kearns, *No Ordinary Time, Franklin and Eleanor Roosevelt: The Home Front in World War II*, New York, Simon & Schuster, 1994.

Harrison, Gordon A., *Cross-Channel Attack*, Center of Military History, Washington DC, 1951.

Heidenheimer, Arnold, *Vanguard to Victory*, Aschaffenburg, Germany: Main Echo Verlag, 1954.

Howard, Michael and Sparrow, John, *History of the Coldstream Guards, 1920-1946*, London: Oxford University Press, 1951.

Jeffers, Paul H., *Theodore Roosevelt, Jr: The Life of a War Hero*, Novato, CA: Presidio Press, 2002.

Johnson, Franklyn A., *One More Hill*, New York, NY: Funk & Wagnalls Company, 1949.

Katcher, Phillip, *US 1st Infantry Division*, 1939-45, London, Osprey Press, 1978.

Kelly, Orr, *Meeting the Fox: The Invasion of Africa, from Operation Torch to Kasserine Pass to Victory in Tunisia*, New York, John Wiley & Sons, Inc., 2002.

Kesselring, Albert, *A Soldier's Record*, Westport CT, 1970

Kirkland, Jr., William B., *Destroyers at Normandy – Naval Gunfire Support on Omaha Beach*, Naval History Foundation, Center of Military History, Washington DC, 1994.

Knickerbocker, H.R., et al, Society of the First Division, *Danger Forward: The Story of the First Division in World War II*, Atlanta GA: Albert Love Publishers, 1947.

Life Magazine, Time Incorporated, November 13 1939, November 20, 1939, June 10 1940, June 17 1940, November 25 1940, December 30 1940, March 16, 1942, November 9 1943, October 25 1943, December 13, 1943, December 20, 1943, May 29 1944, June 19 1944, New York NY.

Liddell Hart, B.H., *The Rommel Papers*, New York NY: Harcourt, Brace, 1953.

Marshall, Malcolm and Many Authors, *Proud Americans: Men of 32nd Field Artillery Battalion in Action, World War II*, New London, NH, Self-published by Malcolm Marshall, 1994.

Mason, Stanhope, *Reminiscences and Anecdotes of World War II*, 1947. Unpublished manuscript provided to author by his grandson.

McManus, John C., *The Dead And Those About To Die: D-Day: The Big Red One at Omaha Beach*, New York, NY: Penquin Group, 2014.

Milano, Vince, *Normandiefront, D-Day to St. Lo Through German Eyes, Volume 1, Invasion*, Zurich, Switzerland: Spiess Publishing Co., 1994.

Mitcham, Jr., Samuel W. and Stauffenburg, Friedrich, *The Battle of Sicily: How the Allies Lost Their Chance for Total Victory*, New York NY, Orion, 1991.

Morison, Samuel E., *History of the United States Navy in World War II, Volume 2: Operations in North African Waters October 1942 to June 1943*, Urbana IL, University of Illinois Press, 2001.

Nicolson, Nigel and Forbes, Patrick, *The Grenadier Guards in the War of 1939 to 1945, Volume II, The Mediterranean Campaign*, Adershot, UL: Gale & Ploden, 1949.

Organization Day, 18th Regiment of United States Infantry, Fort Devens MA, May 3 1941.

Perret, Geoffrey, *Eisenhower*, New York, Random House, 1999.

Petrow, Richard, *The Bitter Years: The Invasion and Occupation of Denmark and Norway April 1940-May 1945*, New York NY: William Morrow & Company, Inc., 1974.

Phillips, Henry G., *El Guettar: Crucible of Leadership, the 9th Infantry Division Against the Wehrmacht in Africa, April 1943*, Penn Valley CA, Published by Henry G. Phillips, 1991.

Playfair, J.S.O., and Molony, C.J.C., *The Mediterranean and the Middle East, Vol. IV, The Destruction of Axis Forces in Africa*, History of the Second World War United Kingdom Military Series, London, Her Majesty's Stationery Office, 1966.

Pyle, Ernie, *Here Is Your War*, Cleveland, OH: The World Publishing Company, 1943.

Reynolds, Quentin, *Dress Rehearsal: A Stirring First Hand Account of the Raid at Dieppe*, New York, Random House, 1943.

Robson, Adam, *Tunisia, The 2nd Battalion of the Coldstream Guards 1942-1943*, Published by Adam Robson, 2015.

Rogers, Edward K., *Doughboy Chaplain,* Boston MA: Meador Press, 1946.

Severloh, Hein, *Erinnerungen an Omaha Beach, Normandie, 6 Juni 1944*, Hanover, Germany: Creativ Verlag, 2000.

Summersby, Kay M., *Past Forgetting: My Love Affair with Dwight D. Eisenhower,* New York, Simon and Schuster, 1975.

The Stars and Stripes, *History of One Day's Battle*, May 1 1943.

Votaw, John F., with Steven Weingartner, *Blue Spaders: The 26th Infantry Regiment, 1917-1967*, Wheaton, IL: Cantigny First Division Foundation.

Walker, Robert W., *The Namesake: The Biography of Theodore Roosevelt, Jr.,* New York, Brick Tower Press, 2008.

Williamson, John, *North Africa, Sicily and England*, diary entries transcribed in 2003 from original by family members Kathleen Williamson Barmon, Ward D. Barmon and Peter Williamson, provided to Author in 2003.

Wilmot, Chester, *The Struggle for Europe*, London England: The Reprint Society, 1953.

Wortman, Marc, *1941 – Fighting the Shadow War: A Divided America in a World at War,* New York, Atlantic Monthly Press, 2016.

~ABOUT THE AUTHOR~

ROBERT W. BAUMER HAS BEEN WRITING about World War II for over twenty years. He is the coauthor with Mark Reardon of *American Iliad: The 18th Infantry Regiment in World War II*, author of *Aachen: The U.S. Army's Battle for Charlemagne's City in World War II*, and *Old Hickory: The 30th Division—The Top-Rated American Infantry Division in Europe in World War II*.

Robert is a graduate of the University of Illinois in Champaign-Urbana, and is a former columnist who wrote "The Tip of the Spear" for *Armchair General* magazine when it began circulation in 2004.

Robert's advocacy for veterans was first recognized in 2005 by an order of the Secretary of the Army, wherein he was made an honorary member of the 18th Infantry Regiment First Infantry Division of World War II; in 2017 he was inducted for life into the Order of the Old Hickory Society for actions that "forever enhanced the reputation, honor, and legacy of the famous combat unit known as Old Hickory."

Today Robert lives in Ormond Beach, Florida, and when not writing he's riding motorcycles.

www.hellgatepress.com

Printed in Great Britain
by Amazon

27240989R00304